ESSAYS ON INDUSTRIALIZATION IN COLOMBIA

Contributors

Albert Berry is Professor of Economics at the University of Toronto and was formerly a member of the Economic Growth Center at Yale University. He has written extensively on Colombia and was an advisor to the National Planning Commission.

David Chu is Director of Project Analysis and Evaluation for the U.S. Department of Defense in Washington, D.C. He was formerly the Assistant Director for National Security and International Affairs for the Congressional Budget Office and prior to that was Associate Head of the Economics Department of the Rand Corporation in Santa Monica, California.

Carlos F. Díaz-Alejandro is Professor of Economics at Yale University. Among his many writings on Latin America is *Foreign Trade Regimes and Economic Development: Colombia*.

Leonard Dudley is Professor of Economics at the Université de Montreal in Montreal, Canada. He has been an advisor to the National Planning Commission in Colombia and a visitor at the International Labour Office's employment program (PREALC) in Santiago, Chile.

Manuel Ramírez is a member of the Corporación Centro Regional de Población in Bogotá, Colombia, and formerly taught at the Universidad de Los Andes in Bogotá. He has written extensively on technological change in industry and on other aspects of the Colombian economy.

Francisco Thoumi is head of the Social Studies Section of the Interamerican Development Bank and Visiting Professor at the American University, Washington, D.C. He was formerly a member of the World Bank and of the Department of Economics of George Washington University, Washington, D.C.

John Todd is Director of the Short Term Information Division, Energy Information Administration, U.S. Department of Energy. He formerly worked at the Department of Health, Education, and Welfare, and prior to that taught economics at Williams College in Williamstown, Massachusetts.

ESSAYS ON INDUSTRIALIZATION IN COLOMBIA

ALBERT BERRY, EDITOR

Published by
Center for Latin American Studies
Arizona State University
Tempe

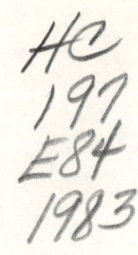

Library of Congress Cataloging in Publication Data

Berry, Albert
  Essays on industrialization in Colombia.

  Includes index.
  1. Colombia--Industries--Addresses, essays, lectures.
2. Industry and state--Colombia--Addresses, essays,
lectures. I. Berry, E. Albert.
HC197.E84 1983   338.09861   83-5175
ISBN 0-87918-053-6

Copyright © 1983--Arizona Board of Regents
Arizona State University
Center for Latin American Studies
Tempe, Arizona 85287

All rights reserved. No part of this publication may be
reproduced or transmitted in any form or by any means,
electronic or mechanical, including photocopy, recording,
or any information storage or retrieval system, without
permission in writing from the publisher.

Published in the United States of America.

Typing by Lynnette Winkelman

Printed by Affiliated Lithographers, Inc.

Bookbinding by Roswell Bookbinding

Bureau of Publications • 23121

Table of Contents

Chapter		Page
	PREFACE	
1	INTRODUCTION *Albert Berry*	1
2	A DESCRIPTIVE HISTORY OF COLOMBIAN INDUSTRIAL DEVELOPMENT IN THE TWENTIETH CENTURY *Albert Berry*	7
	PART I NINETEENTH CENTURY STAGNATION	7
	PART II A QUANTITATIVE OVERVIEW OF TWENTIETH CENTURY INDUSTRIAL DEVELOPMENT	9
	PART III A CHRONOLOGICAL RECORD OF INDUSTRIAL GROWTH AND INDUSTRIAL POLICY IN THE TWENTIETH CENTURY	18
	PART IV A BRIEF SUMMARY OF TWENTIETH-CENTURY INDUSTRIAL POLICY	49
	PART V SOME FEATURES OF THE INDUSTRIALIZATION PROCESS: THE EVOLUTION OF INDUSTRY BY SIZE AND JURIDICAL FORM	51
	PART VI EFFECTS OF INDUSTRIAL GROWTH	61
	SUMMARY	71
3	THE GREAT DEPRESSION AND INDUSTRIALIZATION IN COLOMBIA *David S. C. Chu*	99
	APPENDIX A INDUSTRIAL PRODUCTION AND PRICES: NONTRADITIONAL MANUFACTURING	134

TABLE OF CONTENTS (continued)

Chapter		Page
4	THE EFFECTS OF LEARNING ON EMPLOYMENT AND LABOR PRODUCTIVITY IN THE COLOMBIAN METAL PRODUCTS SECTOR . . . . *Leonard Dudley*	143

PART I
ALTERNATIVE EXPLANATIONS OF PRODUCTIVITY CHANGE 143

PART II
A SPECIFICATION OF THE LEARNING HYPOTHESIS FOR METAL PRODUCTS 145

PART III
THE IMPORTANCE OF LEARNING 150

PART IV
TYPES OF LEARNING. 160

PART V
PRODUCTIVITY AND EMPLOYMENT. 162

PART VI
CONCLUSIONS 164

5	TECHNOLOGICAL CHANGE IN THE THERMAL ELECTRICITY GENERATING INDUSTRY . . . . *Manuel Ramirez G.*	171
6	PLANT SIZE, FACTOR PROPORTIONS, AND EFFICIENCY IN COLOMBIAN INDUSTRY. . . . . *John Todd*	191

PART I
THEORY AND METHODOLOGY 192

PART II
ESTIMATING NET SOCIAL BENEFIT BY SIZE OF PLANT 198

PART III
EXPLANATION OF DIFFERENCES IN EFFICIENCY BY PLANT SIZE 217

PART IV
POLICY IMPLICATIONS. 220

TABLE OF CONTENTS (continued)

Chapter		Page
7	THE UTILIZATION OF FIXED INDUSTRIAL CAPITAL IN COLOMBIA: SOME EMPIRICAL FINDINGS. . . . . *Francisco Thoumi*	241
8	TRADE AND THE IMPORT CONTROL SYSTEM IN COLOMBIA: SOME QUANTIFIABLE FEATURES . . . . *Carlos F. Díaz-Alejandro*	263
	ANNEX A COMPANIES IMPORTING MORE THAN ONE MILLION DOLLARS, 1970	293
9	THE EXPERIENCE OF INDUSTRIALIZATION IN COLOMBIA: SUMMARY AND CONCLUSIONS . . . . . *Albert Berry*	297
	LIST OF ACRONYMS	317
	INDEX	319

List of Figures

Figure		Page
2.1	Labor Force Share in Factory Manufacturing and in Cottage-Shop	55
3.1	Relative Price Movements of Nontraditional Manufactures and New Inputs, 1925-45	111
4.1	Learning and Total Factor Productivity	159
5.1	Efficient and Basic Processes	173
5.2	Alternative Forms of Learning Curves	178
6.1	Factor Proportions and Level of Production Under Constant Returns to Scale and Equal Factor Price Ratios	195
6.2	Factor Proportions and Level of Production Under Increasing Returns to Scale, A Homothetic Production Function, and Equal Factor Price Ratios	196
6.3	Factor Proportions and Size Under Increasing Returns To Scale, A Non-Homothetic Production Function, and Equal Factor Price Ratios	197
6.4	Factor Proportions and Size Under Increasing Returns To Scale, A Non-Homothetic Production Function, and A Higher Relative Price of Capital for Small Firms	199
6.5	The Foreign Exchange Market	213

List of Tables

Table		Page
2.1	TWENTIETH-CENTURY TRENDS IN THE MANUFACTURING SECTOR..................................	10
2.2	A GROWTH ACCOUNTING EXERCISE FOR LABOR PRODUCTIVITY, 1925/27-1969/71 AND SUBPERIODS..	16
2.3	CHARACTERISTICS OF ESTABLISHMENTS REPORTED IN THE 1945 MANUFACTURING CENSUS, BY YEAR FOUNDED...	23
2.4	SECTOR AND CAPITAL INVESTED FOR MANUFACTURING PLANTS LISTED IN COLOMBIA STATISTICS, 1915...	24
2.5	MANUFACTURING EMPLOYMENT OVER TIME, BY FACTORY/COTTAGE-SHOP AND BY SEX.............	25
2.6	SHARE OF GROWTH OF FACTORY MANUFACTURING ASSOCIATED WITH IMPORT SUBSTITUTION, DOMESTIC DEMAND AND EXPORTS, BY SELECTED PERIODS...	27
2.7	COMPOSITION OF COTTAGE-SHOP EMPLOYMENT BY INDUSTRY, 1938, 1951, and 1964.....................	29
2.8	GROWTH OF THE MANUFACTURING SECTOR BY INDUSTRY, 1925-68................................	31
2.9	EFFECTIVE PROTECTION ESTIMATES FOR SELECTED INDUSTRIES AND PRODUCTS........................	33
2.10	CUSTOMS DUTIES AS A SHARE OF THE VALUE OF IMPORTS, 1924-69...................................	38
2.11	CREDIT TO MANUFACTURING IN RELATION TO TOTAL CREDIT AND TO MANUFACTURING OUTPUT, 1940-72...	40
2.12	COMPOSITION OF INDUSTRIAL OUTPUT AND ITS GROWTH OVER TIME................................	41
2.13	ROUGH ESTIMATES OF FOREIGN CAPITAL IN COLOMBIAN MANUFACTURING BY INDUSTRY, 1969..	43
2.14	COMPOSITION OF REGISTERED COLOMBIAN EXPORTS, 1945-72....................................	46
2.15	ASPECTS OF COLOMBIAN MANUFACTURING BY SIZE OF ESTABLISHMENT, 1964	52

LIST OF TABLES (continued)

Table		Page
2.16	MANUFACTURING EMPLOYMENT BY TWO-DIGIT INDUSTRIES AND BY FACTORY/COTTAGE-SHOP, 1938-64	56
2.17	RELATIVE PRICE TRENDS OF MANUFACTURED PRODUCTS VIS-À-VIS THE PRICE DEFLATOR OF GDP, BY TWO-DIGIT INDUSTRY	63
2.18	A GUESS AT RELATIVE TOTAL FACTORY PRODUCTIVITY BY TWO-DIGIT INDUSTRY, FACTORY SUBSECTOR, 1969	64
2.19	ESTIMATES OF CAPITAL PRODUCTIVITY, SELECTED YEARS, 1925-69	67
2.20	THE OUTPUT ELASTICITY OF EMPLOYMENT IN FACTORY MANUFACTURING: RATES OF GROWTH OF VALUE ADDED AND EMPLOYMENT IN FACTORY MANUFACTURING	68
2.21	LABOR SHARES IN MANUFACTURING INCOME, 1950-77	70
2.22	INCOME DISTRIBUTION AND EMPLOYMENT IN NON-TRADED, EXPORT, IMPORT-COMPETING, AND NONIMPORT-COMPETING MANUFACTURING	72
3.1	RATIO OF GROWTH RATE OF INDUSTRIAL OUTPUT TO GROWTH RATE OF GDP; LATE TWENTIES, THIRTIES, AND WORLD WAR II	102
3.2	THE COMPOSITION OF EXPANSION OF NONTRADITIONAL MANUFACTURING; LATE TWENTIES, THIRTIES, AND WORLD WAR II	102
3.3	RATIO OF ACTUAL TO "NORMAL" VALUE ADDED, SELECTED YEARS, 1924-45	103
3.4	COMPONENTS OF INDUSTRIAL GROWTH, TWENTIES, THIRTIES, AND WORLD WAR II	105
3.5	IMPORTS AS A PERCENT OF DOMESTIC DEMAND 1927/28, 1938/39, AND 1944/45	106
3.6	REGRESSIONS OF INDUSTRIAL OUTPUT PER CAPITA (Q_j/N) ON INCOME PER CAPITA (Y/N) AND POPULATION (N): $\ln(Q_i/N) = \ln A_i + b_{1i} \ln(Y/N) + b_{2i} \ln N$	107

LIST OF TABLES (continued)

Table		Page
3.7	TEST OF THE HYPOTHESIS OF EQUAL COEFFICIENT VECTORS FOR 1920-29 AND 1930-45, I.E., THAT $\begin{bmatrix} \ln a_i \\ b_{1i} \\ b_{2i} \end{bmatrix} 1923\text{-}29 = \begin{bmatrix} \ln a_i \\ b_{1i} \\ b_{2i} \end{bmatrix} 1930\text{-}45 = \begin{bmatrix} \ln a_i \\ b_{1i} \\ b_{2i} \end{bmatrix} 1923\text{-}45$	108
3.8	THE RELATIVE PRICE MODEL.........................	116
3.9	EFFECT OF PRICE CHANGES ON INDUSTRIAL OUTPUT, BY INDUSTRY, 1928-45....................	117
3.10	SOURCES OF FUNDS OF INDUSTRIAL CORPORATIONS, BY INDUSTRY, 1943-45......................	119
3.11	ENTREPRENEURIAL CHARACTERISTICS BY SIZE OF FIRM..	121
3.12	CONTRIBUTION OF ESTABLISHMENTS TO CHANGE IN OUTPUT DURING 1930-45, BY YEAR FOUNDED AND INDUSTRY.......................................	122
3.13	VALUE OF MATERIALS INPUTS AS A PROPORTION OF VALUE ADDED AT WORLD PRICES, BY INDUSTRY, UNITED STATES 1947 AND COLOMBIA 1944/45........	123
3A.1	METHODOLOGY FOR CONSTRUCTING PRODUCT INDICES..	136
3A.2	NET VALUE ADDED, BY PRODUCT CLASS, 1944-45...	137
3A.3	OUTPUT INDICES BY TWO-DIGIT INDUSTRY, 1923-45.	138
3A.4	PRICE INDICES BY TWO-DIGIT INDUSTRY, 1923-45...	139
3A.5	PRICE INDICES FOR MATERIAL INPUTS BY TWO-DIGIT INDUSTRY, 1923-45............................	140
4.1	PRINCIPAL CHARACTERISTICS OF METAL PRODUCTS PRODUCTION, BY ACTIVITY..........................	145
4.2	PREDICTED CHARACTERISTICS OF LEARNING IN METAL PRODUCTS, BY ACTIVITY.....................	149
4.3	RATIO OF FIXED CAPITAL TO HORSEPOWER IN COLOMBIAN MANUFACTURING, 1957-67...............	152
4.4	FOUR TYPES OF LEARNING IN METAL PRODUCTS, AND A POSSIBLE MEASURE OF EACH..................	153

LIST OF TABLES (continued)

Table		Page
4.5	COEFFICIENTS OF COBB-DOUGLAS PRODUCTION FUNCTIONS FOR COLOMBIAN METAL PRODUCTS, WITH AND WITHOUT LEARNING, FOR TWENTY-FIVE THREE-DIGIT INDUSTRIES, 1959-66	155
4.6	ESTIMATED BREAKDOWN OF PRODUCTIVITY CHANGES IN COLOMBIAN METAL PRODUCTS FOR TWENTY-FIVE THREE-DIGIT INDUSTRIES, 1959-66	158
4.7	COMPARISON OF THE EFFECT ON LABOR PRODUCTIVITY OF FOUR TYPES OF LEARNING FOR FOUR COLOMBIAN METAL PRODUCTS GROUPS, 1959-66	162
4.8	AVERAGE ANNUAL CHANGE IN LABOR PRODUCTIVITY AND IN EMPLOYMENT FOR FOUR COLOMBIAN METAL PRODUCTS GROUPS, 1959-66	163
4A.1	A TEST OF STRUCTURAL DUALISM IN COLOMBIAN METAL PRODUCTS, 1959-66	166
5.1	AVERAGE VALUES OF TECHNICAL EFFICIENCY ESTIMATES, TWENTY THERMOELECTRIC PLANTS	175
5.2	AVERAGE VALUES OF SOME INDEPENDENT VARIABLES, TWENTY THERMOELECTRIC PLANTS	176
5.3	PARTIAL CORRELATION COEFFICIENTS AMONG INDEPENDENT VARIABLES EMPLOYED: TWENTY THERMOELECTRIC PLANTS	180
5.4	CAPITAL/OUTPUT, LABOR/OUTPUT AND FUEL/OUTPUT RATIOS: TWENTY THERMOELECTRIC PLANTS	184
6.1	INDICATORS OF THE CAPITAL/LABOR RATIO, BY GROUPED SIZE CLASSES, 1966	192
6.2	PERCENT DISTRIBUTION OF TOTAL EMPLOYMENT BY SIZE CLASS, 1956-67	200
6.3	PERCENT DISTRIBUTION OF VALUE ADDED BY SIZE CLASS, 1956-67	201
6.4	VALUE ADDED PER WORKER, BY SIZE CLASS, SELECTED YEARS	203
6.5	PERCENT DISTRIBUTION OF FIXED INVESTMENT AND HORSEPOWER, BY GROUPED SIZE CLASSES, 1956-67	204

LIST OF TABLES (continued)

Table		Page
6.6	ESTIMATES OF THE FIXED CAPITAL/HORSEPOWER RATIO, BY GROUPED SIZE CLASSES, 1957-67	206
6.7	ALTERNATIVE ESTIMATES OF THE FIXED CAPITAL/HORSEPOWER RATIO, BY GROUPED SIZE CLASSES, 1967	207
6.8	OUTPUT/FIXED CAPITAL RATIOS, BY GROUPED SIZE CLASSES, 1956-67	208
6.9	$\frac{\text{VALUE ADDED} - (\text{PAID} + \text{IMPUTED WAGES})}{\text{HORSEPOWER}}$, BY SIZE CLASS, 1956-67	209
6.10	$\frac{\text{VALUE ADDED} - (\text{LABOR FORCE} \times \text{CRAFT WAGE})}{\text{HORSEPOWER}}$, BY SIZE CLASS, 1956-67	211
6.11	COMPARISON OF INDICATORS OF EFFICIENCY FROM TABLES 6.8, 6.9 and 6.10, BY SIZE CLASS	212
6.12	WAGES AND FRINGE BENEFITS (PAID & IMPUTED), AS A PERCENTAGE OF VALUE ADDED, BY SIZE CLASS, 1956-67	214
6.13	PERCENT OF INTERMEDIATE INPUTS IMPORTED, BY SIZE CLASS, 1964	215
6.14	$\frac{\text{VALUE ADDED} - \text{ONE HALF OF IMPORTED RAW MATERIALS}}{\text{HORSEPOWER}}$ BY SIZE CLASS, 1956-67	216
6.15	ESTIMATES OF THE RATIO OF NET SOCIAL BENEFIT TO FIXED CAPITAL, BY SIZE CLASS, 1956-67	218
6.16	WAGES AND FRINGE BENEFITS PER PAID WORKER, BY SIZE CLASS, 1956-67	220
6.17	HORSEPOWER/TOTAL EMPLOYMENT AND VALUE ADDED/HORSEPOWER, BY ORGANIZATIONAL FORM AND SIZE CLASS, 1966	222
6.18	PERCENT DISTRIBUTION OF VALUE ADDED AMONG FOUR-DIGIT INDUSTRIES CLASSIFIED BY WHETHER DOMINATED BY LARGE PLANTS, SMALL PLANTS OR NEITHER, 1960-65	224
6.19	VALUE ADDED/HORSEPOWER BY SIZE CLASS AND BY WHETHER FOUR-DIGIT INDUSTRY DOMINATED BY LARGE OR SMALL PLANTS, 1960 AND 1965	225

LIST OF TABLES (continued)

Table		Page
6.20	RELATIVE VALUE ADDED/HORSEPOWER (R), PLANTS OF SIZE CLASSES 0-8 COMPARED TO PLANTS OF SIZE CLASS 9, SELECTED FOUR-DIGIT INDUSTRIES, 1966	227
6.21	PERCENT DISTRIBUTION OF VALUE ADDED, BY SIZE CLASS, SELECTED DEPARTMENTS, 1958	228
6.22	VALUE ADDED PER HORSEPOWER, VALUE ADDED PER WORKER, AND HORSEPOWER PER WORKER, BY DEPARTMENT AND SIZE CLASS, 1958	229
7.1	GENERAL UTILIZATION PARAMETERS, 1970	246
7.2	ALTERNATIVE UTILIZATION PARAMETERS, BY INDUSTRY, 1970	248
7.3	SHARE OF MAXIMUM POSSIBLE HOURS WHICH ENTREPRENEURS BELIEVE THEIR PLANT SHOULD WORK (U/U_e), AVERAGE BY INDUSTRY, 1970	249
7.4	CORRELATION MATRIX OF UTILIZATION MEASURES	249
7A.1	CORRELATION MATRIX OF THE EXPLANATORY VARIABLES ENTERED IN FINAL EQUATIONS	261
8.1	MAJOR INDUSTRIAL IMPORTERS IN COLOMBIA, BY LEVEL OF IMPORTS AND BY NATIONALITY, 1970	266
8.2	MAJOR COMMERCIAL IMPORTERS IN COLOMBIA, BY LEVEL OF IMPORTS AND BY NATIONALITY, 1970	267
8.3	MAJOR COLOMBIAN IMPORTERS, BY LEVEL OF IMPORTS AND BY NATIONALITY, 1970	268
8.4	SOME CHARACTERISTICS OF MAJOR INDUSTRIAL IMPORTERS, BY LEVEL OF IMPORTS AND BY NATIONALITY, 1970	270
8.5	REASONS GIVEN BY INCOMEX FOR REJECTING APPLICATIONS FOR IMPORT LICENSES, AND TABULATION OF SAMPLE OF REJECTED LICENSES (TOTALLY OR IN PART), SECOND SEMESTER, 1971	272
8.6	AVERAGE CHARACTERISTICS OF APPROVED, REJECTED, AND PARTIALLY REJECTED APPLICATIONS FOR IMPORT LICENSES, SECOND SEMESTER, 1971	274

LIST OF TABLES (continued)

Table		Page
8.7	INDUSTRIAL FIRMS: REGRESSIONS EXPLAINING APPROVAL (1) OR REJECTION (0) OF IMPORT REQUESTS IN SAMPLE..............................	276
8.8	COMMERCIAL FIRMS: REGRESSIONS EXPLAINING APPROVAL (1) OR REJECTION (0) OF IMPORT REQUESTS IN SAMPLE..............................	277
8.9	INDUSTRIAL FIRMS: APPROVALS AND COMPLETE REJECTIONS OF IMPORT LICENSE REQUESTS, ACCORDING TO EMPLOYMENT SIZE AND REIMBURSABLE OR NONREIMBURSABLE CATEGORIES.....	279
8.10	INDUSTRIAL FIRMS: APPROVALS AND COMPLETE REJECTIONS OF IMPORT LICENSE REQUESTS, ACCORDING TO LEVELS OF REGISTERED IMPORTS IN 1970 AND REIMBURSABLE OR NONREIMBURSABLE CATEGORIES...	280
8.11	INDUSTRIAL FIRMS: APPROVALS AND COMPLETE REJECTIONS OF IMPORT LICENSE REQUESTS, ACCORDING TO EMPLOYMENT SIZE AND GEOGRAPHICAL LOCATION......................................	282
8.12	INDUSTRIAL FIRMS: APPROVALS AND COMPLETE REJECTIONS OF IMPORT LICENSE REQUESTS, ACCORDING TO REGISTERED MINOR EXPORTS IN 1970 AND GEOGRAPHICAL LOCATION................	283
8.13	INDUSTRIAL FIRMS: PERCENT OF IMPORT LICENSE REQUESTS APPROVED ACCORDING TO LOCATION OF FIRM AND LEVEL OF 1970 IMPORTS...................	284
8.14	INDUSTRIAL FIRMS: MULTIPLE REGRESSIONS "EXPLAINING" IMPORTS, EXPORTS, WAGES, AND TAXES PER EMPLOYEE.............................	285
8.15	COMMERCIAL FIRMS: MULTIPLE REGRESSIONS "EXPLAINING" IMPORTS, WAGES, AND TAXES PER EMPLOYEE..	286

Preface

Industrialization is accepted by nearly all economists as a major, perhaps pivotal, aspect of the development process. In the two centuries since the dispute over the wisdom of industrialization by protection was first seriously joined in countries like the United States and Germany, the question has been reargued in nearly all countries reaching comparable stages of development. The discussion has become more sophisticated in many respects, but has remained unsatisfactory due to the lack of empirical studies of the processes of change and cost reduction in specific industries. More recently attention has been directed to the wide range of technologies which coexist in many industrial branches in less developed countries, usually associated with the parallel coexistence of large and small establishments with a wide range of labor intensities. Vigorous debate has arisen on the relative merits of traditional labor-intensive technologies and modern capital-intensive technologies for countries at various stages of development. Again, the empirical evidence is too sparse to permit many valid policy conclusions.

This volume will contribute in the search for answers to these and other questions. As a semi-industrialized country, Colombia's experience is of relevance to many other nations, especially those currently at an earlier stage of that process.

Most of the essays included here were written while the authors were affiliated with the Economic Growth Center and/or the Department of Economics at Yale, whose stimulation we gratefully acknowledge.

Toronto

September 1981

Chapter 1

Introduction
Albert Berry

The series of essays in this volume attempts to throw some light on several broad issues surrounding the process of industrialization in a country like Colombia. The central issue is the role played by industrialization in the development of the economy as well as in such particulars as the evolution of real income per capita and the determination of income distribution. Industrialization is a natural concomitant of development in the world at large; what requires analysis is how the success of overall development is affected by how soon industrialization comes to a country, how vigorously it is pushed, and what tools are used to encourage it. Clearly, there is no general presumption that industrialization should be achieved as fast as possible in each and every country. In order to approach these broad questions, it is necessary to have as detailed an understanding as possible of the process of growth within the industrial sector; sources of growth, bottlenecks to growth, and interactions among factors and industries form the essence of such a background.

Over time a body of information has been built up on the process of industrialization and its contribution to overall growth. As a result, a few issues may be deemed largely settled, even in underdeveloped countries. Unfortunately, many other hypotheses have been developed without the basis of much relevant empirical information and are thus less convincing than might be hoped. We try here to focus on some of these unresolved issues.

Industrialization is usually pursued through a policy of protection, the use of which has generated much debate and criticism among academic economists. As the major policy affecting the rate and nature of industrialization, protection is traditionally carried out by tariffs, although in more recent years it has been increasingly implemented by quotas, exchange controls, and other direct interventions. The normal justification for protection is the infant industry argument, or some more complicated variant like the infant sector[1] or infant economy arguments. Several empirical issues bear on the validity of these arguments. One is the extent and predictability of learning associated with the experience of production.[2] Another is the problem of capital market imperfections forcing a firm to self-finance its early growth with family savings and profits, rather than using the capital market. Finally, the degree of risk aversion characterizing potential entrepreneurs is also relevant.[3] Some of these phenomena are very difficult to quantify, others less so.

It seems quite plausible that the extent and nature of risk and uncertainty should vary as industrialization proceeds. Increasing information about industrial processes and about the rest of the industrial sector should permit entrepreneurs to make better estimates of their own costs, the nature of the competition, and so on. Ospina Vasquez felt that risk aversion was a real problem and substantial protection a necessity for inducing industrialization in early twentieth century Colombia. (See Chapter 2). Other observers have felt that this need was less powerful in later periods, such as after World War II. Unfortunately the evidence on the degree of risk aversion and other characteristics of Colombian enterpreneurs discussed in Chapters 2 and 3 allows only for impressionistic judgments to be made.

Chapters 4 and 5 focus upon the extent and nature of learning-by-doing in two selected industries, metal products and thermal electricity generation. In both cases learning is clearly identified. None of the essays presented here focuses upon the capital market characteristics most relevant to the infant industry argument, although Chapter 6, in discussing the issue of why factor proportions differ so much between large and small plants, touches upon the issue by providing circumstantial evidence of considerable capital market imperfection. Whether capital market imperfections raise the costs of some firms and industries that exist as a result of high tariffs is another question; the answer is not obvious, for some are certainly favored by those imperfections.

Assuming some degree of validity for the infant industry argument and protection, the question of an appropriate combination of policy tools for stimulation of domestic industry remains. The choice of such tools is wide and includes tariffs, quotas, easy access to subsidized credit, and tax exemptions. Some observers feel that industrial output is relatively elastic to price, so that the best way to encourage industrialization is by simply using the price incentive of tariffs; others argue for more direct forms of risk reduction and profit stimulation. David Chu's evidence in Chapter 3 tends to support the former contention, at least during the period 1930-45.

The industrial sector in countries like Colombia is frequently characterized as dualistic, or more generally as involving highly heterogeneous technology. For example, Richard Nelson et al.[4] argue that it is meaningful to distinguish within the industrial sector a modern, usually large-scale, subsector in which the technology applied is similar to and the labor productivity near that of developed countries, and a craft or small-scale sector tending to apply relatively traditional, unchanging, and usually (if not always) labor-intensive technologies. The authors hypothesize that the industrialization process involves predominantly the displacement of the latter type of firm and its technology by the former in relative, if not in absolute terms. Frequently accompanying the modern-craft distinction is the proposition that the larger firms dominate the smaller ones in some technological sense, or in the economic sense of having higher total factor productivity when factor costs are measured at appropriate shadow prices (possibly equal to their market prices). John Todd's essay (Chapter 6) advances our understanding of the basic differences between large, capital-intensive plants and small, labor-intensive ones. His conclusion that the former have lower total factor productivity across a substantial range of possible shadow factor prices raises serious questions about the widely accepted view that large firms are in general more efficient in the economic sense. Todd's work shakes credibility in the idea that a simple, positive relationship exists between size, factor intensity, and total factor productivity. The possible advantages of small firms over large ones are striking, especially when the greater labor intensity of the former is taken into account. Among the more plausible interpretations of the wide range of factor proportions observed across firms producing similar products is the existence of highly imperfect factor markets.

One approach to a better understanding of the structure and dynamics of a sector is to focus upon those observed characteristics which seem particularly surprising because they do not fit into the conventional picture of the sector. Attempts to explain the surprisingly wide variance of factor proportions across firm sizes have undoubtedly helped in our understanding of the industrial sector by precipitating a long overdue attack upon the assumption that firms in a given industry operate on a given homogeneous production function and face perfect factor markets. These are handy assumptions indeed for building simple models, but dangerous if one neglects to test their realism in a specific situation. Another striking characteristic of manufacturing in many countries is the presence of widespread excess capacity in economies presumed to be short of capital. To what extent is this due to small markets, to what extent to oligopolistic market structures and the "maintenance of market share" behavior pattern which characterizes them, and to what extent to a situation involving some competition among firms together with the inability of individual enterpreneurs to predict who else is going to enter? Francisco Thoumi's essay (Chapter 7) is a quantitative test of these and other hypotheses in the Colombian context; directly, it indicates to us which characteristics appear to be associated with excess capacity; less directly but perhaps more importantly, it gives us new hints as to the nature and behavior patterns of industrial firms in Colombia.

As discussed above, the major issue of debate for many years in the developing countries was the wisdom of import-substituting industrialization, the optimal level of protection, and the optimal way to grant it. Always at the extreme were the free traders whose theoretical arguments might have been compelling had their assumptions been plausible and subjected to sufficient empirical testing to generate confidence that they were close to the mark. At the other extreme, many of the protectionists were strikingly unpersuasive because they used either interest group arguments or incorrect economics. The more sophisticated protectionist proponents had little interest in engaging the free trade theorists, since the arguments of the latter group never had enough realism to warrant serious discussion. So protection has continued to be an academic issue, as successive generations of countries vigorously protect their industry while very little relevant empirical evidence on the wisdom of the policy has been accumulated.

With the recent manufacturing export booms of a number of developing countries whose industrial sectors had up to that point been highly protected, the same two groups have once again taken the floor. Economists oriented toward free trade argue that the only mistake these countries made was their protected, import-substituting industrialization. These nations should have allowed their industries to evolve in a free trade situation, to develop when they were capable of competing, and to start exporting when they were ready. Since some protectionists have argued that industries in less developed countries (LDCs) cannot easily be competitive in world markets, their position does not appear on the surface to imply that substantial manufactured exports would be likely at early stages of development. Free traders frequently consider the relatively easy arrival of some LDCs on the manufacturing export stage, and its association with a move to realistic exchange rates in many of these countries, as evidence against the wisdom of the previous import-substituting policies. To some extent, of course, this is to attack a straw man. What we may call the sophisticated protectionist arguments have always focused on the phenomena of risk, learning-by-doing, capital market imperfections, and so on. Protection is undertaken on the presumption that the industries so fostered will become competitive; the manufacturing export stage is, therefore, quite consistent with the serious protectionist argument.[5] Accordingly, the opposite position[6] to that of the free traders is that the process of import substitution *has* involved learning and risk reduction, both at the individual level and at the sectoral level. It is this "learning *cum* risk reduction" process, fostered by import substitution under protection, which has permitted the sector to reach the stage where it could compete in export markets.[7] The free trade position is often linked to a Heckscher-Ohlin or factor abundance theory of international trade, and lends itself to the expectation that efficient industrial exports will be labor intensive and that their expansion can accordingly be expected to raise labor's share in the national income. The protectionist position has less obvious implications for the factor proportion and income distribution effects of manufacturing exports.

Chapter 8, while it does not attempt an overall evaluation of the relative validity of these two positions, does probe the characteristics of the new manufacturing exporters and raises particular doubts about the expectation that industries able to move into the manufacturing export stage will be labor intensive. This expectation is not borne out in Colombia. The fact that most manufactured exports come from large firms that have long been producing for the domestic market may support some version of the infant industry or the infant sector argument. As with some of the other essays, Chapter 8 tends to raise more questions than it resolves, but this is perhaps an apt reflection of the state of our understanding with respect both to the new export booms and to the industrialization process in general. We have harbored some naive expectations because of naive and oversimplified models; the first step in evolving helpful explanations of the phenomenon will probably be that of describing the firms involved, and in the process modifying our current frameworks and concepts.

Each chapter in this volume points either explicitly or implicitly to research areas which must be pursued before our understanding of the functioning of Colombia's industrial sector will be adequate. The final chapter, as it reviews the results presented in earlier ones, discusses some of these areas in greater detail.

ENDNOTES FOR CHAPTER 1

1. The proposition that an industrial sector becomes more efficient as different industries become aware of each other's capacities and get practice in interacting and in doing business with each other. Lowering of costs in specific industries may be dependent on the growth of other industries and on the experience of coordinating activities with them.

2. The broad category of learning under discussion here includes learning by the workers, by entrepreneurs, and perhaps by individuals, not yet entrepreneurs, who realize that certain types of entrepreneurship can have high payoff. At early stages of development, when it is necessary to induce this last group into action, such learning may be the most important.

3. Various combinations of conditions are sufficient to imply the validity of the infant industry argument, depending on the surrounding context. For discussions, see G. M. Meier, *The International Economics of Development* (New York: Harper and Row, 1968), and H. G. Johnson, *Economic Policies Toward Less Developed Countries* (New York: Praeger, 1967).

4. Richard Nelson, T. Paul Schultz, and Robert Slighton, *Structural Change in a Developing Economy: The Case of Colombia* (Princeton: Princeton University Press, 1971).

5. It is important to distinguish between protectionist arguments which never warranted serious consideration in the first place and others which are plausible and logically consistent.

6. See, for example, Gustav Ranis and Benjamin Cohen, "Import Liberalization and Growth: The Second Postwar Restructuring" in Gustav Ranis, ed., *Government and Economic Development* (New Haven: Yale University Press, 1971).

7. We disregard here the proposition that the LDC industrial exports are not basically competitive, but are related to very high subsidies or consist of surpluses which are transitorily exported. In the early years of the export booms of several of the countries like Colombia, the idea that the exports were largely related to excess capacity was not patently false, although now it appears to be so.

Chapter 2

A Descriptive History of Colombian Industrial Development in the Twentieth Century
Albert Berry

Most of the chapters in this volume focus on specific issues in the industrial development of Colombia, issues of interest to policy-makers or of importance in understanding the nature of industrial growth. This chapter provides a backdrop of general information on the history of the manufacturing sector in Colombia. Its basic organization is chronological. The key role of world trade conditions both in overall growth and in industrialization is reflected in our delineation of the following subperiods: 1900-30, growth based on coffee exports; 1930-45, Depression and World War II; and since 1945, postwar expansion in a healthy world economy. Manufacturing exports began to take on major significance during this last subperiod, especially in the late sixties.

Within this framework, selected aspects of industrial evolution are probed, including sources of demand expansion (import substitution, domestic demand, and exports), sources of output growth (increases in factor inputs, technological change, changes in sectoral and size structure of output), sources of key inputs (capital and entrepreneurship), and distribution of the fruits of industrialization as among capital, highly paid employees and lower paid workers. This analysis will help in drawing tentative conclusions as to the quality of public policy towards industry in twentieth-century Colombia.

PART I
NINETEENTH CENTURY STAGNATION

The generally successful growth path since the turn of the century followed a lengthy period of relative stagnation. The reasons for this turnaround are worth noting. Colombia's relatively late start toward sustained economic growth and the low income level at the turn of the century were the culmination of a period of stagnation, possibly even decline, during the second half of the nineteenth century. Ospina Vasquez estimated that the purchasing power of a year's labor in agriculture fell dramatically between 1848 and 1892; the income from such labor would buy less corn, meat, flour, or potatoes in 1892 than in 1727 or any subsequent year for which he effected the calculation.[1] William McGreevey related this apparent decline to important changes in land tenure during the nineteenth century. Land passed from communal tenure to large haciendas, from church lands (*mortmain*) to cattle raising, and from public lands to fee-simple tenure; each of these developments had the effect of concentrating the ownership and control of land.[2] Given the low land productivity on large farms, this would be expected to diminish total agricultural output; the greater land concentration would generate greater income inequality, lower wages, and smaller markets for mass consumer goods.

McGreevey cited the switch to free trade around the middle of the century as a second source of economic loss. He argued that, given the substantial small-scale production of manufactured items for domestic consumption, the growth of exports and the consequent expansion of manufactured imports lowered the income of the artisan class (the main loser) much more than it increased the income of the merchant class (the main gainer).[3] He estimated that imports rose by eightfold between 1845 and 1890, but local production of importables, although undergoing substantial fluctuation, showed no net increase.[4] While the erratic export booms of the nineteenth century damaged the artisan sector, contemporary government policy was such that the import capacity that those booms created worked to the disadvantage rather than the advantage of modern industrial development. Some factories did exist in the first half of the nineteenth century. The landed elite of Bogotá, for example, made numerous efforts to create industrial as well as commercial enterprises in the interior. Frank Safford notes that

> between 1821 and 1842, with government encouragement, members of the traditional aristocracy attempted to establish an iron works and a variety of small consumer goods factories, using machinery of the latest European models. These ventures either failed, or had only modest success, for lack of a sufficient internal market and because of competition from imported goods.[5]

Gradually, the Granadan leaders concluded that the effort to establish manufacturing in Bogotá had been a mistake because they could not compete with the more efficient European industries. Influenced in part by the free-trade ideas emanating from Great Britain, the opinion-makers began to see the country's salvation in international trade. Steps were taken to facilitate tropical exports; new emphasis was placed upon steam navigation on the Magdalena River. Protective tariffs were dropped; investments in manufacturing were left unprotected and were even condemned as wrong-headed and quixotic.[6] Although a scattering of entrepreneurs did set up small plants—such as soap and candle factories and a French-owned lamp and lamp oil factory—most of these failed. The many civil conflicts of the second half of the nineteenth century, which also had a negative impact on industrialization, internal trade, and specialization, finally culminated at the turn of the century in the Thousand Days War.

The above basic elements in Colombia's nineteenth-century economic evolution manifested themselves at the start of the twentieth century in the country's relatively low capacity for external payments, small foreign investment,[7] and physical isolation of major economic regions from one another. These factors, in the view of the Economic Commission for Latin America (ECLA), contributed directly to the delayed onset of industrialization in Colombia.

Whatever the precise contribution of these and other factors to Colombia's stagnation and decline during much of the nineteenth century, her economic base was indeed limited at the turn of the century and her successful twentieth-century growth is striking in contrast to what went before. The contrast is perhaps especially sharp in industry, where the wave of growth, as nearly as we can ascertain with figures, lagged somewhat behind that of exports.[8] Coffee was already a substantial export during the last two decades of the nineteenth century. Small export booms during the nineteenth century in tobacco, quinine, and indigo had failed to generate self-sustained growth and expanding manufacturing industry. The reversal of previous trends is most often linked to the advent of coffee as a major export, the associated transportation improvements, and the creation of sizable domestic markets for local manufacturers.[9]

ECLA estimated that the share of manufacturing in the gross national product (GNP) of Colombia had been quite low in the early twentieth century, only reaching about 10 percent in 1925.[10] Industrialization came later to Colombia than to Chile, Argentina, Brazil, and Mexico. In Argentina and Chile, manufacturing accounted for almost 20 percent of total production around the turn of the century, in Mexico 10-15 percent.

PART II
A QUANTITATIVE OVERVIEW OF TWENTIETH CENTURY INDUSTRIAL DEVELOPMENT

Industrial development, stimulated by the protectionist policies of General Rafael Reyes and subsequent governments, received a push during the boom years of the twenties. The change in relative prices resulting from the Depression created a different stimulus during the thirties. In the post-World War II period, import substitution became a highly conscious policy; in the late sixties this strategy began to give way to export promotion as a source of industrial growth.

Table 2.1 summarizes major developments over this century. For the first seventy years of the century, the average annual growth rate of output was about 5.5-6.3 percent;[11] labor productivity rose by about 4.0-4.7 percent per year, and the labor force by almost 1.5 percent.[12] As a proportion of the total labor force, employment in the manufacturing sector appears to have fallen during the latter part of the nineteenth century and possibly during the first years of the twentieth, a fairly frequent phenomenon in countries at the early stages of development when factory manufacturing is beginning to replace artisanry[13] and cottage-shop production. In 1870 perhaps 20 percent or more of the labor force was in manufacturing; by 1938, the share had fallen to around 14 percent.[14] This decline appears to have come to an end around 1950, when only about 12 percent of total employment was in manufacturing. Subsequently, the trend has been positive, and the share was probably 16-17 percent in June, 1978. Table 2.1 reflects these trends in more detail. The manufacturing share of nonagricultural employment tended downward until the sixties. In 1938 it approached 40 percent; in 1964 it was less than 25 percent, but by 1978 it had moved back up to about 28 percent. The secular decline reflected the rapid growth of employment in the service sector.

Employment in factory manufacturing (plants of 5 workers or more) as a share of the labor force has risen secularly from perhaps 1 percent in 1870,[15] to a little better than 3 percent by the mid-twenties, to about 7 percent in 1970, and 9 percent or higher in 1978. The share of the labor force employed in artisan or cottage-shop activities appears to have fallen dramatically between 1870 and 1925, from around 20 percent to perhaps 13-14 percent. Since then, it decreased further, although as of 1970 it was still about 8 percent; the secular decline seemed to end in the early fifties. Some fluctuation may have occurred subsequently; although figures for the seventies are still uncertain, a reasonable guess for 1978 would be 7-8 percent. As discussed in greater detail below,

TABLE 2.1
TWENTIETH-CENTURY TRENDS IN THE MANUFACTURING SECTOR: ALL MANUFACTURING

Year	Employment (thousands)	Output (millions of 1958 pesos)	Labor Productivity (1958 pesos)	Physical Capital Stock	Output/Capital	Manufacturing Employment/Total Employment[g]	Output/G.N.P. Current Prices	Output/G.N.P. Constant Prices[h]
1870	275.0 – 325.0[a]	---	---	---	---	≈ 20.0[a]	---	---
1900	300.0 – 400.0	103.9 – 167.2[e]	346– 418	---	---	≈18.0–18.5	na	na
1925–1927	405.8[b] – 439.4[c]	473.0	1076–1166	3,464.9	.13	15.9–17.2	na	8.9
1929–1931	421.8[b] – 460.1[c]	520.1	1130–1233	4,487.2	.12	15.4–16.8	na	8.2
1939–1941	≈451.3	1,010.5	2239	5,076.2	.20	13.5	13.3	10.6
1949–1951	473.0	2,112.7	4467	8,336.1	.25	≈ 12.1	≈ 16.9	≈14.5
1959–1961	607.5	4,131.1	6800	13,023.0	.32	13.1	18.2	17.8
1969–1971	853.0	7,425.3	8705	18,816.0	.39	14.9	18.8	19.0
1978	≈1,300.0[d]	12,315.0[f]	9473	na		16.2	na	19.2
Growth Rates (1900–1970)	1.1–1.5	5.5–6.3	4.3–4.7	3.97[j]	---	---	---	---

(continued)

TABLE 2.1 (continued)

TWENTIETH-CENTURY TRENDS IN THE MANUFACTURING SECTOR: FACTORY MANUFACTURING

Year	Employment[i]	Output	Labor Productivity	Physical Capital Stock	Output/Capital	Employment / Total Employment[g]	Output G.N.P. Current Prices	Output G.N.P. Constant Prices
1870	---	---	---	---	---	---	---	---
1900	---	---	---	---	---	---	---	---
1925–1927	≤70	---	---	---	---	≤2.74	---	---
1929–1931	---	---	---	---	---	---	---	---
1939–1941	95–115	660.2	5,740–6,950	---	---	2.84–3.44	8.7	6.93
1949–1951	178.8	1,574.8	8,808	7,033	.22	4.57	12.6	10.8
1959–1961	267.1	3,303.8	12,369	11,509	.29	5.75	14.6	14.2
1969–1971	395.4	6,286.9	15,900	16,950	.37	6.90	16.2	16.3
1978	723.0	10,796	14,932	na	na	9.01	17.8	17.0
Growth Rates (1900–1970)	≥3.9[j]	7.77[k]	2.95–3.6[k]	4.43[l]				---

(continued)

TABLE 2.1 (continued)

TWENTIETH-CENTURY TRENDS IN THE MANUFACTURING SECTOR: COTTAGE-SHOP

Year	Employment	Output	Share of Manufacturing Output	Share of Total Employment[g]
1870	---	---	---	---
1900	---	---	---	---
1925–1927	≈350–390	---	---	---
1929–1931	---	---	---	---
1939–1941	336.3–356.3	350.3	34.7	10.1–10.7
1949–1951	294.2	537.9	25.5	7.5
1959–1961	340.4	827.3	20.0	7.3
1969–1971	≈ 457.6	1,099.4	15.4	8.0
1978	577.0	1,519.0	12.3	7.2
Growth Rates (1900–1970)	0.55[j]	3.95[k]	---	---

(continued)

TABLE 2.1 (Continued)

Sources and Methodology: Output figures are from Banco de la República, *Cuentas Nacionales* for recent years, and Table A-13 for earlier years; the splice is effected in 1950. Constant price output figures for years after 1970 are expressed in 1970 pesos in the national accounts and are spliced to the earlier figures in 1970. Employment figures are based on those of Table 2.5, except as noted. Capital stock estimates are based on Tables A-46, A-47, and A-55.

na = not available

[a] For a discussion of the labor force around and before 1900, see Fernando Gomez, "Los Censos de Colombia antes de 1905" in Miguel Urrutia M. and Mario Arrubla, eds., *Compendio de estadísticas históricas de Colombia* (Bogotá: Dirección de Divulgación Cultural, Universidad Nacional de Colombia, 1970).

[b] Interpolated on the basis of a lower limit estimate of 380,000 employment in 1918 (see Table 2.5).

[c] Interpolated on the basis of a upper limit estimate of 435,000 employment in 1918 (see Table 2.5).

[d] This is tentative. Employment figures for the seventies are not yet sorted out. The June, 1978 survey presents a figure of 1,417,000 persons employed in manufacturing. As we have argued elsewhere, this figure is probably too high and 1,300,000 appears to fall in the middle of the probable range. For further details see A. Berry, "The Evolution of Small Scale Industry in Colombia" (1980), Table 2, mimeographed.

[e] Assuming growth rates of 6 percent and 4 percent respectively over 1900-1925.

[f] Provisional

[g] Total labor force is that of ECLA for 1925-1953, with a subsequent series of the author's spliced on at 1951. As a result, the labor force shares shown here are a little different from those of Table 2.5 below. For the 1925-1953 series, see ECLA *Analyses and Projections*, Statistical Annex. For 1959-61 and since we have used employment (as distinct from labor force); for earlier years for which the distinction was vaguer and the difference smaller, we have used estimates for the labor force.

[h] For years before 1950, ECLA's economy-wide growth rate was used to project the 1950 GDP backwards.

[i] Note that ECLA's series, which may have been based on data unavailable to us, was much higher in 1939-41 (156,000 and thus 36 percent above our upper estimate), although also much higher in 1953 (32 percent).

[j] Since 1925/27

[k] Since 1939/41

[l] Since 1949/51

this reversal of the long-run decline in the labor-force share of cottage-shop manufacturing has been related to substantial changes in the composition of output in this subsector, away from popular items like clothing and textiles towards modern, small-scale activities like repairs for transportation equipment.

The measured trends in labor force and labor productivity reflect, among other things, a significant substitution of more highly skilled male workers for less skilled female workers, and possibly of full-time workers for part-time ones. The 1870 census reported between two and three times as many women in the artisan and *fabricante* categories as men. By 1938 the proportions were roughly equal, and by 1964 men far outnumbered women. The women in rural and urban artisan industries who were gradually replaced often had relatively simple skills, and the same was true of those upon whom the early, low-wage factory sector in Medellín was based. Some part of the increase in average labor productivity over time is a reflection of the higher skill level of today's workers.

In any case, labor productivity in manufacturing has risen rapidly during the twentieth century as can be seen in Table 2.1. Our rough data suggest an average increase of around 5 percent per year between 1900 and 1950. This may be an overestimate, but there is no reason to doubt that the true figure is high. The rate of growth of labor productivity has declined markedly since 1950. A comparison of the subperiods 1951-64 and 1964-78 reveals a considerably faster growth over the first subperiod, about 3.8 percent, as contrasted with only about 1 percent over the second. The latter figure, however, is open to some question since the employment estimates come mainly from labor force surveys rather than from population censuses, and may therefore not be fully comparable to the earlier figures. Nonetheless, the range of error is not such as to reverse the conclusion that labor productivity growth slowed significantly. As we shall see later, different rates of change in the composition of the industrial labor force between large and small plants are probably the main cause of the differing rates of labor-productivity growth over time. The thirties and forties witnessed wholesale replacement of traditional small-scale manufacturing by larger-scale,[16] with large, positive effects on average labor productivity. After the absolute level of cottage-shop employment stabilized in the fifties, and then began to rise again in the late sixties, the increase in the share of manufacturing workers in establishments with five workers or more has been less. Although productivity increased in both the factory and cottage-shop subsectors, the average increase for all manufacturing was slower than before.

Trends in the share of manufacturing in total output are similar to those for employment, but not identical since the relative productivity of manufacturing vis-à-vis the rest of the economy has risen over time as indicated in Table 2.1. McGreevey estimated that the approximately 22 percent of the labor force in manufacturing in 1870 produced only 12 or 13 percent of output;[17] according to our revised ECLA figures, the 15 percent or so of the labor force in manufacturing in 1925 produced about 11 percent of output. Subsequently, of course, average labor productivity in manufacturing has risen above that for the economy as a whole; the ratio vis-à-vis nonmanufacturing reached about 1.3 in 1970 (current prices). This positive trend has been closely associated with the increase in the share of manufacturing output coming from modern factories and the decrease in share from small-scale artisanry and cottage-shop. In 1925 ECLA estimated that the 3.4 percent of the labor force in the factory subsector produced 7.6 percent of output; in 1970 the approximately 7 percent of the labor force so occupied produced about 16 percent of value added at current market prices.

The share of cottage-shop in total output has undergone a secular decline according to the limited evidence available. McGreevey estimated roughly[18] 9 percent of total output generated by cottage-shop in 1870; the ECLA estimate for 1925 was a shade below 5 percent. In 1970 the share of value added at market prices may have been about 3 percent.[19]

The manufacturing capital stock has risen rapidly; in 1925 ECLA's estimates of both the capital/labor (K/L) and capital/output (K/O) ratios were below the economy-wide average.[20] By 1967 the K/L ratio in manufacturing appeared to be about a third higher than for the economy as a whole, while the K/O ratio was marginally higher.[21] Our estimate in Table 2.1 suggests that capital per worker rose by about 160-180 percent over the period 1925-27 to 1969-71;[22] it had no doubt risen somewhat during the first quarter of the century as well. Meanwhile, output per worker rose much faster, by about eightfold, over the same period;[23] most of this measured increase must therefore be due not simply to capital formation in manufacturing but to some combination of technological and organizational improvements, complementary public investment, economies of scale,[24] and high relative prices of new manufactures.[25] What are the relative contributions of these various sources of labor-productivity growth? The evidence suggests that the last factor cited could not easily have accounted for more than one-quarter of the observed growth.[26] The contribution made by the increase in K/L depends upon the nature of the production function, specifically upon the elasticity of substitution. Given a Cobb-Douglas production function (and therefore unit elasticity of substitution) as well as a capital share of 50 percent and no economies of scale, one could explain a labor-productivity increase of at most 75 percent,[27] or less than one-fifth of the total increase, even after scaling that increase down to allow for artificial output gains related to protection and the high domestic prices. With a capital share of 60 percent and an elasticity of substitution of 2, the increase in K/L would explain labor-productivity growth of up to 100 percent; even with infinite elasticity of substitution, it would explain an increase of only about 140 percent.[28] With all plausible assumptions, then, it appears that increases in K/L, while important, have not been the key to rising labor productivity.[29] The same holds for the period 1944/5-69, for which better data are available.

Rising labor quality, related both to higher educational levels and to increasing average experience, has also contributed to rising labor productivity. Another factor—which may partially overlap with the previous one[30]—is the gradual shift of output toward industries characterized by high labor productivity. Data on trends in the composition of the labor force by educational and occupational levels, coupled with evidence on the effect of experience on labor income, permit a rough guess as to the labor-productivity gains associated with rising labor skills. As shown in Table 2.2, these data suggest a positive impact on labor productivity of perhaps 40 to 80 percent[31] over the period 1925-69, and about 20 to 35 percent from 1944/5 to 1969. About 10-20 percent of the labor-productivity increase in the factory subsector over this latter period was associated with shifting output composition by two-digit industry; some or all of this increase could have been related to increasing physical or human capital per worker.

The above figures taken together loosely suggest that something over half and possibly up to three-quarters of the increase in labor productivity over time was due to better technology or improved organization, public investment, and economies of scale. The proportion is somewhat less when productivity increase is calculated with output valued at world prices. The role of the last two factors taken together is unlikely to be more than a fraction of that of private capital formation, permitting

TABLE 2.2

A GROWTH ACCOUNTING EXERCISE FOR LABOR PRODUCTIVITY, 1925/27-1969/71 AND SUBPERIODS

Growth of Labor Productivity	LP Increase, Output Valued at:		LP Increase Attributable to Rising Capital/Labor Ratio			LP Increase Associated with Rising Labor Skills[c]	LP Increase Associated with Shifting of Industrial Composition within the Factory Subsector	Residual: LP increase presumably attributable to intra-industry technological improvements,[g] other organizational improvements,[h] public investment, and economies of scale	
	Colombian Prices	World Prices (lower limit)[a]	$S_k=.50$ $\Sigma=1$	$S_k=.70$ $\Sigma=2$	$S_k=.70$ $\Sigma=\infty$			Total Increase Measured at Colombian Prices	Total Increase Measured at World Prices
1925/27-1969/71: Percentage points	676	512	58-64	97-110	127-143				
Share of total increase, at Colombian prices	100		.086–.095	.143–.163	.188–.212				
Share of total increase, at world prices		100	.113–.125	.189–.215	.248–.279				
1944/45-1969/71: Percentage points	185	137[b]	27	41	42	20-35[d]	18.3[e]	95-138[f]	47-90
Share of total increase, at Colombian prices	100		.146	.221	.229	.108–.189	.099	.513–.747	
Share of total increase, at world prices		100	.197	.298	.309	.146–.255			.344–.657

Source: Table 2.1 and the assumptions noted in the footnotes.

LP = labor productivity

S_k = the capital share of income generated in manufacturing

Σ = the elasticity of substitution between labor and capital in manufacturing

(continued)

Descriptive History - 17

TABLE 2.2 (continued)

[a] Assuming the bundle produced in 1925/27 was priced at 5 percent above world prices.
[b] Assuming the bundle produced in 1944/45 was priced at 10 percent above world prices.
[c] Either from better preparation (education) or learning on the job.
[d] Based on the share of wage increases over the period which appears to be related to increasing skills. Evidence used included wage differentials between large plants and small ones, between high-skill industries and low-skill industries, and between persons of different educational levels, along with data on the number of persons at each level at various points of time. None of these approaches gives more than a rough range within which the variable in question may lie, but there was some consistency across the various methodologies. Since each of the differentials cited probably includes also an element of rent not associated with skills (perhaps least likely in the case of the educational differential, but still quite possible) we subtracted five percentage points (from each of the upper and lower limits) as a rough approximation of the effect of this factor. Note that DANE's upward bias in the estimation of value added (due to failure to subtract certain inputs) probably biases the first two wage differentials cited upwards, and by an increasing amount over time. But this factor would not appear to loom large in these calculations. It is possible, on the other hand, that we have underestimated the importance of labor skills gained through experience.
[e] 7.61 percent of 1969 factory output is associated with the shift in question (i.e., 6.41 percent of total output and 9.87 percent of the increase in labor productivity). This calculation is based on the assumption that relative prices did not change among two-digit sectors over this period.
[f] For the high estimate, the low estimates for increases in K/L and in labor skills are used, and it is assumed that the labor productivity increase associated with shifting composition of factory output by two-digit sector is completely due to those two factors. For the low estimate, the high estimates of the first two components were used and an additional 15 percentage point increase was assumed to be related to the composition shift.
[g] Either embodied in capital stock or not; may come in the form of cheaper capital goods, when industries change the type of capital goods they use.
[h] In other words, fuller use of capacity.

the conclusion that improvements in technology and organization were of major importance and possibly accounted for half or more of the labor-productivity gains.[32]

With output measured at Colombian prices, total factor productivity rose by an average of perhaps 3 percent per year between 1925 and 1970. This rise seems to have been particularly rapid in the pre-World War II period; our figures suggest over 4 percent per year, with a gradual decline to only a little over 2 percent per year during the sixties.[33] Measured at international prices, the rates of output growth and of factor-productivity increase would probably be lower, since some of the recently initiated industries appear to be more inefficient than were the nascent industries which Colombia protected in earlier periods, although the difference would not be dramatic.[34]

PART III
A CHRONOLOGICAL RECORD OF INDUSTRIAL GROWTH AND INDUSTRIAL POLICY IN THE TWENTIETH CENTURY

While manufacturing output has increased continuously in the twentieth century, the rate and especially the pattern of growth has varied in response to:

(1) the availability of savings,
(2) the availability of foreign exchange permitting imports of capital goods and raw materials,
(3) the relative price of output, often affected by tariffs and other trade policies,
(4) the supply of entrepreneurial talent, and
(5) the adequacy of market demand.

These factors tend, in their turn, to reflect the level of income and its rate of growth. A helpful, although inevitably arbitrary breakdown by subperiods is:

(1) 1900-30: the first adventure into modern manufacturing on a significant scale, the victory of protectionism over free-trade sentiment, rapid growth of coffee exports, expansion of the railroad system, substantial capital inflow (though not direct investment).
(2) 1930-45: manufacturing growth under the natural protection of the Depression and World War II.
(3) 1945-60s: import-substituting industrialization by use of legislated import controls and other incentives, advance into complex and capital-intensive sectors, substantial direct foreign investment.
(4) 1960s-present: increasing export focus, continued direct foreign investment, and import substitution.

While the character of manufacturing and its growth process have changed markedly during this evolution, the sectoral growth rate has been remarkedly stable, at least since the twenties. Growth was probably below 6 percent per year or even 5 percent per year before that time but, since 1930, the slowest growth decade was the sixties with an average of 6 percent per year, and the fastest was the seventies (through 1978) with an average of 8 percent per year.

The first three subperiods are delineated by changes in the conditions of external trade; one could alternatively distinguish stages of industrialization according to complexity. ECLA, for example, has characterized the industrial process as involving first a focus upon "traditional" industries, such things as primary food processing, tobacco, beverages, textiles, cement and other simple building materials, simple chemical preparations, and containers for pharmaceutical products (still largely based upon imported raw materials).[35] This phase is characterized by a sharp reduction in cottage employment and the formation of sizable nuclei of factory employment while artisan industry and small-scale plants increase. Colombia was not definitely launched in this stage until the Depression.[36]

The next stage in ECLA's scheme involves the development of basic industries and of simple equipment manufacturing, including steelmaking, simple iron and steel transformation, the chemical industry with inorganic products, oil refining, and vehicle assembly.[37] Assimilation of technology is stepped up and the capital/labor ratio rises. Market size becomes a problem, as many new lines have relatively large minimum efficient levels of production; the greater technological complexity and the shortage of needed skilled labor can also constitute barriers. Foreign investment and technical assistance, direct state promotion and intensive training programs help to overcome these obstacles. A further, more complex stage involves complicated intermediate products like the metal transforming industries. In the early sixties, ECLA placed only Brazil, Argentina, and Mexico in this category, but by the late seventies Colombia was moving close to it. Distinguishing such stages of industrialization is helpful in many contexts; but in analyzing the overall pace and effects of industrialization, the criterion chosen here seems preferable.

1900-30: Background to The New Experiment of Industrialization

The turn of the century was a low-water mark for Colombia's economy; from then on the combination of growing exports and stable government ushered in the sustained growth of the twentieth century. Forces for economic growth were building up in the late nineteenth century but were counterbalanced by population increase, political disorganization, and other negative factors. From an economic point of view, the rapid expansion of coffee exports, the associated decreases in transportation costs, and the relatively even distribution of the coffee income seem to have been key factors in turning the tide.

Rising coffee exports benefited a substantial share of the population. Especially after 1857, tobacco income had been concentrated in the hands of a rentier class,[38] with the result that a large share of the foreign exchange was spent on luxury imports. This combined with British-merchant control of some of the best tobacco fields to produce a substantial capital outflow.[39] The rising coffee income, in contrast, fueled a greater demand for cheap cotton textiles than for luxuries. As importing firms were faced with a growing demand for textiles, they saw the budding opportunities for domestic production in modern plants. Roads or railroads to the main population centers in the highlands, irrelevant in the export of tobacco, were now needed since coffee production was located in those highlands.[40] These new roads and rail lines simultaneously contributed to industrialization. Thus McGreevey argued that:

> "the railway played an . . . important role in promoting the Medellín textile industry. Although lower transport costs cut the price of imported manufactures, the price of raw materials and machinery fell even more; and since Medellín re-

> lied initially on the importation of almost all the components required for textile manufacture, transport improvements favoured industrial growth. This effect was greatest, moreover, in coarse grades of cotton cloth of the kind in which Medellín came to specialize."[41]

The availability of savings out of coffee-related income and the absence of strong competition from artisans in the Medellín area raised the attractiveness of investment in industry.

> "Capital and entrepreneurial skills were made available to the new industries directly from the export sector: the same family which began the first textile enterprise was headed by the owner of one of the largest coffee exporting and processing houses. This same individual ran one of the largest importing firms. With such a wide variety of economic enterprises held within one family, neither supply of capital nor of managerial skills proved to be bottlenecks preventing the expansion of manufacturing."[42]

These export-related trends in Colombia's economic situation were doubtless crucial to the onset of industrialization; they were also complemented by policy steps. The Reyes Presidency (1904-09) is something of a watershed in terms of public policy towards industry. Reyes's major goal was to insure Colombia against recurrence of the continuous and disastrous civil wars of the nineteenth century, culminating in The Thousand Days War at the turn of the century. Out of this determination, and the idea that a concerted attempt to industrialize might focus the nation's energies more constructively than in the past, emerged Colombia's first solid program in support of modern industrialization.

The government had been moving in these directions for some time on a timid scale. Reyes's policy, which was in considerable measure the application of the protectionist system sketched a couple of decades earlier by Rafael Núñez, gave the definitive push.[43] Complementing the specific protectionist tools and equally crucial in getting industrialization under way, according to Enrique Caballero, were other steps that helped create an appropriate atmosphere, particularly public works (especially transport improvements), stable money and credit, and political and social peace.[44] Reyes created the Ministry of Public Works, substantially extended the rail system of the country, and regularized and speeded up navigation on the Magdalena River.[45]

The political feasibility of the new protectionist policy was greatly facilitated by the coincidence of the major coffee-exporting and manufacturing interests in Medellín, often within the same family. McGreevey contrasted the accommodation of this period, when both industrialists and coffee growers were favorable to a more rapid expansion of manufacturing with protection, with the internecine conflicts of the tobacco period,[46] and with the disharmony during the second half of the nineteenth century between the protectionist artisans of Santander and the free-trade merchants and land owners of Bogotá and Cundinamarca. Regional conflict, rural unrest, and civil war were due in considerable measure to such differences of interest.

The tariff was the major policy tool of the period. Law 63 of 1903 changed the tariff structure in order to simplify some very complicated and confused legislation. Reyes quickly passed a law in 1905, supplemented by decrees, designed to make protection effective. Tariffs on some final goods were raised while those on raw materials were lowered. Other incentives given to specific firms by Reyes included subsidies and a guarantee of return to capital. Taken together these concessions created an ample margin of potential profits. Ospina felt that very high tariff protection was needed since the country suffered from a severe scarcity of entrepreneurship (or better, a disproportion between the risks and the willingness to assume them) as well as a serious lack of knowledge. Keeping the margin of gains high and limiting productive activity to the later stages of assembly helped to resolve these two shortages. [47]

Most commentators conclude that the other special concessions yielded very little result, although it is true that the period of experimentation was very short since Reyes's fall caused most of these privileges to disappear also. [48] Contemporary critics of Reyes's policies tended not so much to attack the tariff protection per se as these privileges, monopolies, and subsidies which complemented the policy and which naturally lent themselves to abuses. [49] The Mexican example, generally viewed as a success, was a factor in the positive attitude of some Colombians to protection. The increase in urban unemployment, especially of women, also worked in this direction. How important these disinterested positions were, compared to the vested interests emphasized by McGreevey, is hard to say.

Ospina considered that the administrations between Reyes and Pedro Nel Ospina (August, 1922–August, 1926) were timid in terms both of fiscal and administrative matters and of material (infrastructural) improvements. Between the fall of Reyes and the beginning of World War I, the free traders had perhaps their last chance to retake the field, and the debate was heated. Protectionism was now attacked on the grounds that it spawned "exotic" industries. [50] Meanwhile, the usual arguments were presented in favor of industrialization: it creates jobs; it represents a way to get ahead, and so on. In these pre-World War I years the political discussions involved regional jealousies, political blackmail, and all sorts of noneconomic factors. Apparently workers were clamoring for protection for the national industry. [51] The Kemmerer Mission of 1923 was completely pro-free trade, but in this area, as distinct from others, no attention was paid to it.

After the war, President Pedro Nel Ospina brought renewed vigor to economic policy, with more emphasis on improvements in infrastructure, the fiscal system and practices, and the monetary/banking regime. The rearrangement of the monetary system, following the recommendations of the Kemmerer Mission, quickly brought rates of interest down. [52] Colombia had a dramatic 70 percent increase in quantum of exports over 1925–29, and the commodity terms of trade also improved markedly; exports now accounted for about 15-20 percent of gross product in 1950 prices, [53] substantially more in current prices perhaps. [54] Significant capital inflows accompanied this growth, constituting one-third of the purchasing power of exports and representing mainly government borrowing in the international capital markets. [55] The investment coefficient was very high, exceeding 25 percent of gross product; public investment was a quarter of the total for Colombia, and four-fifths of this was for the transportation system, especially railroads and highways. In short, the economy was booming.

The Nature of Industrial Growth, 1900-30

At the turn of the century, although a sizable share of the labor force was engaged in manufacturing (perhaps 18 percent), probably less than 2 percent was in plants of five or more workers. The major industries were textiles, food processing, beverages, furniture, nonmetallic minerals, tobacco, and leather and other cottage-shop production supplying local markets. In textiles and a number of other industries, most workers were women. Most of the limited investment in factories was concentrated in food and beverages.

No serious estimates are available for the growth of manufacturing (either factory or total) prior to the early twenties.[56] McGreevey suggested that the output share of manufacturing probably remained roughly constant between 1870 and 1925.[57] This guesstimate would imply that the growth of manufacturing output was moderate. Of factories still present in 1945, few were established during 1901-05, which is not surprising given The Thousand Days War. Judging again by establishments existing in 1945, the next five-year period saw the boom in textile starts. Something of a lull followed on Reyes's overthrow in 1909, then a recovery over 1916-20, another lull, and finally the expansion of the late twenties. The middle and late twenties are widely regarded as the first real "boom" years of the nonagricultural economy.[58] The boom was aided by the combination of rapid export growth, capital inflow on a scale not seen previously, and prior improvements of the transportation system.[59] During 1925-28, ECLA statistics indicate that industrial output grew at an annual rate of 8 percent, the cottage-shop sector at perhaps 7 percent,[60] and the factory sector at 12.1 percent.[61] In 1929 growth stopped and decline began for many industries.

Whatever the precise timing, factory manufacturing clearly expanded rapidly in percentage terms over the early decades of this century. In 1900 Colombia probably had no more than five to twenty plants of fifty or more workers, in 1925 perhaps forty to eighty,[62] and in 1930 perhaps 150.[63] Textiles and food processing dominated this expansion, as suggested by data from the 1945 Industrial Census in Table 2.3 and from a study by P. T. Bell, The United States trade commissioner in Colombia. Bell's data in Table 2.4 show the considerable range of items produced in factories, the great majority nondurable consumer goods.

Expanding factory production[64] was based partly on substitution of imports, partly on substitution of cottage production for home consumption and cottage-shop production for sale, and partly on the growth of total domestic demand. For products such as matches and glass, factory growth was mainly at the expense of imports; for other products such as some textiles, it was mainly at the expense of traditional production. The latter situation was the more common one,[65] if we may judge from the apparent downward trend in total employment in the nonfactory (cottage-shop) subsector over an extensive period (perhaps from the late nineteenth or early twentieth century to the fifties)[66] (Table 2.5). David Chu's finding that in the twenties, the decade of fastest modern-sector growth, import substitution played no role in expansion of demand in the industries he analyzed corroborates this conclusion (Table 2.6).

Some contemporary observers were intrigued by the fact that the traditional industries (composed of small-scale operators with traditional technologies) did not simply disappear at this time. Ospina observed that, as the traditional textile industry faced the onslaught of factory manufacturing, it tended to withdraw to the sites of its first major flowering in colonial times, the cold lands of the Andean Meseta. Small-scale production of woolen cloth remained competitive; traditional cotton-cloth producers did not give way easily either. In the early years of the

TABLE 2.3

CHARACTERISTICS OF ESTABLISHMENTS REPORTED IN THE 1945 MANUFACTURING CENSUS, BY YEAR FOUNDED

Year Founded	Number of Establishments	Patrimony in 1945 (Millions)	Average 1945 Patrimony Per Establishment (Thousands)	Major Industrial Sectors and Their Share of Total Patrimony of Establishments					
By Decades:									
Up to 1880	35	8.6	246	Food	70.8				
1881–1900	93	67.7	728	Beverages	87.3	Nonmetallic minerals	4.5		
1901–1910	169	72.5	311	Textiles	67.7	Food	11.0	Beverages	10.0
1911–1920	454	94.9	209	Textiles	27.6	Food	16.9	Tobacco	14.4	Petroleum	12.7
1921–1929	809	85.3	105	Food	31.5	Nonmetallic minerals	18.8	Beverages	18.0	Metal Work, Machinery	11.5
1930–1939	4,316	155.0	36	Textiles	29.8	Food	17.6	Metal	11.2		
By Quinquennia:									
1901–1905	75	8.8	117						
1906–1910	94	43.8	466						
1911–1915	190	31.9	168						
1916–1920	264	63.0	239						
1921–1925	375	27.7	74						
1926–1929	434	57.6	133						

Source: Contraloría General de la República, *Primer censo industrial de Colombia, 1945, resumen general* (Bogotá 1947), pp. 18–19.

TABLE 2.4

SECTOR AND CAPITAL INVESTED FOR MANUFACTURING PLANTS LISTED IN COLOMBIA STATISTICS, 1915

Establishments	Number	Capital Invested (U.S. Dollars)
Textiles and thread	21	3,530,000
Sugar	2	2,000,000
Oil refining	1	1,200,000
Electric light and power	5	1,086,000
Flour mills	6	780,000
Matches	5	750,000
Chocolate and candies	8	515,700
Cigars and cigarettes	8	428,000
Cement and artificial stone, tiling, etc.	3	420,000
Beer and ice	5	433,000
Soap and candles	18	330,000
Shoes	6	255,000
Tanning extract	2	200,000
Glass and glassware	3	150,000
Iron foundries	3	53,000
Carbonated beverages	7	38,200
Distilled liquors	1	22,000
Perfumery	1	10,000
All others	16	205,100
TOTAL	121	12,406,000

Source: P. T. Bell, *Colombia: A Commercial and Industrial Handbook*, (Washington: United States Department of Commerce, Bureau of Foreign and Domestic Commerce, Special Agents Series, No. 206, 1921), p. 180.

TABLE 2.5

MANUFACTURING EMPLOYMENT OVER TIME, BY FACTORY/COTTAGE-SHOP AND BY SEX

	All Manufacturing			Factory Manufacturing						Cottage-Shop Manufacturing					
	Employ-ment	Percent of Total Employ-ment	Percent of Non-Agricul-tural Employ-ment	Total	Men	Women	As Share of Total Employ-ment	As Share of Non-Agricul-tural Employ-ment	As Share of All Manu-facturing Employ-ment	Total	Men	Women	As Share of Total Employ-ment	As Share of Non-Agricul-tural Employ-ment	As Share of All Manu-facturing Employ-ment
1918	380-435	18.72-21.43	63.4 72.6[a]												
1938	449.0	13.91	37.76	80-100	50-64	30-36	2.48-3.10	6.73-8.41	17.82-22.27	349.0-369.0	116.2-130.2	232.8-238.8	10.82-11.44	29.34-31.02	77.73-82.18
1944/45	464.0	12.72	31.66	155.6	104.6	51.0	4.26	10.62	33.53	308.4	185.7		8.44	21.04	66.47
1951	474.7	11.82	26.36	185.5	127.1	58.4	4.62	10.30	39.68	289.2	185.7	103.5	7.20	16.06	60.92
1953				199.1	126.5	62.6	4.77	10.14							
1964	637.5	12.68	23.54	310.0	227.0	83.0	6.17	11.60	48.63	327.5	235.8	91.7	6.51	12.26	51.37
1970	853.0	14.9	25.1	395.4			6.9	11.6	46.4	457.6			8.0	13.5	53.6
1978[b]	1,416.8	17.66	26.9	747.7			9.32	10.14	52.8	669.1			8.34	12.7	47.2

Sources and Methodology: Figures for total manufacturing employment are adjusted population census figures or sample figures (1970) or interpolations (1944/45). For details, see A. Berry, "The Evolution of Small Scale Industry in Colombia," Tables 2 and 4.

[a] The agricultural labor force was calculated as 70.5 percent of the total labor force. ECLA's estimate of this ratio in 1925 was 68.54 and in 1932, 65.42. The agricultural share was doubtless declining during the late twenties under the rapid economic growth, but since there was substantial displacement of traditional or artisan manufacturing workers, it is not clear that a percentage point fall as high as that characterizing 1925-31, 3 percent, would be a logical assumption. Our estimate of the total labor force in 1918, following more or less ECLA's inclusion criteria was 2,030,000. Accordingly, our estimate of the agricultural labor force was 1,431,200. The estimate for non-agricultural labor force was 598,900 or 599,000. The resulting estimate of the percentage of the non-agricultural labor force engaged in manufacturing is so high as to be not too credible. This result may, per se, suggest that a more accurate estimate of total manufacturing employment might be in the neighborhood of 330,000; this would be 55 percent of the non-agricultural labor

TABLE 2.5 (continued)

force. It would still be far above ECLA's estimate, however. Only analysis of the service sector in 1918 on the basis of the population census would permit a more accurate estimate. A 55 percent figure is not particularly high by world standards, especially at the early stages of development and figures as high as 65 percent and 70 percent have been observed in some countries.

[b]The 1978 figures appear to be implausibly high relative to those of earlier years; there may be some noncomparability between the household survey based on figures of 1978 and the census based figures of most of the earlier years. For a more detailed discussion of these statistical problems, see A. Berry, "The Evolution of Small Scale Industry in Colombia."

TABLE 2.6

SHARE OF GROWTH OF FACTORY MANUFACTURING ASSOCIATED WITH IMPORT SUBSTITUTION, DOMESTIC DEMAND AND EXPORTS, BY SELECTED PERIODS

Industry	1923/24 - 1927/28			1927/28 - 1944/45			1944/45 - 1965		
	Import Substitution	Domestic Demand	Exports	Import Substitution	Domestic Demand	Exports	Import Substitution	Domestic Demand	Exports
Food				.87	.10	.03	.03	.96	.01
Beverages							.02	.98	-0-
Tobacco							-.01	1.01	-0-
Textiles	-290	390	-0-				.27	.68	.05
Clothing/Footwear							-0-	1.00	.01
Wood Except Furniture							⎫	⎫	⎫
Wooden Furniture							-.02	.93	.08
Paper	- 51	151	-0-	.45	.55	-0-	.58	.40	.02
Printing							.01	.97	.02
Leather							.02	.64	.19
Rubber							.37	.49	.14
Chemicals	- 35	135	-0-	.26	.73	.01	.50	.47	.03
Petroleum	-0-	100	-0-	.35	.64	.02	.51	.49	-0-
Nonmetallic Minerals	- 24	124	-0-	.76	.24	-0-	.26	.67	.06
Base Metals	56	44	-0-	1.02	-.02	-0-	.66	.22	-0-
Metals Except Machinery Products	19	81	-0-	.56	.44	-0-			
Nonelectric Machinery	10	90	-0-	1.87	-.87	-0-	⎫	⎫	⎫
Electric Machinery							.40	.58	.01
Transport Equipment				1.69	-.69	-0-			
Miscellaneous							na	na	na
Total	- 30	130	-0-	.34-.37[a] (.80)[b]	.61-.64[a] (.17)[b]	.02[a] (.03)[b]	.235	.738	.027
Industries Considered by Chu				.75 (.80)[b]	.23 (.17)[b]	.02 (.03)[b]	.400	.563	.037

Sources and Methodology: Data for 1923/24 to 1927/28 and 1927/28 to 1944/45 are taken from Chu's work. For 1927/28 to 1944/45 aggregation across the industries he considers was performed by the author (see Table A-38). Data for 1944/45 to 1965 are from Table A-43a. The estimate for 1967-70 is from Table A-35.

na = not available

Note: Figures do not always add to 100 percent because of rounding.

[a] The figure for exports is a guess. The figure for import substitution is calculated on the assumption that this phenomenon accounted for 5-10 percent of the growth of the "traditional" industries not analyzed by Chu, which in turn constituted 56 percent of the growth over 1927/28-1944/46.

[b] Using an alternative estimate for 1944/45 petroleum output from that used by Chu.

1909-30 period, a large majority of the imported yarns—80 or 85 percent—were still used in small textile firms, although not just in the manufacture of cloth.[67]

Considerable change did appear over time in the composition of non-factory employment. The trends reflected in Table 2.7, which presents data for 1938 and on, probably characterized earlier decades also; while cottage-shop employment in textiles fell, that in wooden and metal products rose. The manufacturers of fique sacks for coffee exports prospered—World War I made jute packing scarce and induced the custom of packing in cabuya. This was primarily a household industry; the great bulk of the cabuya came from single plants or rows sown along field borders as part of the fence. Although widespread, the industry was particularly prevalent in Santander. Attempts at larger-scale production were not successful.[68] Straw-hat production, a thriving export industry for decades, remained an important employer, although exports fell during this period. The original foreign market for straw hats (jipas) was Cuba, but in the first years of the twentieth century this market disappeared and the United States became the major destination. Hurt by World War I, the industry never regained its 1912 level of exports; the principal market then became Colombia itself. Nonetheless, the decline was gradual. As of 1938, the population census still reported 35,311 people employed in this industry (2,647 men and 32,664 women).[69]

Although considerable exports were generated by the cottage-shop sector, the share of factory industry related to agricultural exports was relatively small.[70] As of 1945 the major such industries and their percentage of total value added[71] (excluding profits) were: coffee threshing and toasting, 3.2 percent; production of machinery for coffee processing, probably less than 1 percent;[72] production of petroleum derivatives 1.6 percent; packing materials (coffee sacks), part of 0.4 percent. A few other products may have received some stimulation, but it is unlikely that more than 5 percent of 1945 output could be related directly to these original export activities. The share of output so related in 1925 or 1930 would presumably have been higher, possibly in the range 5-10 percent.

During these decades textiles became the dominant factory industry in Colombia. Associated with their preeminence was that of Medellín as industrial center. Much discussion has centered on why Antioquia provided the locale for the first burst of industrial growth in Colombia.[73] Whatever the causes, the benefits of this growth soon became apparent. Medellín exercised a strong attraction on the surrounding rural and semi-rural population; the city offered opportunities absent in the countryside. For those people who could get jobs in the city, urban salaries were higher than rural ones. While in these early days the factory workers did not constitute a highly privileged class in comparison with other manual workers, it was at the same time true, according to Ospina Vásquez, that those terrible conditions which marked the early stages of industrialization in some countries, such as Great Britain, did not occur. The stage of cheap and abundant factory labor was short. Before too long several factories pioneered the use of such worker benefits as food on the job, housing, and medical assistance. This was especially the case in Antioquia.[74]

Factory growth was stimulated during this period by the rapid growth of domestic demand, the protection from imports, the availability of investment funds, imported capital and intermediate goods, and cheap labor. These inducements had to outweigh the limited supply of entrepreneurship and the numerous and daunting technical problems to be overcome. Ospina felt that the provision of strong incentives to entrepreneurs was crucial, since few people were willing to bear the risks involved in founding and operating a factory.[75] Market size was often a

TABLE 2.7

COMPOSITION OF COTTAGE-SHOP EMPLOYMENT BY INDUSTRY, 1938, 1951, and 1964

	Industry	1938 No. of Workers	1938 % of Total	1951 No. of Workers	1951 % of Total	1964 No. of Workers	1964 % of Total
20	Food	≤ 22,540	5.62	7,956	2.92	32,328	8.68
21	Beverages	≤ 4,383	1.09	1,073	.39	2,796	.75
22	Tobacco	≤ 5,108	1.27	3,555	1.30	4,771	1.28
23	Textiles	≤ 103,133	25.70	25,564	9.38	18,263	4.90
24	Clothing and Footwear	≤ 157,998	39.37	117,937	43.30	121,755	32.70
25	Wood, Cork, and Products					76,021	20.41
26	Wooden Furniture	≤ 44,356	11.05	48,398	17.77	58,491	15.71
27	Paper and Products	-0-		162	.06	128	.03
28	Printing	≤ 7,132	1.78	3,504	1.29	5,123	1.38
29	Leather and Products	≤ 7,024	1.75	4,139	1.52	5,006	1.34
30	Rubber and Products	-0-		49	.02	-1,475	-.40
31	Chemicals	≤ 2,655	.66	2,188	.80	5,933	1.59
32	Petroleum and Coal Products	-0-		132	.05	2,854	.77
33	Nonmetallic Minerals	≤ 13,710	3.42	8,752	3.21	11,414	3.06
34-38	Metals and Metal Products	≤ 23,809	5.93	40,575	14.89	87,877	23.60
34	Base Metals					6,655	1.79
35	Metal Products, except Machinery					9,667	2.60
36	Nonelectric Machinery					13,229	3.55
37	Electric Machinery					4,708	1.80
38	Transportation and Equipment					51,618	13.86
39	Miscellaneous	≤ 9,502	2.37	5,769	2.12	8,361	2.24
	TOTAL	≤ 401,350	100.00	272,400[a]	99.03[b]	372,390	100.00

Source: Figures come from Berry, "The Relevance and Prospects of Small-Scale Industry in Colombia," p. 20 (reproduced as Table A-134), and are based on the population and industrial censuses. For 1938 only lower-limit estimates of factory employment were available, so "equal to or greater than" estimates are presented; total factory employment was probably about twice the 40,000 which could be allocated to the various two-digit sectors. Since our main concern here is the composition of the cottage-shop sector, column 2 is probably not as weak an estimate as it might appear to be at first sight; it would be accurate if the share of cottage-shop employment in a given two-digit sector is overestimated by the same percentage in each industry.

[a] Greater than the sum of the figures in the column, as it includes territories (nondepartmental) for which no attempt to break the employment down at the two-digit level was made.

[b] Does not sum to 100 percent because of the factor mentioned in a.

problem, and long, costly technical adaptations to the physical conditions and the available labor force were necessary.[76] Just getting the equipment into place was a major task in the beginning.[77] Chu also argued that entrepreneurial ability was important for long-run success; early companies that did not remain in the vanguard were either absorbed by others or slipped, often because of failure to modernize equipment and move to new products.

Much of the earliest factory manufacturing, especially in textiles, appears to have been based upon the availability of very cheap labor. While heavy use of imported raw materials was typical in the early years, the trend towards use of local resources seems to have begun with little delay. The early textile industry focused more on weaving than spinning (so the yarn had to be imported), but this tendency was less strong than in many other countries. The textile companies tried from the beginning to stimulate domestic cotton production, but each one worked independently and the results were not very successful.

The growing industry was owned almost in its totality by Colombians, with the exception of the exploitation of hydrocarbons, petroleum, and gas. In some cases firms belonged to foreigners who had settled in the country and were now regarded as Colombians. In a very few cases—Bavaria was the most important—a more or less large block of foreign capital existed, but overall its influence was very small. Industry was essentially regional; ownership of a company in one region by a person from a different region was still rare.

Growth Under "Natural Protection": The Depression and World War II

The Depression wrought a major change in the context of Colombian industrialization:[78] declining export markets, a worsening of the terms of trade for Colombia,[79] the end of the substantial capital inflows of the twenties.[80]

During the late twenties overall prosperity of the economy had been clearly linked to the rapid growth of primary product exports, mainly coffee. In the early thirties, the export quantum leveled off; it rose again in the late thirties, dropped back after the outbreak of World War II, and rose to a 1945 level of 50 percent above that of 1929. Since both the terms of trade and capital inflow remained well below their levels of the late twenties, the sharply lowered contribution of the foreign sector pulled output growth down to only 3.3 percent per year over 1930-45, 1.2 percent on a per capita basis.[81] Gross domestic income fell by 5 percent between the onset of the Depression and the low point in 1931. The import coefficient [the ratio of imports to gross domestic product (GDP)] dropped sharply;[82] the coefficient for imported intermediate products was less affected during the period than that of imported capital goods. Despite these untoward events, growth of the manufacturing sector in the thirties was about the same as that of the previous boom period in middle and late twenties. Although the Great Depression did interrupt industrial expansion, by 1933 growth had resumed at rates comparable to those of the twenties. ECLA's estimate of the average annual rate over 1930-40 was 6.9 percent, and over 1940-45, 6.7 percent.[83] Given the much slower growth of GNP, this meant that the elasticity of manufacturing production with respect to GNP rose dramatically.[84] Although the growth rates of new intermediate and capital-goods industries such as base metals, chemicals, and petroleum were high, most of the growth during this period came in the nondurable, consumer-good sector (Table 2.8). Food, beverages, tobacco, textiles, and clothing (including footwear) accounted for 70 percent of the output increase, while registering

TABLE 2.8

GROWTH OF THE MANUFACTURING SECTOR BY INDUSTRY, 1925-68
(Absolute Values in Thousands of 1953 Pesos)

Industry	1925-30 Growth	1925-30 Share of Total Growth	1925-30 Annual Growth Rate	1930-45 Growth	1930-45 Share of Total Growth	1930-45 Annual Growth Rate	1945-57 Growth	1945-57 Share of Total Growth	1945-57 Annual Growth Rate	1957-68 Growth	1957-68 Share of Total Growth	1957-68 Annual Growth Rate
20 Food	23,228	35.71	6.6	75,351	13.22	4.3	199,167	12.23	7.0	504,758	21.53	8.3
21 Beverages	20,588	31.65	8.95	93,334	16.38	6.5	221,352	13.59	7.75	230,421	9.83	4.45
22 Tobacco	-8,571	-13.18	-6.65	9,635	1.69	2.4	36,947	2.27	6.6	46,548	1.99	4.8
23 Textiles	-7,053	-10.84	-10.3	145,593	25.55	19.25	224,015	13.75	7.7	254,771	10.87	4.75
24 Clothing and Footwear	22,515	34.62	6.0	75,570	13.26	4.2	158,778	9.75	5.8	277,108	11.82	5.8
25 Wood Products	{7,895	{12.14	{4.6	{28,498	{5.00	{3.7	{95,365	{5.85	{7.6	{124,721	{5.32	{5.3
26 Wooden Furniture												5.15
27 Paper Products	143	.22	8.2	2,613	.46	13.8	59,092	3.63	28.5	45,703	1.95	4.15
28 Printing, etc.	3,466	5.33	5.1	16,146	2.83	4.8	12,947	.79	2.9	25,204	1.08	3.9
29 Leather Products	474	.73	5.0	19,273	3.38	16.45	46,939	2.88	10.1	35,575	1.52	6.4
30 Rubber	---	---	---	5,064	.89	---	132,859	8.16	32.0	134,951	5.76	8.0
31 Chemicals	399	.61	.5	14,358	2.52	4.3	18,089	1.11	3.9	65,239	2.78	4.7
32 Petroleum & Coal Products	1,381	2.12	17.65	7,035	1.23	9.4	117,610	7.22	24.0	82,793	3.53	5.1
33 Nonmetallic Minerals	-0-	-0-	-0-	40,920	7.18	13.55	48,516	2.98	6.0	70,427	3.00	5.0
34 Base Metals	46	.07	6.2	4,485	.79	24.5	57,122	3.51	24.0	44,293	1.89	
35 Metal Products, except Machinery and Transport Equipment	485	.75	2.55	8,305	1.46	7.6	66,342[a]	4.07[a]	16.6[a]	180,010	7.68	11.4
36 Nonelectric Machinery	-298	-.46	-.9	23,125	4.06	10.45	-9,523[a]	-0.58[a]	-3.2[a]	40,259	1.72	10.45
37 Electric Machinery	-0-	-0-	-0-	-0-	---	---	42,669[a]	2.61[a]	∞	111,210	4.74	11.8
38 Transportation Equipment	345	.53	13.05	490	.09	3.4	61,364[a]	3.77[a]	38.5[a]	49,153	2.10	9.0
39 Miscellaneous	---	---	---	---	---	---	36,110	2.22	---	20,757	.89	4.2
TOTAL	65,043	100.00	4.05	569,795	100.00	6.5	1,629,026	100.00	8.8	2,343,898	100.00	6.1

Source: Data of Table A-13 and Banco de la República, *Cuentas Nacionales*.

[a]Due to difficulties in reconciliation of categories between the 1945 and 1953 Industrial Censuses, it is not possible to estimate with precision the output level and growth rates of these categories. For metal products as a whole, however, there is no reason to believe that difficulties exist. The same goes for the earlier and later periods, during each of which internal consistency was maintained in terms of product classification.

an annual growth rate of 6.3 percent. Paper, rubber, chemicals, petroleum, and the metal- and mineral-based industries accounted for 18.7 percent of the growth, and grew at an annual rate of 9.3 percent.[85]

Output growth of the factory subsector, at an average of about 7-7.5 percent per year, once again exceeded that of the cottage-shop subsector, about 5-6 percent.[86] Factory employment grew rapidly, from 100,000 or less to 155,000 or so workers.[87] Since total manufacturing employment appears to have been expanding very little, cottage-shop employment may have fallen on balance over this period.[88]

How does one explain the rapid growth of manufacturing output under the generally depressed conditions of the thirties and the shorter supply of imported raw materials and capital goods? The substantial base of experience and investable funds built up earlier was a major plus. Notable improvements in transportation occurred during the thirties, and helped to widen markets as well as lower costs. Up to the twenties, regional isolation had been quite extreme,[89] but in the thirties highway construction led to the incorporation of many outlying regions into the market economy. Meanwhile, prices of manufactured imports rose relative to export prices as the commodity terms of trade deteriorated, and relative to prices of nontraded and import-competing goods as national currencies were devalued. With improving infrastructure and availability of needed inputs from domestic sources, the relative price advantage which this implied for local producers led to a vigorous substitution of domestic production for imports of manufactured goods, and to the impressive growth recorded. Although the scarcity and higher price of imported inputs and capital equipment was undoubtedly a constraint for some industries, imported inputs were only around 15 percent of value of production in factory manufacturing as of the late thirties, probably somewhat higher in the early thirties.[90] The changes in tariff structure were less general in their impact upon relative prices, but still important for some industries. The provision of revenue for the central government was still, according to Ospina, the primary function of tariffs during the twenties. The completely new tariff schedule adopted in 1931[91] was in large part a response to the threat to this source of funds.[92] The effect of the revisions was to increase absolute levels of protection quite substantially; a weighted average for the modern industries[93] analyzed by Chu rose from 25.3 percent in 1927 to 75.5 percent in 1936.[94] The impact on effective protection was naturally more diverse than that on nominal protection; according to one measure it actually declined for about one-half of the sectors analyzed by Chu (Table 2.9). The median level fell from 19 percent to 17 percent, while the mean rose from 36 percent to 123 percent due to large increases for a few products.[95] Tariffs and effective protection were increased substantially for cotton and rayon yarn, rayon fabrics, and cement. In fact, effective protection from all sources increased more than the above figures indicate, since exchange controls were instituted to maintain the overvalued exchange rate. They were frequently administered so as to favor importation of intermediate materials at the expense of final goods.

Although these policies were important, exogenous events were the primary influence on the course of economic events in this period. With the sharp decline in import capacity, the opportunity cost of imports relative to home goods simply had to be increased by some combination of devaluation, tariff increases, and quantitative restrictions. The potential contribution of tariff policy in such a situation lay mainly in providing particularly high incentives for goods that could be produced in Colombia.[96] Judging from the effective tariff rates presented in Table 2.9, the 1931 legislation clearly increased the variance of effective tariff rates among industrial goods, and included increases for such industries

TABLE 2.9

EFFECTIVE PROTECTION ESTIMATES FOR SELECTED INDUSTRIES AND PRODUCTS
(Expressed in Percent)

Industry	Effective Protection Provided by Tariff[b] 1927	Effective Protection Provided by Tariff[b] 1936	Total Effective Protection 1969
Textiles			
Cotton Yarn	15	29	
Cotton Cloth	63	64	
Wool Yarn	1	5	} 113.1 } 3.8
Wool Cloth	81	120	
Rayon Yarn	60	126	
Rayon Cloth	67	714	
Paper			
Pulp	(17)	(48)	
Paper Except Newsprint	(46)	(0) } (31)	} 12.1
Paperboard	(22)	(30)	
Paper, Paperboard Articles	40	31	
Rubber			
Tires	−25	−24	} 18.9 } −31.3
Shoes		23	
Other Rubber Articles	10		
Chemicals			
Basic Industrial Chemicals	11	21	
Quebracho Extracts	NA	NA	
Vegetable/Animal Oils/Fats	19	31	
Paints	38	17	} 101.5 } 60.8
Pharmaceuticals	24	8	
Cosmetics	(93)	(493)	
Soap	108	377	
Miscellaneous Chemical Products NEC	6	−1	

Industry	Effective Protection Provided by Tariff[b] 1927	Effective Protection Provided by Tariff[b] 1936	Total Effective Protection 1969
Petroleum Products	6	95	95 −4.9
Nonmetallic Minerals			
Structural Clay Products	21	3	
Glass	36	104	
China	32	25 } 87.4	} −8.2
Cement	−9	148	
Nonmetal Mineral Products NEC	29	−11	
Basic Metals			
Iron and Steel[a]	(9)	(21) } (19.1)	} 150.7
Nonferrous Metals	(11)	(−7)	
Metal Products			
Containers	33	−1	9.5 47.3
Other Metal Products	25	11	
Nonelectric Machinery	1	1	1 −7.3
Electric Machinery			
Light Bulbs	(−20)	(−45)	
Electric Motors	(−16)	(−24)	d e
Radios and Telephones	(−16)	(−17)	
Other Electric Machinery	(− 5)	(− 6)	
Transport Equipment			
Automobile Assembly	(− 4)	(2)	NA 610.2

(continued)

Descriptive History - 33

TABLE 2.9 (continued)

Sources: For 1927 and 1936, see Chu, *The Great Depression*, p. 25. Input-output data are based on DANE, *Primer Censo Industrial de Colombia 1945: Resumen General* (Bogotá,1947). For these estimates, the nominal tariffs for Colombia were adjusted to reflect a possible undervaluation of imports in 1927 and 1936, by assuming that the true CIF value of imports was 12 percent higher than the reported value in both years. For details of the methodology, see Chu, *The Great Depression*, Annex 1 of Chapter 2. We estimated weighted average effective protection by two-digit sectors in 1936, using as weights Chu's 1944/45 value added figures by sector. See Ibid., Chapter 3, Table A-1. The 1969 estimates are from Thomas Hutcheson, "Incentives for Industrialization in Colombia" (Ph.D. dissertation, University of Michigan, 1973).

( ) = Approximate

NA = not available

[a] Excludes rails in 1927 and 1936.

[b] Chu's estimation technique did not take account of protection from quantitative restrictions, and assumed domestic prices were equal to world prices plus the tariff. For the possible biasing effects of these problems, see Chu, *The Great Depression*, pp. 23-4.

[c] Since world and domestic prices were measured independently, these estimates are conceptually free of the specific problems cited in note b, to which Chu's 1927 and 1936 figures are subject.

[d] Undefined, since there was no recorded production in this two-digit industry.

[e] Negative value added, implying very high protection.

as textiles and nonmetallic minerals which contributed importantly to growth over 1930-45.

Whatever the relative roles of exogenous events and government policy in protecting domestic industry; import substitution did become important during this period, accounting probably for something over 30 percent of manufacturing growth.[97] Import substitution focused mainly on nondurable consumer goods. Such goods probably comprised half or more of all imports in the late twenties, but only 20 percent by 1945.[98] Marked reductions occurred in textiles, foodstuffs, beverages, and tobacco. Textiles represented more than a quarter of all imports during 1925-29, and 19 percent in 1944/45.[99] Foodstuffs, beverages and tobacco accounted for 15 percent of all imports over 1925-29 and 7.4 percent in 1946. Imports of hides and leather goods, lumber and wooden manufactures, and goods manufactured from nonmetallic ores practically ceased by the late forties or early fifties. The relative share of imports of paper and paper products, chemicals, nonedible oils and fats, and fuels and lubricants showed moderate increases. ECLA attributed the more rapid domestic growth of consumer-goods industries largely to size of domestic market (a more serious problem for intermediate and some capital goods) and partly to a preferential tariff policy.[100]

The shift in the character of growth towards import substitution was especially characteristic of a set of technologically modern industries analyzed by Chu. These included textiles, paper, rubber, chemicals, petroleum and coal products, nonmetallic mineral products, basic metals, metal products, electrical and nonelectrical machinery, and transport equipment. He concluded that import substitution was the major proximate source of their growth in the thirties, but had contributed nothing in the mid to late twenties when domestic demand was the sole source of increase in demand. In Chapter 3 of this volume, Chu shows the power of a relative price model in explaining the growth of nontraditional manufacturing during the Depression-World War II period to be superior to Hollis Chenery's per capita income model.[101] Unlike the twenties, a period of declining relative prices for nontraditional manufactures (Chapter 3, Figure 3.1) and the materials used in producing them, the early thirties brought a jump in the former and a smaller increase in the latter. Chu finds relative price to be a significant determinant of output growth in industries like textiles, paper, and rubber which led the expansion of nontraditional manufacturing during the period 1928-45.

As World War II ended, Colombia found itself poised for a decade of rapid growth because of a high level of international reserves due to the limited availability of imports during the war, and an expanding industrial sector ready to make use of those reserves. Although still predominantly small-scale and technologically traditional, the sector had by this time about 425 plants of fifty workers or more. The share of the manufacturing labor force in plants of five workers or more had risen from 15-20 percent in 1930 to about a third, and the share of output from those plants now constituted perhaps 70 percent of the total. As of 1944/45 the modern manufacturing industries analyzed by Chu accounted for about 40 percent of the total value added in factory manufacturing as reported in the 1945 industrial census, and for 33 percent of our estimate of total manufacturing output. The renewed domination of textiles in this period was striking. Textiles accounted for about 60 percent of the total increase in value added of these modern industries; petroleum and chemicals followed well behind. The share of the manufacturing labor force found in urban areas rose from perhaps 35 percent in 1930[102] to about 55-60 percent by the end of the war.[103] The rapid advance of the factory sector seems primarily to have displaced rural cottage-shop employment, which may have fallen by over 50 percent in the intercensal period of 1938-51. As far as can be ascertained, urban cottage-shop employment continued to rise.

Postwar Industrialization: 1945-68.
The Later Phases of Legislated Import Substitution

In the two decades after World War II, Colombia's manufacturing sector grew increasingly complex and quite modern. During 1945-56, buoyant coffee prices contributed to an annual increase in net national income of 6.2 percent, while output rose by 5.1 percent. Coffee prices then fell sharply and income growth dropped to 4.2 percent per year during the period 1956-68. Growth of manufacturing output was rapid during the coffee boom with an annual average rate of 8.3 percent; it continued at a reasonably successful annual average of 5.6 percent during the 1956-68 period despite the continuously tight balance-of-payments situation. The first part of the period was characterized by continuing absolute decline in cottage-shop employment, presumably in the face of competition from modern factory industry. This trend was reversed some time in the fifties when the two had become more complementary (Table 2.5).

This postwar period saw a more conscious pursuit of industrialization in Colombia. The period of foreign-exchange ease was similar in many ways to the earlier boom period of the twenties—incomes rose rapidly; imports were available; rural to urban migration proceeded rapidly. But the intervening decades had brought important changes. The distribution of power between agrarian and industrial interests was shifting gradually towards the latter. Acceptance of the proposition that industrialization was the inevitable handmaiden of development had gradually become more common among politicians and interest groups alike. The need to create industrial employment was forcefully dramatized by the widespread rural violence of the forties and fifties which drove many families to the towns and cities, by the rise of Jorge Gaitan to a position of political power on the shoulders of a prolabor rhetoric, and by the explosion of frustration precipitated by Gaitan's assassination in 1948. Recognition of the need for orderly decision making was reflected in and fostered by the World Bank Mission report of 1951, the first such comprehensive strategy piece on the Colombian economy.[104]

The key policy instrument in a now more varied arsenal supporting import substitution was the control of imports. Although import-substituting industrialization was, as in the earlier period 1930-45, partly a direct reaction to the scarcity of foreign exchange manifested in periodic balance-of-payments crises,[105] the government's desire to industrialize for its own sake appears to have been stronger than before.[106]

Even by 1945, import substitution had been largely completed in most of the fairly obvious consumer-good areas. According to ECLA statistics, the domestic share of total availability (domestic absorption plus exports) was 92 percent for nondurable consumer goods, 69 percent for durable consumer goods, 66 percent for intermediate goods, and 36 percent for capital goods. Colombia was still dependent on imports for the vast bulk of its "sophisticated" capital goods; as late as 1950 more than 90 percent of all machinery and equipment was imported.[107] It was apparent that further import substitution would need to focus more on products other than consumer nondurables, and that at least in the early phases of production, many processes would be heavily dependent on imported inputs. Until late in the period, little attention was paid to the development of manufactured exports, even though market size was a clear obstacle to the development of numerous lines.[108] Colombia's interest in the formation of the Andean Group in the sixties reflected a step in this direction.

Control of foreign trade and development of public-sector enterprise were the major components of industrial policy during this period. The relative importance of the tariff, of import prohibitions, of prior deposits, and of import controls induced by exchange crises varied over the period. Tariff levels and regular prohibitions were the main ingredients over 1945-57, while quantitative restrictions (including temporary ones) became more important in the tight balance-of-payments period which followed. By the late forties, the protective effect of the tariff structure inherited from the thirties had been eroded by inflation (most of the tariffs were specific rather than *ad valorum*) to the point where collections were less than 10 percent of the value of imports (see Table 2.10). In 1950 a new tariff was adopted; its timing was related to a balance-of-payments deficit (which led also to the devaluation of 1951), but protection was a specific objective, according to Hernán Jaramillo.[109] Tariffs became less uniform than before, with final goods having high rates and capital and intermediate goods low ones;[110] a list of prohibited imports was also adopted. Average collections rose to 22 percent of the value of imports in 1951.[111]

A period of almost systematic balance-of-payments crises was ushered in by the collapse of coffee prices in 1957; Colombia was caught beneath a heavy burden of short-term debt accumulated by the Rojas government. The next decade saw two more devaluations as a pernicious devaluation-inflation cycle made the context for economic activity increasingly unsatisfactory. The first crisis made tight import controls necessary. In 1959, midway through a recovery period (1957-62) during which GNP grew at 4 percent a year, the National Front adopted a revised tariff. The document supported the continuation of import-substituting growth as in the fifties, but anticipated foreign exchange limitations permitting only modest growth.[112] Nonessential imports were to be eliminated and import composition further shifted towards intermediate and capital goods, especially those necessary in the production of certain previously imported intermediate and capital goods. Capital and intermediate goods for agriculture would continue to be imported rather freely at low tariffs. As in 1950, the average tariff level was increased and rates were made less uniform. The government established an import licensing agency, the Superintendencia de Comercio Exterior (SUPERCOMEX), later renamed Instituto Colombiano de Comercio Exterior (INCOMEX), and the percentage of imports on the free list was sharply reduced between 1960 and 1965. A further fall in coffee earnings in 1962 led to another exchange crisis, provoking a sizable devaluation, but easy monetary policy and a legislated increase in wages inflated prices so that the positive effect on the real exchange rate was gone within a year. A tariff reform in 1962 reinforced the import-substituting emphasis by lowering tariffs on intermediate goods not already produced in the country and raising those on final goods. After a devaluation in 1965, a combination of gradually increasing awareness of the inadequacies of the "flexible peg *cum* devaluation" system and a dispute between the International Monetary Fund (IMF) and the government of Colombia led to the 1967 switch to a floating rate.[113] This switch contributed importantly to the successful move into exports discussed in the next section.

Increasingly important as a tool of industrialization policy has been the Instituto de Fomento Industrial (IFI), created in 1941 to encourage the development of certain basic industries by doing initial studies, providing financial resources, and eventually transferring the industry to private capital. The major early enterprise of IFI was the Paz del Río Iron and Steel Works,[114] but it also had a hand in rubber tires, cement,

TABLE 2.10

CUSTOMS DUTIES AS A SHARE OF THE VALUE OF IMPORTS,[a] 1924-69

Year	Customs Duty /Imports	Year	Customs Duty /Imports	Year	Customs Duty /Imports
1924	30.8	1941	17.9	1958	7.6
1925	22.8	1942	17.8	1959	13.6
1926	20.9	1943	14.8	1960	16.5
1927	20.9	1944	14.9	1961	15.1
1928	22.8	1945	14.7	1962	14.1
1929	25.1	1946	12.2	1963	12.6
1930	26.1	1947	10.3	1964	12.6
1931	38.4	1948	10.0	1965	12.7
1932	50.9	1949	8.3	1966	15.0
1933	40.4	1950	13.7	1967	22.5
1934	25.1	1951	21.8	1968	13.0
1935	23.0	1952	18.9	1969	14.2
1936	22.3	1953	18.3	1970	15.5
1937	20.2	1954	20.0	1971	14.5
1938	19.5	1955	16.1	1972	14.6
1939	22.2	1956	13.4	1973	14.8
1940	18.7	1957	9.4	1974	≈ 11.5[b]
				1975	≈ 12.0[b]

Sources and Methodology: Figures for custom duty collected (this includes customs duty and any extra charge which may be imposed at a given time based on the duty) are from DANE, *Estadísticas Fiscales*, for recent years, and from ECLA, *Analyses and Projections*, Statistical Annex, p. 60 for earlier years. ECLA's original source was also the *Estadísticas Fiscales*. Only basic customs revenues are included (i.e., surcharges such as the 1.5 percent charge on imports to finance PROEXPO are not included), which biases downward the figures from the late sixties on. In the early seventies this surcharge was over 10 percent of the basic customs duty. Data on imports come from DANE, *Anuario de Comercio Exterior*, various years.

[a] Both values expressed in pesos.
[b] Tentative

fertilizer, paper, metal working, and a number of other industries during the forties and fifties. Its portfolio was rapidly expanded during the sixties (assets rose forty-five fold in real terms between 1958 and 1972), and it had a strong orientation toward capital-intensive industries. By 1969 chemicals and petrochemicals accounted for 53 percent of the portfolio while smelting and transportation equipment constituted another 32 percent.[115] By the end of the sixties, IFI was important in overall industrial financing, and was a major factor in the capital-intensive direction of industrial growth during that decade. IFI's tendency to focus on large-scale, capital-intensive projects ran the risk of both inefficiency (given the scarcity of capital in the country) and a negative income-distribution effect. Only an intensive analysis of a number of specific projects, their characteristics, and their interactions with the rest of the economy would permit a serious evaluation of IFI on these counts. A number of IFI's major projects, such as the Paz del Río steel works and Forjas de Colombia, a metalworking plant in Bucaramanga, have generally been considered as dubious investments. In some cases, including Forjas, political pressures have affected the locations selected for projects, with unfortunate impact on their economic viability. IFI, like other development finance corporations, typically provided long-term industrial credit at real interest rates which were barely positive, creating an inducement towards capital-intensive technologies. Public enterprises were also frequently favored in their access to foreign exchange for imports.

Credit allocation reflected the increasing attention to industrialization during this period, although credit policy could not be described as a key factor in that process. The ratio "commercial bank loans outstanding to manufacturing/manufacturing output" showed no trend over 1952-68 (Table 2.11). The share of commercial bank credit going to industry averaged below 25 percent over 1952-62 and around 30 percent during 1963-67; this upward trend was roughly parallel to the increase in share of GDP generated in the manufacturing sector. No data seem to exist on credit to manufacturing from the financial system as a whole,[116] but it seems likely that trends were similar to those for commercial banks alone until the late sixties when the role of the financial corporations very quickly became important.

What was the nature of industrial growth during this period and how successful were the above-cited policies? On the positive side, the growth rate averaged a creditable 7 percent per year and industry became quite diversified. Whether the nature of the expansion during this period was responsible or not, a number of industries subsequently made successful entries into world markets.

Prior to 1945, at least 70-75 percent of the growth of manufacturing was in nondurable consumer goods (food, beverages, tobacco) and textiles (see Tables 2.8 and 2.12). Over 1945-68 this percentage fell to under 60 percent, as production moved increasingly into the areas of intermediate and capital goods. Whereas ECLA estimated the breakdown among nondurable consumer, durable consumer, intermediate (including fuels and lubricants), and capital goods production to be 71.3, 3.1, 18.9, and 6.7 in 1945,[117] by 1968 the comparable figures were 57.1, 4.8, 23.4, and 14.7 percent.[118] The share of output growth occurring in a group of intermediate products (rubber, paper, chemicals, products of petroleum and coal) rose sharply from 5.1 percent in 1930-45 to 20.1 percent in 1945-57, dropping to 14 percent in 1957-68. The contribution of the metal-metallurgical industries rose from 5 percent in 1930-45 to 13.6 percent in 1945-57 to 18.1 percent in 1957-68. In this latter period, the share of the food sector temporarily reversed its downward trend, due in part to the rapid expansion of sugar processing and in part to the subcategory "various," including many individually unimportant items

TABLE 2.11

CREDIT TO MANUFACTURING IN RELATION TO TOTAL CREDIT AND TO MANUFACTURING OUTPUT, 1940-72
(Values in Millions of Pesos)

Year	Commercial Bank Loans Outstanding to Manufacturing / Total Commercial Bank Loans Outstanding[b]	New Loans by Commercial Banks to Manufacturing / Output in Manufacturing[a]	Commercial Bank Loans Outstanding to Manufacturing[b] / Output in Manufacturing	Loans Outstanding to Manufacturing from Commercial Banks, Financial Corporations and the Corporación Financiera Popular[b] / Output in Manufacturing[a]
1940		11.4		
1941		13.5		
1942		16.8		
1943		17.4		
1944		12.1		
1945		13.6		
1946		14.2		
1947		18.2		
1948		20.9		
1949		19.3		
1950		21.4		
1951		28.0		
1952	26.6	26.6	15.2	
1953	23.7	23.7	14.1	
1954	21.6	25.4	14.2	
1955	23.4	25.9	17.0	
1956	25.9	30.0	20.5	
1957	28.9	26.8	19.2	
1958	27.9	24.6	16.7	
1959	21.9	27.3	12.4	
1960	24.1	23.5	13.6	
1961	24.7	26.4	14.9	
1962	25.7	22.0	14.4	18.3
1963	28.9	23.8	14.9	20.1
1964	31.4	27.1	15.5	21.7
1965	29.8	25.6	14.3	20.3
1966	31.1	24.4	13.8	20.0
1967	31.3	27.3	14.6	22.3
1968	26.6	28.2	15.7	30.9
1969	26.5	26.8	15.2	34.7
1970	23.0	22.5	13.0	33.4
1971	21.8	17.6	11.7	32.3
1972	20.4	14.3	10.4	32.2
1973	28.3	18.8	13.6	31.4
1974	28.0		12.9	27.0
1975	27.0		12.9	27.4

Sources and Methodology: Commercial bank credit data are from *Revista del Banco de la República*, various issues except for 1973-75, for which data are from the World Bank. For the financial corporations and the *Corporación Financiera Popular*, the data for 1970-75 are also from the World Bank. For previous years the data were taken from Banco de la República, *Análisis Preliminar de las Cuentas de Flujo de Fondos Financieras de la Economía Colombiana, 1962-1969* (Bogotá: Banco de la República, 1971), p. 35. Output data are from Banco de la República, *Cuentas Nacionales* for years from 1950 on; for earlier years a series based on Tables A-13 and A-5 is spliced to the series beginning in 1950.

[a] Measured at factor cost.
[b] As of December 31.

TABLE 2.12

COMPOSITION OF INDUSTRIAL OUTPUT AND ITS GROWTH OVER TIME
(Values Expressed in Millions of 1958 Pesos)

Sector	1937		1937-45		1945		1945-53		1953		1955-68		1968	
	Output	Percent of Total Output	Increase in Output	Percent of Total Increase	Output	Percent of Total Output	Increase in Output	Percent of Total Increase	Output	Percent of Total Output	Increase in Output	Percent of Total Increase	Output	Percent of Total Output
Consumer Goods	1,126.39	77.90	722.90	69.57	1,849.29	74.40	1,716.84	67.18	3,566.13	70.70	6,396.67	55.20	9,962.60	59.90
Nondurable	1,090.50	75.40	581.49	65.58	1,771.99	71.30	1,599.34	62.58	3,371.33	66.80	5,593.53	48.27	8,964.86	53.90
Durable	35.89	2.50	41.41	3.99	77.30	3.10	117.50	4.60	194.80	3.90	803.14	6.93	997.94	6.00
Intermediate Goods	234.99	16.30	234.44	22.56	469.43	18.90	526.03	20.58	995.46	19.90	2,842.62	24.54	3,842.08	23.10
Fuels and Lubricants	25.52	1.80	19.99	1.92	45.51	1.80	74.88	2.93	120.39	2.40				
Capital Goods	84.18	5.80	81.79	7.87	165.97	6.70	315.76	12.36	481.73	9.50	2,345.78	20.26	2,827.51	17.00
TOTAL	1,445.56	100.00	1,039.12	100.00	2,484.68	100.00	2,555.63	100.00	5,040.31	100.00	11,592.08	100.00	16,532.39	100.00

Sources and Methodology: Figures for 1937, 1945, and 1953 are taken from ECLA, *Analyses and Projections; Statistical Annex*, p. 138. They are converted to 1958 pesos. Although ECLA's allocation of output in 1968 is different from that of most subsequent series, we allocated output in 1968 as nearly as possible according to the rules used by ECLA in 1953 and earlier years. Other sources have broken industrial output down by two or three-digit sectors, and come out with somewhat different breakdowns by type of product, (e.g., the World Bank, whose estimates are reproduced in Table A-25). The category definitions as between intermediate goods and capital goods are strikingly different, the latter category being much smaller according to the World Bank definitions.

with a collective weight in the budget that rises as the diet becomes more complex and as factory production replaces household production.

Although import substitution remained the major strategy during this period, problems of market size and technology became more serious as the process advanced, and its relative contribution was less than in the previous period. Import substitution accounted for about a third of the growth during 1930-45 and about a quarter during 1945-68.[119]

Between 1945 and 1968, the domestic share of total availability (domestic absorption plus exports) rose from 92 percent to 98 percent for nondurable consumer goods, from 69 percent to 96 percent for durable consumer goods, from 66 percent to 68 percent for intermediate goods, and from 36 percent to 51 percent for capital goods. Nondurable consumer goods and intermediate goods still accounted for the bulk of manufacturing output growth, with capital goods becoming much more important towards the end of the period.

Most of the fastest growing industries in this phase of industrialization, including metal products, rubber products, and paper products, were strongly dependent on imported inputs; in 1953 each of the cited industries imported about 80 percent of all raw materials used.[120] As a result of the increasing range and complexity of the consumer and capital goods produced, no trend was apparent in the share of manufactured intermediate goods which were imported (see above), nor in the relative importance of imported and domestically produced inputs[121] used by the manufacturing sector; the latter ratio remained between 20 percent and 23 percent.[122] The new industries also tended to be capital intensive. Calculations by Hutcheson indicate a definite relationship between capital intensity and level of effective protection as of the late sixties; over 1962-68 he also found the average annual growth rate across industries to be associated with the level of effective protection, suggesting that the shift towards more capital-intensive industries was due in part to differential tariff incentives.[123]

The diversification of Colombian industry into technologically complex and capital-intensive lines, and the positive attitude of the Colombian government led to substantial foreign investment, mainly since the mid-fifties.[124] Whereas in 1955 foreign-controlled companies employed 4-6 percent of the factory labor force,[125] by 1970 this share was 12-15 percent.[126] Foreign capital concentrated in chemicals, paper, rubber, electrical machinery and equipment, food, and textiles (Table 2.13). Of investments made before Decree 444 of 1967, the first four industries accounted for 59.5 percent and all six accounted for 78.1 percent.[127] The growth of foreign investment during this period made its impact on Colombia an increasingly important issue.[128] No detailed evaluation of this impact has been undertaken as yet, although a few relevant bits of information are available. A report presented to the United States Agency for International Development (AID) in 1962 found that United States business interests in Colombia lived in isolation from the Colombian business community and operated on a bare minimum of capital from the United States, though other evidence seemed inconsistent with this.[129] Decree 444 of 1967 may have affected such patterns. It is sometimes argued that the technology and skills foreign investment brings are more important, for good or ill, than the inflow of capital. The effect is exceedingly difficult to measure because judgments must be made as to the social benefits of the technology and whether as well as how much of it would have been borrowed in the absence of the foreign firms.[130] One reasonably safe conclusion is that the rate of return on foreign capital in Colombia has been relatively high, with a share of profits often taken out in such hidden forms as overinvoicing of imported inputs.[131] But these facts give no particular clue as to the effect of

TABLE 2.13

ROUGH ESTIMATES OF FOREIGN CAPITAL IN COLOMBIAN MANUFACTURING BY INDUSTRY, 1969

Industry	Foreign Capital (millions of dollars)	Foreign Capital as Share of Total Physical Capital
Food	27.777	10.4
Beverages	1.405	0.9
Tobacco	NA	NA
Textiles	21.529	6.5
Clothing and Footwear	.604	1.0
Wood and Products / Wooden Furniture	3.320	11.5[a]
Paper and Products	37.488	62.7
Printing	.900	1.8
Leather and Products	.536	2.1
Rubber and Products	31.408	70.2
Chemical Products	88.738	45.5
Petroleum and Coal Products	18.797	10.6
Nonmetallic Minerals	10.306	8.3
Basic Metals	----	----
Metal Products, including Machinery and Transport Equipment	51.143	26.7
Miscellaneous	16.616	36.3[b]
TOTAL	310.567	16.4

Sources and Methodology: Estimates of total fixed capital were based on the 1958 estimates presented in the Ten Year Plan (Consejo Nacional de Política Económica y Planeación, Departamento Administrativo de Planeación y Servicios Técnicos, *Plan General de Desarrollo Económico y Social, II Parte: Industria* (Bogotá: Imprenta del Banco de la República, 1967), p. 181 and on) plus our estimates for net investment over 1958-69 (Table A-58) and an average of DANE's reported value of inventories on January 1, 1969, and December 31, 1969 (DANE, *Industria Manufacturera Nacional 1969*, Bogotá: DANE, 1972, pp. 62-75).

[a] Foreign investment is located in the wood industry, where its share might be over 30%, but not in wooden furniture, where its share is probably close to zero.

[b] May not be reliable as category may be differently defined as between the two sources used here.

foreign capital on Colombian welfare. Since the share of manufacturing output produced by foreign firms[132] rose rather rapidly during the late fifties and the sixties, the output growth rate of national firms was below the overall average, perhaps 4-4.5 percent over 1955-70 instead of the overall rate of 5.6 percent.[133] Does this suggest a negative impact of foreign investment on the growth of Colombian-controlled industry and on labor absorption? Possibly, but not obviously.

Evaluating Import-Substituting Industrialization

The benefits of an import-substitution strategy depend on how rapidly initially high-cost production can be made competitive with world prices and on whether protected industries, via their "linkages" to other industries, bring into use factors which would otherwise go unused or less productively used.[134] This postwar period probably saw more products with internal prices far above world prices than did earlier periods. It is interesting to note that in a 1960-62 study ECLA found the ratio of manufactured product prices to food product prices (in urban areas) to be only a shade higher in Colombia than in the United States; in other Latin countries (except Guatemala) the ratio was significantly higher.[135] The relative price of manufactured consumer goods to food prices differed less from the United States rate than did the relative price of investment goods; the former difference was only about 15 percent.[136] Colombian prices were lower for nonalcoholic beverages, tobacco (much lower), textiles and clothing (a little), footwear (more than 25 percent), pharmaceuticals, and construction materials. Machinery and equipment prices were generally higher, anywhere from a third to 200 percent, as in the case of transportation equipment. Consumer durables appeared without exception to be higher priced than in the United States, with much greater discrepancies than in the nondurable manufactures.

Although the sectors of recent import substitution were then characterized by high prices, examples of successful cost reduction are not hard to find. Leonard Dudley's analysis of several metal products industries in Chapter 4 points to considerable learning-by-doing in that sector. A comparison of aggregate input and output growth is consistent with rather rapid technological improvement for manufacturing as a whole, as discussed earlier in this chapter. The experience of the textile industry in the first decades of this century exemplifies the transition from alleged white elephant to efficient industry with export potential. The real issue in judging import substitution is perhaps not so much whether protected industries eventually become reasonably efficient—probably a majority eventually do—but rather whether the loss suffered by the country while they remain inefficient outweighs the subsequent gains,[137] and whether the experience of production is really a condition for ultimate efficiency. When foreign capital and management are extensively involved, this latter contention seems particularly open to question. Much careful analysis will be needed to judge whether import substitution should have been more restricted before the emphasis was switched to exports, and whether other policy tools than those used would have been more effective.

Shortage of Imports as a Constraint on Industrial Growth

Import substitution, although it substitutes domestically produced goods for some imports, requires additional imports of intermediate and capital goods to foster the increases in local production; accordingly, its impact on the total demand for imports is not clear a priori. The numerous balance-of-payments crises afflicting Colombia during the 1957-66 period highlighted the dependence on imports of growth in the manufacturing sector and of growth in general. Many new industries purchased 60-80 percent of their inputs abroad, and their capital intensity meant that large imports of capital equipment were needed.[138] Colombia got a taste of the import intensity of import substitution.[139] The balance of payments became a prime preoccupation and the "two gap" model[140] was used to interpret the situation. The model implied a particularly strong dependence of growth on imports; increases in domestic savings could make little or no contribution to growth if foreign exchange was short.[141]

Industrial growth was a considerably faster 7.7 percent per year in the easy balance-of-payments period 1948-56 than during 1956-68, when the rate was 5.7 percent. There is no reason to doubt that, other things being equal, the more imports are available the more rapid will be industrial and overall growth.[142] But except for unusual and short periods, the Colombian evidence does not suggest that import shortages need have a traumatic effect on growth either of industry or of the economy as a whole.[143] On the one hand the *ex post* relation between the availability of imports and overall economic growth appears to be surprisingly weak; during "the expansion" of 1948-56 gross output (GDP) increased at only 5.2 percent per year while during the "stagnation" of 1956-67 it grew at 4.6 percent per year.[144] Díaz-Alejandro found no simple relation between imports (or capacity to import) and growth on an annual basis. Since one would in any case expect distributed lags, perhaps of varying length, in the import-growth relationship, this may not be surprising.[145] More importantly, import shortages are not a "given"; some of the excess capacity and excess demand for imports during this period must be attributed to the serious overvaluation of the exchange rate and the continued tendency to subsidize capital in general and imported inputs in particular even when these resources were quite scarce. Also, events since 1967 suggest considerable price response of exports and hence that the import shortages were to some degree avoidable.

To say that all Colombia needed was an equilibrium exchange rate was cold comfort in a situation where devaluations, increasingly associated with inflation, had become such a hot political issue that President Valencia felt obliged in 1963 to promise no devaluation during the rest of his term (through 1966). The basic question of how much further import substitution could be pushed without curtailing growth was now paralleled by a dilemma of short-run, balance-of-payments policy. The solutions to these two problems were by no means generally obvious in the mid-sixties.

From Import Substitution to Exporting:
The Late Sixties and Early Seventies

Fortunately, the solution was just around the corner—growth through diversification into new "minor" exports, including manufactured products.[146] In the late sixties manufacturing exports became an important source of manufacturing sector growth. (Table 2.14 shows the composition of exports by major categories). They grew at a rate of 20-25 percent per year between 1965 and 1972,[147] attaining by the latter year 5-6 percent of total value of industrial product,[148] and accounting during 1968-72 for about 11-12 percent of manufacturing output growth. Although rapid percentage growth dates back to the fifties and early sixties, the absolute level of these exports was at that time too small for their growth to have a significant overall impact. But by the

46 - Berry

TABLE 2.14

COMPOSITION OF REGISTERED COLOMBIAN EXPORTS, 1945-72

Year	Percent of Value of Exports of Goods					Value of Exports[a]		
	Coffee	Petroleum	Bananas	Minor Agri-cultural or Mineral Exports	Manufactures	Total	Minor Agricultural or Mineral Exports	Manufactures
1945	73.98	15.82	.79			140,511		
1946	76.57	11.85	1.11			201,255		
1947	70.51	13.51	1.63			276,324		
1948	70.67	14.14	1.90			306,647		
1949	72.28	17.36	2.58			335,177		
1950	77.84	16.39	2.42			395,583		
1951	74.29	15.18	1.81	7.93	.78	484,301	38,400	3,800
1952	78.64	14.80	1.91	3.74	.91	483,037	18,053	4,400
1953	81.30	12.60	1.90	3.09	1.11	605,458	18,707	6,700
1954	82.22	11.33	1.97	2.90	1.57	669,082	19,436	10,500
1955	81.68	10.30	2.82	3.50	1.69	596,685	20,866	10,100
1956	74.88	12.96	5.09	6.82	2.07	551,623	37,597	11,400
1957	76.06	14.92	5.13	1.70	2.17	511,108	8,704	11,100
1958	76.92	14.44	3.36	1.81	3.43	460,715	8,334	15,800
1959	76.37	15.49	2.93	1.90	3.30	473,004	8,989	15,600
1960	71.51	17.21	2.95	5.13	3.19	464,578	23,844	14,800
1961	70.85	15.70	3.23	6.50	3.71	434,467	28,246	16,100
1962	71.69	13.07	2.30	8.26	4.68	436,403	38,255	21,700
1963	67.86	17.28	2.97	7.25	4.66	446,657	23,397	20,800
1964	71.97	13.67	2.26	5.62	6.49	548,136	30,807	35,600
1965	63.78	16.35	3.45	8.49	7.92	539,144	45,754	42,700
1966	64.67	14.12	3.94	6.96	10.30	507,591	35,352	52,300
1967	63.22	12.00	4.90	9.11	10.75	509,923	46,467	54,800
1968	62.95	6.51	4.42	13.10	13.02	558,278	73,111	72,700
1969	56.61	9.33	3.25	15.90	14.91	607,511	96,593	90,600
1970	63.45	7.97	2.46	26.13		735,657	192,222	
1971	57.30	6.63	2.12	33.95		690,009	234,234	
1972	50.76	3.71	1.58	43.96		845,067	371,446	

Source: Most of the absolute figures on which these percentages are based have been taken from Banco de la República XLIV,*Informe del Gerente a la Junta Directiva, Segunda Parte*, 1967, p. 167. For years since 1967 data are from DANE, *Anuario General de Estadística* and *Boletín Mensual de Estadística*. For all years the estimates of manufactured exports are from Díaz-Alejandro, *Foreign Trade Regimes*, p. 39. Generally more accurate figures (including estimates of nonregistered exports) are presented in Table A-117.

[a]Thousands of U.S. dollars.

late sixties, Colombia clearly joined the group of minor export success stories; the leading industries were textiles, food products (especially sugar), chemicals, glass and cement, and paper products. As this export performance has become solidly entrenched, optimism with respect to the future of the Colombian economy has spread. The obstacle to growth created by the increasing complexity and capital costs of further import substitution seems to have been circumvented by the outward-looking approach. Rapid growth of minor exports and of manufacturing have been reflected in rapid overall growth since 1968. Although the precise mechanisms through which the export boom has contributed to rapid growth have not been fully worked out, the hypothesis of a strong causal link is plausible.[149]

Important policy steps appear to have contributed to the minor export boom, complementing the increasing underlying competitiveness of manufacturing.[150] A major event was the switch in 1967 from a system of pegged exchange rates and the periodic devaluations which must accompany them in an inflationary economy to a gradually devaluing exchange rate; this significantly increased real exchange rate stability. Also, policy was consciously shifted to favor export promotion, involving such financial incentives as the certificado de abono tributario (CAT)—a roughly 15 percent subsidy to minor exports, improved credit availability for exporters, easier access to imports via removal of administrative roadblocks to the use of Plan Vallejo,[151] and speeding up of contract signing under that plan. A well funded export promotion agency (PROEXPO) was established; it holds fairs, researches markets, and finances exports. The excess capacity which characterized the economy in 1967, partly as a result of the recent exchange crisis, and the gradual advent of an export mentality, complemented the effects of these policies. Increasingly, businessmen felt a need to export, partly as a bargaining lever with the bureaucracy, and partly because of a general moral suasion to do so.

Even with the gradually increasing awareness of the joint problems of high-cost import substitution and recurring balance-of-payments crises less and less amenable to devaluations, the transition to a flexible exchange rate was somewhat accidental. President Carlos Lleras Restrepo (1966-70) happened to be more concerned with the details of economic development than most of his predecessors; further, his choice of this particular policy was in part an outcome of a dispute with the International Monetary Fund over appropriate financial policy.[152] It was probably only a matter of time until Colombia would have adopted a set of policies broadly similar to those which entered into force in the late sixties, given the continuation of the pressures of the early sixties plus increasing evidence from other countries that export booms were achievable, and that exchange rate stability might be one important factor in generating them. But the switch to a flexible rate was perhaps the least obvious of these policies, so its occurrence at this time was particularly significant.[153]

Although they constituted a watershed in decreasing the relative disincentives to the production of exports vis-à-vis import-competing and home goods, the 1967 reforms left the incentives for import substitution very high (i.e., production of import-competing goods was still strongly favored over nontraded goods). The key instrument was the licensing system. Imports of goods with adequate domestic production were prohibited, while many goods with inadequate domestic production were placed in the "prior license" group on the grounds that if they were allowed to enter freely the demand for foreign exchange would exceed the supply.

After the balance-of-payments crisis and policy changes of 1967, manufacturing growth accelerated rapidly. Between 1955, when the growth fostered by the coffee-price bonanza began to decelerate, and 1968 annual growth was usually in the neighborhood of 5-7 percent, with two-year averages seldom rising above 6 percent.[154] During most of the post-1950 period and especially since 1957, there had been a tendency for years or short periods of rapid growth to alternate with years or short periods of slower growth, due in part to the running down of foreign exchange reserves in periods of rapid growth and the need to tighten up thereafter.[155] But between 1968 and 1974, average growth was nearly 8 percent with only 1974 falling below 7 percent. Minor exports, both of manufactures and of nonmanufactures, grew dramatically, so an obvious hypothesis was that they had been simply waiting for the appropriate price inducements. Some indirect support for this position comes from regression analyses undertaken by Carlos Díaz-Alejandro which indicate that the growth of minor exports between 1950 and 1970 was related to the real exchange rate and to its stability, although the share of variation of exports so explained is not particularly high.[156] Doubtless the complementary export-promotion policies had their effects as well, and quite distinct factors may also have played a role. José Francisco Escandon has argued that more or less simultaneously with the proexport policies of the late sixties, small and medium firms were beginning a vigorous expansion which created increasing competition in the domestic market for previously dominant larger firms and gave these latter an additional push into the export market.[157]

The two significant regional trading arrangements of the sixties, the Latin American Free Trade Area (LAFTA) and the Andean Group, appear to have made some contribution to export growth, especially the latter. Colombia's manufacturing export growth has been directed in a moderate degree to Latin and Andean-group countries; as of the late sixties, 13-15 percent went to the Andean Group.[158] Of total registered exports, the share going to Andean-group countries rose from about 5-6 percent in 1968 to 16.5 percent in 1975, with the average annual growth rate exceeding 25 percent. But it appears that Colombia's export drive and the increasing oil wealth of the Group members (especially Venezuela) were more important factors than the creation of the Group. The rate of export growth to members was greater over 1965-70, before the Group began to function, than over 1970-75.[159]

It is noteworthy that the production of manufactured exports has come disproportionately from foreign firms and from large firms. The former fact makes necessary a careful evaluation of their potential contribution to Colombia.[160] The latter introduces a further interesting facet into the question of the relative merits of large and small firms. By apparently going counter to the proposition—based on a Heckscher-Ohlin interpretation of trade patterns—that exports of less-developed countries will tend to be labor intensive, it raises concern about the income-distribution impact of such exports.[161] In Chapter 8 of this volume, Díaz-Alejandro discusses characteristics of the firms with high imports and exports. Tentative estimates by the author confirm the rather high capital/labor ratio in most of the exporting industries, but suggest at the same time that both that ratio and the share of inputs which are imported are noticeably lower than in most of the recent import-substitution industries.[162] A recent study by Francisco Thoumi (discussed further below) finds labor intensity considerably higher in export-oriented industries than in import-competing ones.[163]

PART IV
A BRIEF SUMMARY OF TWENTIETH-CENTURY INDUSTRIAL POLICY

Before taking a more detailed look at specific aspects of Colombia's industrialization process and attempting an evaluation of its success, we will summarize the broad outlines of industrial policy discussed in a more dispersed fashion in the previous sections. As in most countries, international trade restrictions have been the main policy tools. Trade policy went through several phases during the twentieth century. In the first, which may be regarded as ending early in the thirties, Colombia resorted mainly to tariffs with a principal aim being government revenue;[164] since this goal was complementary (at least up to a point) with the promotion of certain types of manufacturing, it is difficult to detect the relative importance placed on the two objectives at the time. The relative importance of the fiscal motive declined gradually as other forms of government revenue increased; the share of tariff revenues in the national government's current revenue fell from around 50 percent in the mid-twenties to 16.9 percent in 1969; as a share of national government tax revenue it fell from around 80 percent to 17.7 percent. The ratio of tariff revenue to value of imports has shown no trend since 1950 (see Table 2.10); it fell significantly between the late twenties and mid-forties.

The crisis of the early thirties accentuated both the fiscal and balance-of-payments problems in Colombia (as in most other Latin countries); exchange controls were introduced in 1931 as was the new tariff; the peso was devalued in 1933-35, and a variety of other instruments were introduced. The net result was an important boost to domestic industry; Ospina doubted that the protectionist effect was planned. In the wartime period, with the difficulties in getting many imports, it was definitely unplanned. After the high, foreign-exchange reserves of early postwar years were depleted, Colombia ran briefly into a foreign-exchange crisis, met by the devaluation of 1951, but did not then have to face comparable pressures till the dramatic fall of the coffee price in 1957. During these years of balance-of-payments ease, Colombian industry had no natural protection, but a deliberately protectionist tariff had been introduced in 1950. Since that time, it has been revised a number of times, always with the protective effect the foremost consideration. The numerous balance-of-payments crises necessitated exchange controls, and by the sixties the import licensing/exchange control activity had become a locus of considerable discretionary power. It is natural to wonder whether this power has been used to benefit larger, well-connected firms; in Chapter 8 Díaz-Alejandro throws some empirical light on this issue, confirming the suspicion just noted but concluding that as of 1970 the bias in question was by no means overwhelming.

As discussed above, the bias against exports built into the import-substitution strategy which had dominated other objectives was quickly attacked in the late sixties by the shift to a gradually devaluing exchange rate and a set of complementary policies. This phase in Colombia's foreign trade policy lasted at least until the late seventies, by which time the coffee and drug bonanzas led to an appreciation of the real exchange rate and a decrease in the competitiveness of Colombia's manufactured exports on world markets.

Another important component of industrial policy is the scope, terms, and selectivity of credit. Most firms must finance themselves largely via internal savings or flotation of stocks and bonds, but the banking system can play an important role, especially with respect to short-term credit. Judging by the ratio of loans outstanding to output, overall credit availability improved markedly during the forties; since that time no obvious trend was apparent until the late sixties when financial corporations (especially) and other intermediaries became important sources of credit and total availability again improved measurably (see Table 2.11). Prior to that time the commercial banks were the dominant suppliers, and a higher share of credit was short-term.

Because commercial bank credit is essentially a source of short-run or working capital, the majority of industrial capital comes from elsewhere. For corporations the major sources of capital during the thirties and the war were internal funds and sale of equity (Chapter 3). Funding became somewhat more diversified over time but even as of 1964 less than 10 percent of corporations' debt and equity capital took the form of bank loans.[165] Internal funding seems to have remained the major source through the fifties—over 1953-58 it accounted for 61 percent of all sources and over 1958-62 for 50 percent[166]—but to have become less important in the sixties; Superintendencia de Sociedades Anónimas data indicate that over 1962-66 reserves and undistributed profits accounted for about 35 percent of additions to capital.

Financing through the stock market is essentially restricted to larger firms and credit flows disproportionately to these firms as well;[167] the small producer must rely much more on his own funds or on those of relatives or friends. A rough estimate suggests that in 1964 proprietorships were much less able to avail themselves of external sources than the corporations, for perhaps 20-35 percent of total capital as contrasted with about 55 percent for the latter. The problem is especially severe for small firms. Before the programs undertaken by the Caja de Crédito Agrario, the Corporación Financiera Popular and the Fondo Financiero Industrial were begun in the middle and late sixties, the access of small firms must have been very limited.[168] With the initiation of these programs, the supply of funds to medium and small plants did improve.[169]

As is true of most countries, Colombia's industrial promotion policy outside the trade and credit areas has been piecemeal, made by different agencies and seldom thought through as a unified whole.[170] No specific industrial development legislation exists; the incentive measures are dispersed among different laws and decrees dating back to the subsidy arrangements, guarantees, and so on of the early industrialization effort during 1904-30. Tax incentives have been provided for firms engaged in basic industries, iron-related industries, and a variety of other import-substituting lines.[171] The few recent appraisals of such incentive plans tend to conclude that their impact is small,[172] just as most observers felt that the devices used by General Reyes and his successors had little effect on the speed or direction of industrialization.

In terms of technical assistance, the Instituto de Investigaciones Tecnológicas was established in 1955 and continues to operate on a rather small scale.[173] It prepares specific projects for various types of industries by contract with the interested parties, and provides technical assistance to small and medium-scale industry in respect of organizational problems. More recently the Fundación para el Fomento de la Investigación Científica y Tecnológica (FICITEC) has begun to provide technical and administrative advice to medium-sized firms. Several other organizations are doing so on a small scale. The Instituto Colombiano de Administración, a private foundation created under the sponsorship of AID, offers courses for executive personnel and provides technical assistance to them on a small scale. In the area of training centers for workers already in employment, Colombia has Servicio Nacional de Aprendizaje (SENA), an institution of generally good reputation. The Corporación

Financiera Popular has, in connection with its credit activities, a natural assistance role on more administrative and financial aspects of businesses.

IFI has been the key institution of direct state promotion. Its participation in iron and steel, petroleum refining, manufacture of alkalies, fertilizers, tires, spirits, and salts tends to reflect a focus, typical for Latin America, on basic industrial activities calling for relatively high investment and entailing considerable risks, a focus which would suggest that it was not competing with private capital but rather complementing its activities. IFI has operated through subscriptions for shares, concession of credit, and endorsement of loans; by the mid-sixties it had promoted about twenty important industrial concerns. Its portfolio has expanded dramatically since the late fifties. Most operations have been transferred to the private sector. IFI's orientation toward capital-intensive industries raises questions about the economic efficiency of its investments, especially since the minor export boom provided an alternative to increasingly difficult import substitution.

The country's policy with respect to foreign investment is difficult to evaluate, partly because some negotiations and understandings are never published and partly because both the true profits and the treatment given to foreign firms are hard to gauge even *ex post*.[174] Broadly speaking, the policy can be described as positive but moderate; foreign investment has been welcomed and given certain concessions, but not comparable to cases like Puerto Rico with its tax holiday. Colombia was one of the pioneers in the idea of automatic reversion of foreign petroleum fields and refineries to the national government after a certain period and is, of course, part currently of the Andean Group with its reversion principle. Only occasionally have there been limitations on profit remittances (imposed, for example, by Carlos Lleras during the balance-of-payments crisis in 1967). In general, Colombian law has been remarkably free of discriminations against foreigners. Foreigners have been subjected to the same minute regulation of business as nationals, but no more so.[175] While the Andean Group has made treatment asymmetrical between the two groups, it remains to be seen how important the modifications are in practice.

PART V
SOME FEATURES OF THE INDUSTRIALIZATION PROCESS:
THE EVOLUTION OF INDUSTRY BY SIZE AND JURIDICAL FORM

An important feature of the process of rising labor productivity has been the gradual replacement of cottage-shop by the factory as the characteristic mode of production. By 1900 plants of five or more workers probably accounted for no more than 5-10 percent of the manufacturing labor force and 1-2 percent of the total labor force; in 1970 these shares were 45-50 percent and about 7 percent respectively. The share of the total labor force in cottage-shop production had eased down gradually up until the sixties, but since then appears to have moved up a little (Table 2.5). Some activities have seen wholesale displacement of cottage-shop operations by factories (e.g., textiles). Other industries have provided increasing opportunities for small operators (e.g., transportation equipment repairs[176] and wooden furniture).

The marked effect on average labor productivity in manufacturing of increases in the share of employment found in factories is due to the very wide differential in labor productivity by plant size,[177] as much as seven or eightfold between independent workers and large firms in 1964 (Table 2.15).[178] It is due in part to a higher capital/labor ratio in the larger plants; whether other factors (e.g., a better production function, economies of scale) also play a role is more difficult to judge. Differences in wages and in marginal productivity of labor are much less.

TABLE 2.15

ASPECTS OF COLOMBIAN MANUFACTURING BY SIZE OF ESTABLISHMENT, 1964: COTTAGE-SHOP SUBSECTOR

	Independent Workers (1)	Establishments of 2-4 Workers			All Establishments of <5 workers (5) = (1) + (2)
		Total (2)=(3)+(4)	(Not reported by DANE) (3)	(Reported by DANE) (4)	
Number of Establishments				3,637	
Number of Workers (thousands)	169.3	153.2–163.2	142.5–152.6	10.7	322.5–332.5
Gross Value Added (millions of pesos)	1,073	1,036–1,100	903–967	133	2,109–2,173
Salaries (Including Fringe Benefits) per Paid Worker (thousands of pesos)		3.5–3.9	3.4–3.8	4.7	3.5–3.9
Gross Value Added/Occupied Person (thousands of pesos)	8.0–9.0	7.4	≈7.0	12.5	7.7–8.2
Gross Value Added/Horse Power (thousands of pesos)			n.a	7.9	
Paid Labor Share of Gross Value Added (percent)		20.54–22.02	20.03–21.75	24.00	10.09–11.15

(continued)

TABLE 2.15 (continued)

ASPECTS OF COLOMBIAN MANUFACTURING BY SIZE OF ESTABLISHMENT, 1964: FACTORY SUBSECTOR

	Size of Establishment (Number of Workers)							Total Establishments of ≥ 5 workers	All Manufacturing
	5-9	10-25	25-49	50-74	75-99	100-199	≥200		
Number of Establishments	6,100– 7,635	2,961	869	315	167	261	223	10,896– 12,431	
Number of Workers (thousands)	40– 50	40.7	29.6	18.9	14.2	36.0	115.2	294.6– 304.6	627
Gross Value Added (millions of pesos)	580– 725	749	765	637	452	1,841	5,407	10,431– 10,576	12,540– 12,749
Salaries (Including Fringe Benefits) per paid Worker (thousands of pesos)	6.0	7.0	9.3	11.2	11.2	14.0	16.1	11.9 12.4	10.5– 10.7
Gross Value Added/Occupied Person (thousands of pesos)	14.5	18.4	25.8	33.7	31.8	51.2	46.9	35.9	20.3
Gross Value Added/Horse Power (thousands of pesos)	10.4	9.8	8.0	14.3	14.8	15.2	9.3		
Paid Labor Share of Gross Value Added (percent)	33.69	35.69	35.43	33.07	35.02	27.31	34.30	33.17– 33.18	28.81– 29.91

Sources and Methodology: For details see Berry "The Relevance and Prospects. . ." Table 1. A few figures have been revised from that source. The basic source for all but the independent workers and the small establishments (2-4 workers) not surveyed by DANE is DANE, *Anuario General de Estadística*, 1964. A number of adjustments were made to the DANE figures, because of certain biases they are known to have. Data for the smaller plants and independent workers are based primarily on Urrutia and Villalba, "El Sector Artesanal."

54 - Berry

Rural cottage-shop employment appears to have decreased or been stagnant over several decades, especially during the thirties and forties, before increasing again in the sixties and seventies.[179] Urban cottage-shop employment appears to have risen at about the same rate as urban factory employment.[180] Meanwhile, small-scale factories decreased in importance with respect to large-scale factories[181] up until around 1970; during the seventies this pattern appears to have been reversed, as employment in small plants rose very fast.[182]

Although cottage-shop is important in all the major factory manufacturing departments (Cundinamarca, Antioquia, Valle, and Atlántico), its relative importance is greatest where factory manufacturing is unimportant and, correspondingly, where per capita productivity in industry is low, as in Bolívar, Magdalena, Nariño, Tolima, Caldas; these are in general the poorer departments[183] (Figure 2.1). In 1964 only Antioquia, Cundinamarca, and Atlántico had more people in factory industry than in cottage-shop, with Valle being about half and half. Nevertheless departments with an above average percentage increase in the number of factory workers between 1953 and 1964 had also above average increases in the number of cottage-shop workers. Thus, the four leading manufacturing departments showed an increase of 56.7 percent in factory employment versus an increase in 1.4 percent for the other departments, and an increase of 36.8 percent in cottage-shop employment as contrasted with 21.6 percent for the other departments. This suggests that the factory and cottage-shop subsectors may in the aggregate be more complementary than competitive.[184]

Almost all departments suffering sharp decreases in the number of rural cottage-shop workers between 1951 and 1964 (Valle, Tolima, Huila, Bolívar, Caldas, Cundinamarca) saw a rapid increase in the absolute number of urban workers.[185] This could indicate some direct transfer of cottage-shop activities like clothing, leather, and carpentry from the rural to the urban setting, plausible in view of the better facilities in the latter.[186] But some of the traditionally rural cottage-shop activities, such as fique coffee sacs and straw hats, tended to disappear rather than transfer to an urban setting,[187] while such expanding shop activities as auto repair were never rural but rather emerged with urban development and wealth. Recent studies have found urban cottage-shop activities to be more market oriented than rural ones; whether this was true in the days of the extensive production of coffee bags and straw hats is another question. A study of the Ubate Valley found the great majority of the rural artisans to be women, and an important part of their production destined for household consumption; relatively few were full-time and production systems were sometimes primitive.[188]

Evolution of the potential and competitiveness of cottage-shop production differs widely by industry. Of the sectors which in 1964 accounted for almost three-quarters of all cottage-shop workers, over the period 1938-64 employment in textiles fell sharply, that in clothing and footwear fell moderately, that in food showed little trend, while that in wood and wood products trended up moderately and that in transportation materials sharply[189] (Table 2.16). The relative and absolute decline of employment in both textiles and clothing/footwear is evidently a result of competition from factory industry; the growth of wood/furniture employment is in spite of such competition. Some small-scale metal-working activities appear to be complementary to new consumption patterns (especially the automobile) and some to expanding factory industry. Of the two-digit, cottage-shop industries still important in 1964, only in clothing/footwear was employment on the decline.

Has the maintenance of high employment in cottage-shop been mainly a safety valve phenomenon, the result of poor employment prospects

FIGURE 2.1
LABOR FORCE SHARE IN FACTORY MANUFACTURING AND IN COTTAGE-SHOP

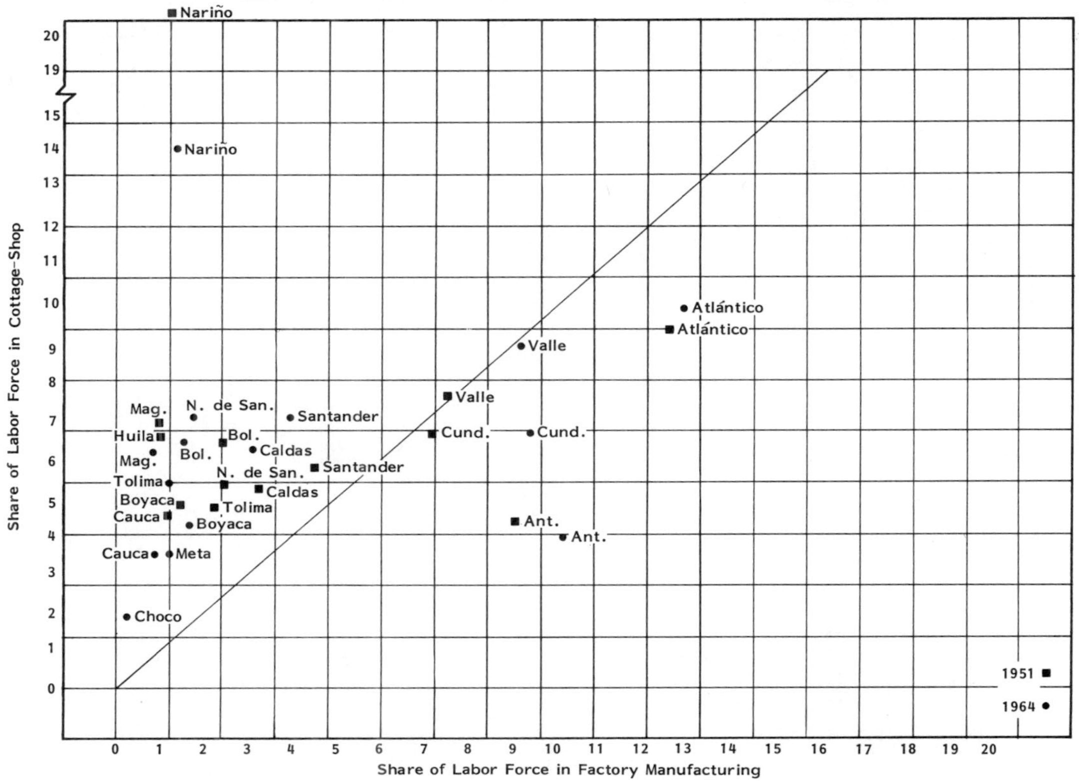

TABLE 2.16

MANUFACTURING EMPLOYMENT BY TWO-DIGIT INDUSTRIES AND BY FACTORY/COTTAGE-SHOP, 1938-64

Industry	1938	1944/45	1951[c]	1964	Industry	1938	1944/45	1951[c]	1964
Food-Total	29,387	32,172	47,311	73,889	Leather & Products-Total	7,024[d]	3,409	8,006	9,488
Factory	≥ 6,153		39,355	41,561	Factory	NA		3,867	4,482
Cottage-Shop	≤ 23,234		7,956	32,328	Cottage-Shop	≤ 7,024		4,139	5,006
Beverages-Total	6,358	9,671	11,772	19,216	Rubber & Products-Total		5,764[d]	2,329	5,425
Factory	≥ 1,975		10,699	16,420	Factory			2,280	6,900
Cottage-Shop	≤ 4,383		1,073	2,796	Cottage-Shop			49	-1,475
Tobacco-Total	10,167	8,560	10,654	8,574	Chemicals-Total	4,722	5,890	11,146	25,752
Factory	≥ 5,059		7,099	3,803	Factory	≥ 2,761		8,958	19,819
Cottage-Shop	≤ 5,108		3,555	4,771	Cottage-Shop	≤ 1,961		2,188	5,933
Textiles-Total	114,684[b]	29,961	60,691	62,362	Petroleum & Coal Products-Total		1,142	1,607	4,880
Factory	≥ 11,551		35,127	44,099	Factory			1,477	2,026
Cottage-Shop	≤ 103,133		25,564	18,263	Cottage-Shop			132	2,854
Clothing & Footwear-Total	160,788	18,347	143,933	153,265	Nonmetallic Mineral Products-Total	16,517	13,291	25,592	36,907
Factory	≥ 2,790		26,056	31,510	Factory	≥ 2,807		16,840	25,493
Cottage-Shop	≤ 157,998		117,877	121,755	Cottage-Shop	≤ 13,710		8,752	11,414
Wood & Products-Total	44,356	10,154	57,202	78,245	Metal & Metal Products - Total	25,226	9,414	55,754	139,426
Factory	NA		8,804	10,989	Factory	≥ 1,417		15,179	51,549
Cottage-Shop	≤ 44,356		48,398	67,256	Cottage-Shop	≤ 23,809		40,575	87,877
Paper & Products-Total		610[d]	1,798	5,613	TOTAL	435,863	151,700	460,900[a]	655,961
Factory			1,636	5,485	Factory			185,500[a]	283,571
Cottage-Shop			162	128	Cottage-Shop			272,400[a]	372,390
Printing-Total	7,132	5,552	10,767	16,935					
Factory	NA		7,263	11,812					
Cottage-Shop	≤ 7,132		3,504	5,123					

TABLE 2.16 (continued)

Sources and Methodology: The 1964 figures, including the factory-cottage-shop breakdown, are those of Berry, "The Relevance and Prospects," Table A-2b; the two-digit totals are unadjusted figures from the 1964 population census and the factory employment is from DANE, *Anuario General de Estadística, 1964*. The 1944/45 factory employment data are from the Industrial Census of that year, with an upward adjustment to allow for unpaid workers. (Contraloría General de la República, *Primer Censo Industrial de Colombia*.) The 1938 total employment figures are from the population census of that year. The factory employment figures (lower limits, as indicated) are based on a survey reported in the *Anuario General de Estadística, 1938* and designed only to give a feel for the possible magnitudes. For 1951 estimates of total employment at the two-digit level had to be based on data for 9 departments where that breakdown was available; for the other 6 departments estimates were made by interpolation between 1938 and 1964; a given industry was assumed to account for a percentage of the total manufacturing labor force in 1951 equal to the unweighted average of its percentages in 1938 and 1964. Total error introduced by this methodology would appear to be small. Factory employment in 1951 was interpolated between the 1944/45 figures and 1953 values from the official DANE statistics corresponding to the industrial census of that year and published in various issues of DANE *Boletín Mensual de Estadística*, assuming a linear growth path.

[a] Greater than the sum of the figures in the column as it includes territories (nondepartments), for which no attempt to break the employment down at the two-digit level was made, and a few industries classified as miscellaneous.

[b] Includes 90,559 persons listed in "Industries of Animal and Vegetable Fibres," of which 81,409 were men.

[c] Figures do not correspond to those of Table 2.5 because of adjustments made in that table which would not be affected at the industry level and are therefore not included here.

[d] Some possibility of error, since category definitions were not the same in 1944/45 as in succeeding years.

elsewhere and consistent with stagnant or declining real earnings, or does it reflect rising productivity and continuing ability to compete? While both interpretations have some validity, on balance the second appears closer to the truth. A striking recent finding (at the level of the urban economy, not just manufacturing) is that the income gap between employees of small scale establishments (five workers or less) and those of larger establishments (plus persons with a university education or who are government employees) is relatively small, perhaps 20 percent, after allowing for differences in levels of education and skill.[190] This suggests that, unless manufacturing is quite atypical of the urban sector as a whole, earnings of workers in small-scale establishments must have been rising at least moderately, a proposition borne out by the available wage statistics. Over the period 1953-70, the increase in average real earnings of paid workers in establishments of less than five workers was nearly 60 percent, as compared with over 200 percent for employees in the factory subsector.[191] The widening gap would suggest increasing differences between the two subsectors in the skill and education levels of workers, partly associated with the increasing inputs of white-collar workers and professionals in the factory sector. For the period 1953-64, Urrutia and Villalba estimated that average cottage-shop incomes (for paid workers and self-employed) rose by 24 percent, while real wages in factory industry rose by 66 percent. In some departments where the factory subsector grew least, the figures indicate income decreases for cottage-shop workers, as in Caldas, Cauca, Tolima, and Norte de Santander. On a cross-departmental basis, however, little relationship appeared between the percentage increase in real factory wage and real artisan income. Urrutia and Villalba found that cottage-shop income levels varied widely by sector; the lowest incomes were those of women working in *confecciones* (clothing) and the highest those of mechanics in automobile repair shops. Clothing and furniture used primitive techniques while food and auto-mechanics were more advanced. Such evidence is consistent with the plausible, but at this point unprovable, hypothesis that average cottage-shop earnings have trended upwards over much of the century. Changing composition of employment from lower to higher productivity activities and from rural to urban would be expected to exert an upward push on average earnings. Evidence on labor mobility, especially in recent decades, would also suggest that when other laboring groups are gaining, it is unlikely that this one would be losing.

Small-scale industry (defined for the moment as plants of five to twenty-four workers) tends to be important in the same industries as cottage-shop production, though with some interesting differences. In 1964 the major employers in this size range were food (19,000), clothing and footwear (14,000), nonmetallic minerals (7,700), and metal products excluding machinery (5,400). Wooden furniture, where cottage-shop production is so important, had few small factories (only 3,000 workers in the size range cited), and transport equipment relatively few (5,100).[192] In these two industries the growth process involved increasing numbers of cottage-shop producers rather than the growth of cottage-shop establishments into small factories; economies of scale are apparently unimportant. In the cases of the other two major cottage-shop industries, clothing/footwear and food, small-scale industry is fairly and very important respectively. The gradual decrease of cottage-shop employment in textiles was probably associated with a shift of workers to larger plants rather than with the growth of cottage-shop firms into small factories, if the lack of contemporary small plants is at all indicative. The apparent stagnation of cottage-shop employment in the food sector might more likely be associated with expansion of cottage-shop establishments into small factories.

Within the factory subsector the share of both output and employment in the larger plants has gradually increased. Whereas in 1953 about 47 percent of employment was in plants of less than fifty workers, by 1957 this proportion had fallen to about 34 percent, and a full 46 percent were in plants of 200 or more workers. It is not known whether large firms and plants have tended to grow faster than small ones, or whether the increasing share of employment at the larger sizes is due mainly to smaller producers graduating into the higher size categories with the passage of time.

The trend toward larger plants is paralleled by a trend toward the corporate form, as opposed to proprietorships, partnerships and other juridical forms. In 1950 probably 40-45 percent of factory output was produced by corporations; by 1975 the figure had risen to around 65 percent.[193] Corporations are larger in almost every respect than firms run by individuals or partners, while limited companies fall between the two. As noted elsewhere, large size usually implies relatively high capital intensity and modernity. Interestingly, plants owned by corporations tend to be more capital intensive than the same size plants under some other juridical form, suggesting a considerable range of possible capital intensities even at fairly small plant sizes, with availability of capital (greater for corporations) and familiarity with capital-intensive technologies being important determinants.[194] (See Table A-87).

The process whereby large-scale plants or firms increase their share of output and employment at the expense of smaller factories or of cottage-shop, and the relative productive efficiency of these different-sized operations are important and related issues. The greater availability of data on smaller factories has made it possible to analyze their relative growth and productivity vis-à-vis larger plants in a way not possible for cottage-shop producers. Nelson et al. have emphasized the technological dualism of Colombian manufacturing and argued that the process of growth has been essentially the growth of the larger more modern and more efficient plants at the expense of the smaller ones.[195] In John Todd's analysis of relative social efficiency of plants by size in Chapter 6, however, the small and medium sizes come out ahead of the largest (above 200 workers). This apparent contradiction is discussed further in Chapters 6 and 9; it is evident that our understanding of the relationships in question remains seriously incomplete.

The Entrepreneur

Much discussion has surrounded the origins and characteristics of the industrial entrepreneur. In the early industrializing countries, especially Great Britain and northern Europe, religious nonconformity and lower social class along with artisan background are frequently cited as characteristics of this group during incipient industrialization—continuing in Great Britain to perhaps the middle of the nineteenth century. Industrialization was a new phenomenon, one on which the elite classes would be expected to look with disdain and disfavor, perhaps also with relatively little concern; it was not initially self-evident that the fulcrum of their economies would increasingly shift to the industrial sector. In North America, the wealthy families had from the start diversified commercial, financial, and industrial holdings and the period during which industrial structure was dominated by small competitive firms was short-lived. Correspondingly, the American business elite have been largely born to their positions of wealth and power.[196] The Latin American pattern, to the extent that a single one exists, seems characterized by the greater relative importance of immigrants than in the United States and many European countries;[197] as in the United States, a traditional wealthy group dominates, with the difference that in Latin America this group sits at the top of a more rigid social system.

In Latin America, in contrast to early Europe, it would be surprising if alert, traditional families did not recognize the inevitably increasing importance of industry and try to swim with the tide. Because import-substituting industrialization in Latin America tends to be based upon large firms owing their success substantially to factor and product market imperfections (trade controls, financial contacts, and the like), one would expect it to be difficult for persons of humble origins to reach the top, even in the absence of a constraining social system.

Who have been Colombia's entrepreneurs, and do they fit any of the above molds? The Antioqueño has contributed greatly to Colombian industrialization both in the early twentieth century and in the post-World War II period; an extensive literature extols the Antioqueño's business abilities.[198] Foreigners have also had an increasing role to play during this period.[199] Chu found that of eighty entrepreneurs running large firms in the period 1920-45, 67 percent were native born and 26 percent foreign born; of forty small-firm entrepreneurs the corresponding ratios were 77 percent and 18 percent. Most of the foreign-born entrepreneurs were immigrants, not employees of foreign companies.[200] The number of foreign entrepreneurs rose sharply during World War II, due to the turmoil in Europe. When Aaron Lipman sampled 461 Bogotá industrial leaders [members of The Asociación Nacional de Industriales (ANDI)] in 1962,[201] he found 41 percent to be foreign born; almost all were from Europe, most arriving since 1933 and a good number during 1943-45 when religious persecution in Europe was rife.[202] Alan Gilbert's 1970 sample of company founders listed in ANDI included 378 firms.[203] Among these companies were fifty-five foreign corporations, while ninety-nine founders were first or second-generation immigrants. These two categories therefore covered 41 percent of all the companies, although this ratio varied widely by city (19 percent in Medellín, 54 percent in Cali, 57 percent in Bogotá, and 79 percent in Barranquilla). Foreign entrepreneurship is much less prominent in the smaller cities; in Cartagena, Manizales, Pereira, and Bucaramanga taken together, the ratio was 19 percent. Lack of full comparability among the surveys by Chu, Lipman, and Gilbert makes it hard to judge whether the share of industry operated by foreign-born persons has trended up or down; in any case, it has been substantial through most, if not all, of this century.

Little information is available on the class, occupational, and income antecedents of the entrepreneurial group. It is known that considerable capital for early industrialization came from the commercial sector, especially import-export activities, and that the entrepreneurship came with it.

Since the private sector dominates Colombian industry, the government has played little direct role in the provision of the entrepreneurial function. In 1968, the output of manufacturing plants classified as "official" and semiofficial" was 8.2 percent of the total, concentrated in beverages (departments have a monopoly on certain alcoholic beverages), chemicals, and base metals, with a scattering of plants in other sectors. The Colombian government has had a nondogmatic point of view with respect to property and the relationship between government and private sectors.[204] IFI was designed to complement the development of private sector manufacturing. IFI's involvement has more frequently involved financial support, though in some cases direct management as well.

PART VI
EFFECTS OF INDUSTRIAL GROWTH

The contribution of a country's industrialization to overall development and welfare depends on its short and long-run effects on total output of the economy and on income distribution. A major determinant of the effect on total output is the efficiency achieved by industry (reflected by its competitiveness) and the resource mobilization which it induces. Analysis of trends in the prices of manufactured products and of the level of profits and the use to which they are put, is useful in this context. An indication of the income distribution impact may be provided by evidence on the amount of employment created and the corresponding wage levels. Other important considerations include the level of taxes and transfers to the government, and the effects on the balance of payments. We turn first to the matter of price trends.

The Relative Price of Manufacturing Output Over Time: Static Efficiency and International Competitiveness

Many traditional industries in Colombia have long been price competitive with imports (e.g., some beverages, textiles, clothing, leather products, wood products, and others). Few entered the export ranks until recently because of the small scale of production, dispersed markets, and uneven quality. Success in the industrialization process is more a matter of improving the competitiveness over time of those larger-scale, modern production lines which in the beginning need protection, textiles being the best example earlier in the century. In this sense industrialization appears to have been at least reasonably successful; a fair share of industries have approached or reached international competitiveness without too long a delay. The rapid export growth of the sixties and early seventies is very encouraging. Overall, Colombia's industrial performance compares favorably with that of many other Latin and Asian countries.

Trends in the relative price of value added in manufacturing vis-à-vis the other sectors of the economy provide another measure of the sector's changing competitiveness over time and its contribution to overall growth. In the early stages of industrialization, one expects to see prices of manufactured goods and of value added in manufacturing above world levels; but learning-by-doing and rising capital/labor ratios may be expected to lower these prices. Our estimates suggest a substantial decrease in the relative price of manufactured goods between 1939 and 1950; an index of the manufacturing/total price ratio fell from 125 in 1939 to 100 in 1950.[205] National accounts data indicate a further substantial decline of about 15 percent in the ratio of the price of value added in manufacturing to the implicit GDP price deflator over 1950-70. Despite the substantial error which could be involved in these statistics, a trend seems clear. Since a secular increase in the relative price of services, at least as captured in the national accounts, is common to almost all countries, it is relevant to ask whether this fall in the relative price of value added in manufacturing has been atypically fast; over 1950-70 the trends vary widely among less-developed countries and no general pattern seems to emerge.[206] Colombia's experience is not exceptional. Since 1970 the previous trend has been reversed and the price of value added in manufacturing has risen faster than the GDP deflator, by 6.6 percent over 1970-77.

Across two-digit industries, trends in the relative price of manufactured products have varied substantially over 1950-70. (Table 2.17). Measured prices in the newer industries producing intermediate and capital goods showed no tendency to decline more than those of the traditional, consumer-oriented ones. Of nine long-standing industries (numbers 20 through 29, except paper), the relative price index fell by more than 10 points in four and did not in five; of the ten modern ones, it fell this fast in four and did not in six. The weighted (by 1960 value added) decline was 16.5 percent in the first group and about 10 percent in the second group. Overall, then, the price performance of manufacturing appears to have been acceptable, although one might have expected more declines in the newer industries relative to the older ones; this conclusion must remain tentative given the doubtful quality of the price data.

Some feel for the static efficiency of various industries is provided by Table 2.18, which presents estimates of capital productivity and total factor productivity in 1969. The most relevant measures are value added at world prices minus labor costs, all divided by capital (Column 2a), and total factor productivity with capital costed at its average rate of return in all manufacturing and with value added measured at world prices (Column 3a). Both indicators imply that as of 1969 the most efficient sectors were food, clothing and footwear, wood and wooden furniture (especially the latter), paper, rubber, nonmetallic minerals, metal products except machinery, textiles (more marginally). (The figures for beverages and tobacco are so affected by the heavy taxes that they are of little help in evaluating efficiency.) Most of these combine at least reasonably high labor intensity with a relatively long history in production. The dramatically inefficient industries appeared to be base metals, electrical machinery, transportation equipment, and miscellaneous (of which plastics is an important component). The petroleum products sector was less inefficient than those just cited. Comparable calculations at the three-digit level would be needed to avoid the averaging of unlike industries; some textiles and chemicals could emerge as quite efficient, while others were very inefficient. Limited evidence suggests that the broad pattern emerging in 1969 held also in 1958.[207]

Many of the industries which were still inefficient in 1969 were cases of recent import substitution. If these estimates are close to being accurate, base metals, electrical machinery, and especially transport equipment were a long way from being competitive.

Capacity Utilization as a Determinant of Efficiency

An important aspect of efficiency in resource utilization is the utilization of capital, a scarce resource in developing countries. Many observers find it anomalous that such countries frequently appear to leave much capital idle by operating plants only one turn.[208] The first organized data for Colombia were provided by the 1945 Industrial Census, which revealed that of 7,523 reporting firms, 187 operated two turns, 143 three turns, and the rest one turn. The share of total capital operated on two or three turns was perhaps 50-60 percent, much higher than the share of firms.[209] Between this 1945 Census and a mail survey conducted by Oscar Gómez in 1959, the increase in multiple-shift plants appears to have been more or less proportional to the total increase in plants.[210]

Thoumi's recent research, reported in Chapter 7 and elsewhere, has cast new light on the underutilization phenomenon, although it does not provide data directly comparable to that cited above, since the sample

TABLE 2.17

RELATIVE PRICE TRENDS OF MANUFACTURED PRODUCTS VIS-À-VIS THE PRICE DEFLATOR OF GDP, BY TWO-DIGIT INDUSTRY
(Indices Have 1958=100)

Industry	1950	1955	1960	1965	1970
20 Food	95.9	95.3	95.2	98.3	87.6
21 Beverages	112.0	112.6	96.1	105.9	122.4
22 Tobacco	117.9	115.9	97.5	100.9	74.2
23 Textiles	121.3	97.4	91.6	77.1	81.5
24 Clothing and Footwear	125.6	103.7	97.3	89.8	87.0
25 Wood	121.1	111.9	117.1	128.5	135.8
26 Wooden Furniture	147.9	116.5	102.6	108.1	105.2
27 Paper and Products	73.3	76.4	94.3	85.9	71.8
28 Printing and Related	67.3	59.2	95.9	77.1	72.1
29 Leather and Products	102.1	95.3	126.2	96.1	108.3
30 Rubber and Products	116.1	87.7	93.3	79.5	70.4
31 Chemical Products	96.3	79.8	87.6	76.4	74.0
32 Petroleum Derivatives	65.6	57.3	96.3	78.8	71.8
33 Nonmetallic Minerals	118.9	101.7	100.8	99.0	105.9
34 Basic Metals	66.9	64.8	105.9	89.2	113.9
35 Metal Products except Machinery & Equipment	91.6	79.2	96.8	85.0	87.4
36 Nonelectric Machinery	104.7	85.0	105.3	110.7	109.6
37 Electrical Machinery	102.1	77.7	97.4	81.3	72.4
38 Transport Equipment	93.3	79.7	98.2	87.4	86.4
Total (including coffee)	98.1	90.5	91.7	85.8	86.8
Total (excluding coffee)	106.0	93.3	97.0	90.0	90.1

Source: Banco de la República, *División de Cuentas Nacionales*, unpublished data. These price series are usually based on a narrow sample of products within each sector, and are in general unweighted.

TABLE 2.18

A GUESS AT RELATIVE TOTAL FACTORY PRODUCTIVITY BY TWO-DIGIT INDUSTRY, FACTORY SUBSECTOR, 1969
(Absolute Values in Thousands of Pesos)

Industry	Capital Productivity: Output/Capital		Rate of Return to Capital: Output-Payments to Labor/Capital		Total Factor Productivity: Output/Estimated Value of Inputs	
	$\frac{VA}{K}$	$\frac{VA_W}{K}$	$\frac{VA-WB(TO/R)}{K}$	$\frac{VA_W-WB(TO/R)}{K}$	$\frac{VA}{K(r_a)+WB(TO/R)}$	$\frac{VA_W}{K(r_a)+WB(TO/R)}$
	(1)	(1a)	(2)	(2a)	(3)	(3a)
Food	.248	>.248[a]	.143	>.143[a]	.911	>1.244[a]
Beverages	.567	.256	.445	.134	1.959	1.185
Tobacco	.681	.350	.583	.252	2.566	1.819
Textiles	.284	.273	.146	.136	.931	1.180
Clothing & Footwear	.486	.486	.229	.229	1.145	1.383
Wooden Products except Furniture	.259	.292	.108	.140	.814	.915
Wooden Furniture	.604	.807	.251	.454	1.162	1.805
Paper	.219	.195[b]	.132	.109[b]	.863	1.081[b]
Printing	.344	>.344[b]	.129	>.129[b]	.901	>1.114[b]
Leather	.307	.278	.173	.144	1.020	1.219
Rubber	.291	.423	.138	.271	.910	1.718
Chemicals	.314	.195	.189	.070	1.074	.891
Petroleum Products	.085	.090	.065	.070	.456	.787
Nonmetallic Minerals	.249	.271	.118	.140	.834	1.204
Basic Metals	.152	.061	.096	.004	.681	.403
Metal Products except Machinery and Transport Equipment	.322	.219	.155	.052	.965	.838
Nonelectric Machinery	.342	.368	.145	.171	.939	1.266
Electrical Machinery	.317	neg.	.151	neg.	.951	neg.
Transport Equipment	.370	.052	.117	neg.	.880	.150
Miscellaneous	.348	.161	.187	neg.	1.061	.629
TOTAL	.290	.217	.167	.094	1.000	1.000
TOTAL (excluding beverages & tobacco)	.270	.208	.147	.082	1.000	1.000

TABLE 2.18 (continued)

Source: Data on value added, employment, and wages are from DANE, *Industria Manufacturera Nacional 1969*. Foreign capital figures are those of Table 2.13, and the data on value added at world prices are based on Hutcheson, *Incentives for Industrialization*.

Symbols: VA is value added at domestic market prices; VA_W is value added converted to world prices using Hutcheson's effective protection rates; WB is wage bill; TO is total persons occupied; R is persons remunerated; K is capital stock (including capital in financial forms); r_a is the average return to the capital in factory industry, excluding beverages and tobacco, 14.7 percent as calculated in Col. (2).

[a] Did not permit the calculation of an average effective protection rate from Hutcheson's data. But since coffee and sugar had strongly negative protection, it seems clear that the average is negative. (Excluding these two items, Hutcheson's figure is 2.2 percent).

[b] Assuming negative protection for this industry. Hutcheson made no estimate since the output is not traded.

was not random. His findings suggest that capacity utilization in 1970 was relatively high compared to the few other developing countries with data, and that the capital-intensive industries in particular tended to operate on a three-shift basis. It seems likely that, for manufacturing as a whole, a higher share of total output is now produced in multiple-shift plants than was the case several decades ago, partly because the relative importance of some of the multiple-shift industries has risen.

Thoumi concludes that high utilization is associated with the corporate form of management, or conversely, that low utilization often reflects the high cost of night plant operation on the manager's leisure and tranquility.[211]

Capital Income and Its Uses

Returns to capital in the manufacturing sector have been high, as suggested by the modest labor share. It appears that a considerable share of such income has gone into savings and taxes. Direct statistics on the rate of return are virtually nonexistent so estimates must be based on comparisons of total capital income in manufacturing and the capital stock.[212] Such comparisons suggest a healthy rate of return. With a gross output/capital ratio usually in the .3 to .5 range, even after deduction of a labor share of 30-40 percent of gross value added and allowance for depreciation and indirect taxes, the average rate of profit on capital would appear to have been in the range of 11-17 percent.[213] The data are more consistent with higher profit rates in the late forties and early fifties than in the sixties, given the equal or higher output/capital ratios (Table 2.19) and the probably lower labor and definitely lower total tax shares (indirect plus direct) in the earlier period. Rough calculations based on data presented by the Superintendencia de Sociedades Anónimas for national corporations suggests a gross before tax profit rate on net real assets of 15-35 percent;[214] the estimated net after tax rate fell in the range 8-18 percent for the years 1950, 1957, and 1964.

During most of this century, industrial capital formation has in the main been financed internally. Some savings data exist for corporations, which generate a higher share of output in manufacturing than in any other major sector. As of 1950, the national accounts estimated net corporate saving, a majority of which was probably by manufacturing corporations, as 10.2 percent of net savings and 1.25 percent of national income; in 1970 the comparable values were 18.4 percent, and 3.22 percent, and in 1975 29.5 percent and 3.18 percent. Since then these shares have fallen again. These estimates of corporate savings are probably biased downward substantially, due to the underestimation of corporate profits.[215] If true profits of manufacturing corporations in 1950 were two to three times those calculated in the Superintendencia's accounting-type measure,[216] then they constituted perhaps 25-30 percent of value added in the sector. With a majority of this saved by the corporations themselves,[217] and a good share of that paid out as dividends probably saved by the high-income recipients,[218] the contribution to total savings was clearly sizable. At that time, about 40-45 percent of factory output was produced by corporations; even if the savings ratio out of other manufacturing output was lower, the average must have been substantial. By 1970, over 60 percent of factory output came from the corporations. In earlier decades, the behavior of proprietorships and partnerships was the key determinant of sectoral savings, but we have little evidence apart from the observed fact of fairly rapid growth of the capital stock.

TABLE 2.19

ESTIMATES OF CAPITAL PRODUCTIVITY, SELECTED YEARS, 1925-69

Year	$\dfrac{\text{Output}}{\text{Capital}}$ (1958 prices)	$\dfrac{\text{Output}}{\text{Capital}}$ (Current prices)
1925	.137	(.566)[a]
1938	.182	(.299)[a]
1945	.252	(.434)[a]
1951	.243	.427
1958	.289	.289
1962	.338	.424
1964	.355	.455
1967	.347	.356
1969	.376	.358

Source: Table A-84, where details of the methodology are presented.

[a] Tentative.

Because of the importance of corporations and the relatively high incomes generated in manufacturing, the sector contributes disproportionately to taxes. In 1950 direct and indirect taxes paid by manufacturing corporations accounted for about 15 percent of all government revenues, many of which are not sector specific (e.g., the income tax). This ratio had risen to 18 percent in 1964. Before 1950 we have only estimates of direct taxes paid by these corporations, which ran around 2-3 percent of government tax revenue before 1940, rising toward 10 percent at the end of the forties. No systematic data are available on tax payments of noncorporations.

Employment

As noted earlier, the share of manufacturing employment in the total labor force appears to have declined moderately from at least the turn of the century, falling to a low of 12 percent around 1950, followed by an increase to around 15 percent in 1970 and 17 percent in 1978. The decline was associated with the replacement of cottage-shop production (for home use and for sale) by factories. In the factory sector itself, employment has grown at an annual rate probably exceeding 4 percent since 1900, thereby increasing from perhaps 2 percent of the labor force to 8-9 percent in 1978. Over 1950-78 factory labor absorption was a healthy 4.5-5 percent per year, although between 1962 and 1968, it appears to have fallen to about 2.6 percent, helping to generate serious worries about the future of manufacturing employment.[219] A number of observers have related the low labor absorption of these years to the high share of investment going to quite capital-intensive industries.[220] Almost 40 percent of total fixed investment over 1962-67 was in the capital-intensive chemical sector or the even more capital-intensive petroleum sector.[221] Over 1958-61, these two industries accounted for 11.5 percent of fixed investment in manufacturing; over 1968-72 their share was again substantially lower than in 1962-67, at 17.6 percent.[222] The output elasticity of employment in factory manufacturing reached a low of about 0.5 in 1962-67[223] then rose in 1967-70, and reached a strikingly high level over 1970-78 (Table 2.20). One factor in the improved employment experience since 1967/68[224] was probably the greater focus on exports, since even though exports are not highly labor intensive (as discussed in greater detail in Chapter 8), they could hardly fail to be more so than such industries as petrochemicals and chemicals, prominent in the growth picture for 1962-67.[225] The main factor, however, was the resurgent growth of small and medium industry with greater labor intensity than large industry.

The growth of some strikingly capital-intensive industries and a general rapid increase in the K/L ratio during the sixties led some observers to believe that overpriced labor and/or underpriced capital were steering industrial growth in an undesirable direction; others felt that government policies and/or other factors were more important than relative factor prices in determining which industries would grow fastest.[226] Neither hypothesis has yet received detailed empirical investigation in Colombia.

TABLE 2.20

THE OUTPUT ELASTICITY OF EMPLOYMENT IN FACTORY MANUFACTURING: RATES OF GROWTH OF VALUE ADDED AND EMPLOYMENT IN FACTORY MANUFACTURING
(Percentage)

Period	Rate of Growth of Value Added[a] (1)	Rate of Growth of Employment (2)	Output Elasticity of Employment (3)
1953-78	7.00	4.7-5.3	0.67-0.76
1953-62	7.55	4.17	0.55
1962-67	5.45	2.65	0.49
1967-70	7.92	6.45	0.81
1970-78	7.00	6.0-7.8	0.86-1.11

Sources: Output data from Banco de la República, *Cuentas Nacionales*. Employment data from Table A-131 and Table 2.1. The employment growth rate for 1970-78 is presented as a range due to lack of a firm figure for 1978.

[a] 1958 prices.

[b] Col. (2) divided by Col. (3).

The Wage Rate, The Wage Share, and Income Distribution

Wages of blue-collar workers in factory manufacturing appear to have risen on the order of 200-250 percent between the early twenties and 1970.[227] Rapid increases occurred in the twenties (if we may judge from the evidence for Medellín) and from 1945 to the late sixties. Over 1930-45 increases were substantially less, and some groups suffered losses. Earnings of white-collar workers rose faster over 1945-53 than those of blue-collar workers, but more slowly thereafter.[228] The period from the early fifties to around 1963, one of very rapid employment growth, was also characterized by dramatic wage increases; during the late sixties the advance was modest, and the seventies have seen declines, probably related to sharply higher rates of inflation than had characterized earlier periods.[229]

The wage increases were widely distributed across industrial sectors and regions from 1944/45 to 1967; labor earnings per worker (white and blue-collar) in most industries rose by between 100 percent and 250 percent, and in most departments by between 100 percent and 200 percent. Regionally, some tendency towards equalization appeared between the four most industrialized departments and the other departments. As a group, the former saw an average wage rise of 135 percent, while the average wage rose in the latter by 164 percent.[230] Evidence on wage trends by firm size for the period 1953-66[231] indicates rapid wage increases for plants above 100 workers (about 80 percent or so), relatively small increases for plants of up to twenty-five workers (perhaps 30 or 35 percent), and intermediate gains for the medium-sized plants.[232]

Over 1953-68 the change in two-digit composition of employment had virtually no effect on the industry-wide average wage. Wage increases within the typical size category and industry were also almost as great as the average increase. Had size composition remained the same as in 1953, given the observed wage increases in each size category, the average wage would have been only about 20 percent lower in 1966 than was in fact the case.

Given developments in other sectors,[233] one might speculate that unskilled wages in manufacturing rose relatively little over the first half of the twentieth century, and that the increase in average wages was due to rising average skill levels. Data for certain unskilled categories in the Fenicia plants in Bogotá are consistent with this, at least over the twenties and thirties. Most available data are too aggregated to permit separation of the unskilled workers.

The wage share reflects both a sector's labor intensity and average remuneration. Crude estimates for 1925-36, necessarily based on wage and output trends, strongly suggest a declining share for factory manufacturing. One would expect the same result for all manufacturing, since the labor share was probably lower in the factory sector than in small-scale operations, with imputed wages duly taken into account. Subsequently, over 1936-53, the labor share appears to have moved upward somewhat in modern factory manufacturing and possibly, but with less assurance, in manufacturing as a whole.

Between 1950 and 1970 the paid labor share of gross value added in factory manufacturing increased markedly from 27.5 percent to nearly 42 percent according to National Accounts estimates.[234] (See Table 2.21). After 1970 a dramatic reversal occurred as the labor share fell back by 1977 to the level of the mid-fifties.[235]

The impact of industrialization on income distribution has probably not been dramatic, since usually no more than 15 percent of the labor force has been employed in manufacturing. Distribution of income within the sector is not dissimilar to that in the rest of nonagriculture. In

TABLE 2.21

LABOR SHARES IN MANUFACTURING INCOME, 1950-77

	Estimates Based on the National Accounts		Estimates Based on DANE Data			
	Paid Labor Share of Gross Value Added[a] in Manufacturing	Paid Labor Share of Gross Value Added[a] in Factory Manufacturing	Paid Labor Share of Gross Value Added in Factory Manufacturing:			Total Labor Share of Gross Value Added in Factory Manufacturing, All Workers
Year	(1)	(2)	All Workers (3)	Blue-Collar (4)	White-Collar (5)	(6)
1950	27.5					
1951	28.3					
1952	29.5					
1953	30.1					
1954	30.8		28.72	19.37	9.35	31.54
1955	32.4		29.16			
1956	32.7					
1957	34.0					
1958	34.8					
1959	35.0		31.65			
1960	34.9	36.24	31.41			32.69
1961	36.2	37.16	32.09			33.48
1962	36.3	36.96	32.12			33.51
1963	36.5	37.00	32.18			33.50
1964	38.1	38.11	32.96			34.34
1965	38.1	37.67	32.89	20.95	11.93	34.25
1966	37.8	37.86	32.82	20.84	11.98	34.13
1967	38.9	39.77	34.03	21.01	13.01	35.33
1968	40.1	39.27	31.80	19.49	12.31	32.99
1969	39.9	41.49	32.99	20.29	12.71	33.80
1970	41.8		35.41	21.43	13.98	
1971	40.8		33.52	19.71	13.81	
1972	40.2		33.60	19.54	14.07	
1973	35.2		33.58	20.74	12.85	
1974	30.4		30.31	NA	NA	
1975	31.2		31.43	18.17	13.26	
1976	31.6		30.62	17.70	12.92	
1977	31.6					

Sources and Methodology: Basic sources are the Banco de la República, *Cuentas Nacionales*, and DANE's annual industrial survey. Banco labor share estimates are higher because of a lower estimate of value added than that used by DANE and because the DANE estimates are at market prices rather than at factor cost. Columns (2) and (6) are the author's estimates based on adjustments to the other columns. For further details, see Table A-148.

[a] At factor cost.

Descriptive History - 71

1970, the first household survey undertaken by the Departamento Administrativo Nacional de Estadística (DANE) implied an average income about 12 percent higher for persons engaged in the manufacturing sector than for persons in other nonagricultural activities, and a coefficient of concentration (Gini coefficient) of .509, about the same as for nonagriculture as a whole.[236] The high skewness of income, reflecting the technological heterogeneity of the sector, was thus neither markedly worse nor better than the general pattern for the economy as a whole. At the same time, no reason exists for doubting that certain aspects of the evolution of the manufacturing sector have done their share to promote the high level of inequality in Colombia. Possibly the import-substitution process had a negative impact, as one would suppose given the capital intensity of the process, especially in its later stages. The blue-collar labor share, at least of gross value added, has been relatively low, usually around or below 20 percent.[237] And, given the frequency of monopoly or oligopoly power under protection from imports, the returns to capital have often been both high and concentrated. It is thus a plausible conjecture that import-substituting industrialization may have been one factor in the probable worsening of income distribution between the mid-thirties and the mid-fifties.[238] By the same token, one might anticipate that the expansion of minor exports would have a positive effect on distribution, or at worst a less negative effect than import substitution.[239] Since Colombia's level of manufactured exports is not of the same order of magnitude, relative to the size of the economy, as in a case like Taiwan, a comparable impact could not be expected. As noted earlier, the large size of the major exporting firms raises doubts about the export activity being very labor intensive,[240] but it is probably considerably more so than the import-competing activity. Thoumi's recent study of the employment content of various types of manufactured goods throws further light on this issue.[241] He classifies four-digit industries into export oriented, nontraded, import competing, and nonimport competing, according to the value of the ratio of imports minus exports to absorption in 1970. Labor-intensity is defined by the ratio of employment to value added. The export-oriented industries are found to be much more labor intensive, especially in blue-collar labor, than the other categories, although their labor share is lower than for non-import-competing industries. (See Table 2.22). Since no study has yet identified factor use in actual exports (as opposed to the two or four-digit industries from which the exports come) or taken account of indirect effects, no propositions can be taken as proven in this area. But Thoumi's findings create a strong presumption that the distribution impact of the export activity is superior to that of import substitution.

SUMMARY

Output of Colombia's manufacturing sector has grown at a healthy 6 percent per year in the twentieth century, based mainly on increases in labor productivity; the labor force itself only grew at about 1.5 percent, so the share of manufacturing workers in the total labor force fell somewhat, although not continuously. The rapid increases in labor productivity were due to the replacement of cottage-shop activities by factories, or more generally by the increasing share of the latter in the manufacturing labor force. Still, as late as 1970, a majority of manufacturing workers were employed in the cottage-shop sector (5 workers or less).

Manufacturing output rose with surprising continuity, with few decades for which adequate data are available diverging much from the

TABLE 2.22

INCOME DISTRIBUTION AND EMPLOYMENT IN NONTRADED, EXPORT, IMPORT-COMPETING, AND NONIMPORT-COMPETING MANUFACTURING

Category of Manufactures	Total employment per million pesos of VA	Blue-collar employment per million pesos of VA	White-collar employment per million pesos of VA	Ratio of white to blue-collar employment	Total labor remuneration as percent of VA	Blue plus white-collar remuneration as percent VA	Average labor remuneration	Direct plus indirect wages and salaries per peso VA
Nontraded	10.9	7.7	2.6	.338	27.4	24.6	24,460	.307
Exports	29.1	23.9	3.6	.151	50.0	43.3	26,200	.576
Import-competing	15.5	11.0	3.2	.291	40.8	35.8	28,580	.523
Nonimport-competing	21.7	16.3	3.8	.233	55.6	46.5	28,200	.643

Source: Thoumi, "Estrategias de Industrialización," p. 141.

VA = value added

long-run average growth rate. Growth was probably slower before 1925 and has been faster since about 1968.

Most of the increase in demand for manufactured goods came from the growth of domestic demand, although over a third came from import substitution during the Depression and World War II (less in later periods); exports accounted for over 10 percent between 1968 and 1974. In production function terms, most of the increase in labor productivity since 1925 has been due neither to increases in the capital/labor ratio (probably no more than a quarter) nor to upgrading of labor skills, but to other factors of which the chief is presumably technological improvements within industries. This "residual" seems to have been particularly large before World War II, as much as 4 percent per year with a gradual decline to a little over 2 percent in the sixties.

The main policy tools in aid of factory manufacturing were trade restrictions of one sort or other, although the natural protection of the Depression and World War II were important in their day. Import substitution became a more explicit policy in the postwar period and by the early sixties some of the new industries were quite capital intensive. The decision to make policy more equitable as between export promotion and encouragement of import substitution, highlighted by the switch to floating exchange rates in 1967, ushered in a period of rapid growth both for manufacturing and for the economy as a whole. Exports were an important component of the increase in demand for manufactured goods.

The mid-seventies saw another striking change in the pattern of manufacturing growth. Exports declined as a source of growth as Colombia's chronic need for more foreign exchange was replaced by a surplus resulting from rapid increases in coffee prices and high revenues from the drug trade (marijuana and cocaine). The real exchange rate was allowed to appreciate, cutting the price incentive to export. At the same time, domestic demand for many products was buoyant due to the rapid increase in income levels, so manufacturing output continued to grow satisfactorily until 1979. It remains to be seen when the foreign-exchange bonanza from primary products will recede, and if manufacturing exports will then regain the dynamism of the pre-1974 period.

The efficiency of Colombia's manufacturing development and its contribution to overall growth are discussed in Chapter 9, with emphasis on the insights and evidence presented in Chapters 3 to 8. On the basis of the discussion in this chapter, there would seem to be no reason to question that it has been reasonably satisfactory.

ENDNOTES FOR CHAPTER 2

The appendix tables cited in this chapter (Tables A-1 to A-156) are available in mimeographed form from the author on request.

1. Luis Ospina Vásquez, *Industria y Protección en Colombia, 1810-1930*, (Medellín: Editorial Santa Fe, 1955), p. 429. Unfortunately the data are based on the records of just one highland hacienda.

2. William P. McGreevey, *An Economic History of Colombia, 1845-1930* (Cambridge: Cambridge University Press, 1971), Chapter 6.

3. Ibid., Chapter 7.

4. As far back as 1860, the artisans were feeling the pinch of expanded trade. In the second half of the nineteenth century this sort of displacement seems to have occurred on a large scale. See the discussions by McGreevey, *An Economic History*, Chapter 7; Luis Nieto A., *El Café en la Sociedad Colombiana*, Bogotá: Ediciones La Soga al Cuello, 1971) and *Economía y Cultura en la Historia de Colombia* (Bogotá: Ediciones Tercer Mundo, 1962).

5. Frank R. Safford, "Commerce and Enterprise in Central Colombia, 1821-1870" (Ph.D. dissertation, Columbia University, 1965), pp. 1-2.

6. Ibid., p. 179.

7. "It was not until the second half of the twenties that there were any appreciable contributions of foreign capital. In other Latin American countries foreign capital assisted in financing the expansion of productive capacity not only in export activities but also in the development of means of transport, power etc. Colombia, on the other hand, had to finance even the expansion of exports—the chief of which was coffee—mainly from domestic savings, which naturally reduced the possibilities of any serious investment in the manufacturing sector." United Nations, Economic Commission for Latin America (ECLA), *Analyses and Projections of Economic Development: The Economic Development of Colombia*, (New York, United Nations, 1957), pp. 261-262.

8. As of the mid-twenties it appeared that Colombia's modern industrial sector was, by international standards, still small relative to her income level. David Chu's calculations (in Table 3.3 of the next chapter) imply for 1923/24 an average ratio of actual to what Hollis Chenery terms "normal" output levels of about 60 percent in the modern industries considered. (Based on the cited Table, with weights for the various industries according to their normal output levels).

9. See McGreevey, *An Economic History*; Ralph Harbison, "Colombia" in W. Arthur Lewis, *Tropical Development 1880-1913* (Evanston, Northwestern University Press, 1970).

10. United Nations, Economic Commission for Latin America (ECLA), *The Process of Industrial Development in Latin America* (New York, United Nations, 1966).

11. According to our revision of ECLA's estimates, the average annual growth rate of output for 1950-70 was 6.2 percent and for 1925-50, 6.6 percent. Before 1925 the rate was perhaps 4-6 percent, but data are very skimpy for this first period (see below). Assumption of a 4 percent growth rate over 1900-25 implies a rate of 5.55 percent for the seventy years, while 5 percent implies 5.91 percent and 6 percent implies 6.27 percent.

12. A conservative reading of the 1870 census suggests 275-325,000 persons engaged primarily in manufacturing; a low estimate for 1900 would appear to be 300,000 while 400,000 would seem to be an upper limit. Our reading of the 1918 population census suggests a manufacturing labor force in that year of around 400,000. Placing some limited confidence in the 1875 and 1918 estimates, it seems not incautious to accept the range 300-400,000 workers for the year 1900. Using these two bases, and an estimate of 850,000 in 1970, we find a minimum total growth of 110 percent and a maximum growth of over 200 percent. In terms of annual growth rates, these are 1.1 percent and 1.5 percent. A best guess would be somewhere in the middle of this range.

13. Although ambiguous and confusing given the historical context, the custom in Latin America is to use the term "artisanry" for plants of less than five workers.

14. These figures are based on the population censuses of the respective years; for 1938, the census figure was adjusted to make the labor force definition equivalent to that of subsequent censuses.

15. McGreevey, *An Economic History*, p. 298.

16. The term "replacement" is used here in the broad sense to include, for example, displacement of the cottage jute industry by other factory-produced types of packing.

17. This is a rough estimate by the author based on diagrams presented in McGreevey, *An Economic History*, p. 299. Our estimate of 20 percent or higher was similar.

18. This estimate is implicit in his Figure 18.

19. The Banco de la República figure from the national accounts is 2.7 percent, but its figure may have underestimated cottage-shop production substantially. In 1953 and 1964, Urrutia and Villalba generated alternative estimates of this output, which fell 20-100 percent above those of the Banco. A best guess would put the underestimation toward the lower end of this range. Miguel Urrutia M. and Clara Elsa Villalba, "El Sector Artesanal en el Desarrollo Colombiano," *Revista de Planeación y Desarrollo* (octubre 1969):68.

20. Our capital stock estimates, both for manufacturing and for the economy as a whole, are less accurate than those of output or the labor force. Accordingly, it should be borne in mind that any ratios based on the capital stock figures are best estimates, and could be biased upward or downward.

21. Our estimate of K/L for the two sectors is 22.6 and 15.2 thousand pesos respectively; for K/O, 2.88 and 2.75 respectively, all values

in 1958 prices. Note that some of the capital stock included in the economy total is not sector specific, so a comparison of manufacturing and nonmanufacturing would show bigger differences than those just cited. The total capital stock figures used are cited in the next endnote.

22. Accepting ECLA capital stock figures for 1925-53 and estimates by Harberger for 1953-67, it would appear that for the economy as a whole the comparable ratio rose by only about 80 percent, capital rising by about fourfold while labor was rising by 125 percent. For capital figures see ECLA *Analyses and Projections, Statistical Annex*, p. 7, and Arnold C. Harberger, "La Tasa de rendimiento de capital en Colombia," *Revista de Planeación y Desarrollo*, (October 1969).

23. In 1925 output per worker (using our labor force and output estimates in manufacturing rather than ECLA's) was about 75 percent that of the economy as a whole; by 1969 it was about one-third above the average for the economy. Thus, while labor productivity was rising by about eightfold in manufacturing, it was rising by four-fivefold overall, and by less than fourfold in the nonmanufacturing sector.

24. Investment which raises industrial output may include that in public infrastructure as well as that in manufacturing establishments themselves; the former is not part of our capital stock figures. Some industries may show increasing returns to scale. Both factors are likely to account for some output growth.

25. When a good entering the production bundle is highly protected, factor productivity can rise in terms of local prices even though it does not do so in world prices. Suppose that when first introduced, the technology used to produce a good is only equally productive with the representative technology used to produce other goods when world prices are used, but more productive when local prices are used. Its inclusion in the bundle would raise productivity (e.g., labor productivity) of the sector at Colombian prices but not at world prices. As of 1969, Thomas Hutcheson's estimate of effective protection indicates that Colombia's factory manufacturing output would have been worth 30 percent less at world prices than it was at Colombian prices (assuming overvaluation of 34 percent), or 24 percent less assuming no inefficiency in tobacco or beverages. Our own estimate, using the latter assumption and Hutcheson's figures at the two-digit level applied to 1968 output figures, is 20 percent.

26. If we accept that the 1969 bundle was worth 25 percent less at world than at domestic prices (see previous endnote) and place a comparable estimate of 5 percent (10%) on 1925 output (designed to be downward biased), then output measured at world prices would in 1969 have reached 12.41 (13.10) instead of 15.65 times its 1925 level. Output per worker would have risen more than twice as fast as capital per worker, indicating that capital formation could not account for as much as half of the output growth (viewed in simplistic growth-accounting terms).

27. This assumes that the K/L ratio tripled over this period, whereas our estimate (Table 2.1) is that it rose only by 160-180 percent.

Descriptive History - 77

28. This again assumes a K/L increase of 200 percent as in the previous endnote, and a capital share of .6 to .7.

29. Partitioning total output growth—to 15.70 times its 1925 level, or as little as 12.41 times assuming the artificial growth related to protection has been quite large—one would attribute 100 percent of the original base to the joint doubling of labor and capital, perhaps another 200 percent (see endnote 27), to the rising capital/labor ratio, and the remaining 840-1,260 percent of the original base to increase in total factor productivity. Thus a majority of the total output growth must also be attributed to increased total factor productivity.

30. It would be a separate source of rising labor productivity if, for reasons not related to the quality of the factors themselves, total factor productivity is higher in some industries than others, and the high productivity industries take on increasing relative importance over time.

31. This is only a very rough guess since we have only impressionistic evidence prior to 1944/45; it is based mainly upon the 1944/45-60 events, and the debatable assumption that differences in remuneration across individuals reflect differences in their productivity. If productivity differences tend to be less than earnings differences, these figures would be upward biased.

32. Apart from the studies by Leonard Dudley and Manuel Ramirez in Chapters 4 and 5, the only attempt to measure technological change in Colombian manufacturing appears to be Alejandro Vivas B., *Cambio Tecnológico en la Industria Manufacturera Colombiana 1955-68*, BA thesis, Departamento de Economía, Universidad Nacional de Colombia.

33. Other attempts to measure technological change, limited to the more recent period, are broadly consistent with this result. Vivas focused on embodied technological change. When he assumed a labor share of .3 it was estimated at .15-.17 over the period 1955-68, Ibid., p. 27. With a higher labor share, the estimate would also have been a little higher. Since he did not estimate nonembodied technological change, his results are not fully comparable to mine. For the seventies one can only speculate since the increase in manufacturing employment is not known with any precision, nor has a capital-stock series been estimated.

34. Even as uncompetitive new industries are founded, however, effective protection on earlier established ones has often fallen, so it is not obvious that the average ratio of "output measured at Colombian prices/output measured at international prices" has risen much. A rough calculation given in endnote 26 suggested that between 1925 and 1969 the output of factory manufacturing might have grown about 0.5 percent less annually at international prices than at domestic prices (i.e., 5.9 percent per year rather than 6.4 percent). This would imply that total factor productivity measured at international prices was rising at about 2.5 percent instead of about 3 percent. Such a performance is still impressive, although it could doubtless have been somewhat more so had some of the industries of large comparative disadvantage been avoided, especially since protection and other incentives doubtless drew a portion of

the best human resources away from the industries with the highest potential and into those at considerable comparative disadvantage.

35. ECLA, *The Process*, p. 19.

36. According to ECLA, Colombia was never in what has been called the prefactory stage, when local manufacturing activities are confined to cottage industries and some industrial establishments are engaged in processing or simple transformation of primary export products, but have few if any linkages with the rest of the internal economy.

37. ECLA notes that in Colombia, as in Latin America in general, within each branch of manufacturing that has expanded, the tendency has been to cover the widest possible range of products in quest of a high level of self-sufficiency; thus specialization was not an objective of industrial policy in Latin America. This may be a factor in the long period of sluggish export performance of these countries.

38. The relevance of the income-distribution implications of different exports, and in particular of coffee as contrasted to Colombia's earlier exports, is argued by McGreevey, *An Economic History*, Chapter 9. Availability of foreign exchange and savings was not, in McGreevey's judgment, a sufficient condition for industrialization. He contrasts the ultimate use of the savings and foreign exchange generated by coffee, and the market potential for industrialization created by the rising coffee incomes, with the failure of any significant industrialization to follow from earlier export booms like that of tobacco over the 1845-75 period. The competing hypothesis, that coffee had more marked effects simply because the value of exports was greater, also merits attention.

39. The income generated by the export of tobacco left no real improvements in the country's productive potential save for the introduction of steam navigation on the Magdalena. "After 1857 the only commercial group that benefited from tobacco was situated in Barranquilla and they were oriented more outwards in the direction of Europe than inwards toward Cundinamarca, Tolima, or Antioquia. The active commercial interests with their abiding faith in *laissez faire* and operating in an expanding capitalistic economy, dominated the tobacco industry from 1846 to 1857. After this date the land owners, with their high interest rate and static society controlled the cultivation and marketing of tobacco." John P. Harrison, "The Colombian Tobacco Industry from Government Monopoly to Free Trade, 1778-1876," (Ph.D. dissertation, University of California, Berkeley, 1952), pp. 356-357. McGreevey cites other factors which may have helped prevent the tobacco boom from inducing industrialization (e.g., the dominance of artisan industrial activity in the eastern part of the country where tobacco was produced, and difficulties in mechanizing wool cloth production for the cooler eastern climate). He feels the lack of innovation due to a sort of planter-class mentality contributed to the small amount of industrial growth. McGreevey, *An Economic History*, p. 239.

40. Transport costs were a significant share of the delivered cost of production. They fell from 20 percent of delivered price to less than 5 percent after the introduction of the railway.

41. McGreevey, *An Economic History*, p. 237.

42. Ibid., p. 200.

43. It appears from the policy record of the second half of the nineteenth century, and from the strong opposition of upper-class consumers to paying high tariffs for their imported goods, that "turning the attitudes around" vis-à-vis protection must have been a real task. Rafael Núñez made a substantial contribution in this direction; Reyes, whose protectionist program is sometimes described as "Núñez program applied," took the major practical steps.

44. Enrique Caballero, *Historia Económica de Colombia*, 2nd ed. (Bogotá, Italgraf, 1971), p. 188.

45. McGreevey notes that "All during the second half of the nineteenth century transport innovations actually adopted by Colombia were biased in favor of the expansion of international trade and increased dependence on the vicissitudes of external markets. . . . However, from 1905 onward the Colombian government was also making investments in a system of feeder roads and other highways tending to lower the nation's transport bill and to enlarge the size of market areas. These improvements may have had an even greater impact on Colombia's rate of economic development than did the railways." McGreevey, *An Economic History*, pp. 277-278.

46. Ibid., p. 238.

47. Ospina, *Industria y Protección*, p. 333.

48. Ibid., p. 338 and Caballero, *Históra Económica*, p. 188.

49. Among the firms which were subsidized by one technique or another at this time were several yarn and clothing companies in the Medellín area and around Cartagena, the textile factory at Samacá, refineries, and a match factory. In the cases of sulphuric acid and glass, exclusive rights were given to companies which did not produce; presumably the aim was to create obstacles for any potential competitors of Bavaria and Fenicia.

50. The minister of finance, in his 1913 report, strongly supported increasing the tariffs on yarn, considering an integrated domestic textile industry more valid and a greater contributor to national development than one using imported inputs. Manufacture of candles was also considered to be on an artificial base. Petroleum refineries on the Atlantic coast were heavily criticized as was the match industry. The profit margin of the wheat millers on the north coast was considered to be extremely large—60 percent or 80 percent rather than the alleged 20 percent or 25 percent typical elsewhere in the world. Ospina, *Industria y Protección*, p. 379.

51. Finance Minister Restrepo Plata considered this ironical; he felt that the high protection for shoes and harnesses would work against the small-scale producers. Ospina, *Industria y Protección*, p. 380.

52. Ibid., p. 347. Note that concentration of the banking system occurred in 1925-30.

53. ECLA figures suggest a share in the range of 20-25 percent, but the gross domestic product (GDP) was probably underestimated by 15-25 percent. ECLA, *Analyses and Projections*, Statistical Annex, p. 1-20.

54. ECLA's figures suggest that the ratio "price of exports/price of GDP" was 49 percent higher over 1925-29 than in 1950, implying a share of exports in gross domestic product at current prices of 25-30 percent. Ibid., p. 38.

55. David S. C. Chu, "The Great Depression and Industrialization in Latin America," (Ph.D. thesis, Yale University, 1972), p. 8; based on ECLA's balance of payments calculations for these years.

56. The 1945 industrial census presents data on year of foundation of factories still extant in 1945. Unfortunately, the early decades were punctuated by numerous failures, so the census misses many firms which were producing during some interval prior to 1945. The number of establishments surviving through 1945, when classified by decade when founded, more than doubled with each decade except the twenties.

57. See chart in McGreevey, *An Economic History*, p. 299.

58. See, for example, the discussion referring to the twenties in Vernon L. Fluharty, *The Dance of the Millions* (Pittsburgh: Pittsburgh University Press, 1957), pp. 31-32.

59. For a discussion, see McGreevey, *An Economic History*, Chapter 11.

60. Since existing estimates for most of the traditional sector are of little meaning for such a short period of time, this figure is very approximate.

61. The sectors studied by Chu were estimated by him to have grown by 15 percent per year during 1923/24 to 1927/28. Chu, *The Great Depression*, p. 47.

62. In 1922, Medellín had nine coffee processing plants employing 1,480 workers. McGreevey, *An Economic History*, p. 214.

63. The *Anuario General de Estadística, 1936*, based on the survey of that year, reported 118.

64. Recall that factories are defined throughout this study as establishments with five or more workers.

65. Usually there is a reasonably close traditional substitute for a factory-produced nondurable good (e.g., panela for refined sugar, chicha for beer, and so on).

66. For an extensive discussion of the numbers and output of artisans during the second half of the nineteenth century, see McGreevey, *An Economic History*, Chapter 7.

67. Ospina, *Industria y Protección*, p. 406.

68. Ibid., p. 408.

69. These figures include persons producing felt as well as straw hats, but the former group was probably small.

70. Some countries have received substantial pulls along the industrialization path via the processing of agriculturally based exports. In the case of Argentina, for example, Díaz-Alejandro notes that in the early part of the twentieth century a high share of industrial production was related to the export industries; "it may be estimated that before 1930, between 15 percent and 20 percent of the gross value of manufacturing production was directly exported," and probably at least 10 percent of manufacturing value added was directly linked to exports. During the period 1900-29, growth of exports and domestic demand were the main direct sources of output growth, rather than import substitution. Meat-packing plants, wool-washing establishments, and the like were engaged in the processing of exports. (Carlos F. Díaz-Alejandro, *Essays on The Economic History of The Argentine Republic*, New Haven: Yale University Press, 1970, p. 211.)

71. Comparisons in terms of gross value of production are potentially misleading since some goods receive very little processing. If coffee is included in Colombia's figures, the share becomes very high indeed.

72. This is part of the category "machinery," which accounted for about 4 percent of total value added. In 1953 the category "machinery for treatment of coffee" accounted for only 0.1 percent of value added.

73. See, for example, Everett E. Hagen, *On the Theory of Social Change*, (Homewood, Illinois: The Dorsey Press, Inc., 1962) Chapter 15. Among factors frequently cited for Antioquia's becoming the first factory center are (1) the depleted mines, (2) the difficulties of importing during the 1900 to 1904 crisis, (3) the small effect of the War of the Thousand Days in Antioquia relative to other departments, (4) previous experience with associations of capital to handle the risky mining business, and (5) the poor soil. Population density was particularly evident in Antioquia. William McGreevey observes in his *An Economic History*, p. 214 that "Antioquia and by extension Colombia, began economic development through a process involving mutual interdependence between export expansion and manufacturing activity. The intervening variables of transport improvement, financial intermediaries and related processing activities were themselves important in the process. The degree to which the process was successful in each of the regions of Colombia was a function of the expansion of exports from that region and the preparation of that region to undergo the changes implied by industrialization. Antioquia maintained a position of leadership in part because of the superior system of education as well as the experience in entrepreneurial activities gained in nineteenth-century mining and export activities."

74. Ospina, *Industria y Protección*, p. 414.

75. Chu notes that companies were usually started by a small number of business associates, usually no more than five or six, who put up the initial risk capital. Others were involved via "commercial houses" to which the promoters belonged, and which were often the

82 - Berry

legal representatives of the family business. Some of these were coffee exporters, others were importers. The principal firms incorporated not long after their start and sold stock to the public in order to get additional capital and because of the lack of any tax on dividend income. Chu, *The Great Depression*, p. 216.

76. Ospina, *Industria y Protección*, p. 340. Caballero (*Historia Económica*) also places great emphasis on the size of the internal market, arguing that while regional isolation protected artisanry, it held up industrialization.

77. See the stories of the early textile plants and sugar mills presented in Hagen, *On the Theory of Social Change*, Chapter 15.

78. The story of the growth of the factory sector under the impact of the Great Depression and World War II is told in greater detail in Chapter 3.

79. ECLA estimated a fall of about 25 percent between 1925 and the midthirties. (ECLA, *Analyses and Projections*, Statistical Annex, p. 4.)

80. Long-term capital inflows to the economy in the thirties were only one-eighth their earlier level.

81. Chu, *The Great Depression*, p. 12, based on ECLA statistics.

82. The import substitution process is normally characterized by a declining import coefficient. This has been true of Latin America, which was an exceptionally open economy before 1929 (imports accounted for 20-25 percent of the total product) but had become a particularly closed one by 1963, with a coefficient of barely 10 percent. (ECLA, *The Process*, p. 21.) Within Latin America, coefficients are related to size of country, with Brazil's less than 5 percent in the early sixties. Colombia's had moved down substantially from the late twenties to fall below 10 percent.

83. These figures were calculated by using, in each case, three-year averages centered on the cited year. Although the figures are at best approximations, there is no doubt that industry grew rapidly during these years.

84. Over 1930-45 the output elasticity was about 1.8 percent, over 1945-57 about 1.6 percent, and over 1957-68 about 1.1 percent.

85. The renewed domination of textiles in this period was striking. The industry accounted for about 60 percent of total increase in value added of these nontraditional industries; petroleum and chemicals followed well behind.

86. According to ECLA figures (see Table A-130) cottage-shop employment and output both rose substantially during these years.

87. In Table 2.5 the higher estimate for 1938 is probably roughly comparable to the 1944/45 estimate, which in turn was constructed with a view to its being comparable to the 1953 and subsequent figures.

Descriptive History - 83

88. Our benchmark estimates of employment do not coincide with the beginning or end of this period. We do know that there were large declines in the number of workers in such lines as vegetable fiber products between the 1938 and 1951 population censuses.

89. Jorge Zalamea notes: "Until 1925 Colombia had little more than the Magdalena River and the Pacific Railway, with the Quindio Pass, as international traffic routes. The Departments of Nariño, Huila, Norte de Santander and Magdalena were practically isolated from the center of national life, and among the remaining departments there was no possibility of establishing any voluminous commercial interchange." Jorge Zalamea, "Progress and Problems of Colombian Industry," *Pan-American Union Bulletin* LXXV (August 1941): 454.

90. See Tables A-100 and A-107. Note that this economy-wide ratio of imported inputs to GDP fell only moderately from the previous period. The ratio of capital imports to GDP did fall more sharply, but apparently this was not a crucial obstacle to manufacturing over this middle-term period.

91. Some modification took place in subsequent years due to pressure from principal trading partners—in 1935 a commercial treaty was signed with the United States.

92. Ospina argues that the Liberal Party's protectionist measures of this time were not so designed at the start. He comments as follows on the 1931 revision of the Colombian tariff and subsequent import controls: ". . . if the Liberal Party took measures which implied an extreme protection, because they practically denied entrance to certain foreign products, they had taken them not as part of a program of stimulus to the national economy, deliberate and permanent, but as emergency measures. . . .But much later occurred a curious change: they wanted to make it appear as the start of a deliberate policy of tariff protection. . . .They tried to claim for the Liberal Party the initiative in protectionist policy. . . ." Ospina, *Industria y Protección*, pp. 458-59.

93. Chu distinguishes modern and traditional industries according to their technological complexity. (See Chapter 3). This classification should not be confused with that between factory and cottage-shop subsectors, which we employ.

94. The weighting done here is by size of the pre-Depression market. See Chu, *The Great Depression*, p. 22.

95. This was calculated using the 1944/45 value added as weights. Ibid., p. 26.

96. Even if tariff increases had been the only tool used to raise import prices, one would not attribute the new higher protection to that tool since in its absence some other tool would have had to be used. In the event the principal import exchange rate rose by 71 percent over 1927-36 and the tariff increase had the effect of raising prices by 28 percent, given the 1927 import bundle. Ibid., p. 39.

97. Over 1927/28-1944/46, the nontraditional industries analyzed by Chu accounted for an estimated 41 percent of output growth. About 75-80 percent of this growth was accounted for by import substitu-

tion. (Table 2.6). Its share in the growth of the more traditional industries, harder to measure because figures are less accurate, was probably only 5-10 percent. Together, these figures imply that import substitution accounted for a little over 34-37 percent of total growth.

98. ECLA, *Analyses and Projections*, p. 272.

99. Based on Chu's estimates of textile imports compared to official figures for total imports. See Chu, *The Great Depression*, p. 291.

100. Between 1937 and 1953, a period partially overlapping the one considered here, ECLA estimated that the share of manufactured imports in total availability fell from 33 percent to a little more than 20 percent. For nondurable consumer goods the fall was from 17.5 percent to only 4 percent, for durable consumer goods from 56 percent to 41 percent, for capital goods from 73.9 percent to 58.3 percent. (All figures are approximate due to the difficulty of comparing the values of domestic and imported goods.) The share of imported fuels and lubricants in total availability rose from one-third to 38 percent.

101. Chu has analyzed in detail the development of textiles, paper, rubber, chemicals, petroleum and coal products, nonmetallic mineral products, basic metals, metal products, electrical and non-electrical machinery, and transport equipment, branches which normally grow substantially more rapidly than the total of manufacturing. Chu excluded the other industries from his analysis on the grounds that they were generally dominated by small establishments using locally produced materials and keeping few records. Chu, *The Great Depression*, p. 4. Partial exceptions, both on these counts and in terms of the modernity of production techniques would be beverages, and parts of the food-processing industry. See Hollis B. Chenery and Lance Taylor, "Development Patterns: Among Countries and Over Time," *Review of Economics and Statistics* 50 (November 1968).

102. These figures are based on the estimate of about 40 percent for 1938. (See Table A-140).

103. In 1951 the figure was about 70-75 percent. The population census indicates 75 percent, but there was no doubt a relative under-enumeration of the rural as opposed to the urban labor force in manufacturing. For census-based estimates see Urrutia and Villalba, "El Sector artesanal", Table 4a.

104. International Bank for Reconstruction and Development, *The Basis of a Development Plan for Colombia*, (Washington, D.C.: International Bank for Reconstruction and Development, 1950).

105. It is difficult, if not impossible, to disengage the deliberate from the unplanned in retrospect. Some policy-makers no doubt recognized the fact that import limitation, for whatever immediate reason, would provide an inducement to domestic producers.

106. Note that, according to ECLA's calculations, Colombia's industrial output in 1960 was over 20 percent below what would be predicted on the basis of the experience of other Latin American countries

and Colombia's per capita income, population, level of urbanization, and import coefficient.

107. ECLA, *The Process*, p. 53. See Table A-107. Care must be taken in the use of these figures since there is probably some underestimation of domestically produced small-scale capital goods, and since in any case the classifying procedure for imports is not very precise. In any case, the share of machinery and equipment imported was very high in the early postwar years and has since declined quite substantially.

108. Relative to the per capita income level, the move into intermediate and capital-goods industries came later in Colombia than in larger Latin American countries such as Argentina, Brazil, and Mexico. As of 1960, ECLA calculations revealed that although countries like Chile, Venezuela, and Colombia had higher per capita incomes than Brazil or Mexico, a much smaller share of their industrial output was in each of these categories; size of country would seem to be the key difference. ECLA, *The Process*, pp. 84-85.

109. Hernán Jaramillo Ocampo, "Conferencia sobre la política arancelaria del gobierno" introduction to *Arancel de Aduanas*, Ministerio de Hacienda (Bogotá, 1950), p. 17.

110. Thomas L. Hutcheson, "Incentives for Industrialization in Colombia," p. 4; see also "Historia de la Industrialización en Colombia" (Medellín: *Revista Trimestral de la Asociación Nacional de Industriales*, October 1970), p. 64.

111. The figures of Table 2.10 are somewhat misleading in that the value of imports expressed in pesos (the denominator for the ratio) increases abruptly when devaluation occurs. A more meaningful series could be constructed by converting dollar imports to pesos by a less erratic exchange-rate variable, one which reflects more closely the trends in the purchasing power of the peso. But we have not attempted construction of such a series.

112. Ministerio de Hacienda, "Memorando Sobre el Proyecto de Arancel de Aduanas" (Bogotá, 1959), p. 21.

113. The very unsatisfactory results of exchange-rate policy as it was pursued prior to 1967 are detailed in Harold Dunkerley, "Exchange Rate Systems in Conditions of Continuing Inflation: Lessons from Colombian Experience" in Gustav Papanek, ed., *Development Policy: Theory and Practice* (Cambridge, Massachusetts: Harvard University Press, 1968). The IMF-government dispute is discussed in Richard Maullin, *The Colombia-IMF Disagreement of November-December 1966: An Interpretation of Its Place in Colombian Politics*, Memorandum RM 5314 (Santa Mónica: The Rand Corporation, 1967).

114. For an early discussion see Eduardo Wiesner D., *Paz del Río* (Bogotá: Centro de Estudios sobre el Desarrollo Economico, Universidad de Los Andes, Monografía 16, June 1963).

115. Francisco E. Thoumi, "Industrial Development Policies During The National Front Years" in R. Albert Berry, Ronald G. Hellman, and Mauricio Solaun, eds., *Politics of Compromise: Coalition Govern-

ment in Colombia (New Brunswick, New Jersey: Transaction Press, 1980), p. 333.

116. Discussions of the financing of industry include Instituto de Fomento Industrial, *El Financiamento de la Industria Manufacturera en Colombia* (Bogotá, 1970); Alvaro Gonzalez, *Financiación Industrial y Mercado de Capitales en Colombia* (Medellín: Asociación Nacional de Industriales, mayo, 1974).

117. ECLA, *Analyses and Projections*, Statistical Appendix, p. 135.

118. Following ECLA's figures with respect to the share of the various two-digit industries falling in each category.

119. ECLA estimates that between 1929 and 1963, 36 percent of the expansion of industrial product in Latin America was directly related to the import-substitution incentive; in Argentina, Chile and Colombia as a group this was 50 percent or more. ECLA, *The Process*, p. 27. This conclusion is at considerable variance with ours; for 1930-45 we concluded that import substitution accounted for something over 30 percent of output growth; over 1945-65 our estimate is about 25 percent. The source of this discrepancy could only be traced down by a detailed comparison of ECLA's figures and methodology with our own.

    The most detailed study of recent import substitution in Colombia is Jairo Ramírez R. *Sustitución de Importaciones en la Industria Manufacturera de Colombia, 1950-1970: Cuantificación* (Bogotá, 1977), mimeographed. It presents a critique of traditional measures of the phenomenon, and proposes a new measure. Ramírez's estimates of the share of output growth resulting from decreases in the ratio of imports to domestic supply, using the Lewis-Soligo definition (similar to that used by Chu and in this chapter) was .25 for 1950/51-1969/70; .25 for 1950/51-1959/60; .12 for 1959/60-1969/70. For five-year intervals the pattern was .06 for 1950/51-1954/55; .43 for 1954/55-1959/60; .23 for 1964/65; and .09 for 1964/65. Ibid., Cuadro VIII. The period of balance-of-payments ease in the early fifties was thus, like the late twenties, one of negative import substitution. It was important from the mid-fifties to mid-sixties and became less so as economic growth and exports accelerated in the late sixties.

120. Extensive raw-material importing had, it should be noted, characterized nearly all of the more modern industries during their early stages. In 1936, when capital goods and intermediate imports were relatively more expensive, textile and beverage firms reporting used, respectively, 73 percent and 58 percent foreign inputs. (See Table A-106). Since the reporting firms were above average size, a complete census of firms would presumably have generated somewhat lower imported input ratios. The originally dominant food industry presumably never had a very high imported input ratio (in 1936 reporting firms had a ratio of 28 percent), but in textiles the ratio prior to 1936 was probably even above the 73 percent reported in that year.

121. Whether manufactured or not.

122. See Table A-106.

123. Hutcheson, *Incentives for Industrialization*, p. 15.

124. Foreign capital has obviously played a substantially smaller role in Colombia than in many other countries such as Puerto Rico and Canada, but neither has this role been insubstantial. It mainly involved transportation (railroads) in the nineteenth century, and then petroleum and other mining projects in the pre-World War II period. Manufacturing became the main sector of foreign investment only in the postwar years.

125. Companies controlled by the United States employed 3.2 percent. Banco de la República, División de Análisis Económico de la Oficina de Cambios, "Empleo en Empresas con Inversión Extranjera Directa", *Revista del Banco de la República* XLVII (mayo 1974): 388. In the middle and late sixties American capital was about 70-75 percent of all foreign capital in manufacturing. The ratio may have been lower in the fifties.

126. Depending on whether only firms categorized as "foreign" by Decree 444 of 1967 (i.e., 50 percent or more of paid capital in foreign hands) or all firms with some foreign capital are included. There were 47,200 employees of "foreign" companies, and 58,100 employees of firms with some foreign capital. Ibid., p. 388.

127. Miguel Angel Betancur, et al., "Capital Extranjero en Colombia" in DANE, *Boletín Mensual de Estadística*, No. 239 (June 1971), pp. 70-79.

128. The literature on foreign investment is extremely varied in its conclusions with respect to the effects of the phenomenon, and extremely thin in terms of empirical verification. An interesting point of view has been expressed by Hirschman. Albert O. Hirschman, "How to Divest in Latin America and Why," International Finance Section, Department of Economics, Princeton University, *Essays in International Finance No. 76* (November 1969). He argues that foreign investment in Latin America is currently a very mixed blessing since (1) it tends to involve less the introduction of a missing factor of production complementary to those available locally than the introduction of a bundle of factors, some at least of which are locally available; it can therefore be competitive with such local resources as entrepreneurs, technicians, and savers, whose domestic supply may be much more elastic than is usually suspected; (2) the new local industrialists do not speak with as strong and influential a voice on certain issues of public decision making as they might in the absence of the foreign individuals, who in turn may tend to be too quiet on these things because of their political vulnerability in the modern world; (3) policy making may be less carefully undertaken when the fruits of good decision making may accrue in substantial part to foreigners.

Studies of foreign investment in Colombia include Beatriz Abad de Tirado, *El Capital Extranjero en Colombia en Sus Modalidades de Inversión Directa y Financimiento* (Medellín: Centro de Investigaciones Económicas, Universidad de Antioquia, 1973); Constantine Vaitsos, "Transferencia de Recursos y Preservación de Rentas Monopolisticas", *Revista de Planeación y Desarrollo* III (July 1971); Seymour W. Wurfel, *Foreign Enterprise in Colombia: Laws and Policies* (Chapel Hill: University of North Carolina Press, 1965); Hector Melo, "Observaciones sobre el Papel del Capital Extranjero y sus Relaciones con los Grupos Locales de Capital en Colombia", (Bogotá: Universidad Nacional de Colombia, Centro de Investigaciones para el Desarrollo, April 1974).

129. Wurfel, *Foreign Enterprises in Colombia*, p. 462. In particular, the reported results of a survey carried out by the American Embassy in 1962 of ninety firms (excluding petroleum) with at least 95 percent American stockholding, which found that (1) seven out of ten (excluding some who did not borrow out of principal) maintained debts with local banks, but (2) the capital brought to Colombia by these firms exceeded their local credit in a ratio of 8 to 1. At the same time, American banks had extended credits to many Colombian businessmen. Based on a speech of Ambassador Fulton Freeman before the Colombo-American Chamber of Commerce, August 16, 1962. More recently ECLA referred to an increasing tendency of American firms to finance themselves in local capital markets, but did not present data. See Naciones Unidas, Comisión Económica Para América Latina, *Estudio Económico de América Latina 1970* (New York: Naciones Unidas, 1971), p. 312. See Table A-68 for reported net inflow of private direct investment and the return flow of profits, as estimated by the IMF.

130. One of the channels by which technology is borrowed is the joint venture. These have in general been successful in Colombia. For an early discussion see Columbia University School of Law, *Public International Development Financing in Colombia*, Report 6 (New York, 1963).

131. Vaitsos, "Transferencia de Recursos", p. 68. In rubber, Vaitsos calculated that whereas the stated profit rate was 16 percent, a better measure—declared profits plus royalties plus overpricing, divided by resources transferred from abroad—was 43 percent. For pharmaceuticals, these figures were 6.5 percent and 136 percent.

132. The definition of a foreign firm is, of course, somewhat arbitrary. Here we have tried to stick to the criterion that more than half of paid capital be held by foreigners.

133. For all manufacturing. Since, on balance some national firms were sold to foreign interests, the former range presumably understates the vegetative growth rate of output in national firms.

134. For appraisals in other countries or in general, see, for example Ian Little, Maurice Scott, and Tibor Scitovsky, *Trade and Industry in Some Developing Countries* (London: Oxford University Press, 1970); Benjamin Cohen and Gustav Ranis, "The Second Post-War Restructuring" in Gustav Ranis, ed., *Government and Economic Development* (New Haven: Yale University Press, 1971); Santiago Macario, "Protectionism and Industrialization in Latin America," *Economic Bulletin for Latin America* IX (March 1964). Schultz, Slighton and Nelson, *Structural Change*, have a few limited comments on the process in Colombia.

135. See ECLA, *A Measurement of Price Levels and the Purchasing Power of Currencies in Latin America, 1960-62*, (Santiago, Chile: ECLA, 1963).

136. Ibid., p. 130. In 1970, Kravis et al. reported that with United States price relatives defined as unity the relative price of clothing and footwear (vis-à-vis that of food) was 1.13 in Colombia, that of furniture and household appliances was 1.43, that of producers' durables 2.35, and that of construction 0.53. Irving B. Kravis, Alan Heston, and Robert Summers, *International Comparisons of Real Product and Purchasing Power* (Baltimore: The Johns Hopkins University Press, 1978), pp. 90-92.

137. An industry causes losses (gains) to the nation when it uses resources less well (better) than they would be used elsewhere in its absence, and/or its presence decreases (increases) the total supply of available resources in the economy.

138. In the only detailed study of investment behavior, R. Bilsborrow found the availability of foreign exchange to be the single most important influence on aggregate investment. Accelerator, cashflow, and risk variables also helped to explain the level of investment in the up to 120 corporations studied over part or all of the period 1950-65. R. Bilsborrow, "The Determinants of Fixed Investment by Manufacturing Corporations in Colombia," (Ph.D. dissertation, University of Michigan, 1968), pp. 137-139.

139. An issue analyzed by Carlos Díaz-Alejandro, "On the Import Intensity of Import Substitution," *Kyklos* 18 (1965): 495-508.

140. Developed originally by Hollis Chenery and Alan Strout, "Foreign Assistance and Economic Development," *American Economic Review* 56 (September 1966).

141. See especially Jaroslav Vanek, *Estimating Foreign Resource Needs for Economic Development* (New York: McGraw-Hill, Inc., 1967); Richard R. Nelson, "The Effective Exchange Rate, Employment, and Growth in a Foreign Exchange Constrained Economy," *Journal of Political Economy* 78 (May/June 1970): 546-564.

142. See Carlos Díaz-Alejandro, *Foreign Trade Regimes and Economic Development: Colombia* (New York: Columbia University Press for The National Bureau of Economic Research, 1976), Chapter 1.

143. Since reliable data on imports of inputs for the manufacturing sector do not exist on an annual basis, it is not possible to analyze the effects of their scarcity in a very direct way. It is of interest to note that the ratio of imported inputs to value of production in factory manufacturing appears to have been about the same in the second subperiod (1956-68) as in the first one (1948-56). See Table A-107.

144. John Sheehan has argued that there was a tight relationship between exchange availability and economic growth; he relates the cyclical tendency of the economy during these years in considerable measure to fluctuations in the price of coffee, and to the government's tendency to relax the controls on imports during easy exchange situations, thus leading to overabsorption, the reduction of their availability a couple of years later, and new restrictions. His argument that growth is closely associated with the amount of imports is not the same as the two-gap theory, as it is possible that savings are easy to convert into imports. John

Sheehan, "Imports, Investment and Growth" in Gustav F. Papanek, ed., *Development Policy: Theory and Practice* (Cambridge, Massachusetts: Harvard University Press, 1968).

145. Another analysis of the imports-growth relationship comes to the conclusion that a significant relationship does exist between the two variables, but that, because it is not evident in each period or takes on a different form across periods, it does not show up when the period 1950-68 is analyzed as a whole. Alberto Corchuelo and Luis Bernardo Flores, "El Sector Externo y las Fluctuaciones de Corto Plazo de la Economía", *Boletín Mensual de Estadística*, DANE, No. 244 (November 1971), p. 9.

146. The best study including an analysis of this export performance is Carlos F. Díaz-Alejandro, *Foreign Trade Regimes*, Chapter 2. In Chapter 8 of this volume Díaz-Alejandro focuses on some characteristics of firms heavily involved in the exporting business.

147. Probably around 25 percent over 1968-72. There is some ambiguity in the figures due to the fact that emeralds were recycled (i.e., exported more than once) during the period when the CAT export subsidy was higher than the black market/official exchange rate differential. There are also arbitrary matters of where the line is drawn between manufactured and nonmanufactured goods. We use here data of Calvo and Escandon updated to 1972. See Haroldo Calvo and José Francisco Escandón, *Las Exportaciones Colombianas de Manufacturas 1963-1971* [Bogotá: Fundación para la Educación Superior y el Desarrollo (FEDESARROLLO), 1973].

148. The lower limit comes from assuming an export of 125 million dollars in 1972, of which one half was value added, and total manufacturing value added of 36.55 billion pesos (at market prices) according to national accounts statistics; this latter figure includes cottage-shop production of probably something under 5 billion pesos. An exchange rate of 25 was used to convert dollars to pesos; the minor export exchange rate was a little over 22 and the 15 percent CAT was applied. The export figure, that of Calvo-Escandón (presented in Table A-119) may be low; Díaz-Alejandro's figures, which go only to 1969, are substantially higher (Table A-118).

149. The most detailed analysis of the evolution of Colombia's foreign sector in the last couple of decades is found in Díaz-Alejandro, *Foreign Trade Regimes*.

150. Replacement of the previous tax deduction for exporters (a program instituted in 1961) with a relatively simple subsidy was a substantial improvement.

151. As of the late sixties, about 70 percent of manufacturing exports were carried out under the Plan Vallejo system. The relevance of the other fiscal and tax incentives has received wide discussion. See Díaz-Alejandro, *Foreign Trade Regimes*, Chapter 2.

152. For a detailed discussion see Richard Maullin, "The Colombia-IMF Disagreement."

153. Decree 444 of 1967, which institutionalized many important changes, was preceded by a disastrous attempt at import liberalization. With

good intentions and with the support of some of the international institutions, the government attempted after the 1965 devaluation to lower the degree of import restrictions, perhaps to the level prevailing in 1962. But in the interim the real exchange rate had fallen by over 20 percent and there was substantial pent-up real and speculative demand for imports. The surge of imports quickly produced negative foreign-exchange reserves and in 1967 ushered in the most stringent licensing in history, but it came with Decree 444. Hutcheson, *Incentives for Industrialization*, p. 8.

154. See Table A-12.

155. See Fedesarrollo, *Principales Aspectos de la Evolución Económica Colombiana, 1961-1971* (Bogotá: Fedesarrollo, 1972), p. 1. The stop-go nature of growth in manufacturing was reminiscent of the Argentine pattern described by Carlos Díaz-Alejandro, *Essays on the Economic History of the Argentine Republic*, Chapter 7.

156. Díaz-Alejandro, *Foreign Trade Regimes*, Chapter 2. For a review of studies of this relationship see A. Berry, "Política Económica Internacional de Colombia" in Hernando Gómez O. and Eduardo Wiesner D. *Lecturas sobre Desarrollo Económico Colombiano* (Bogotá; Fedesarrollo, p. 74).

157. José F. Escandon S., "Análisis de los Factores que han Determinado el Desarrollo de la Pequeña Empresa en Colombia: Una Interpretación Histórica", (September 1979), mimeographed.

158. Table A-120.

159. Albert Berry and Francisco Thoumi, "Import Substitution and Beyond: Colombia," *World Development* 5 (1977): pp. 104-106.

160. See Chapter 8, where Díaz-Alejandro finds that the 134 foreign firms in his study had exports of 26.8 million dollars in 1970 or 30 percent of the total exports of manufactures in that year. At the same time these firms had imports of 202.4 million dollars, 20-25 percent of the grand total for that year. A Banco de la República study aimed specifically at measuring the exports of manufacturing firms with foreign capital (except those in petroleum refining) came up with a total of 28 million dollars. Banco de la República, División de Análisis Económico, Oficina de Cambios, *Exportaciones Manufacturadas por Empresas con Inversión Extranjera Directa* (Bogotá, julio 1973), Cuadro 3B. While foreign firms have been important participants in the export boom, a boom has certainly occurred for the national firms as well. INCOMEX reported total exports (all sectors) by firms with foreign capital as 6.3 percent, 5.5 percent and 5.3 percent of all exports in 1967, 1968, and 1969, respectively. See Abad de Tirado, *El Capital Extranjero*, p. 69. Most of these were of manufactured products.

If one guessed that Colombia's participation in the Andean Group would lower national income, then the effect of Group directed exports could be unclear. But if the Group is a *fait accompli*, it is of course desirable to export as much as possible, as long as more exports are not tied to more imports. And in some cases such exports may be the first step to exporting to the rest of the world. These are all complicated empirical questions.

161. For a discussion see Albert Berry and Carlos Díaz-Alejandro, "The New Colombian Exports: Possible Effects on the Distribution of Income" in Albert Berry and Ronald Soligo, eds., *Economic Policy and Income Distribution in Colombia* (Boulder, Colorado: Westview Press, 1980).

162. See Tables A-12 and A-108.

163. Francisco E. Thoumi, "Estrategias de Industrialización, Empleo, y Distribución del Ingreso en Colombia", *Coyuntura Económica* (April 1979).

164. For a detailed description of the evolution of instruments of import control in Latin America as a whole see Santiago Macario, "Protectionism and Industrialization in Latin America," *Economic Bulletin for Latin America* (1964).

165. See Table A-77.

166. Presented in ECLA, *The Process*, Statistical Annex, Table III-7, and citing the *Revista de la Superintendencia de Sociedades Anónimas* as the source.

167. Disproportionately to output and labor force in any case; the ratio of bank credit to capital stock, however, appears to be lower for the larger establishments than for medium-sized ones. (See Table A-78).

168. Even in 1969, the ratio of institutional credit (long and short term) to value added for very small plants (less than ten workers) might have been one-third as high as that of plants with more than 100 workers. (See Table A-78).

169. See Planeación, *El Desarrollo de la Pequeña y Mediana Industria a Través del Crédito y Medidas Complementarias* (Bogotá, 1970), p. 64.

170. One should add that this may not necessarily be bad, although usually the conflicting or offsetting signals which tend to result do cause inefficiency.

171. See ECLA, *The Process*, p. 166.

172. See, for example, R. E. Bilsborrow and R. C. Porter, "The Effects of Tax Exemption on Investment in Industrial Firms in Colombia," *Weltwirtschaftliches Archiv* (Kiel), 108 (1972).

173. Colombia clearly does less in this area than do some other Latin countries. The I.I.T. has indicated on a number of occasions that it prefers to concentrate on research, and has discouraged several efforts to engage it more actively in trouble-shooting technical assistance to small and medium industries, even when funds would have been provided by outside agencies for this purpose. Chile's development corporation, in contrast, had already become fairly important by the end of the forties, although it subsequently declined.

174. Rules and regulations affecting foreign firms as of the mid-sixties are presented in detail in Seymour W. Wurfel, *Foreign Enterprise in Colombia*, p. 165.

175. Wurfel, *Foreign Enterprise*, p. 367.

176. This pattern of continuing importance of small scale enterprise, along with changes in its composition by industry, is the typical one according to Eugene Staley and Richard Morse, *Modern Small Industry for Developing Countries*, (New York: McGraw-Hill, 1965).

177. That large firms have somewhat greater average productivity per worker is not surprising; it seems to characterize all or almost all countries and would be expected on the basis of what is known about factor market imperfections, the relationship between firm size and the type of industry, and so on.

178. Meanwhile, relative labor productivity in the cottage-shop sector as compared to the factory sector appears to have been about 1:5 or 1:6. The ratio for 1960 was estimated at about 1:7 or 1:8 in Colombia's Ten Year Plan. See Consejo Nacional de Política Económica y Planeación, Departamento Administrativo de Planeación y Servicios Técnicos, *Plan General de Desarrollo Económico y Social, II Parte: Industria* (Bogotá: Imprenta del Banco de la República, 1967), p. 7 and p. 19.

179. Table A-139 gives circumstantial evidence of the earlier decline. Population census based estimates for 1951 and 1964 are 100,000 and 105,000 respectively, while the June, 1978 household survey of DANE indicated a figure of 160,000. (See Berry, "The Evolution of Small Scale Industry," mimeographed.)

180. There is little rural factory employment.

181. Note that this is not to say that small firms grew less rapidly; rapid growth of a small firm moves it out of that category entirely.

182. Berry, "The Evolution of Small Scale Industry," Table 2-26.

183. But, as Urrutia and Villalba note ("El Sector Artesanal," p. 50), where cottage-shop was relatively important it had tended to grow least over 1951-64.

184. Possibly much of the positive association may be explained by joint causation (i.e., growth of both factory and cottage-shop subsectors may be in part effects of overall income growth from whatever source).

185. Only in Nariño—where there was a decrease in both rural and urban workers—was this not the case. (See Table A-141).

186. Recall that "rural," in the parlance of the Colombian population censuses, includes towns of up to 1,500 inhabitants. It would be unusual for carpenters to be found in the countryside per se, but some locate in small villages.

187. For a discussion of these activities in their heyday (early twenties) see Bell, *Colombia: A Commercial and Industrial Handbook*, pp. 180-184.

188. Rafael Prieto, Marco Ruiz Carmona, and Bill Hanneson, *Estudio Agro-económico de la Hoya del Río Suárez* (Bogotá: Centro de Estudios Sobre Desarrollo Económico (CEDE), Universidad de Los Andes, 1965).

189. As indicated in Table 2.7, the cottage-shop figures are biased upward, being calculated as total labor force in the industry minus those known to be in factories. If the factory figure is underestimated by more than the all-industry average, the cottage-shop share is overestimated in a given industry. This could have happened in textiles (or any other sector); as a result, conclusions based on these data must remain somewhat tentative.

    Probably such products as bakery items, candy, *panela*, and so on, were very important in food; wooden furniture was the "growth" part of the wood industries.

190. Francois Bourguignon, "Pobreza y Dualismo en el Sector Urbano de las Economías en Desarrollo: El Caso de Colombia," *Desarrollo y Sociedad*, No. 1 (1979): 54. Bourguignon used a DANE seven-city household survey of 1975 in his analysis.

191. Based on Berry, "The Evolution of Small Scale Industry," (1980), p. 30, mimeographed.

192. See Berry, "Relevance and Prospects," p. 18. These figures are adjusted upward from those of DANE to allow for underreporting in this size range.

193. Based on DANE's somewhat upward biased figures for 1975 (implying 66 percent) and for 1950 extrapolating back from 1957 (the first year DANE presented a breakdown of output by juridical form), using data from *Superintendencia de Sociedades Anónimas, Revista de la Superintendencia de Sociedades Anónimas*, various issues.

194. See Table A-87.

195. See R. Nelson, R. Slighton, and T. P. Schultz, *Structural Change in a Developing Economy: Colombia's Prospects and Problems* (Princeton: Princeton University Press, 1971), Chapter 4.

196. Dale L. Johnson, "Industrialization, Social Mobility, and Class Formation in Chile," (St. Louis: Studies in Comparative International Development, Washington University, Social Science Institute, vol. 3, no. 7 (1967-68): 134.

197. The later start would lead one to expect this. From the beginning much technology was borrowed. (See, for example, Frank Safford, "Foreign and National Enterprise in Nineteenth Century Colombia," *The Business History Review*, XXXIX (Winter 1965).

198. See Hagen, *On the Theory of Social Change*, Chapter 15 and Frank Safford, *Commerce and Enterprise*. Safford contends that a greater supply of mobilizable capital may explain the Antioqueño's

more evident business success. In his view, entrepreneurial attitudes were common enough in most of Colombia. (Safford, "Foreign and National.")

199. Their presence was notable in the nineteenth century too, although less than in some other Latin American countries. Safford feels that their clearest advantage over Colombians was in knowledge of certain mining, manufacturing, and marketing techniques, to some extent in capital at their disposition, but not in basic entrepreneurial inclinations. (Safford, "Foreign and National.")

200. For more details, see Chapter 3.

201. Aaron Lipman, *El Empresario Bogotano* (Bogotá: Ediciones Tercer Mundo y Facultad de Sociología, Universidad Nacional, 1966), p. 44. Lipman's sample constituted 26 percent of the total companies affiliated with ANDI at that time; he interviewed the person at the top of the hierarchy.

202. Note that the relative importance of foreign entrepreneurs has always been lower in Medellín, which was relatively more important as an industrial center in the period considered by Chu.

203. See Alan G. Gilbert, "Industrial Growth in the Spatial Development of the Colombian Economy Between 1951 and 1964" (Ph.D. thesis, University of London, 1970) pp. 260-261.

204. Frank Brandenburg, *The Development of Latin American Private Enterprise,* The National Planning Association, (Washington: 1964), Chapter 3.

205. See Table A-3. It is interesting that ECLA felt there had been no long-run trend towards a decreasing manufactured price/total price ratio. ECLA, *The Process,* p. 144. Data for Colombia were not presented.

206. See Table A-7.

207. See Table A-91, which presents calculations for 1958, but only at Colombian prices.

208. A considerable literature has recently addressed this issue. See Chapter 7.

209. If it be assumed that fixed assets/plant were, within each three-digit sector, twice (three) times as high for plants with two (three) turns as for plants with one turn, then the approximate shares of such assets in plants of one, two, and three turns is 54 percent, 22 percent and 24 percent, respectively. The assumed differentials in assets per plant would appear to be on the conservative side.

210. Gómez's survey elicited replies from about 225 plants of 100 or more workers; of these, 41 percent operated one turn, 22 percent two turns and 37 percent three turns. A much smaller and probably less representative response from plants of 25-99 workers revealed shares of 73 percent, 18 percent, and 9 percent. If the samples were representative, and if no plants of less than twenty-five

workers operated on a multiple-shift basis, the total number of two and three-shift plants in 1959 would have been 321 and 267, respectively. But it seems likely that selectivity of response would be such as to bias the figures upward and best guesses would be perhaps 210-270 and 195-240, respectively.

211. Chapter 7, p.

212. The *Superintendencia de Sociedades Anónimas* presents accounting figures for the rate of return, but their relation to the economic rate of return has not received much analysis.

213. See Table A-84.

214. The rate is gross of both taxes and depreciation. Intangibles are excluded from assets, hence "real assets." See Table A-80.

215. Family savings are also biased severely downward in the national accounts, at least for some years.

216. In 1950, profits were listed as 17.1 percent of paid-in capital and 7.54 percent of assets. Capital in the economic sense would probably lie between the values of paid capital and of assets.
    In the period 1956-67, Todd's analysis suggested that the output/fixed capital ratio was about the same for corporations as for manufacturing as a whole. In 1950 it might have been somewhat lower as the relative importance of official and semi-official establishments (with very low output/capital ratios) was probably smaller; in 1945 they had 4.4 percent of total patrimony; in 1958, their share of horsepower was 3.6 percent and their share of fixed capital is estimated at about 10 percent. If corporations had had an average output/physical capital ratio in 1950, their share of physical capital would have been perhaps 40-45 percent of the total.

217. Although a majority of officially calculated corporate savings are paid out, only a minority of true profits are, if our estimates of the latter variable are reasonably accurate.

218. As of 1959/60 a study by the *Superintendencia de Sociedades Anónimas* indicated that .13 percent of the stockholders of 483 corporations held 54 percent of the stock. This figure is not easy to interpret since corporations were also among the stockholders. But it is consistent with the high concentration believed by most observers to exist.

219. It should be noted that the labor-absorption problem was somewhat exaggerated due to statistical problems in DANE's survey procedure during the sixties, which led to an increasing downward bias in the estimate of total factory employment since about 1962; DANE data indicated growth of only 1.5 percent per year over 1962-68.

220. For example, Manuel R. Agosín, "Price Distortions, Development Pattern, and Labor Absorción in Colombian Manufacturing" (1973), mimeographed.

221. See Table A-58.

222. An unweighted average of the share of these four years.

223. The chemical industry (31) was not particularly capital intensive prior to this period, but became so.

224. An interesting aspect of the situation in Colombia is that the Verdoorn effect (lower output elasticity of employment when output growth is faster) does not hold when the output elasticity of employment is taken for the period of years shown in Table 2.20; 1962-67 showed markedly slower output growth than periods both before and after, but also showed the lowest output elasticity of employment.

225. See the discussion below.

226. Feldl's position with respect to the reasons for the low marginal output/capital and labor/capital ratios in Colombian industry was that public policy had favored branches of production which by nature must be capital intensive, and that there was a disequilibrium not between costs of capital and costs of labor, but between the availability of credit for fixed investment and for working capital, a result of the credit policy. He believed that excess capacity and high capital intensity were the problems, but that they were produced not by a distorted factor price ratio, but rather by the effect of government policy on the direction of investment. See Peter Feldl, *Relación sobre la Situación Actual de la Industria Manufacturera Fabril de Colombia* (Bogotá: Ministerio de Desarrollo Económico, República de Colombia, May 1970), p. 7.

227. Wages of specific occupational categories have, in general, risen somewhat less rapidly but still substantially. Urrutia's figures indicate real wage increases of 32-54 percent for various specific occupational categories in Bogotá over 1934-65; the figures appear to exclude fringe benefits and therefore underestimate gains. See M. Urrutia, "Los Salarios Reales en Bogotá" in CEDE, *Empleo y Desempleo en Colombia* (Bogotá: Ediciones Universidad de Los Andes, 1968), pp. 202-205.

228. A. Berry, "Real Wage Trends in Colombian Manufacturing and Construction During the Twentieth Century," University of Western Ontario, Department of Economics, Research Report 7403, p. 34.

229. See A. Berry, "The Effects of Inflation on Income Distribution in Colombia: Some Hypotheses and a Framework for Analysis," in R. Albert Berry and Ronald Soligo, eds., *Economic Policy and Income Distribution in Colombia* (Boulder, Colorado: Westview Press, 1980).

230. See Table A-149.

231. As a result of certain statistical biases in DANE data, information for more recent years is not yet interpretable.

232. A. Berry, "Real Wage Trends," p. 24. It must be remembered that these are comparisons of the average real wage in plants of a given size category at two different points in time; the set of plants in a given category will generally be different at the two points of time, so the figures do not tell us directly anything about the growth of real wages at a point of time or over a period of time for plants in a given size category.

233. Studies have suggested that real wages in agriculture fell in the late thirties and early forties, rising gradually thereafter but only in the early sixties surpassing the level of the mid-thirties; the labor share underwent a secular decline over most of this period. Meanwhile unskilled construction worker wages in 1950 appear to have been only at about the same level as in the mid-thirties. A. Berry and M. Urrutia, *Income Distribution in Colombia* (New Haven: Yale University Press, 1976), Chapters 3 and 4.

234. DANE data show a paid labor share of about 29 percent in 1953 and 35.5 percent in 1970; the presumably more reliable central bank estimate of value added in the factory subsector (market prices) is below that of DANE by an increasing percent over time.

235. If, as is likely, depreciation has been an increasing share of gross value added over time, the labor share of net value added would have risen faster or fallen less than the share of gross value added. The reason for the greater variation in the labor share in central bank figures than in DANE figures is not immediately clear.

236. DANE, *Boletín Mensual de Estadística*, No. 237 (April 1971), pp. 69-71.

237. See Table A-148.

238. Berry and Urrutia, *Income Distribution in Colombia*, Chapter 7.

239. In the cases of Korea and, especially, Taiwan it has been argued that the growth of manufacturing exports contributed significantly to improvements in income distribution. See John C. H. Fei, Gustav Ranis, and Shirley W. Y. Kuo, *Growth With Equity: The Taiwan Case* (New York: Oxford University Press, 1979).

240. A point emphasized in R. Albert Berry and Carlos Díaz-Alejandro, "The New Colombian Exports: Possible Effects on Income Distribution" in Albert Berry and Ronald Soligo, eds., *Economic Policy and Income Distribution in Colombia* (Boulder, Colorado: Westview Press, 1980).

241. F. E. Thoumi, "Estrategias de Industrialización, Empleo y Distribución del Ingreso en Colombia," *Coyuntura Económica* IX (April 1979): 119-142.

Chapter 3

The Great Depression and Industrialization in Colombia[1]
David S. C. Chu

One of the themes in the development literature is the close association between industrial expansion and increases in gross national product (GNP) per capita. The work of Hollis Chenery perhaps best elaborates this theme.[2] Chenery concedes that the growth of the industrial sector is ultimately linked to changes in factor prices (for capital, labor, skills, and natural endowments), but he argues that factor price changes are associated with changes in the capital stock and in human skills both of which in turn are correlated with increases in per capita income. Chenery therefore predicts a close relationship between increases in per capita income and the growth of industrial output.

A second theme is the disappointing nature of import substitution industrialization, especially in Latin America. Many Latin American governments have sought to stimulate industrialization by relative price changes initiated through a policy of tariff protection and trade controls. Despite the substantial import substitution induced, the industrial sector has for the most part failed to play the intended leading role. The inefficiency of the sector necessitated large changes in relative prices (i.e., very high effective protection); industries have typically been unable to expand beyond the import substitution phase and compete in world markets. Moreover, foreign firms, and not indigenous entrepreneurs, have frequently been the ones to respond to the price incentives.

These themes are usually developed with data from after World War II. Although it is difficult to assemble material for earlier periods, the concentration on the postwar years neglects the rather substantial growth that preceded World War II and that may be important to understanding postwar developments. Colombia is a specific example of the general case. Between World War I and the end of World War II, Colombia developed a substantial manufacturing sector, accounting for perhaps one-seventh of the gross domestic product (GDP) by the end of the period.[3] Much of this growth appears to have taken place during the Great Depression and the Second World War, despite the sluggish performance of the economy as a whole.

One explanation for this "depression industrialization" rests on changes in relative prices. Prices of industrial imports rose relative to export prices as the commodity terms of trade deteriorated, and rose relative to prices of nontraded and import-competing goods as the peso was devalued. These relative price changes gave domestic manufacturers a substantial incentive to expand their output; the result was a vigorous substitution of domestic production for imports of manufactured goods.

Other observers have advanced this scenario for Latin America in general,[4] and for Argentina, Brazil, and Chile in particular.[5] Although it represents a distinct alternative to the Chenery model, few attempts to test the relative price hypothesis have been made.[6] Attempting such a test is the purpose of this essay. Not only is the test important to our understanding of the process of industrial growth, but it may help to illuminate developments in the years since World War II.

As an introduction to the interwar period, I shall describe general economic conditions, then sketch the growth of the manufacturing sector. I test the Chenery model and, finding it deficient, analyze the changes that took place in the structure of input and output prices. I then formulate and test a model that relates these changes to industrial growth. To further illuminate the development process, I explore the possible contribution from changes in the supply of industrial credit and from changes in the supply of entrepreneurship. Because the efficiency of industries created by import substitution has been an issue, I conclude by offering some data that bear on this question.

General Economic Conditions

The Colombian economy expanded rapidly during the twenties, with real GDP growing at better than 7 percent per year in the latter half of the decade.[7] This prosperity rested on a strong export sector. Between 1925 and 1929 the volume of exports grew almost 70 percent, and the commodity terms of trade reached levels not seen since the late nineteenth century.[8] A significant influx of capital added to the country's import capacity, with net inflows on the long-term account averaging one-third the purchasing power of exports in the years 1925-29. Given this capacity for external payment, the quantum of imports rose more than 60 percent while the import coefficient (imports as a fraction of GDP) jumped from 20 percent in 1925 to 29 percent in 1928.

The collapse of the international economy after 1929 terminated the export boom. The growth of export volume slowed considerably, gaining only 50 percent between 1929 and 1945. The commodity terms of trade also deteriorated sharply. At the nadir in 1933, the terms-of-trade index stood at two-thirds its 1928 level. The collapse also choked off the long-term capital inflow that Colombia had enjoyed in the twenties; during the thirties, this averaged only one-eighth its earlier rate. In addition, the heavy burden of debt service and profit remittances remained.

The twofold result of these developments was to curtail prosperity and strangle imports. Because Colombia was a primary product exporter with inelastic short-run supply responses, and because devaluation helped maintain the domestic purchasing power of exports, the effect on real production was not too severe. From peak to trough, real GDP declined less than 3 percent between 1929 and 1931. The repercussions of the international collapse can be seen more clearly in the slower rate of growth between 1929 and 1945, and in the abrupt drop in the import coefficient. The growth of real output declined to 3.3 percent per year (1.2 percent per year on a per capita basis), and the import coefficient fell to two-thirds its former level.

Development of the Manufacturing Sector

In contrast to the slowdown in the economy as a whole, real manufacturing output continued to expand vigorously, growing at better than 7 percent per year throughout the thirties, and slipping only slightly to 6.5 percent during the Second World War.[9] In analyzing this development, I shall focus on what might loosely be called nontraditional manufacturing; that is, sectors shown by other studies to grow most rapidly as industrialization proceeds.[10] The choice of focus is dictated by limitations of data; these are the sectors for which it is possible to construct reasonably reliable real output indices. Construction of these indices required making several rather strong assumptions about input-output relationships in Colombian manufacturing. It also required a heavy reliance on Colombian foreign trade data, and data from the 1945 industrial census. Therefore any limitations in these underlying sources apply as well to the indices presented here. In some cases it was possible to validate the general conclusions drawn from these data with information from other materials. The alternative to constructing new estimates of industrial production was to use the series prepared by the United Nations Economic Commission for Latin America (ECLA).[11] Unfortunately, the ECLA indices are incomplete and of uncertain quality.[12] The new indices of real output, together with a general description of how they were prepared, are presented in the appendix to this essay.

The nontraditional sectors dominated the industrial expansion that took place in this period. They accounted for better than three-fifths of the growth in value added between the pre-Depression peak in 1928 and the end of World War II, thereby raising their share in manufacturing value added from 41 to 55 percent. This growth is particularly impressive when viewed against the slower expansion of total output. The ratio of the industrial growth rate to the growth rate of GDP jumps from 1.3 during the late twenties to 2.5 in the thirties, remaining at the same high level during the war years. When this ratio is disaggregated to two-digit sectors (Table 3.1), it is quickly apparent that the increase was not uniformly distributed. In such sectors as textiles, paper, and probably rubber, the thirties saw a dramatic spurt; chemicals and transport equipment advanced only modestly; petroleum products were unable to match their performance of the twenties. World War II had substantially different effects on different industries. Basic metals and nonelectric machinery benefitted considerably from wartime conditions; paper, metal products, and transport equipment were severely hurt—the latter two even experiencing declines in production.

Because of size differences among industries, these ratios cannot tell us which sectors were most important to the growth of nontraditional manufacturing; for this we need the contribution of each industry to the total increase in value added (Table 3.2). Although the expansion of the twenties was sustained by the development of several industries, after 1930 a remarkable proportion of growth was concentrated in textiles. Textiles provided over half the increase in value added during the thirties and two-thirds of the increase during World War II. Only petroleum products contributed more than 10 percent in either period.

A fair question is whether these changes were normal for a country at Colombia's stage of development. Chenery and Taylor's work suggests that "normal" can be defined by reference to the level of GNP per capita, and to the share of primary and manufactured exports in GNP.[13] Their estimated equations allow us to compute normal value added at the two-digit level using this definition.[14] Table 3.3 presents the ratio of actual to normal value added in benchmark years. The most striking aspect of Table 3.3 is the low level of actual value added relative to normal value added in the twenties, and the substantially higher ratio in both 1939 and 1945. The closing of the gap suggests an abnormally high rate of growth, especially between 1929 and 1939, particularly in the case of textiles, the leading industry. The principal exceptions to this pattern are chemicals and petroleum products, and metal manufactures. The former enjoyed a high ratio even during the twenties, reflecting Colombia's domestic petroleum resources, whereas the 1945 ratio for metal manufactures was probably depressed by wartime shortages.

TABLE 3.1

RATIO OF GROWTH RATE OF INDUSTRIAL OUTPUT TO GROWTH RATE OF GDP; LATE TWENTIES, THIRTIES, AND WORLD WAR II

Sector	Late Twenties[a]	Thirties[a]	World War II[a]
Textiles	0.0	4.0	3.5
Paper	2.2	5.4	0.6
Rubber	NA	(11.3)	8.5
Chemicals	0.8	1.0	0.5
Petroleum Products	4.9	2.4	2.2
Nonmetallic Minerals	2.7	2.3	3.0
Basic Metals	2.0	-1.1	22.0
Metal Products	3.1	2.9	-3.4
Nonelectric Machinery	4.9	-0.1	3.0
Transport Equipment	1.7	2.0	-0.6

Sources: Computed as the ratio of annually compounded growth rates between period endpoints. For underlying data, see the appendix to this chapter, and ECLA, *Statistical Appendix*, p. 1.

[a] 1925/26-27/28, 1927/28-38/39, 1938/39-44/45, where "/" denotes average of years indicated.

NA = not available.
( ) = less than full period

TABLE 3.2

THE COMPOSITION OF EXPANSION OF NONTRADITIONAL MANUFACTURING; LATE TWENTIES, THIRTIES, AND WORLD WAR II
(Percent of Increase in Total Value Added)

Sector	Late Twenties[a]	Thirties[a]	World War II[a]
Textiles	8	56	67
Paper	0	1	0
Rubber	NA	1	3
Chemicals	20	9	3
Petroleum Products	35	19	16
Nonmetallic Minerals	12	8	10
Basic Metals	0	0	2
Metal Products	6	6	-5
Nonelectric Machinery	18	0	5
Transport Equipment	1	0	0
TOTAL	100	100	100[b]

Source: Appendix to this chapter.

[a] 1923/24-27/28, 1927/28-38/39, 1938/39-44/45, where "/" denotes average of years indicated.

[b] Column does not add to 100 due to rounding.

TABLE 3.3

RATIO OF ACTUAL TO "NORMAL" VALUE ADDED, SELECTED YEARS, 1924-45

Sector	1924^a	1928^a	1939^a	1945^a
Textiles	.64	.55	2.19	3.57
Paper	.12	.14	.86	.65
Rubber	.00	.00	.20	.56
Chemicals and Petroleum Products	1.36	2.04	3.07	3.45
Nonmetallic Minerals	.19	.35	.73	1.04
Basic Metals	.03	.14	.08	.71
Metal Manufactures[b]	(.27)	.52	.66	.53

Sources: For actual value added, the chapter appendix; for normal value added, Chenery and Taylor, "Development Patterns," pp. 406-407.

[a] 1923/24, 1927/28, 1938/39, 1944/45, where "/" denotes average of years indicated.

[b] ISIC 35-38: Metal products, nonelectric machinery, electric machinery, and transport equipment.

( ) = approximate

These trends suggest that the structure of industrial development differed fundamentally before and after 1929. A shift occurred in the leadership of industrial expansion as measured by the rate of growth of output. Growth concentrated in a few sectors; in the twenties it had been more broadly based. The rate of expansion was extremely high and reversed the position of several industries from a below-average contribution to GDP to a more normal level, or even one much above average.

The context of industrial development also changed after 1929. In the twenties, nontraditional manufacturing grew as part of a rapid overall expansion generated by an export boom. The export boom and large capital inflows permitted a high level of imports, especially consumer goods. With the collapse of the boom, the economy stagnated. The structure of imports began to change, moving away from consumer goods and toward raw and intermediate materials.

These parallel developments suggest that the industrial growth of the thirties and early forties arose more from import substitution than from the expansion of domestic demand. Instead of importing the finished product, Colombia turned toward importing the raw materials—or exploiting domestically produced inputs—and manufacturing the finished product herself.

To measure the contribution of import substitution to the growth of industrial output, I use the identity:

$$X_2 - X_1 \equiv (a_2 - a_1)D_2 + a_1(D_2 - D_1) + (E_2 - E_1)$$

where:

    X is domestic production (value of production),

    D is domestic demand (equal to domestic production plus imports less exports, or $X + I - E$),

    E is exports,

    a is the proportion of domestic demand satisfied by domestic production, or $(X-E)/(X + I + E)$, and

    1,2 refer to benchmark years.

The first term on the right-hand side of the identity measures the contribution of import substitution to the growth of domestic production; the second term measures the contribution of increases in domestic demand; the third term measures increases in exports.

Table 3.4 presents the components of industrial growth as computed from this identity for each two-digit sector, and expressed as a percent of the change in value added during each period. (If the components add to -100, then value added declined.) The source of industrial growth changed dramatically after 1929. During the twenties, increases in domestic demand were largely responsible for the growth of nontraditional manufacturing, but after 1929 growth was predominantly the result of import substitution. This is a very strong change, occurring not only for nontraditional manufacturing as a whole, but in almost every two-digit sector. And in every two-digit sector but one, import substitution accounted for more than half of the increase in value added achieved during the thirties.

During the war years, the importance of import substitution as a source of industrial growth began to weaken. To a certain extent, the slack was taken up by increased exports. This essentially wartime boom peaked in 1943. Colombia's industrial exports were concentrated in textile products, especially cotton cloth, and most went to neighboring countries—Venezuela, Ecuador, Panamá, and Curaçao.

As a result of this import substitution, Colombia sharply reduced her dependence on foreign supply of nontraditional manufactures. The change can be seen in the dramatic fall of import coefficients (Table 3.5). Imports met three-quarters of domestic demand for nontraditional manufactures in 1929, but by 1945 local industry supplied more than half of Colombia's needs. Although some of the low import coefficients for 1945 may reflect wartime conditions, this was not the case in many sectors, since much of the reduction in import dependence had already been achieved by 1939.

The Chenery Model

Can the Chenery model be used to explain Colombia's industrial growth in the three decades before 1945? In his 1960 article, Chenery used only two variables to explain the growth of manufacturing output per capita: income per capita (to test his basic thesis) and national population (as a proxy for market size, to test the effects of economies of scale). His more recent formulation (1968) added another set of exogenous variables: the shares of primary and manufactured exports in national income (to test the effects of trade patterns). In either formulation, the basic hypothesis being tested is the existence of a regular and stable association between changes in per capita income and manufacturing output. The evidence in Table 3.1 already suggests a possible

TABLE 3.4

COMPONENTS OF INDUSTRIAL GROWTH, TWENTIES, THIRTIES, AND WORLD WAR II
(Percent of Change in Value Added)

Sector	(1) Twenties[a] (2) Thirties (3) World War II	Import Substitution	Domestic Demand	Exports
Textiles	(1)	-290	390	1
	(2)	81	19	0
	(3)	62	32	6
Paper	(1)	-51	151	0
	(2)	59	41	0
	(3)	-2056	2156	0
Rubber	(1)	NA	NA	NA
	(2)	NA	NA	NA
	(3)	45	55	0
Chemicals	(1)	-35	135	0
	(2)	104	-5	1
	(3)	-99	195	4
Petroleum Products	(1)	0	100	0
	(2)	31	69	0
	(3)	26	70	4
Nonmetallic Minerals	(1)	-24	124	0
	(2)	91	9	1
	(3)	21	79	0
Basic Metals	(1)	56	44	0
	(2)	64	-164	0
	(3)	99	1	0
Metal Products	(1)	19	81	0
	(2)	66	34	0
	(3)	-38	-62	0
Nonelectric Machinery	(1)	10	90	0
	(2)	1486	-1586	0
	(3)	107	-7	0
Transport Equipment	(1)	NA	NA	NA
	(2)	160	-60	0
	(3)	-1054	954	0
Nontraditional Manufacturing	(1)	-30	130	0
	(2)	76	24	0
	(3)	50	45	4

Sources: Chapter appendix, and Chu, "Depression and Industrialization," Appendix B-2.

[a] 1923/24-27/28, 1927/28-38/39, 1938/39-44/45, where "/" denotes average of years indicated.

NA = not available.

TABLE 3.5

IMPORTS AS A PERCENT OF DOMESTIC DEMAND
1927/28, 1938/39, AND 1944/45

Sector	1927/28	1938/39	1944/45
Textiles	81	39	18
Paper	81	51	70
Rubber	(99)	81	50
Chemicals	52	40	48
Petroleum Products	36	21	15
Nonmetallic Minerals[a]	75	41	33
Basic Metals[b]	97	99	86
Metal Products	82	71	78
Nonelectric Machinery	88	79	64
Electric Machinery	100	100	100
Transport Equipment[c]	100	99	99
Nontraditional Manufacturing	77	50	35

Sources: Chapter appendix, and Chu, "Depression and Industrialization," Appendix B-2.

( ) = approximate

[a] Excludes structural clay products.

[b] Excludes rails.

[c] Vehicles only.

---

discontinuity in that relationship around 1930. The model should therefore be tested for the entire period 1923-45, and separately for the subperiods 1923-29 and 1930-45.

Both the original and later versions of the Chenery model were estimated for 1923-45, and separately for both subperiods, using annual data. Only the simpler formulation is reported in Table 3.6, since most of the trade coefficients either were insignificant or had an incorrect sign. (Otherwise, the two sets of results are quite similar.) With the exception of basic metals, all the results in Table 3.6 can be classified into two groups. In the first group, the income coefficient is positive and significant[15] for the period 1930-45, but not for 1923-29. This group includes paper, petroleum products, and nonelectric machinery. Textiles, chemicals, nonmetallic minerals, metal products, and transport equipment constitute a second group; in these industries the income coefficient was significant in both subperiods. The important question for this group is whether the relationship between industrial output, per capita income, and market size was the same before and after 1930. To answer this question, we test the hypothesis that the coefficient vectors for 1923-29 equal those for 1930-45. In every industry but transport equipment, the hypothesis is rejected (Table 3.7), indicating that the coefficients differ significantly between the subperiods. In other words, some difference in the economic environment is not being captured by the variables in the Chenery equation.

TABLE 3.6

REGRESSIONS OF INDUSTRIAL OUTPUT PER CAPITA (Q_j/N) ON INCOME PER CAPITA (Y/N) AND POPULATION (N): ln (Q_i/N) = ln A_i + b_{1i} ln (Y/N) + b_{2i} ln N

Industry	Period	b_{1i}	b_{2i}	R^2	Durbin-Watson Statistic
Textiles	1923-29	6.51*	-21.30*	.66	2.40
	1930-45	4.74**	3.53**	.90	1.10
	1923-45	-1.95	7.35**	.85	.52**
Paper	1923-29	1.45	1.34	.74	2.67
	1930-45	12.80**	-1.32	.75	1.04
	1923-45	1.65	4.72*	.70	.52**
Rubber	1933-45	7.33**	9.39**	.94	1.63
Chemicals	1923-29	2.41***	-4.96	.82	2.30
	1930-45	2.65**	-.25	.86	1.74
	1923-45	.61	.35	.52	.52**
Petroleum	1923-29	.64	1.24	.96	2.56
	1930-45	2.89*	2.02*	.87	1.11
	1923-45	3.87**	.69	.93	1.25
Nonmetallic Minerals	1923-29	6.03***	-9.81	.90	2.96
	1930-45	4.75**	2.21**	.98	1.64
	1923-45	1.55*	2.79**	.88	.49
Basic Metals	1923-29	13.25	-26.75	.76	1.94
	1930-45	-8.78**	15.89**	.83	1.10
	1923-45	-1.94	6.45	.44	.35**
Metal Products	1923-29	7.31**	-14.71**	.98	2.21
	1930-45	11.68**	-5.91**	.87	1.98
	1923-45	4.13**	-1.29	.71	.37**
Nonelectric Machinery	1923-29	6.27	-8.21	.86	2.63
	1930-45	7.42**	-1.95	.69	1.48
	1923-45	3.37*	-1.84	.31	.84**
Transport Equipment	1925-29	2.29**	-1.58	.99	3.26
	1930-45	3.94**	-1.87**	.70	.85**
	1925-45	2.95**	-.90	.81	1.01

Sources: Chapter appendix, and ECLA, *Statistical Appendix*, pp. 1, 6, with GNP estimates for 1923-24 obtained by extrapolating backward growth rates for 1925/26-27/28.

*Significant at 10 percent.
**Significant at 5 percent or better.
***Significant at approximately 15 percent (1923-29 only).

TABLE 3.7

TEST OF THE HYPOTHESIS OF EQUAL COEFFICIENT VECTORS FOR 1920-29 AND 1930-45, I.E., THAT

$$\begin{bmatrix} \ln a_i \\ b_{1i} \\ b_{2i} \end{bmatrix} 1923\text{-}29 = \begin{bmatrix} \ln a_i \\ b_{1i} \\ b_{2i} \end{bmatrix} 1930\text{-}45 = \begin{bmatrix} \ln a_i \\ b_{1i} \\ b_{2i} \end{bmatrix} 1923\text{-}45$$

Industry	F	Degrees of Freedom
Textiles	7.56*	3, 17
Chemicals	16.67*	3, 17
Nonmetallic Minerals	26.08*	3, 17
Metal Products	14.60*	3, 17
Transport Equipment	1.76	3, 15

Source: Calculations by the author.
*Significant at the 5 percent level or better.

The population variable is positive and significant at 10 percent or better in nine of the twenty-eight equations. As might be expected, it is more usually significant over the longer time periods. However, the effects of market size are probably not as strong as these results suggest. Compared with Chenery's estimates for the post-World War II period, most of my coefficients are much too large. Moreover, they are insignificant (or actually negative) in the metals industries—just those cases where a priori one would predict a strong, positive value.

The poor results of Table 3.6 are quite remarkable when contrasted with the generally successful application of the Chenery model to the postwar years. Part of the explanation is that I am using time-series data, whereas Chenery used cross-section or pooled cross-section and time-series data. The failure of the model when tested with just time-series data is a further reminder that conclusions based on cross-section analysis cannot always be generalized to explain changes in economic structure over time.

Prices and Industrial Growth

The unsatisfactory results from the Chenery model, particularly the marked change in the relationship between industrial output and GNP per capita after 1930, suggest that other events may help to explain the development of manufacturing between 1930 and 1945. One of these is the marked change in the structure of input and output prices and therefore in the incentives facing domestic producers of industrial commodities. The change in the price structure resulted from the implicit and explicit devaluation of the peso, which was caused by the collapse of primary export markets at the start of the Depression, and by the curtailed inflow of capital.

Initially, the Colombian central bank tried to maintain the pre-Depression parity of the peso by using exchange reserves accumulated during the twenties. Reserves soon began to run out, and Colombia started to ration foreign exchange using a permit system (September, 1931), although still maintaining the pre-Depression exchange rate with the dollar.[16] As the backlog of permit applications grew, the peso was devalued 10 percent in February, 1933 and another 9 percent in September, 1933.[17] The latter devaluation was supplemented by a limited auction system for rationing foreign exchange. The central bank continued to receive the exchange proceeds from all exports, issuing in return a foreign exchange certificate which could be used by the holder or sold to the highest bidder, although bidders were still required to have exchange licenses in order to use the certificates.[18] This semifree peso quickly depreciated, reaching a low of 53 percent of the pre-Depression dollar parity in July, 1935, and remained at approximately this level (with varying degrees of government intervention) through the end of World War II.

Even before the peso was devalued, the Colombian government enacted a substantial upward revision of the tariff. During the twenties, the tariff had functioned principally as a source of revenue for the central government, accounting for almost one-half of receipts. The contraction of imports that began in 1929 threatened to restrict this source of funds. For this reason, and as a supplementary measure to improve the balance of payments,[19] Colombia adopted a completely new tariff in 1931. Together, devaluation and the new tariff approximately doubled the price of imported nontraditional manufactures. Their individual contribution to this can be measured with the identity:

$$P_D \equiv P_I \cdot E \cdot (1+T) \cdot R$$

where:

P_D is the domestic price,

P_I is the international price,

E is the exchange rate (domestic currency units per U.S. dollar),

T is the *ad valorum* tariff, and

R is an index measuring the effect of other policies that restrict imports (exchange control, quotas, etc.); a value of 1.00 indicates a neutral effect.

Any change in the domestic price can then be broken into its constituent parts:

$$\frac{(P_D)_t}{(P_D)_{t-1}} \equiv \left[\frac{(P_I)_t}{(P_I)_{t-1}}\right] \cdot \left[\frac{E_t}{E_{t-1}}\right] \cdot \left[\frac{(1+T)_t}{(1+T)_{t-1}}\right] \cdot \left[\frac{R_t}{R_{t-1}}\right]$$

With 1927 and 1936 as benchmarks for pre-Depression and Depression price levels, $(P_I)_{1936}/(P_I)_{1927}$ is .89, E_{1936}/E_{1927} is 1.71, and $(1+T)_{1936}/(1+T)_{1927}$ is 1.28, which indicates that most of the change in the price of imported nontraditional manufactures was due to the devaluation of the peso.[20]

The incentive effects of the change in the price of imported nontraditional manufactures are best measured against the general price level and in comparison with prices for factor and material inputs. In

Figure 3.1, indices for the price of imported nontraditional manufactures and material and factor inputs are expressed relative to the general domestic price level as measured by the GNP deflator. A decline in any index therefore indicates a fall relative to the general price level; a rise indicates an increase relative to the general price level. Measured in this way, the price of imported nontraditional manufactures more than doubled at the start of the Depression, whereas the price of intermediate materials used in their production rose only 50 percent. Both indices declined somewhat in the late thirties but rose again in the early war years, reflecting shortages of finished as well as intermediate industrial products. These indices fell toward the end of the war, as shortages of industrial products began to ease and as the general price level responded to inflationary, monetary and fiscal policies.

The advantage these changes gave to domestic manufacturing was only partially offset by shifts in factor prices. Relative to the general price level, industrial wages rose moderately; in the late thirties, real wages were probably 10-15 percent higher than the late twenties. Although Figure 3.1 suggests great inflation in the relative rental price of machinery, this overstates the change for all capital goods. The 1945 industrial census indicates that about 40 percent of the fixed capital stock in nontraditional manufacturing consisted of land and buildings.[21] If, as seems likely,[22] the prices of land and buildings moved in concert with the general price level, then the rental rate of all capital goods probably increased about as much as the price of imported nontraditional manufactures.

The Relative Price Model[23]

My hypothesis is that the price changes just described—principally the rise in the price of imported manufactures—induced the import substitution of 1930-45. To test this hypothesis, I assume that producers have a target level of real output that is a log-linear function of expected prices for material inputs and final commodities. Thus, in any two-digit sector:

$$\ln Q^* = a_0 + a_1 \ln P^* + a_2 \ln I^* + u \tag{1}$$

where:

Q^* = target level of real output,

P^* = expected level of output prices (equal to the expected level of prices for competing imports),

I^* = expected level of material input prices, and

u = an error term.

Since price changes must be corrected for general deflation,[24] both P^* and I^* are expressed relative to the GNP deflator.

When actual prices change, expected prices follow, but may not adjust instantaneously. A simple lag specification with this property is:

$$\ln P^* - \ln P^*_{-1} = \beta_P \cdot (\ln P_{-1} - \ln P^*_{-1}) \tag{2a}$$

$$\ln I^* - \ln I^*_{-1} = \beta_I \cdot (\ln I_{-1} - \ln I^*_{-1}) \tag{2b}$$

FIGURE 3.1

RELATIVE PRICE MOVEMENTS OF NONTRADITIONAL
MANUFACTURES AND NEW INPUTS, 1925-45

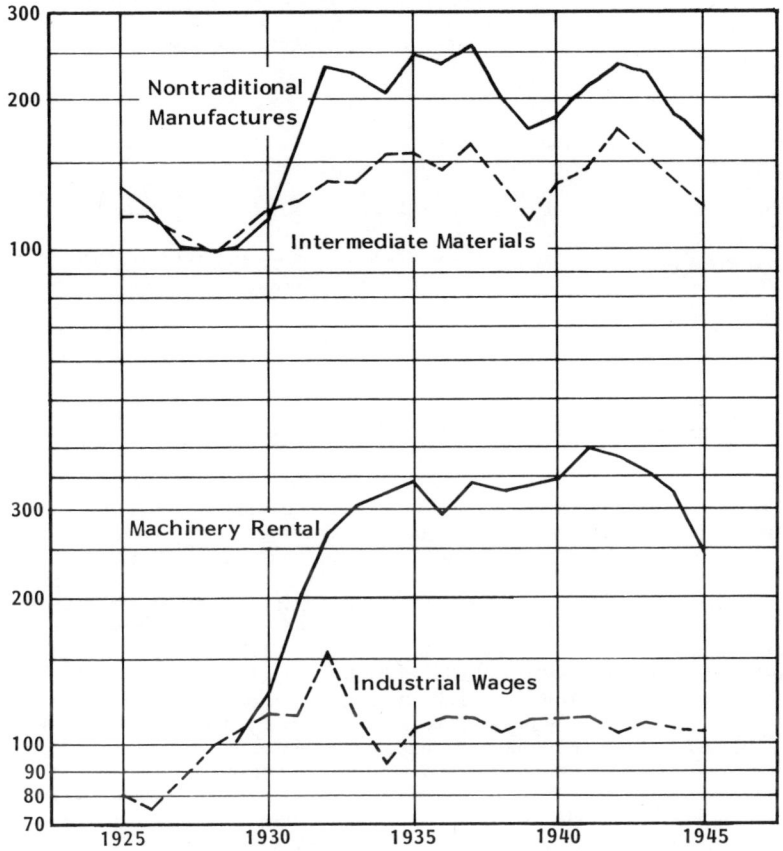

Sources: Nontraditional manufactures and intermediate materials: See chapter appendix.

Industrial wages: Female textile workers, Medellín (Medellín, *Anuario Estadístico del Municipio de Medellín*, various issues).

Machinery rental: Nominal interest rate (Bogotá mortgage rate from Banco de la República, *Revista del Banco de la República*, various issues) plus assumed depreciation rate of 5 percent, all times unit value index for imported nonelectric machinery.

GNP deflator: ECLA, *Statistical Appendix*, p. 38.

where:

P^*_{-1} = the expected level of prices in the previous period,

P_{-1} = the actual level of output prices in the previous period.

Similarly for I^*_{-1}, I_{-1}

and

$$0 < \beta_P \leq 1, \ 0 < \beta_I \leq 1$$

Actual output need not equal target output but can also respond in lagged fashion:

$$\ln Q - \ln Q_{-1} = \gamma (\ln Q^* - \ln Q_{-1}) \qquad (3)$$

where:

$$0 < \gamma \leq 1$$

I assume that expected input and output prices adjust at the same rate, i.e., $\beta_P = \beta_I = \beta$. This seems a reasonable assumption for prices of outputs and material inputs. Moreover, a model of this type cannot be reduced to an estimating equation composed of observable variables unless the expectations lag structure is the same for all elements. Otherwise, the reduced form will include unobservable expected prices.

Factor prices are not included in the specification for two reasons. First, we would expect factor prices to adjust at a different rate than prices for materials and outputs; as just noted, a model of this kind requires assumption of the same expectations structure for all prices. Second, for this period in Colombian history, factor prices are not available at the level of the two-digit industry. Figure 3.1 presented what little evidence is available on changes in factor prices in this period; it indicated a substantial relative increase in machinery rental rates. I will therefore discuss separately below ("Financing Industrial Growth") what is known about the supply of capital to industry in this period.

Two modifications of (1) must be introduced before these equations can be used to explain import substitution industrialization in Colombia. First, if P is the relative price of competing imports, then Q should be interpreted as the production of import-competing goods. Unfortunately, besides import-competing goods, observed output includes both exportables and nontraded goods. Since exports were not important, they can safely be ignored,[25] leaving nontraded goods.

Even before the Depression, domestic producers satisfied a part of domestic demand in some industries (Table 3.5). Presumably much of this output should be considered nontraded goods. Production would be expected to grow with the expansion of income, independent of changes in relative import prices, unless import prices were to fall substantially. To account for this "natural" component of industrial growth, I introduce GNP (Y) into equation (1), yielding:

$$\ln Q^* = a_0 + a_1 \ln P^* + a_2 \ln I^* + a_3 \ln Y + u \qquad (1a)$$

The other modification of equation (1) is to account for the special demand conditions of World War II, which may not be fully reflected in the price series. The basic assumption behind the price series is that the domestic price of an imported good is equal to the international price plus the tariff. The use of price controls and other rationing mechanisms during World War II vitiates that assumption.[26] Thus the price series may not fully capture the surge in demand for certain domestically produced manufactures, nor may they properly reflect shortages of imported intermediate materials. For this reason, I add a dummy variable (D) to (1a), which takes on the value zero for 1928-41, and the value one for 1942-45:

$$\ln Q^* = a_0 + a_1 \ln P^* + a_2 \ln I^* + a_3 \ln Y + a_4 D + u \qquad (1b)$$

Equation (3) may now be rewritten as:

$$\ln Q = (1-\gamma) \ln Q_{-1} + \gamma [a_0 + a_1 \ln P^* + a_2 \ln I^*$$
$$+ a_3 \ln Y + a_4 D + u] \qquad (4)$$

and (2a) and (2b) as:

$$\ln P^* = (1-\beta) \ln P^*_{-1} + \beta \ln P_{-1} \qquad (5a)$$

$$\ln I^* = (1-\beta) \ln I^*_{-1} + \beta \ln I_{-1} \qquad (5b)$$

Substituting (5a) and (5b) in (4) yields:[27]

$$\ln Q = \gamma \beta a_0 + [(1-\gamma) + (1-\beta)] \ln Q_{-1}$$
$$- [(1-\gamma)(1-\beta)] \ln Q_{-2}$$
$$+ \gamma \beta a_1 \ln P_{-1} + \gamma \beta a_2 \ln I_{-1}$$
$$+ \gamma a_3 \ln Y - \gamma(1-\beta) a_3 \ln Y_{-1}$$
$$+ \gamma a_4 D - \gamma(1-\beta) a_4 D_{-1}$$
$$+ \gamma u - \gamma(1-\beta) u_{-1} \qquad (6)$$

or equivalently:

$$\ln Q = \pi_0 + \pi_1 \ln Q_{-1} + \pi_2 \ln Q_{-2} + \pi_3 \ln P_{-1} + \pi_4 \ln I_{-1}$$
$$+ \pi_5 \ln Y + \pi_6 \ln Y_{-1} + \pi_7 D + \pi_8 D_{-1} + W \qquad (7)$$

Estimates for π_1 and π_2 will tell something about the lag structure of the adjustment process. If $\pi_2 = -(1-\gamma)(1-\beta) = 0$, then either $\gamma = 1$ or $\beta = 1$. If $\gamma = 1$, (6) becomes a simple expectations model:

$$\ln Q = \beta a_0 + (1-\beta) \ln Q_{-1} + \beta a_1 \ln P_{-1} + \beta a_2 \ln I_{-1}$$

$$+ a_3 \ln Y - (1-\beta) a_3 Y_{-1} + a_4 D - (1-\beta) a_4 D_{-1}$$

$$+ u - (1-\beta) u_{-1} \qquad (7a)$$

If $\beta = 1$, (6) becomes a strict partial adjustment model:

$$\ln Q = \gamma a_0 + (1-\gamma) \ln Q_{-1} + \gamma a_1 \ln P_{-1} + \gamma a_2 \ln I_{-1}$$

$$+ \gamma a_3 \ln Y + \gamma a_4 D + \gamma u \qquad (7b)$$

If $\pi_1 = (1-\gamma) + (1-\beta) = 0$, this implies both $\gamma = 1$ and $\beta = 1$, and (6) collapses to a simple supply equation:

$$\ln Q = a_0 + a_1 \ln P_{-1} + a_2 \ln I_{-1} + a_3 \ln Y + a_4 D + u \qquad (7c)$$

If the error term W is assumed normally independently distributed, then ordinary least squares applied to (7) will give consistent estimates of the π_i.[28]

As specified here, the model implies at least a modest lag in the response of output to price changes, since expected prices in the present period reflect actual prices in the previous period [equations (2a) and (2b)]. To allow for a more rapid rate of adjustment, expected prices may also react to actual prices in the present period:

$$\ln P^* - \ln P^*_{-1} = \beta (\ln P - \ln P^*_{-1}) \qquad (8a)$$

$$\ln I^* - \ln I^*_{-1} = \beta (\ln I - \ln I^*_{-1}) \qquad (8b)$$

It is a straightforward matter to demonstrate that using (8a) and (8b) will cause $\ln P_{-1}$ and $\ln I_{-1}$ in equations (7) and (7a)-(7c) to be replaced by $\ln P$ and $\ln I$.

Estimation of the model was carried out using ordinary least squares, and annual observations on production, prices, and GNP for the period 1928-45. The model was applied to each two-digit industry using separate series for the input and output prices of the individual industries. The year 1928 was chosen as the starting point since it represents the approximate pre-Depression peak of output levels. The production data used for the estimation have already been described. Most of the output prices are based on prices for competing imports; the input prices are based on import unit values, since imports were an important source of intermediate materials. The appendix provides the details of how the output and price data were constructed.

With several variants to the basic model, the estimation proceeded in a sequential fashion. First, the full model [equation (7)] was tested. If π_1 and π_2 proved significantly different from zero,[29] indicating lags in the adjustment of both expectations and output, testing the variants was unnecessary. If, however, π_2 failed a 10 percent significance test, indicating that *either* expectations or output adjusts fully in one period, then both the simple expectations model [equation (7a)] and the strict partial adjustment model [equation (7b)] were tried. If π_1 failed a 10 percent significance test, indicating that *both* expectations and output adjust immediately, then the simple supply model [equation (7c)] was tried. At each step in this process, the equations were fitted with and without a dummy variable for the World War II years, and the dummy was retained only when significant at 10 percent or better. This entire process was repeated for the specification suggested by equations (8a) and (8b), and the best set of results was selected for reporting in Table 3.8.[30] (The two general specifications—one using I_{-1} and P_{-1}, and one using I and P—are labeled "lagged prices" and "contemporaneous prices" in the table.)

The results reported in Table 3.8 are generally encouraging. The output price variable has the correct sign (plus) in seven of the ten industries, and the coefficient is significant (at 10 percent) in five of the seven cases. Input prices have the correct sign (minus) in six of the ten cases, and the coefficients are significant in three of the six cases. None of the coefficients with incorrect signs are significant.

Moreover, a significant association appears between production and output prices in five of the six industries that grew more rapidly relative to GNP in the thirties than in the twenties (textiles, paper, chemicals, nonmetallic materials, and transport equipment; see Tables 3.1 and 3.3). Rubber is the one disappointment in this respect with a weakly significant output price coefficient but a strongly significant input price coefficient; moreover, the coefficient on the dummy variable is significant and positive. The results for the various metals industries are generally poor, but both production and price data are weakest for these sectors. The lack of significant association between production and relative prices in the petroleum industry could have been predicted from the history of its development.[31]

The coefficients on lagged output imply slow to moderate speeds of adjustment, with values for γ and β in the range of .2 to .5. Some of the variability in the speed of adjustment (γ) can be explained by differences in the product mix of the individual industries, and the degree to which expansion of capacity for manufacture of a particular product involved fixed investment with a longer lead time (longer lead times implying slower adjustment). Similarly, variability in the elasticity of price expectations (β) would be associated with differences in the investment intensity of particular products (with producers reluctant to change their price expectations rapidly in the case of products requiring large fixed investment). The immediate adjustment of output in the paper and rubber industries to changes in relative prices probably reflects the rather simple nature of the items produced; expanding production in these sectors did not require much investment in machinery. Expansion of textile output, in contrast, required importation of spinning and weaving machinery; it is therefore not surprising that output in this industry adjusted more slowly. However, this explanation is not very satisfactory for either the chemical industry (where much of the increase in output took place in simple pharmaceutical products) or the transport equipment sector (dominated by repair of railway equipment). It is plausible to argue that the low elasticity of price expectations in the nonmetallic minerals industry reflects the importance of cement output in that sector. Very substantial fixed investment was required to expand cement production, and producers would obviously not undertake such investment until they were quite sure that any increase in output prices was likely to endure.

The persistent significance of the GNP variable is, at first glance, somewhat troubling. This would seem to undermine the assertion that changes in relative prices lie behind Colombian industrialization in the Great Depression, supporting instead Chenery's view of how industrial growth proceeds. However, since GNP was steadily rising throughout

TABLE 3.8
THE RELATIVE PRICE MODEL

Industry (Model)	ln Q_{-1}	ln P	ln P_{-1}	ln I	ln I_{-1}	ln Y	ln Y_{-1}	Dummy	Adjusted R^2	Durbin-Watson
Textiles (PA-P)	.48** (3.12)	1.01** (2.84)		.13 (.26)		2.24** (3.08)		-.31** (-2.58)	.982	3.18
Paper (SS-P)		1.52** (3.83)		-.40 (-1.26)		4.49** (7.76)			.853	1.38
Rubber (SS-P)[a]		.51 (1.36)		-1.07** (-3.20)		8.45** (11.21)		.86** (3.20)	.977	2.35
Chemicals (PA-L)	.59** (2.83)		.27** (2.18)		-.51* (-1.97)	.38 (.98)			.921	1.93
Petroleum Products (PA-P)	.50** (2.51)	-.06 (-.39)		.03 (.10)		1.39** (2.53)			.909	1.77
Nonmetallic Minerals (SE-L)	.75** (4.87)		.22* (1.93)		NA	3.46* (3.22)	-2.88 (-2.95)		.976	2.46
Basic Metals (PA-P)	.79** (4.16)	-.62 (-.95)		-.01 (-.02)		2.67** (2.97)			.936	2.57
Metal Products			No acceptable results							
Nonelectric Machinery (SE-L)	.56** (3.21)		.09 (.29)		-.53 (-1.07)	12.12** (4.55)	-10.64** (-4.24)		.774	2.31
Transport Equipment (PA-P)	.67** (4.37)	.38** (2.92)		-.53** (-3.82)		.81** (2.88)		-.19** (-3.02)	.949	2.29

( ) = ratio, NA = not available
Models:
PA = Partial Adjustment (equation 7b)
SE = Simple Expectations (equation 7a)
SS = Simple Supply (equation 7c)
P = Contemporaneous prices
L = Lagged prices

[a] 1933-45 (insufficient data to estimate full period).
* Significant at 10 percent.
** Significant at 5 percent.

most of the period 1928-45, a strong correlation with the upward-trending industrial production series exists, regardless of any possible cause and effect relationship. We need GNP as a control for the increase in production of nontraded output that would have taken place in any event, but the estimated elasticities appear much larger than Chenery's work would suggest is reasonable.[32]

One way of dealing with this problem in interpreting the results of Table 3.8 is to accept for the moment the coefficients on GNP, and ask what was the effect of the price changes that actually took place. If the estimated equations of Table 3.8 correctly describe the growth path of Colombian industry, how much would production have increased had prices remained at the 1928 level throughout the period, but GNP grown as actually observed, and how does this increase compare with the growth in output predicted from the price changes that actually took place? These calculations are presented in Table 3.9. It appears that the paper, rubber, and various metals industries would have been better off with 1928 input and output prices.[33] However, had prices remained at 1928 levels, output of nonmetallic minerals would have grown only one-quarter as much as otherwise would have been predicted, textiles and chemicals only one-half as much. Since these three industries contributed three-quarters of the growth in nontraditional manufacturing between 1930 and 1945 (Table 3.2), this confirms the hypothesis that a significant share of the industrial expansion occurred in response to relative price changes.

TABLE 3.9

EFFECT OF PRICE CHANGES ON INDUSTRIAL OUTPUT, BY INDUSTRY, 1928-45

	Predicted Growth of Output With Prices Fixed at 1928 Levels (percent) (1)	Predicted Growth of Output With Actual Price Changes (percent) (2)	Column (1) Divided by Column (2) (3)
Textiles	528	1,106	.55
Paper	1,130	803	1.41
Rubber	2,164	1,792	1.21
Chemicals	42	84	.50
Petroleum Products	331	314	1.05
Nonmetallic Minerals	93	390	.24
Basic Metals	6,502	1,344	4.84
Nonelectric Machinery	172	125	1.38
Transport Equipment	294	134	2.19

Financing Industrial Growth

The relative price model excluded the cost and availability of capital as explanatory variables, not only because it would be difficult to include them in the specification, but also because good data are not available. It is nonetheless important to analyze how these factors may have affected the development of the manufacturing sector, especially because this was a period of significant change among financial institutions. The central bank was enlarging its share in the assets of the financial system, with a concomitant decline in the role of commercial and private mortgage banks, the major lenders to private borrowers. At the same time, an increase in the role of official development institutions reflected the creation of several new agencies: the Agrarian, Industrial and Mining Credit Bank (1931); the Central Mortgage Bank (1932); the Territorial Credit Institute (1939); and the Industrial Development Institute (1940). [34]

A first step in understanding how changes in the supply of credit may have influenced the pattern of growth is to examine the financing of industrial expansion. Table 3.10 summarizes the sources of funds of leading manufacturing corporations during World War II, the earliest period for which data are available covering a significant number of firms. On average, nearly half of all corporate funds arose from internal sources, including depreciation. [35] Those funds not drawn from internal sources came largely from equity issues; [36] neither long- nor short-term debt appears to have been an important source of funds.

World War II, however, was characterized by limited opportunities for the purchase of new equipment because Latin America was cut off from the usual sources of supply in the United States and western Europe. This was also a time of increased profitability for domestic manufacture in some product lines. The greater availability of internal funds and the more restricted opportunity to spend them might imply a higher internal financing ratio during the forties than during the thirties. Such a difference does appear in the few flow-of-funds statements that can be constructed over the entire period 1930-45. Moreover, short-term debt appears to be somewhat more important before 1939 than during the war. [37]

Given this pattern of sources of funds, what can be said about the supply of short-term credit, long-term credit, and equity capital to the industrial sector? First, the funds supplied by commercial banks during these years are essentially the supply of short-term credit. Commercial bank loans were the most significant element among short-term funds, and conversely most commercial bank loans were short term. [38] The real value of commercial bank loans to the private sector remained depressed throughout the period 1930-45, [39] and loans to industry appear to have conformed to this general pattern. Moreover, the marginal share of industrial loans was relatively stable. [40]

Long-term instruments are conspicuously absent in this period for three reasons. First, corporate bonds were unknown as a financial instrument; [41] second, private mortgage banking was disappearing (assets of the private mortgage banks declined from 23 percent of the assets of the financial system in 1929 to 1 percent in 1941); and third, the remaining institutions engaged in long-term operations were government-owned and directed most of their investment elsewhere. [42]

Financial intermediaries furnished very little equity capital; commercial banks were prohibited from doing so. [43] One official institution, the Industrial Development Institute, did purchase the stock of young enterprises, often reselling its holdings to the public at a later date. But the Institute was not created until 1940, and its effect on industrial

TABLE 3.10

SOURCES OF FUNDS OF INDUSTRIAL CORPORATIONS, BY INDUSTRY, 1943-45

(Percent of Total Funds)

Sector	Internal	External		
		Equity	Long-Term Debt	Short-Term Debt
Textiles	68	49	-2	-14
Rubber	0	74	0	26
Nonmetallic Minerals	40	40	0	18
Basic Metals and Metal Products	7	81	0	12
Transport Equipment	11	61	8	2
All Corporations in Sample	47	52	-1	2

Coverage and Sources: Corporations listed on the Bogotá Stock Exchange; balance sheet records of the Bogotá Stock Exchange.

Methodology: The flow of funds from a particular source is the difference in the stock of liability items between the beginning and the end of the period. Negative entries indicate a decline in liabilities. Components may not add to 100 percent because of small unallocated categories.

---

output was just beginning to be felt at the close of World War II. In addition, the total credit it provided to all industry between 1940 and 1945 was only 6.1 million pesos (U.S. $3.5 million).[44] This would have financed less than 10 percent of new stock issues by companies listed on the Bogotá exchange in the same period.[45]

One financial intermediary that did hold corporate stock as part of its portfolio was the insurance company. But insurance companies held only 8.1 million pesos (U.S. $4.6 million) in corporate stock in 1945, or less than 5 percent of the nominal value of shares listed on the Bogotá stock exchange. Between 1941 and 1945, Colombian insurance companies increased their stock holdings by 4.7 million pesos (U.S. $2.7 million), or less than 8 percent of new issues on the Bogotá stock exchange during the same period.[46]

In discussing the supply of equity capital, an understanding of where the initial venture funds came from is important. Although little data can be found to provide an answer, the scanty literature on the origins of industrial enterprises in Colombia suggests that personal funds of the entrepreneur and his acquaintances frequently provided the initial equity. This was the characteristic pattern in the textile, cement, and soap industries.[47]

Once started, many enterprises raised needed additions to equity capital through public stock offerings. The demand for stock by individuals was greatly encouraged by the absence of any tax on dividend income,[48] and dividends rather than earnings were what attracted purchasers of corporate stock. As a result, corporations habitually paid out a high proportion of profits in order to maintain the quotation on their shares.[49] The typical new stock issue of an established firm was floated by offering the shares to existing shareholders at a discount from the market price, and most shareholders chose to exercise rather than sell their rights.[50] In a sense, high payout ratios combined with stock sales to existing stockholders was an indirect technique for the retention of corporate earnings.[51]

To sum up, it does not appear that industry benefited from any important shift in the supply of credit that might account for the rapid growth of nontraditional manufacturing in the period 1930-45. First, the significant change in institutional structure was the expansion of the central bank and the relative decline of institutions dealing with the public (commercial and mortgage banks); the net effect of this change was to improve the access of the government to domestic savings at the expense of other borrowers. Second, industrial firms were partially self-reliant, with perhaps half their funds arising from internal sources. Third, the industrial credit extended by financial institutions consisted chiefly of short-term loans. The real volume of such credit remained depressed throughout the period 1930-45, and the share of the industrial sector was relatively stable. Fourth, the supply of long-term funds was constrained both by legal restrictions and by the government's control of the institutions engaged in long-term operations. Little of their capital was directed to the industrial sector. Finally, although we know much less about the supply of equity capital, a substantial share of stock offerings may have represented the indirect retention of dividends—a combination of high payout ratios and the sale of stock to existing shareholders.

The Supply of Entrepreneurship

It is often argued that underdeveloped countries suffer from a limited supply of entrepreneurial skills. In the case of Latin America, some ascribe this condition to unfavorable cultural characteristics.[52] Might changes in the supply of entrepreneurship—perhaps through immigration—help explain the discontinuity in Colombian growth patterns after 1930?

One approach to this question is to describe the typical entrepreneur and then examine changes in his characteristic attributes. To construct a sample of entrepreneurs, I selected large firms engaged in nontraditional manufacturing from the 1941 and 1947 Industrial Directories,[53] collected the names of their managers and backers, and then searched available biographical sources for career information. To supplement the large-firm data, information on entrepreneurs of smaller companies was culled from business histories. Table 3.11 summarizes the results.[54] When pre-1930 entrepreneurs are compared with those in the post-1930 group, the only difference about which one can be sure is the increased role of the foreign born. Most of these foreign-born entrepreneurs were immigrants rather than employees of international concerns. They possessed high levels of education—all of those for whom we know the educational background had some university training. It may be, therefore, that foreigners were important among the ranks of Colombian entrepreneurs not because of social attitudes derived from a foreign cultural background (and presumably more favorable to the development of entrepreneurial skills), but as a result of noncultural characteristics associated with immigrant status—in this case, a relatively high educational level.

In analyzing changes in the supply of entrepreneurship, we should first examine the pattern of immigration, and then the stock of university graduates. Unfortunately, data on immigration for the years before

TABLE 3.11

ENTREPRENEURIAL CHARACTERISTICS BY SIZE OF FIRM

	Large Firms		Small Firms
	Pre-1930	Post-1930	Post-1930
Number of individuals	25	36	23
Country of birth (%)			
Colombia	92	44	83
Foreign	4	42	13
Unknown	4	14	4
Community of birth (%)			
Urban	40	28	61
Rural	12	8	17
Unknown	48	64	22
Education (%)			
Some Primary	0	0	0
Some Secondary	12	6	26
Some University	16	44	52
Unknown	82	50	22
Previous occupation before association with a firm in the sample (%)			
Business	82	47	22
Farming	8	0	0
Professional	4	6	26
Education	0	3	0
Worker	0	0	8
Unknown	16	44	43
Father's occupation (%)			
Business	12	8	22
Unknown	88	92	78

World War II is limited.[55] Net arrivals were probably less than a thousand per year, and although this rate appears to have risen somewhat during and after World War I (relative to the period 1880-1910), the data are too scanty to draw firm conclusions about trends. The stock of university graduates was growing moderately throughout the period 1925-45.[56] The number of engineers increased notably after 1935, but this timing suggests more a reaction to than a cause of industrial expansion. On balance, it is difficult to see any important shift in the supply of entrepreneurial characteristics.

A second approach to the entrepreneurship question is to examine the role played by firms started after 1930. Because ownership of the typical company was so closely held (frequently controlled by a single family), new firms can be identified with new entrepreneurship. Did the role of new firms vary systematically among industries? Industries are ranked in Table 3.12 by the change in output growth rate; no very good correlation with the contribution of new firms to increases in output is apparent. Most significant, over half the increase in textile output was contributed by establishments started before 1931. If the growth of

TABLE 3.12

CONTRIBUTION OF ESTABLISHMENTS TO CHANGE IN OUTPUT DURING 1930-45, BY YEAR FOUNDED AND INDUSTRY

	Percent Contributed by Establishments Founded		
	Before 1931	1931-41	1942-45
Rubber	5	83	12
Textiles	54	42	4
Paper	-15	110	5
Chemicals	-9	90	19
Nonmetallic Minerals	44	40	16
Petroleum Products	100	0	0
Metals	28	63	9

Sources: Chapter appendix, and DANE, *Primer censo,* pp. 18-19.

industry was related to changes in the supply of entrepreneurship, the relationship cannot be discovered in this simple analysis.

Import Substitution and Industrial Efficiency

Serious questions have been raised about the efficiency of industries created by import substitution in developing countries. One indicator of efficiency is the ratio of material inputs to value of output, both calculated at world prices. Such a ratio measures how well manufacturing firms can turn raw and intermediate materials into final product; one minus the ratio gives us value added per unit of output. Use of this criterion is inspired by the recent literature on effective protection and the finding that negative value added exists (i.e., that in some cases more materials are consumed than final value produced, when both are measured at world prices).[57] Although this criterion has both theoretical and empirical problems,[58] comparing the ratios with similar measures for advanced countries may be helpful in making judgments about efficiency, particularly when large differences are uncovered.

This comparison is made in Table 3.13 with ratios for the United States;[59] the results speak quite favorably for the efficiency of non-traditional manufacturing in Colombia. The ratios are substantially out of line with those for the United States in only a few sectors. In a number of sectors, Colombia is quite competitive with the United States even if the aberrant results for metal and metals manufactures are excluded from consideration.[60]

Before we try to use the results of Table 3.13 to draw lessons from the period 1930-45, four points are worth recalling. First, the causal mechanism I have identified was an exogenously induced change in relative prices, reflecting events in the international marketplace. Second, foreign firms provided little of the required entrepreneurship. Third, growth was accomplished without the help of special institutions to provide direction and capital (contrary to Alexander Gerschenkron's model of late industrialization).[61] Fourth, the government played a fairly passive role in promoting industrial development, especially when one

TABLE 3.13

VALUE OF MATERIALS INPUTS AS A PROPORTION OF
VALUE ADDED AT WORLD PRICES, BY INDUSTRY,
UNITED STATES 1947 AND COLOMBIA 1944/45
(Percent)

	United States 1947	Colombia 1944–45
Textiles		
Cotton Yarn	55	56
Cotton Cloth	50	66
Wool Yarn	62	51
Wool Cloth	55	63
Rayon Yarn	37	46
Rayon Cloth	51	71
Paper		
Paper Articles	57	49
Rubber		
Tires	59	47
Shoes	40	
Other Rubber Articles	46	43
Chemicals		
Basic Industrial Chemicals	52	43
Vegetable/Animal Oils/Fats	76	56
Paints	63	41
Pharmaceuticals	38	36
Cosmetics	39	213
Soap	57	74
Petroleum Products	76	28
Nonmetallic Minerals		
Structural Clay Products	27	15
Glass	37	36
China	26	22
Cement	38	29
Nonmetallic Minerals [not elsewhere classified (NEC)]	43	45
Metal Products		
Containers	66	55
Other Metal Products	44	33
Nonelectric Machinery	43	32

Sources: United States: Bureau of the Census, *Census of Manufactures 1947* (Washington 1949), vol. II; Colombia: Chu, "Depression and Industrialization," p. 191.

considers alternative growth paths faced by Colombia. (With export expansion precluded by the Depression, growth now had to depend on other stimuli.)

These aspects of industrialization contrast with the postwar pattern of active government intervention and a prominent role for foreign firms. In the postwar period, Latin American governments have imposed price changes that favor the industrial sector, arguing that the long-term outlook for primary product terms of trade precludes export expansion. Special institutions have been established to finance industrial activities, and high levels of effective protection have been used to encourage domestic manufacturing. Unlike the period discussed here, however, a substantial part of the response has been provided by foreign firms.

Given this contrast, especially the low level of effective protection in the thirties,[62] it is tempting to compare the conclusions suggested by Table 3.13 with the consensus that postwar import substitution has been inefficient, and to speculate on reasons for the difference. The expansion of the thirties may have involved earlier and easier stages in the process of industrialization. Part of the explanation may also lie in the differences between "exogenous" and "endogenous" import substitution strategies. One point is clear. Contrary to the impression left by postwar experience, the indigenous private sector *can* be efficient in responding to new industrial opportunities and thus move the economy in the direction implied by changing opportunities for trade.

Conclusions

There was a marked change in the pattern of industrial development in Colombia after 1930. Relative to GNP, nontraditional manufacturing grew much more rapidly than it had in the twenties. Import substitution became the basic source of growth, with just a few sectors accounting for most of the increase in value added. In contrast, several sectors shared the leadership role during the twenties, and growth in that decade was based largely upon the expansion of domestic demand.

I have tested two alternative models that seek to explain these events—the Chenery model and a relative price model. In addition, I examined the possibility that changes in the supply of credit stimulated manufacturing development, and the possibility that entrepreneurship was a bottleneck in the development process, and that shifts in the supply of entrepreneurship can be used to explain industrial growth.

The Chenery model links manufacturing output to changes in per capita income, market size, and opportunities for trade. It has been applied successfully to the period after World War II on both a cross-section and a time-series basis. However, my results confirm Kuznets's recent pessimism about applying this kind of model to the historical analysis of manufacturing development.[63] First, postwar coefficients poorly predict both the absolute level of manufacturing output and the relative importance of individual sectors in the period 1920-45 (Table 3.3). Second, when the model is estimated with Colombian data, a significant shift appears in the parameter structure between 1920-29 and 1930-45 (Tables 3.6 and 3.7). This shift must be explained outside the model itself.

Much of the discontinuity can be explained by changes in the relative prices of outputs and material inputs. With the onset of the Depression, prices of industrial imports rose relative to export prices as the terms of trade deteriorated, and rose relative to prices of nontraded and import-competing goods as national currencies were devalued. These changes greatly encouraged domestic production of manufactured commodities. The formal model confirms that there was a significant association between relative prices and output changes in those sectors with the most dramatic growth, especially the textile industry.

Changes in the supply of credit do not explain the growth of nontraditional manufacturing in this period. Internal funds were a principal source of financing for industrial corporations, and the limited evidence available suggests that external funds actually were more difficult to obtain in the thirties. The real volume of short-term credit extended by financial institutions was depressed relative to the late twenties, and the supply of long-term funds was constrained both by legal restrictions and by the decline of private mortgage banking. Government institutions engaged in long-term operations were not especially helpful to the industrial sector. Although changes may have occurred in the supply of equity capital, much of the equity supplied was probably a disguised form of reinvested earnings.

If a shift in the supply of entrepreneurship was responsible for industrial development in this period, we would expect new firms to play a prominent role. In fact, no discernible association between changes in the rate of growth of output and the contribution of new establishments appeared (Table 3.12). As the development literature suggests, industrial entrepreneurs had well-defined characteristics, and the group of entrepreneurs active after 1930 may have included a larger number of the foreign born and the better educated than was characteristic of earlier years. However, it is not possible to link any significant shift in the supply of these traits with the development of 1930-45.

In contrast to what is thought to be true of import substitution industrialization in Latin America after World War II, the growth of Colombian manufacturing between 1930 and 1945 produced a fairly efficient industrial sector. Part of the explanation for this difference may be that growth was concentrated in the "simpler" industries, and that these opportunities were largely exhausted by 1945. It may also be significant that growth in the thirties responded to a general signal from the international marketplace—a devaluation of the peso, which raised the price of all imports. Within this general change in the structure of opportunities, domestic firms successfully sought out the profitable investments. In contrast, the postwar signals have been more specific—individual changes in the tariff made to encourage the development of particular industries. Perhaps the most important policy lesson to be learned from the experience of 1930-45 is not only that the indigenous private sector can be responsive to price incentives, but that its judgment in selecting the truly profitable opportunities may be superior to that of central planners.

ENDNOTES FOR CHAPTER 3

1. The opinions expressed in this study are the authors' and do not reflect those of the U.S. Department of Defense, The Congressional Budget Office or The Rand Corporation. The research upon which the study was based was supported by the Foreign Area Fellowship Program of the Joint Committee of the American Council of Learned Societies and the Social Science Research Council. I am grateful to Shane Hunt for having originally interested me in this topic; the work has greatly benefited from the comments of R. Albert Berry, Carlos Díaz-Alejandro, Hugh T. Patrick, and Edwin M. Truman. They bear no responsibility, of course, for any errors that might remain.

2. Hollis Chenery, "Patterns of Industrial Growth," *American Economic Review* L (September 1960): 624-654; Hollis Chenery and Lance Taylor, "Development Patterns: Among Countries and Over Time," *Review of Economics and Statistics* L (November 1968): 391-416.

3. United Nations, Economic Commission for Latin America (ECLA), *Analyses and Projections of Economic Development,* vol. III: *The Economic Development of Colombia, Statistical Appendix* (E/CN.12/365/add.1/rev.1, Santiago 1957), p. 1.

4. Celso Furtado, *Economic Development of Latin America* (Cambridge: Cambridge University Press, 1970), Chapter 11; Albert O. Hirschman, "Political Economy of Import Substitution," *Quarterly Journal of Economics* LXXXII (February 1968): 1-32; Alexander Kafka, "The Theoretical Interpretation of Latin American Economic Development" in H.S. Ellis and H. C. Wallich eds., *Economic Development for Latin America* (London: Macmillan, 1961), pp. 1 ff.; Santiago Macario, "Protectionism and Industrialization in Latin America," *Economic Bulletin for Latin America* IX (March 1964): 61-63; D. M. Phelps, "Industrial Expansion in Temperate South America," *American Economic Review* XXV (June 1935): 273-282; ECLA, "The Growth and Decline of Import Substitution in Brazil," *Economic Bulletin for Latin America* IX (March 1964): 5.

5. Aldo Ferrer, *The Argentine Economy* (Berkeley: University of California Press, 1964), pp. 164-165; Werner Baer, *Industrialization and Economic Development in Brazil* (Homewood, Illinois: Irwin, 1965), pp. 20 ff.; Werner Baer and Isaac Kerstenetsky, "Import Substitution and Industrialization in Brazil," *American Economic Review* LIV (May 1964): 413; Celso Furtado, *The Economic Growth of Brazil* (Berkeley: University of California Press, 1965), pp. 216 ff., ECLA; "Growth and Decline," pp. 11 ff.; Paul T. Ellsworth, *Chile: An Economy in Transition* (New York, Macmillan, 1945); Oscar Muñoz, "An Essay on the Process of Industrialization in Chile Since 1914," *Yale Economic Essays* VIII (Fall 1968): 1965-1968.

6. One exception is a recent study of the Argentine textile industry, which found that price changes played a substantial role. See Alberto Petrocolla, *Prices, Import Substitution and Investment in the Argentine Textile Industry (1920-39)* (Buenos Aires: Instituto Torcuato Di Tella, Centro de Investigaciones Económicas, 1968).

7. Growth rates are expressed throughout as compound rates. Quantitative comparisons in this section are based on data from ECLA, *Statistical Appendix*.

8. William P. McGreevey, "The Economic Development of Colombia" (Ph.D. dissertation, Massachusetts Institute of Technology, 1965), Appendix Table II-G.

9. These growth rates, and the following comparisons, are based on an index that combines my estimates for the output of nontraditional manufacturing (see below) and the ECLA estimates for traditional sectors after correcting the ECLA indices for splicing errors. See ECLA, *Statistical Appendix*, p. 140. Details are provided in the appendix to this chapter.

10. International Standard Industrial Classification (ISIC) groups 23 (Textiles), 27 (Paper), 30 (Rubber), 31 (Chemicals), 32 (Petroleum and Coal Products), 33 (Nonmetallic Mineral Products), 34 (Basic Metals), 35 (Metal Products), 36 (Nonelectric Machinery), 37 (Electric Machinery; omitted here because it did not exist), and 38 (Transport Equipment). See Chenery and Taylor, "Development Patterns" pp. 410-411; W. G. Hoffman, *The Growth of Industrial Economies* (Manchester, 1958), pp. 2-3, 110-126; Simon Kuznets, *Modern Economic Growth* (New Haven, 1966), pp. 135 ff.

    The term "nontraditional" has been used in some other studies in a rather different sense, to describe "modern" firms, with size of firm frequently used as an indicator of modernity. I wish to distinguish that meaning from the one used here.

11. ECLA, *Statistical Appendix*, p. 140.

12. For a discussion of some of the shortcomings of the ECLA indices, see David S. C. Chu, "The Great Depression and Industrialization in Latin America" (Ph.D. dissertation, Yale University, 1972), p. 45.

13. Chenery and Taylor, "Development Patterns."

14. Their equations for small countries exporting primary products were used to estimate normal value added for Colombia.

15. For the subperiod 1923-29, a significance standard of 15 percent is used in making these classifications because of the crude nature of the per capita income estimate for two of the years (1923-24) in that short period. No per capita income data are available for 1923-24. To generate observations for per capita income in 1923-24, the per capita income growth rate for 1925/26-1972/28 was extrapolated backwards.

16. The United States was Colombia's principal source of imports, followed by Germany and Great Britain. Since the pound was depreciating relative to the dollar, the peso was actually appreciating relative to the pound until 1933.

17. Measured by the dollar price of the peso.

18. Until April, 1935, the exchange certificates were valid for only thirty days in order to prevent exchange speculation. When the limited auction system was introduced, the central bank announced that it would require the sale of 15 percent of all export proceeds at the old buying rate in order to cover the government's exchange needs at a favorable price. The practice of confiscatory sales remained a feature of Colombia's exchange control system throughout 1930-32 with the rate and proportion confiscated changing from time to time.

19. See Colombia, Ministerio de Hacienda, *Informe 1933*, p. 95.

20. Aggregate indices for P_I and T in this calculation are based on product class indices weighted by value added in 1944-45. (For sources of data see the appendix to this chapter; and Chu, "Depression and Industrialization," Appendix B-2. Were weights based on market size, $(1+T)_{1936}/(1+T)_{1927}$ would be 1.40, while $(P_I)_{1936}/(P_I)_{1927}$ would probably be little changed.

21. Departmento Administrativo Nacional de Estadística (DANE), *Primer Censo Industrial de Colombia 1945: Resumen General*, (Bogotá: DANE, 1947), pp. 46-47. This figure should be considered approximate, because of valuation problems.

22. Labor presumably constituted a significant proportion of construction inputs. Wages in construction appear to move parallel with the general price level in the thirties and early forties. See Miguel Urrutia and Mario Arrubla, eds., *Compendio de Estadísticas Históricas de Colombia* (Bogotá: Universidad Nacional de Colombia, Dirección de Divulgación Cultural, 1970), p. 45.

23. The model is a straightforward adaptation of the scheme put forward by Marc Nerlove in *The Dynamics of Supply: Estimation of Farmers' Response to Price* (Baltimore: Johns Hopkins Press, 1958), Chapter IX.

24. If all prices in the economy change by a constant percent, then the incentives facing domestic producers remain unchanged.

25. This is true except during World War II, which will receive special treatment in order to take this and other factors into account.

26. To the extent that exchange controls were used during the Depression years, the assumption is likewise inappropriate for that period. However, the assumption is considerably *more* inappropriate for the war years; hence the dummy variable.

27. Substituting (5a) and (5b) in (4) first gives us:

$$\ln Q = (1-\gamma) \ln Q_{-1} + \gamma [a_0 + a_1 \left\{(1-\beta) \ln P^*_{-1} + \beta \ln P_{-1}\right\}$$

$$+ a_2 \left\{(1-\beta) \ln I^*_{-1} + \beta \ln I_{-1}\right\}$$

$$+ a_3 \ln Y + a_4 D + u]$$

adding $\gamma(1-\beta) [a_3 \ln Y_{-1} + a_4 D_{-1} + u_{-1}]$ to both sides of this equation yields:

$$\ln Q + \gamma(1-\beta) [a_3 \ln Y_{-1} + a_4 D_{-1} + u_{-1}]$$
$$= (1-\gamma) \ln Q_{-1} + \gamma [a_0 + a_1 \left\{(1-\beta) \ln P^*_{-1} + \beta \ln P_{-1}\right\}$$
$$+ a_2 \left\{(1-\beta) \ln I^*_{-1} + \beta \ln I_{-1}\right\}$$
$$+ a_3 \left\{(1-\beta) \ln Y_{-1} + \ln Y\right\}$$
$$+ a_4 \left\{(1-\beta) D_{-1} + D\right\}$$
$$+ u + (1-\beta) u_{-1}]$$

The right-hand side includes the expression for $\gamma \ln Q^*_{-1}$, and with (3), thus yields equation (6).

28. If W is indeed normally independently distributed, this implies that in (6):
$$u = (1-\beta)u_{-1} + \varepsilon, \quad \varepsilon \text{ normally independently distributed.}$$
Although it is reasonable to assume that perhaps $u = \rho u_{-1} + \varepsilon$, no obvious theoretical justification exists for requiring $\rho = (1-\beta)$. However, the alternative to making this assumption (excluding iterative techniques) is to apply a two-stage procedure suggested by Zvi Griliches in "Distributed Lags: A Survey," *Econometrica* XXXV (January 1967): 41 ff. Unfortunately, I am limited to annual observations and am trying to explain events over the rather short time period 1928-45; not enough degrees of freedom can be found to support the alternative estimating procedure.

However, if $\beta = 1$ (i.e., expectations adjust immediately), a much less restrictive assumption about the error term will insure that ordinary least squares (OLS) yields consistent parameter estimates. If $\beta = 1$, then (7) becomes (7b) or (7c), and if u is assumed to be normally independently distributed (a more plausible assumption), OLS will give consistent estimates.

29. At 10 percent.

30. Besides the tests on π_1 and π_2 already described, "best" results were selected by using the following sequence of rules, with significance tests always applied at the 10 percent level:

(1) Equations were discarded when none of the coefficients on P, I, and Y were significantly different from zero.

(2) In choosing between partial adjustment and simple expectations models, I made use of the fact that the form of (9a) differs from that of (9b) only by the inclusion of lagged values of Y (and D, where appropriate). Thus when the Y coefficient was significant in the first, the significance of the lagged Y coefficient in the second was used to discriminate between the two specifications. When the Y coefficients were significant in neither, the equation requiring the simpler assumption on the error term was selected (i.e., a partial adjustment model, 9b).

(3) Results that violated a priori restrictions on γ and β were discarded. (This occurred only once.)

(4) Adjusted r^2 was used to discriminate between equations that survived all other tests.

31. The establishment of petroleum refining in Colombia was the direct result of government development policies. Oil concession contracts required that a refinery be constructed as soon as the exploiting company's crude oil production reached 4000 metric tons per day. The first such refinery began full service in 1922 and a second was inaugurated in 1939. See Ministerio de Minas, *Memoria 1940*, p. 75; *Memoria 1942*, p. XXVI; *Memoria 1946*, vol. III, p. 83.

32. Chenery's more recent estimates of the elasticity of manufacturing output with respect to GNP per capita generally range between 1 and 2 for small countries. See Chenery and Taylor, "Development Patterns," pp. 407-408. The estimates in Table 3.8 imply elasticities with respect to absolute GNP greatly in excess of 2 for most industries; elasticities with respect to GNP per capita would be even higher.

33. Prices for paper outputs actually declined relative to the general price level.

34. For data on the structure of the financial system, see Chu, "Depression and Industrialization," p. 138.

35. These estimates of internal financing are probably biased downward (and the estimates of equity financing biased correspondingly upward) because of the difficulties in distinguishing capitalization of earnings from actual equity financing; only increases in equity issues outstanding which could be unambiguously identified as capitalization of earnings were included in internally generated funds. However, these estimates do agree with postwar experience, especially for large corporations. See Robert W. Adler, "The Organized Financial Markets of Colombia," (Ph.D. dissertation, University of Oregon, 1965), p. 175; *Economic Growth of Colombia, Report of a Mission Sent to Colombia in 1970 by the World Bank* (Baltimore, The Johns Hopkins Press, 1972), p. 114. The exception is ECLA's estimate for 1941-52 that only 22 percent of all corporate funds came from internal sources. See ECLA, *Colombia*, p. 128.

36. Alfonso Manero's 1952 report to the World Bank on Colombian capital markets confirms this point: "The most widely used method of financing industrial enterprises in Colombia during the last twenty-five years has been the sale of common stock in privately-owned corporations." *Report on the Colombian Capital Market* (Washington, International Bank for Reconstruction and Development, 1952), p. 11.

37. Chu, "Depression and Industrialization," p. 149.

38. Commercial banks were not generally permitted to offer loans of more than one year, and most loans were limited to a three-month term. See Robert Triffin, *Money and Banking in Colombia* (Washington, D.C.: Board of Governors, The Federal Reserve System, 1944), p. 9. Of course, short-term credit whose renewal is expected and that is, in fact, renewed becomes long-term credit; some evidence exists to show that this practice was not unknown. See Manero, *Report*, pp. 10-11.

39. Triffin, *Money and Banking in Colombia*, Table VIIb. Triffin's data are in nominal terms, but they can be deflated by the price index for imported nonelectric machinery to get an approximate "real" series. (For the price index, see the Appendix to this chapter.)

40. The first year for which data on industrial loans are available is 1937. Between 1937 and 1945 new loans to industry and all commercial loans moved in parallel; new loans to industry represented about one-fifth of all new loans, and this marginal share was quite stable from year to year. See Chu, "Depression and Industrialization," p. 164.

41. See, for example, Manero, *Report*, p. 16.

42. For a detailed discussion of the role of official agencies in long-term lending, see Chu, "Depression and Industrialization," pp. 166-168.

43. Robert Triffin, "La moneda y las instituciones bancarias de Colombia," *Colombia economica* III (mayo 1945): pp. 593-595.

44. Taken from unpublished balance sheets of the Instituto de Fomento Industrial.

45. See Liborio Cuellar Gomez, *Desarrollo de las Empresas Industriales Inscritas en la Bolsa durante la Guerra* (Bogotá: 1946), pp. 48 ff. This excludes financial corporations.

46. Adler, "Organized Financial Markets," p. 323.

47. See Chu, "Depression and Industrialization," p. 176 and Appendix A.

48. See James K. Weekly, "Security Markets in a Developing Economy: The Case of Colombia," *Inter-American Economic Affairs* XIX (Autumn 1965): pp. 75-76.

49. Analysis of the reports and balance sheets of selected Colombian textile firms for the period 1935-52 indicates that most of the companies distributed as dividends between two-thirds and five-sixths of net (reported) earnings in almost every year. See Manero, *Report*, p. 14. This phenomenon implies no contradiction to my earlier assertion that internal funds provided a substantial base of industrial financing, since internal funds include depreciation.

50. Weekly, "Security Markets," pp. 64-65.

51. In Manero's sample of textile enterprises, sale of new stock over the period 1935-52 equalled almost one-half of dividend disbursements. See Manero, *Report*, p. 14.

52. For example, Thomas C. Cochran, "Cultural Factors in Economic Development," *Journal of Economic History* XX (December 1960): pp. 515-530; Albert Lauterbach, *Enterprise in Latin America: Business Attitudes in a Developing Country* (Ithaca: Cornell University Press, 1966). On Colombia in particular see Seymour Wurfel, *Foreign Enterprise in Colombia* (Chapel Hill: University of North Carolina Press, 1965), pp. 32-33.

53. Ministerio de la Economia Nacional, *Directorio de la Industria Manufacturera de Colombia 1941;* Ministerio de Comercio e Industrias, *Directorio de la Industria Manufacturera de Colombia 1947.* The sample includes any firm with a *capital* (roughly, book value of equity liabilities) of more than 250,000 pesos (U. S. $150,000) in 1941, or 500,000 pesos (U.S. $280,000) in 1947.

54. The characteristics of entrepreneurs in Table 3.10 do not differ significantly from those of entrepreneurs in present-day Colombia or elsewhere in Latin America. See Aaron Lipman, *El Empresario Bogotano* (Bogotá: Ediciones Tercer Mundo y Facultad de Sociología, Universidad Nacional de Colombia, 1966); George Hadley, *Some Characteristics of Colombian Industry* (Bogotá: Universidad de Las Andes, 1965), pp. 1-2; Fernando H. Cardoso, *El Empresario Industrial en América Latina 2. Brazil* (E/CN.12/642/add.2, Santiago 1963); and Guillermo Briones, *El Empresario Industrial en América Latina, 3. Chile* (E/CN.12/642/add.3, Santiago 1963).

55. For the available data, see McGreevey, "Development of Colombia," Appendix Tables I-C-I and I-C-2.

56. Chu, "Depression and Industrialization," p. 124.

57. See, in particular, Ronald Soligo and Joseph Stern, "Tariff Protection, Import Substitution, and Investment Efficiency," *Pakistan Development Review* V (Summer 1965): 249-269.

58. On the theoretical side, Stephen Guisinger and Augustine Tan demonstrate that negative value added can exist even when the economy is "efficiently" operating on the production possibility frontier. Stephen Guisinger and Augustine Tan, "Negative Value Added and the Theory of Effective Protection," *Quarterly Journal of Economics* LXXXIII (August 1969): 425-427; "Differential Tariffs, Negative Value Added and the Theory of Effective Protection," *American Economic Review* LX (March 1970): 109-110. On the empirical side, if domestic input-output data are deflated by import prices (including tariffs) to arrive at world price figures (our procedure), then where the tariff on the final product is redundant, a downward bias appears in the calculated world price value added. The failure to allow for substitution among material inputs may impart a further downward bias. See H. G. Grubel and P. J. Lloyd, "Factor Substitution and Effective Tariff Rates," *Review of Economic Studies* XXXVIII (January 1971): 101. On the other hand, ignoring the possible substitution of primary for material factors of production biases world price value added upward, if such substitution in fact exists. See Bela Balassa, Stephen Guisinger and Daniel M. Schydlowsky, "The Effective Rates of Protection and the Question of Labor Protection in the United States: A Comment," *Journal of Political Economy* LXXXVIII (September/October 1970): 1160.

59. Ratios for the United States are at domestic rather than world prices and thus may sometimes overstate American efficiency. (However, in 1947 tariffs had a doubtful effect on domestic prices in the United States, and in most cases domestic prices were probably the same as world prices.) The use of cost-insurance-freight (CIF) import prices to deflate Colombian values may further slightly understate its competitiveness relative to the United States (assuming that material inputs have a lower value per unit volume than final products).

60. Comparability of the data for metals and metals manufactures is not good. Moreover, the quality of the Colombian estimates is weakest for these sectors.

61. Alexander Gerschenkron, *Economic Backwardness in Historical Perspective* (Cambridge, Massachusetts: Belknap Press of Harvard University Press, 1962), pp. 343-344.

62. See Chu, "Depression and Industrialization," p. 25.

63. Kuznets, *Modern Economic Growth*, pp. 436-437.

APPENDIX A

INDUSTRIAL PRODUCTION AND PRICES: NONTRADITIONAL MANUFACTURING

Physical Production Indices

The United Nations International Standard Industrial Classification (ISIC)[1] was used as the basis for defining two-digit industries, with the following modifications:

(1) Rayon yarn manufacture was included with textiles rather than chemicals so that its development could be considered along with the rest of the textile industry.

(2) Repair activities were usually excluded, because of difficulties in estimating their output. The exception is railway repairs, included in ISIC 38 (transport equipment).

Each two-digit industry was disaggregated into a set of product classes, and each product class into a group of subcomponents, where possible. A physical production index was constructed for each product class or subcomponent.

Frequently, direct output series were not available, and indirect estimates were based on the apparent consumption of inputs. Census data were used to select inputs specific to the industry, and these were weighted based on their relative importance in the period July 1, 1944 to June 30, 1945 (the period covered by Colombia's first industrial census).[2] Thus for a particular product class by subcomponent (p_j) the output index was computed as:

$$p_j = \sum_k w_{jk} m_k$$

where:
m_k is the amount of material input k consumed by the Colombian economy, and

w_{jk} is the amount of input k used to manufacture product j in 1944-45.

Inputs derived entirely from imports were often used because their apparent consumption could be estimated more accurately. The use of imported inputs as a proxy for output is the reason the production series start with 1923. Detailed foreign trade data are not available for earlier years.

In some cases, output series estimated from input data displayed large year-to-year variations around a basic trend. This was particularly true during the war years for series based on imported inputs. To reduce such illusory variation where necessary, an arbitrary smoothing scheme was adopted. The raw estimates for the previous year and the current year were averaged to give a new current year observation ($\hat{P}_{jt}$). Thus:

$$\hat{P}_{jt} = \frac{P_{jt} + P_{jt-1}}{2}$$

The basic method used to compute each product class is presented in Table A-1.[3]

Value Added

Table A-2 presents value added estimates by product class based upon data from the 1944-45 industrial census. The census *excludes* profits from its reported data on value added and value of output. To produce a profit series, I reestimated the value of output to include profits and then deducted the original value of output. Since the census figures on value of output include depreciation, the value added estimates presented here are net of depreciation.

Value of output was reestimated using the detailed input data provided by the census. The census reported inputs and outputs using the same product code; inputs were reported at market prices, including profits (as well as distribution and transportation costs). Therefore, the detailed input data were used to derive a series of implicit prices, and these prices were applied to the physical volume of output to yield revised value of output figures.[4]

One of the problems with the value added estimated in Table A-2 is that they may be distorted by wartime conditions. Compared with estimates of value added in the early postwar period, however, only the estimate for value added in ISIC 32 (petroleum) appears unreasonable.[5]

Two-Digit Indices

The product class indices (p_j) were weighted by the value added estimates (v_{ij}) of Table A-2 to provide two-digit indices (Q_i) of industrial production (Table A-3):

$$Q_i = \sum_j v_{ij} P_j$$

The strongest indices are those for textiles and petroleum; the weakest are those for metals and machinery. The lack of suitable data prevents the construction of transport equipment and rubber industry indices for the early years. The nonelectric machinery index probably picks up some metal product output, but no way could be found to separate these two groups.

Output Prices

Direct observations on the domestic prices of nontraditional manufactures are not available for the period 1928-45. Proxy series were constructed by capitalizing on the fact that imports satisfied a substantial proportion of demand for nontraditional manufactures. Domestic price was assumed to equal the import price plus the tariff. The proxy series for two-digit industries (Table A-4) was built up from product class cost, insurance, and freight (CIF) import unit values using value added in 1944-45 as weights. Because of the nature of the data base, some price indices in Tables A-4 and A-5 may appear unstable when year-to-year comparisons are made. However, the basic trends are clearly discernible.

TABLE A-1
METHODOLOGY FOR CONSTRUCTING PRODUCT INDICES

Product Class	Index Based On:	Product Class	Index Based On:
ISIC 23		**ISIC 32**	
Cotton ginning	(1)	Petroleum products	(1)
Cotton yarn	(2)	**ISIC 33**	
Cotton fabrics	(2)	China	(3)
Wool yarn	(2)	Glass	(3)
Wool fabrics	(2)	Cement	(1), (3)
Rayon yarn	(3)	Nonmetallic minerals NEC	(2)
Rayon fabrics	(2)	**ISIC 34**	
ISIC 27		Iron and steel	(1)
Paper/paperboard articles	(3)	Nonferrous metals	(3)
ISIC 30		**ISIC 35**	
Tires	(3)	Containers	(3)
Other rubber articles	(1), (3)	Other metal products	(1), (3)
ISIC 31		**ISIC 36**	
Basic industrial chemicals	(1), (3)	Nonelectric machinery	(3)
Fertilizer	(3)	**ISIC 38**	
Paints	(3)	Railway repairs	(1)
Pharmaceuticals	(3)	Vehicle assembly	(3)
Soap	(3)		
Cosmetics	(3)		
Miscellaneous chemical products NEC	(1), (3)		

Source: Chu, "Depression and Industrialization," Appendix Table B-1.12.

(1) Actual output data
(2) Input data, including imported inputs
(3) Imported inputs only

TABLE A-2
NET VALUE ADDED, BY PRODUCT CLASS, 1944–45
(In Millions of Pesos)

Industry/Product Class	Profits	Wages	Value Added	Industry/Product Class	Profits	Wages	Value Added
ISIC 23				ISIC 32			
Cotton ginning	16.1	4.5	0.3	PETROLEUM Products	31.07	1.73	32.80
Cotton yarn	34.2	10.1	20.6	ISIC 33			
Cotton fabrics			44.3	China	1.18	0.64	1.82
Wool yarn	1.2	0.2	1.4	Glass	1.26	1.35	2.61
Wool fabrics	8.2	1.8	10.0	Cement	4.70	2.56	7.26
Rayon yarn	2.3	0.6	2.9	Nonmetallic minerals NEC	2.29	1.49	3.78
Rayon fabrics	11.7	3.2	14.9	NONMETALLIC MINERALS			15.47
TEXTILES			94.4	ISIC 34			
ISIC 27				Iron and steel	1.18	0.20	1.38
Paper/paperboard articles	0.66	0.37	1.03	Nonferrous metals	0.03	0.11	0.14
PAPER			1.03	BASIC METALS			1.52
ISIC 30				ISIC 35			
Tires	0.13	0.06	0.19	Containers	0.20	0.24	0.44
Other rubber articles	1.87	0.69	2.06	Other metal products	2.75	0.77	3.52
RUBBER			2.25	METAL PRODUCTS			3.96
ISIC 31				ISIC 36			
Basic industrial chemicals	0.60	0.46	1.06	NONELECTRIC MACHINERY	4.8	4.8	9.6
Fertilizer	0.05	0.09	0.14	ISIC 38			
Paints	0.38	0.16	0.54	Railway repairs	0.0	0.3	0.3
Pharmaceuticals	7.28	2.16	9.44	Vehicle assembly	0.0	0.1	0.1
Soap	3.85	0.83	4.68	TRANSPORT EQUIPMENT			0.4
Cosmetics	0.12	0.24	0.36				
Miscellaneous chemical products NEC	3.47	0.82	4.29				
CHEMICALS			20.51				

Source: Chu, "Depression and Industrialization," Appendix Table B-1.22, and DANE, *Primer Censo Industrial*.

TABLE A-3
OUTPUT INDICES BY TWO-DIGIT INDUSTRY, 1923-45
1945 = 100

Year	Textiles	Paper	Rubber	Chemicals	Petroleum Products	Nonmetallic Minerals	Basic Metals	Metal Products	Nonelectric Machinery	Transport Equipment
1923	9.8	9.0	NA	43.5	6.8	8.5	1.5	18.9	15.0	NA
1924	10.2	7.8	NA	44.6	6.7	9.5	1.7	27.5	15.2	NA
1925	11.6	9.7	NA	51.9	11.6	14.9	2.8	29.3	23.5	32.8
1926	12.2	13.2	NA	57.7	14.7	16.6	7.6	34.8	27.7	37.2
1927	13.5	13.2	NA	62.2	24.1	22.4	8.5	48.2	42.7	44.1
1928	9.6	19.3	NA	62.7	29.5	25.6	5.9	54.8	61.1	48.4
1929	7.9	15.1	NA	58.5	33.8	20.2	5.3	43.1	39.2	49.6
1930	7.1	14.4	NA	53.2	26.1	14.9	3.8	33.2	22.5	60.6
1931	9.8	9.8	NA	46.5	27.6	13.2	2.8	34.8	7.2	54.2
1932	13.8	9.7	NA	46.7	22.3	16.6	2.3	31.9	20.8	52.6
1933	23.6	8.1	1.5	56.6	20.3	19.8	2.5	45.3	20.8	53.6
1934	29.8	14.0	5.7	60.2	32.8	30.9	3.3	59.4	28.1	56.3
1935	34.5	43.2	6.4	62.6	34.6	33.7	4.0	68.6	33.5	60.4
1936	39.9	103.7	8.2	70.9	51.4	40.5	2.8	96.4	45.3	76.9
1937	52.8	131.1	12.3	88.5	59.1	45.3	3.3	104.9	48.0	82.4
1938	49.0	120.4	24.6	84.5	67.2	57.8	4.5	141.1	50.3	98.0
1939	61.5	133.5	29.8	102.2	70.2	64.2	4.5	181.0	50.5	111.3
1940	53.0	110.5	34.1	90.3	73.5	67.2	10.9	170.6	37.0	98.0
1941	99.6	129.4	30.0	98.5	79.9	81.8	14.5	133.4	40.6	103.6
1942	96.5	65.1	47.3	99.4	76.2	72.5	14.9	83.2	39.3	78.4
1943	99.1	116.0	76.1	94.1	84.2	86.8	20.2	78.2	35.4	76.5
1944	91.5	154.2	92.7	101.4	93.3	95.0	55.8	78.2	61.3	89.5
1945	100.0	100.0	100.0	100.0	100.0	100.0	100.0	100.0	100.0	100.0

Source: Chu, "Depression and Industrialization," Appendix Table B-3.2.
NA = not available

TABLE A-4
PRICE INDICES BY TWO-DIGIT INDUSTRY, 1923-45
1928 = 100

Year	Textiles	Paper[a]	Rubber[b]	Chemicals	Petroleum Products	Nonmetallic Minerals	Basic Metals	Metal Products	Nonelectric Machinery	Transport Equipment
1923	106.1	101.7	152.6	97.6	155.0	169.9	100.0	97.3	96.2	65.6
1924	102.5	103.5	122.2	89.0	124.8	139.5	97.7	85.1	103.2	103.2
1925	98.5	100.6	139.9	92.4	142.4	125.3	109.6	85.2	64.5	96.3
1926	89.0	109.4	141.9	104.5	160.1	141.5	103.1	93.3	72.7	146.7
1927	73.8	109.4	146.7	100.2	116.5	115.4	99.9	91.0	85.1	170.8
1928	100.0	100.0	100.0	100.0	100.0	100.0	100.0	100.0	100.0	100.0
1929	89.1	81.8	83.2	101.1	89.6	103.7	93.6	91.2	92.2	106.9
1930	78.1	63.5	66.4	102.3	79.2	107.4	87.4	82.3	84.5	113.8
1931	81.2	48.4	95.4	146.0	109.6	124.7	76.8	93.4	116.4	82.6
1932	84.5	33.2	124.3	189.7	140.1	142.0	66.2	104.4	148.4	51.5
1933	92.6	36.9	124.6	211.8	101.6	160.3	91.9	101.2	181.5	98.7
1934	118.7	41.4	162.2	308.6	111.7	208.3	121.9	168.9	272.6	126.4
1935	114.3	73.3	213.6	341.1	231.3	216.5	129.5	127.0	277.4	149.9
1936	125.3	82.2	202.0	316.3	249.9	206.0	121.6	113.3	258.7	182.7
1937	134.6	116.3	223.4	348.9	283.5	263.2	176.8	118.6	299.5	191.5
1938	133.0	110.2	222.1	339.4	188.4	271.3	183.8	105.7	318.3	198.7
1939	128.8	78.0	208.7	308.0	131.1	257.0	169.8	109.5	334.1	197.7
1940	133.7	117.1	193.8	327.6	154.8	278.5	197.7	121.0	360.6	179.3
1941	148.8	164.0	208.8	345.1	148.2	364.9	187.5	174.5	378.7	190.3
1942	194.4	112.0	269.9	383.2	135.8	557.6	240.5	244.8	399.1	198.0
1943	234.8	91.5	295.7	364.1	181.1	580.6	223.6	216.2	451.3	230.4
1944	233.7	134.7	290.0	366.0	176.5	386.5	173.5	196.2	448.8	214.4
1945	266.5	101.1	219.2	393.5	193.9	398.8	185.6	176.1	422.5	207.2

Source: Chu, "Depression and Industrialization," Appendix Table B-3.2.

[a]Paper articles only.
[b]Excludes tires and shoes.

TABLE A-5

PRICE INDICES FOR MATERIAL INPUTS BY TWO-DIGIT INDUSTRY, 1923-45
1928 = 100

Year	Textiles	Paper	Rubber	Chemicals	Petroleum Products	Nonmetallic Minerals	Basic Metals	Metal Products	Nonelectric/Transport Machinery/Equipment
1923	116.1	89.5	76.3	100.0	141.5	62.2	127.2	100.7	100.0
1924	114.6	87.5	88.1	97.3	141.5	64.8	90.4	99.7	97.9
1925	107.4	81.0	97.5	90.3	85.0	69.7	105.8	110.1	109.4
1926	93.7	88.4	97.5	107.2	141.5	96.4	101.3	104.2	103.7
1927	89.6	87.4	100.0	95.1	114.3	98.3	83.9	100.9	100.4
1928	100.0	100.0	100.0	100.0	100.0	100.0	100.0	100.0	100.0
1929	92.3	82.9	92.4	95.0	102.7	86.5	101.6	94.7	93.6
1930	84.3	65.9	100.0	86.8	96.6	60.6	103.3	89.4	87.3
1931	74.6	70.5	76.3	84.0	65.3	50.6	74.6	79.0	76.1
1932	65.3	74.9	77.1	79.6	75.5	34.5	38.7	67.8	64.9
1933	65.2	84.5	83.1	92.7	64.4	41.3	49.4	92.8	90.8
1934	106.2	91.5	78.8	134.1	113.6	57.6	76.9	120.0	116.5
1935	110.3	93.3	83.1	126.1	119.7	61.1	90.9	130.4	125.8
1936	110.6	90.1	89.8	122.3	117.0	65.4	88.6	122.5	117.8
1937	122.2	115.1	101.7	140.1	136.1	71.6	141.3	173.6	171.4
1938	109.1	114.3	89.8	116.9	136.7	78.4	131.5	182.6	180.2
1939	105.6	103.5	89.8	119.3	112.9	85.4	120.7	167.5	165.4
1940	121.4	128.4	101.7	126.3	121.1	77.0	137.1	192.3	191.6
1941	131.7	144.4	114.4	137.3	124.5	75.6	150.3	184.3	181.8
1942	188.6	182.6	255.9	172.4	131.3	81.5	186.8	237.4	238.2
1943	219.4	200.3	174.6	174.3	128.6	98.2	184.9	214.6	214.0
1944	221.3	177.0	211.9	184.9	136.7	119.3	158.9	172.4	167.4
1945	238.5	62.3	372.9	185.8	136.1	157.0	165.9	183.7	178.9

Source: Chu, "Depression and Industrialization," Appendix Table B-3.6.

Material Inputs for Nontraditional Manufacturing

Indices were constructed for the price of material inputs in each two-digit industry (Table A-5). The method was to weight price indices for the major material input(s) of each product class by the value added of that product class in 1944-45. Since a substantial proportion of industrial intermediates was imported, product class input price indices were generally based on import unit values, assuming that the domestic price equalled the import price plus the tariff.

ENDNOTES FOR APPENDIX A

1. United Nations, *Indexes to the International Standard Industrial Classification of all Economic Activities* (ST/STAT/ser.M/4/rev.1/add.1, New York 1959).

2. DANE, *Primer Censo.*

3. For details of the construction of individual indices see Chu, "Depression and Industrialization," Appendix B-1.

4. For further details, and for tests of the accuracy of the estimates, see Chu, "Depression and Industrialization," Appendix B-1.2.

5. See ECLA, *Colombia*, p. 273.

Chapter 4

The Effects of Learning on Employment and Labor Productivity in the Colombian Metal Products Sector
Leonard Dudley

This chapter examines the learning process in twenty-five industries in the metal products sector, over a seven-year period from 1959 to 1966. The object is to determine both the importance and the nature of this process in Colombia, and to consider its implications for government policy. The period chosen was one of relatively moderate growth for the economy as a whole (gross national product [GNP] increased at about 5 percent annually) but of rapid growth for the metals products sector (value added increased at an average annual rate of over 12 percent). In the discussion of interindustry differences, a distinction will be made both in the type of learning (cumulative output versus elapsed time) and in the learning agent (firm versus worker). Part I below will present various hypotheses of technological change. Part II will discuss in detail the learning hypothesis and its application to metal products production. Part III will then test these hypotheses empirically.

This chapter will have less to say with regard to policy and the optimal form of intervention. Static trade theory states that subsidies are superior to tariffs, so the wall of tariffs and import licenses behind which much of the observed increase in Colombian production occurred might clearly be suboptimal. The types of subsidies warranting consideration will depend upon findings about the nature of the learning process given in Part IV.

Finally, in view of the recent interest in objectives other than output, this chapter will consider the possibility of a conflict between increases in productivity and increases in employment.

PART I

ALTERNATIVE EXPLANATIONS OF PRODUCTIVITY CHANGE

A number of different explanations of productivity change are available in the economic literature. R. M. Solow has suggested a production function in which output per worker, π, is a function of capital per worker, k, and disembodied technological change occurs at a uniform annual rate, t.[1]

$$\pi = f(k,t) \qquad f_1 > 0, \ f_2 > 0 \qquad (1)$$

For a country like Colombia, in the early stages of import substitution, technical change may appear to occur in this embodied form. Over time transformations other than changes in the capital/labor ratio are likely and may lead to a significant relationship between productivity and time. But this catch-all specification indicates little about the nature of such transformations.

A possibility quite readily fitted into this neoclassical framework is that productivity is a function of the scale of the firm or the industry. To equation (1) is added a scale factor, S.

$$\pi = f(k, t, S) \tag{1'}$$

One must ask, however, whether these economies of scale are reversible. Would they disappear if the scale of operation of the industry or firm were reduced? If not, one might suspect that such economies were not so much a function of the static scale of output as a function of past production experience.

Richard R. Nelson has argued that instead of there being a single technology at a point in time, there may be different types of manufacturing firms among which gaps in technology may exist.[2] To state the hypothesis in simplified form, for one group—the modern firms—the productivity function may well be of the type of equation (1').

$$\pi_m = f_m(k, t, S)$$

For the craft firms, productivity is of the simplest neoclassical type with no technical change.[3]

$$\pi_c = f_c(k)$$

At the same capital labor ratio $\pi_c < \pi_m$.

Under these dualism assumptions, the observed productivity increases in Colombian metal products would be interpreted as the consequence partly of expansion in the modern sector at the expense of the craft sector,[4] and partly of technical change within the modern sector.

This simple version of dualism holds only if over time a typical firm in the low-productivity group remains at its initial low level of productivity. If, as time passes, firms are somehow able to acquire whatever factors are missing, they may close the productivity gap. For any particular firm, low productivity may be only a temporary state left behind as the firm gains experience. A dualism model, taking this into account, becomes essentially indistinguishable from a model of learning-by-doing.

A number of empirical studies suggest that learning from production experience is an important explanatory variable. Even with a constant capital/labor ratio and a constant "state of the art," productivity may increase substantially as production experience increases. Productivity is then a function of the capital/labor ratio, of scale, and of the level of experience, G:

$$\pi = f(k, S, G) \qquad f_3 > 0 \tag{2}$$

This learning hypothesis has the advantages of being both consistent with direct observation of metal products activities and capable of explaining substantial increases in productivity over time in various countries.[5] The remaining problem of choosing the most appropriate measure of G will be addressed in the next section.

PART II

A SPECIFICATION OF THE LEARNING HYPOTHESIS FOR METAL PRODUCTS

This section will attempt to extend the learning hypothesis so as to take account of the characteristics of different metal products industries found in Colombia. To do so, it is first necessary to describe the production processes occurring within these industries.

Production Activities in the Metal Products Sector

In distinguishing among these activities, definitions for a number of characteristics of the design, production, and sales processes will be useful (Table 4.1). One of these dimensions is the complexity of the production task of each worker. Complexity of production task is a difficult concept to define precisely. The concept involves both the number of substeps composing the task, and the physical and mental skills required of the worker in each substep. By the latter criterion, the metal-working activity (defined here as machining and milling) probably has the highest ranking because it is characterized by operations requiring considerable skill. Casting, forging, and stamping (CFS) all involve somewhat less difficult operations, while assembly and repair operations are, with some exceptions, intermediate in this regard.

TABLE 4.1

PRINCIPAL CHARACTERISTICS OF METAL PRODUCTS PRODUCTION, BY ACTIVITY

Characteristic	CFS	Metal-working	Assembly	Repair
Production-task complexity	int.[a]-high	high	int.	int.
Production-task interdependence	int.	low	high	low
Importance of non-production tasks	int.	high	low	low
Purchaser-dependence	int.	high	int.	low

[a]Intermediate

Another relevant characteristic is the degree of sequential interdependence among the tasks necessary to finish a product; this could possibly be measured by the total number of tasks in the production process. Assembly operations are characterized by a high degree of production-task interdependence. A failure to perform one task can cause a bottleneck which will prevent the performance of all later tasks in the process. CFS and metalworking have an intermediate degree of interdependence. Interdependence is lowest of all in repair work. In some industries, the relative importance of the various types of tasks depends upon the scale of output, as where scale may determine whether forging or machining is used.

In addition, one should consider the manner in which these production steps are combined with design and sales operations. Another key characteristic, therefore, is the importance of nonproduction tasks in the activity as a whole, measured perhaps by the percentage of the labor force accounted for by nonproduction employees. This percentage is high in metalworking, since at this stage the design specifications must be translated into production operations. The same description applies to CFS, although perhaps to a lesser extent, since the products and the production processes are less complex than in metalworking. Since assembly and repair simply involve bringing together and taking apart already manufactured components, nonproduction tasks should be relatively unimportant in these activities.

Firms specializing in metal products are also characterized by differing degrees of interdependence between themselves and the purchasers of their products. In some branches, a large part of production is custom-made to the specifications of purchasing firms. This fourth characteristic, which might be termed purchaser-dependence, would be measured by the percentage of sales accounted for by such contractual purchases. It is especially critical in developing countries, where the purchasing firm usually has a limited number of alternative suppliers, and probably most important for metalworking firms, with lesser importance for casting, forging, and stamping. In assembly and repair activities, where the products are generally standardized, this characteristic should be least important.

Learning in Metal Products

Given these characteristics of metal products production, what sort of learning processes would be expected in each activity? Who learns, how does learning occur, and who benefits?[6]

First, who learns, individual workers or firms? The simplest hypothesis has workers acquiring production skills through experience, and hence learning is embodied in individual workers. The importance of this worker-embodied learning—measured, say, by the impact on a worker's productivity of a doubling of his experience—is probably a function of the complexity of the task involved. Since complexity is generally high in all metal-products activities, worker-embodied learning should be important in all branches. However, it should be most important in metalworking, because of the high skill requirements of that branch, somewhat less important in CFS, and of intermediate importance in assembly and repair.

In some activities, learning by workers may be less important than learning embodied in firms themselves. Over time a firm may develop a system for training workers and managers, designing products, and coordinating operations of suppliers with its own production operations. The result is a package within which the experience of individual workers and managers is an easily acquired and relatively unimportant component.

One aspect of this firm learning, coordination of production operations, is probably most important where there is a high degree of production-task interdependence and the main problem is one of coordinating sequential production tasks. The classic case is an assembly operation. But firm-embodied learning will also be important in the coordination of nonproduction with production operations. This second aspect of firm learning should be a function of the relative role of nonproduction tasks in the activities. It should, therefore, be important in metalworking, intermediate in CFS, and less important in assembly and repair.

The next question to be answered is how learning occurs. This is a familiar question in the area of industrial psychology, where considerable attention has been paid to the factors influencing the learning curve. This curve typically shows the daily output of a worker from the time he begins a particular industrial task until he achieves an average level of proficiency. Generally these curves are characterized by negative acceleration; that is, the increase in daily output with each successive day of experience declines over time.[7]

Of the two principal theoretical explanations of these learning curves, one suggests that learning depends on cumulative output, and the other that it depends on elapsed time. The studies of Werner Hirsch and William Fellner suggest that each of these hypotheses has explanatory power.[8] On the one hand, it is plausible that learning through repetition of the same simple task be closely related to the level of cumulative output and less closely related to the time period during which that output was produced. Of course some minimum length of time may be needed for cumulative output to lead to learning, but given this minimum period, the learning process in this case may be described tolerably well by a functional relationship between productivity and cumulative output. On the other hand, there may be a process of learning-to-learn which leads to an increase in the rate of learning over time, and which depends less on past production than on time elapsed. Hirsch reported that this learning-to-learn was relatively more important in complex machining operations and less so in assembly.

Why should learning *how* to learn be more dependent on time than on cumulative output? The simplest explanation is that learning-to-learn may be simply a function of the number of different past learning experiences. In learning a number of *different* skills, the individual gradually acquires a more general skill—the ability to learn. If so, what matters in the case of metal products is not the total volume of previous production, since this may all have involved learning one set of skills. Owing to model changes over time, the number of different learning experiences is quite likely to be less a function of cumulative output than of the time over which that output has been spread. In addition, it might be suggested that in any complex cognitive process, such as learning *how* to acquire production skills, time may be the key explanatory variable. The integration of these complex techniques with what the individual already knows may be more difficult and time-consuming than the assimilation of a simple skill.

The answer to the question of how learning occurs in metal-products activities would therefore appear to depend on the relative importance of simple, output-dependent learning on the one hand, and more complex, time-dependent learning-to-learn on the other. These two types seem in large part to be a function of the degree of complexity of the operations involved. Consider the learning that is embodied in individual workers. Where the tasks are relatively simple, as in most assembly operations, worker-embodied learning is most likely to be of the output-dependent type. Where more complex operations are involved, in casting, forging, and stamping, learning may be dependent on time as well as cumulative output. In complex metalworking operations, labor-embodied learning is probably strongly time-dependent.

The conclusions of Hirsch and Fellner may also be relevant to learning by firms. The production-coordination aspect would appear to be a simpler type of learning, akin to the acquisition of a production skill. What is required is simply making sure that each phase in the production chain functions at the same rate, so that the flow of output may continue uninterrupted. The production-coordination aspect may therefore be a function of cumulative output. In contrast, the coordination of production and nonproduction tasks would seem quite complex, involving continual instruction and feedback between the designers and machine operators. It was suggested above that the acquisition of these more difficult skills may not be easily compressed in time. If so, this aspect of firm learning may depend more on the passage of time than on cumulative output. In metalworking, where it has been argued that the coordination of production and nonproduction tasks is the main problem, firm learning should be primarily time-dependent. In assembly, with the simpler problem of coordinating sequential production tasks, firm learning is likely to depend more on cumulative output than on time. Casting, forging, and stamping should demonstrate both of these effects.

The third important question about the learning process is who obtains the benefits. Here it is relevant to distinguish between cases of learning embodied in the workers and learning embodied in firms. In each case, the issue is how the benefits of learning are distributed among the workers, the firm, and others (via externalities).

To begin, consider the case in which all learning is embodied in the workers. Gary S. Becker states that firms will be able to capture all of the benefits from on-the-job learning by their workers.[9] If workers realize that learning will permit them to earn higher wages in the future, they should be willing to pay for this investment by accepting lower wages in the present. The difficulty with this argument is that it depends upon the assumption of long-run equilibrium under conditions of perfect certainty. In the conditions of uncertainty which characterize a newly established industry, a firm is not likely to be able to bid workers away from other industries by offering a wage lower than labor's marginal product. If workers are averse to risk, they will have to be offered a premium to induce them to leave the more certain earnings in existing industries. Moreover, once these workers have learned, new firms entering the industry will be able to capture part of the learning benefits by bidding experienced workers away from the pioneering firm. Under these circumstances, with competitive labor markets, the firm is likely to share the benefits with its workers and with other firms in the same industry. These labor-embodied externalities are likely to vary with the complexity of the production task as shown in Table 4.2.

If learning is embodied not in the workers but in individual firms, the answer to who benefits appears at first to be a simple one—the firm itself. Nevertheless, spillovers may occur through the product market. It is sometimes argued that one of the problems of manufacturers in developing countries is that domestic suppliers are unable to make deliveries on schedule or meet quality specifications. It is probably true that firms purchasing domestically-produced capital goods or intermediate inputs are strongly affected by the experience levels of their suppliers; it follows that these purchasers, whether other firms or consumers, may be able to capture a substantial portion of the benefits of any learning by the supplying firms. Here the externalities should be a function of purchaser-dependence, as Table 4.2 indicates.

An examination of the learning process in metal products, activity by activity, thus suggests several interesting hypotheses:

TABLE 4.2

PREDICTED CHARACTERISTICS OF LEARNING IN METAL PRODUCTS, BY ACTIVITY

Aspect	Casting, Forging, Stamping,	Metalworking	Assembly	Repair
Who learns?				
Workers	int.[a]-high	high	int.	int.
Firms:				
Production-coordination	int.	low	high	low
Production-nonproduction	int.	high	low	low
How?				
Workers:				
Output-dependent	int.	low	int.	int.
Time-dependent	int.	high	low	low
Firms:				
Output-dependent	int.	low	high	low
Time-dependent	int.	high	low	low
Who benefits?				
Labor-embodied externalities:				
Workers and other firms in industry	int.-high	high	int.	int.
Firm-embodied externalities:				
Purchasing-firms	int.	high	int.	low

[a] Intermediate

(1) Because of the discontinuity of the production processes in the metal products sector and the complexity of some of these processes, learning from experience should be important in all branches. The learning version should therefore dominate both the neoclassical and technological-dualism versions.

(2) It may be possible to distinguish between two types of learning, one a simple learning process dependent on cumulative output, the other a more complex process of learning-to-learn dependent more on experience with a variety of tasks, for which elapsed time may be a reasonable proxy. The relative importance of these processes should differ between activities.

(3) It may also be possible to distinguish between two types of learners—firms and their workers—the importance of each type varying across branches.

(4) Finally, a significant portion of the benefits of learning should be passed on to workers and other firms.

Unfortunately, because of the problem of measuring external economies, the fourth hypothesis is difficult to verify. Each of the first three hypotheses, however, may be tested statistically.

PART III

THE IMPORTANCE OF LEARNING

The Model

The model used to test the first of these hypotheses was a single-equation, Cobb-Douglas production function estimated by ordinary least squares. In order to distinguish between the neoclassical approach and learning-by-doing, it was necessary to formulate different versions of the model.

Corresponding to the neoclassical equation (1'), with disembodied technical change and economies of scale, is the version:

$$\ln(V/L)_{jt} = a_o + \alpha_o \ln(K/L)_{jt} + \gamma_o \ln L_{jt} + \lambda_o t + w_{jt} \qquad (3)$$

where:
    V is value added,
    K is the capital stock,
    L is the number of employees,
    j indicates the size class,
    t the year, and
    w is a disturbance.

A second version of the model permits learning, following equation (2).

$$\ln(V/L)_{jt} = a_i + \alpha_i \ln(K/L)_{jt} + \gamma_i \ln L_{jt} + \lambda_i t + \eta_i G_{irt} + w_{ijt} \qquad (4)$$

$$i = 1, 2, 3, 4; \quad r = 1 \text{ if } 1 \leq j \leq 6$$
$$r = 2 \text{ if } 7 \leq j \leq 10$$

Here G_i is a measure of learning, where the subscript i indicates the learning regime as described below. The subscript r indicates the size group.

These functions were fitted separately to each of twenty-five Colombian three-digit metal-products industries, using pooled, cross-section, time-series data. There were ten size classes of firms, (by number of employees per firm), each size class having a maximum of eight observations, one for each of the years 1959-66. Obtaining measures of G_i for each of the ten size classes proved impossible. Consequently, estimates were made on the one hand for small firms of less than fifty employees (r = 1) and on the other for large firms of over fifty (r = 2). In addition, all monetary values were deflated by the same price index for home and imported goods, a procedure which would introduce a bias if prices did not rise by similar amounts for large and small firms.

The use of three-digit industries to classify firms does not, of course, correspond with precision to the distinctions among alternative types of metalworking processes on which the discussion of this chapter has focused. It was unavoidable since the data were available only in this form. The first nine industries (see Table 4.5), falling in the two-digit heading of metal products, comprise a variety of casting, forging, stamping, and metalworking activities. The next four, under nonelectrical machinery, are involved primarily in metalworking and assembly operations. The six electrical products activities are concerned primarily with assembly and the six transportation equipment industries are divided between assembly in the automobile and bicycle industries and repair in the four remaining industries. The relationship between three-digit industry and type of activity, while not really tight, is close enough to provide useful results.

The Measurement of Capital

One of the more difficult problems in estimating production functions is the measurement of the capital stock. In the case of Colombian manufacturing, energy capacity, measured in horsepower, has been used as a measure in a number of previous studies. This variable may be less subject to measurement error than the most acceptable alternative; namely, a capital-stock series constructed from annual investment data.[10]

However, as John Todd argues in Chapter 6, the horsepower series may well contain serious biases which reduce its attractiveness as a proxy for capital stock.[11] In the first place, as equipment becomes more complex over time the ratio "total capital/horsepower of energy capacity" could rise. Secondly, because of the higher quality of their machinery and plant, large firms may have a higher value of fixed capital per horsepower than smaller ones.

The first possibility, that of increases over time in the capital to horsepower ratio, poses the more serious problem in this study. This chapter attempts to explain the increase over time in productivity, that is, in the amount of output per unit of capital and labor. However, if the amount of capital used is increasingly underreported over time, the result will be an overestimate of the rise in the amount of output per unit of capital. The real increase in productivity will consequently be less than that reported.

Table 4.3 attempts to evaluate the importance of this effect by size of plant for the whole of the Colombian manufacturing sector in the period 1957-67. Data are taken from Todd's "best" estimates of the capital stock by size class, using a 10 percent depreciation rate. No clear indication of an increase over time in the capital to horsepower ratio for manufacturing firms as a whole is evident from the right-hand column. In two size categories the ratio increased, whereas in two others the ratio fell. If one may assume that these general tendencies also held in metal products, there would seem to be no reason to give up the horsepower figures as a reasonable proxy for the stock of capital in this study.

The second problem mentioned above is the difference in capital/horsepower ratios between small and large firms. In the time-series estimates of production functions which are the subject of this chapter, such a discrepancy is not likely to affect the general thrust of the results unless it varies systematically over time. Table 4.3 shows no evidence of a widening of the gap between small and large plants. Among the two smaller size classes, the ratio rose in one category and fell in the other; the same can be seen in the two larger size classes.

The gap in capital/horsepower ratios between small and large firms does come into consideration, however, when one attempts to determine the relative social efficiency of small firms compared with large. We will return to this subject later in the chapter.

TABLE 4.3

RATIO OF FIXED CAPITAL TO HORSEPOWER IN COLOMBIAN MANUFACTURING, 1957-67
(1958 Pesos per Horsepower)

Size of Plant (Number of Employees)	Ratio of fixed capital to horsepower	
	Average 1957-67	Average annual increase[a]
Under 15	2.9	.05
15-49	3.7	-.18
50-199	6.2	-.45
Over 200	5.7	.39

Source: John Todd, "Plant Size, Factor Proportions and Efficiency in Colombian Manufacturing," Chapter 6 of this volume, Table 6.8.

[a]Calculated from a linear, time-series regression.

Indices of Learning

It was suggested above that two different types of learning may occur in metal products, one process dependent upon cumulative past production, and the other upon the time elapsed since the beginning of production. It was also argued that each of these types had two possible classes of learners, individual workers and their firms. Table 4.4 shows a four-way breakdown of possible learning processes. In each case, a possible measure of learning suggests itself: the logarithm of cumulative output per worker and per firm, for the output-dependent type; and average years of experience per worker and average age of firm for the time-dependent type. Unfortunately, data were not available at the firm level. However, with the use of available data by size of firm, it was possible to construct indices which approximate the desired measures. These indices were constructed separately for small and large firms.

To obtain the desired indices, a base-year (1959) value was first derived for each index. The data for each succeeding year were then used to modify the index. The procedure used to calculate the base values was highly arbitrary due to the absence of data by size class prior to 1959. In practice, however, the final estimates of the importance of learning are likely to be rather insensitive to the initial values of the indices, the impact of which will be absorbed by the constant term in equation (4).

The method used to modify the indices over the 1959-66 period is more interesting. For cumulative value added this modification consisted simply of adding the current year's value added to the cumulative total.

For the age-of-firm and years-of-experience variables, first differences between the total number of firms or workers in successive years were assumed to constitute new additions to the stock of firms or workers. In the calculation of the average age these new additions were assumed to have an age of zero, while the preceding year's stock was assumed to have an age one year greater than it did in the preceding year.

TABLE 4.4

FOUR TYPES OF LEARNING IN METAL PRODUCTS, AND A POSSIBLE MEASURE OF EACH

Type of Learning	Measure
1. Learning by workers dependent upon cumulative output	Log of cumulative value added per employee (G_1)
2. Learning by firm dependent upon cumulative output	Log of cumulative value added per establishment (G_2)
3. Learning by workers dependent upon elapsed time	Average number of years of experience per employee (G_3)
4. Learning by firm dependent upon elapsed time	Average age of establishment (G_4)

The main problem in these computations was to take account of movements of firms between size groups within the same industry. To handle this problem it was assumed that all new entrants to the industry start as small firms with fewer than fifty employees. Thus all changes in the number of large firms were assumed to be caused by movements into and out of the large-firm group. In defense of this assumption, it might be suggested that it is likely to correspond quite closely to the typical growth pattern of domestically owned firms. In the case of foreign subsidiaries, however, new entrants are more likely to begin operations with fifty employees or more, but foreign-controlled firms generally also have an initial body of production experience accumulated in similar operations in other countries. These assumptions, by assigning accumulated experience to newly entering foreign firms, will therefore take into consideration the initial experience advantage of these firms over their domestic rivals.

A further assumption was essential to assure that moving firms carried their experience along with them. These firms were assumed to have experience levels (in terms of cumulative output and age of firm and worker) which were the average for firms in the size class where the movement originated. This experience was then subtracted from the group of origin and added to the group of destination. For firms moving from the small group to the large group, this assumption presumably implied an underestimation of the experience of the moving firms, since these were probably older and larger than the average small firm, with an experience level greater than average. Conversely, for movements in the opposite direction, the experience of the moving firms will be overestimated, since they were presumably near the bottom of the large-firm size distribution. In both ways, then, this assumption leads to an underestimation of the experience of large firms and helps offset the bias caused by the earlier assumptions.

The Statistical Significance of Learning

Of the five models described in equations (2) and (3), one failed to produce significant results. This was the learning model with average years of experience of workers as an explanatory variable. Possible reasons for its lack of success are discussed below.

The coefficients of the four remaining versions are set out in Table 4.5. On the whole, these results indicate that learning was indeed statistically significant in Colombian metal products. By the t-test, the cumulative-output-per-employee variable was significant at the .05 level with the correct sign in nine out of twenty-five industries, while the variables measuring cumulative output per establishment and average age of establishment were significant in fifteen and twelve industries, respectively.

It is important to note that the learning variables are not simply substituting for the effect of the time variable in the neoclassical version. In the latter version, the coefficient indicating the exponential rate of disembodied technological change was significant in only six industries, in one of which it had a negative sign. However, in the learning versions, one or more of the learning variables was significant in sixteen of the twenty-five industries.

The addition of the learning variables had an interesting effect on λ, the coefficient of the time variable. In many cases where λ had been nonsignificant or even significant with a positive sign in the neoclassical version, the coefficient was significant and with a negative size in the learning versions (as for example, in industry 364 or 371). It would appear that the total learning effect is a combination of the impact of time and the learning index.[12] Since the values and significance of λ in the learning versions are so strikingly different from those in the neoclassical version, it would seem that the learning effect may be a compound one made up of the influences of both the learning variable and the time variable.

The specification of equation (4) permits a test of the relative significance of economies of scale and learning. In the no-learning version, presented in column 2 of Table 4.5, the γ_0 coefficient, which measures the importance of scale economies, is significantly different from zero in twenty industries. It would appear, however, that this result is due in part to misspecification. When the learning variable is added, the statistical significance of scale economies falls, although this effect by no means disappears. In the best-fitting of the learning versions, the scale parameter, γ_2, is significantly different from zero in ten industries, while in the other two learning versions the scale coefficient is significantly nonzero in seventeen industries.

The Economic Importance of Learning

When one tries to appraise the economic importance of learning, interpretation of the statistical results becomes somewhat more difficult. A way is needed to compare the effects of the various causes of productivity change. Two components are necessary for such a comparison. The first is the set of ordinary-least-squares coefficients or elasticities of Table 4.5. The second is the annual rates of growth of the corresponding explanatory variables, k, L, and G_i (i = 1, 2, 4). By combining these two components, one obtains a breakdown of the total change in productivity, with an estimate of the contribution of each of the inde-

TABLE 4.5

COEFFICIENTS OF COBB-DOUGLAS PRODUCTION FUNCTIONS FOR COLOMBIAN METAL PRODUCTS, WITH AND WITHOUT LEARNING, FOR TWENTY-FIVE THREE-DIGIT INDUSTRIES, 1959-66

No. Industry	No Learning			
	α_0	γ_0	λ_0	R^2
35 Metal Products				
351 Tinware products	.33*	.21*	.05*	.49
352 Tools	.44*	.29*	-.02	.80
353 Cutlery	1.19*	.13	.06	.59
354 Nonelectrical kitchen appliances	.22*	.12*	-.03	.28
355 Aluminum products	.28*	.10**	.00	.34
356 Wire products	.32*	.14*	.00	.43
357 Foundries	.62*	.17**	-.01	.62
358 Machine shops	.18**	.18*	.01	.23
359 Other machine products	.48*	.10	.03	.35
36 Nonelectrical Machinery				
361 Turbines	.24	.18**	-.05	.18
362 Agricultural machinery	-.23*	.30*	.04**	.36
363 Industrial machinery	-.62**	-.11	.07	.10
364 Machinery parts	.07	.03	.06*	.17
37 Electrical Products				
371 Electrical machinery	.10	.29*	.02	.16
372 Radio and television	.07	.39*	-.05**	.51
373 Electrical appliances	-.36*	.22*	.08*	.37
374 Electric wire	.38*	.17**	-.03	.57
375 Light bulbs	.01	.12**	.00	.06
376 Electric installations	.18	.46*	-.04	.48
38 Transportation Equipment				
381 Naval repair	.04	.25*	.00	.39
382 Railway repair	.01	.12*	.09*	.64
383 Automobiles	.53*	.10	-.02	.37
384 Bicycles	.17**	.27*	-.01	.47
385 Automobile repair	-.28*	-.19*	-.01	.42
386 Aircraft repair	.09**	.07**	.01	.21
Average	.18	.17	.01	.40
T-score	(2.8)	(3.5)	(1.2)	

* Coefficient significant at the .01 level.
** Coefficient significant at the .05 level.

[a] Time and learning variables perfectly correlated; same results as model with no learning.

α = coefficient of capital/labor ratio

γ = coefficient of labor

λ = coefficient of time

η_i = coefficient of learning index i.

TABLE 4.5 (continued)

	With Learning														
	Cum. Value Added per Employee					Cum. Value Added per Establishment					Average Age of Establishment				
No. Industry	α_1	γ_1	λ_1	η_1	R^2	α_2	γ_2	λ_2	η_2	R^2	α_4	γ_4	λ_4	η_4	R^2
35 Metal Products															
351 Tinware products	.32*	.15*	-.04	.71**	.52	.30*	.12**	.04**	.13*	.55	.29*	.17*	.00	.11**	.52
352 Tools	.43*	.27*	-.07	.18	.80	.42*	.27*	-.04	.97	.80	.41*	.27*	-.04	.06**	.81
353 Cutlery	1.22*	.15	.08	-.08	.60	1.21*	.16	.07	.03	.59	1.13*	.06*	.06	.03	.60
354 Nonelectrical kitchen appliances	.22*	.12*	-.03	.03	.28	.23	.09	-.03	.05	.29	.23*	.10**	-.04	.04	.29
355 Aluminum products	.13*	.05	-.05**	.53*	.46	.12**	.04	-.03	.14*	.48	.18*	.03	-.13*	.24*	.55
356 Wire products	.32*	.14*	-.03	.38	.44	.29*	.12**	.00	.10	.44	.30*	.12*	-.02	.05	.45
357 Foundries	.61*	.16**	-.06	.38	.63	.58*	.12	-.02	.10**	.65	.57*	.14**	-.11*	.15*	.65
358 Machine shops	.12	.09**	-.09*	1.01*	.39	.09	.05	.01	.15*	.49	.12	.09**	-.08*	.15*	.41
359 Other machine products	.44*	.05	-.01	.19	.37	.49*	.01	.02	.08	.37	.47*	.08	.03	.02	.36
36 Nonelectrical Machinery															
361 Turbines	.24	.19**	-.04	.21	.21	.25	.03	-.07	.25**	.26	.27**	-.01	-.16*	.38*	.46
362 Agricultural machinery	-.19**	.26*	.06*	-.28**	.40	-.10	.23*	.01	.19*	.55	-.17**	.25*	-.09**	.21*	.48
363 Industrial machinery	-.61**	.15	.11	-.20	.10	-.62**	-.16	.06	.07	.11	-.60**	-.13	-.01	.10	.10
364 Machinery parts	.07	.01	.12*	-.40	.19	.19*	.03	.02	.16*	.34	.16**	.04	-.07**	.16*	.28
37 Electrical Products															
371 Electrical machinery	.12**	.24*	-.04**	.15**	.16	,14**	.18*	-.03**	.09*	.68	.13**	.22*	-.06*	.09*	.65
372 Radio and television	.07	.30*	-.07*	.29**	.53	.07	.37*	-.05**	.01*	.51	.07	.31*	-.08*	.08**	.53
373 Electrical appliances	-.33**	.22*	.01	.76*	.47	-.32*	.06	.07*	.19*	.45	-.29*	.11**	.01	.23*	.50
374 Electric wire	.34*	.15**	-.05	.17	.58	.35*	.00	-.04	.18**	.63	.36*	.15	-.04	.03	.58
375 Light bulbs	.02	.11	.03	-.37	.08	.00	.10	-.01	.10*	.07	.25**	.10*	-.05*	.07	.07
376 Electric installations	.24**	.41*	-.13*	1.06*	.53	.33*	.34*	.05**	.19*	.53	.25**	.39*	-.11*	.14*	.53
38 Transportation Equipment															
381 Naval repair	.04	.25*	-.01	.30	.40	.05	.24*	-.00	.01	.39	.04	.26*	.01	-.03	.39
382 Railway repair	-.01	.11**	.27	-1.21	.66	.02	.11**	-.09	1.12	.70	.01	.12*	.09*	a	.64
383 Automobiles	.53*	.06	-.06	.41	.38	.54*	.05	-.03	.08	.38	.53*	.08	-.02	.01	.37
384 Bicycles	.17**	.18*	-.14*	.71*	.56	.22*	.08	-.07*	.31*	.65	.17**	.27*	-.01	a	.47
385 Automobile repair	-.22*	-.16*	-.10*	.68**	.46	-.22*	-.16*	-.02	.05**	.45	-.24*	-.17*	-.10**	.10	.44
386 Aircraft repair	.07	.05	.00	.21	.25	.08**	.01	.01	.08**	.29	.07	.04	-.04	.07	.26
Average	.17	.14	-.01	.23	.44	.19	.10	-.01	.15	.47	.18	.12	-.05	.10	.45
T-score	(2.8)	(2.7)	(1.5)	(1.7)		(2.9)	(1.9)	(1.0)	(2.4)		(2.9)	(2.5)	(1.6)	(2.1)	

pendent variables to the total increase. Table 4.6 shows the resulting breakdown of total productivity change for the neoclassical model and the three learning versions.[13]

Whichever measure of learning is chosen, the effect of learning would appear to be considerably more important than the effects of increased capital per worker or larger scale. Learning from experience alone would seem capable of explaining annual productivity increases of from 2 to 3 percent in the metal-products sector as a whole, with considerably higher rates in individual industries. It may be concluded that in terms of both statistical significance and economic importance, the production functions with learning provide a better explanation of productivity change in Colombian metal products than a simple neoclassical production function with either disembodied or capital-embodied technological change.

Some indication of the relative importance of scale economies and learning may be obtained from the bottom line of Table 4.6. If attention is confined to the three learning versions, scale economies, as represented by the effect of a change in L, explain productivity increases averaging 6 to 9 percent over the period. However, the learning indices, G_1, G_2, and G_4, explain average productivity increases of 12 to 34 percent.

Learning and/or Dualism

Despite the apparent superiority of the learning version over the neoclassical version, it is conceivable that the productivity changes in Colombian metal products may be explained equally well by the hypothesis that small and large firms have different neoclassical production functions. The Chow test is one way to distinguish between the learning version and this dualism version by testing the hypothesis that both size groups of firms have the same production function.

If the neoclassical version is used to test for dualism, the hypothesis of identical production functions for small and large firms is rejected at the .01 level in fifteen of twenty-four industries. The metal-products group would therefore appear to be characterized by structural dualism. In the learning versions, however, the hypothesis of identicality is rejected in only twelve, nine, or ten of the twenty-four cases, depending on the index used. Even in these industries for which the hypothesis continues to be rejected, the F-statistics are generally considerably lower in the learning version than in the neoclassical version.[14]

Thus the addition of learning to the production function significantly reduces the evidence of structural dualism in Colombian metal products. Productivity differences between small and large firms would appear to arise as much from differences in experience levels of firms and their workers as from differences in the technology being used.

Total Social Product and Plant Size

The preceding sections have shown evidence that learning has had a positive effect on labor productivity. It might be argued, however, that unless total social product has increased in the process, the effect of learning need not have been beneficial. For this reason, it is necessary to ask what has happened to the productivity of capital.

A problem might occur if a firm gaining in experience and growing in size moved into a factor market with a factor price ratio sharply different from the social optimum. Suppose that due to learning, the firm moves from point A to point B' of Figure 4.1. The latter is on a lower

158 - Dudley

TABLE 4.6

ESTIMATED BREAKDOWN OF PRODUCTIVITY CHANGES IN COLOMBIAN METAL PRODUCTS
FOR TWENTY-FIVE THREE-DIGIT INDUSTRIES, 1959-66

Industry No.	Actual Productivity Change, 1959-66	No Learning			With Learning											
					Cum. Value Added per Employee				Cum. Value Added per Establishment				Average Age of Establishment			
					Estimated Percent Change in Productivity Due To:											
	%	K/L	L	T	K/L	L	T	G_1	K/L	L	T	G_2	K/L	L	T	G_4
351	104	10	10	42	10	7	a	86	9	5	33	15	9	8	a	39
352	33	19	33	a	19	30	a	a	18	29	a	a	17	30	a	8
353	110	4	a	a	5	a	a	a	5	a	a	a	4	3	a	a
354	5	20	5	a	20	5	-27	48	21	a	a	10	21	4	a	124
355	24	5	4	a	2	a	-27	48	2	a	a	a	3	a	-60	a
356	42	8	14	a	8	13	a	a	7	11	a	a	7	12	a	a
357	77	42	12	a	42	11	a	a	39	a	a	a	38	10	-54	98
358	29	4	7	a	a	4	-46	121	a	a	a	13	a	4	-43	75
359	11	-13	a	a	-12	a	a	a	-12	a	a	a	-13	12	-67	a
361	143	a	11	a	-5	12	a	a	a	24	a	28	25	a	-67	105
362	116	-6	37	32	-5	32	50	-10	a	a	a	18	-4	30	-47	117
363	52	10	a	a	10	a	a	a	10	a	a	a	10	-1	a	a
364	48	a	a	52	a	a	135	23	-4	a	a	52	-2	a	-39	122
371	58	a	28	a	3	23	-23	23	4	17	-17	19	-4	21	-34	38
372	43	a	22	-30	a	17	-37	40	a	21	-28	2	-10	17	-43	20
373	145	-12	15	75	-11	16	a	126	-11	a	67	27	-10	7	a	53
374	60	60	13	a	53	11	a	a	53	a	a	30	56	12	a	a
375	11	a	4	a	a	a	a	a	a	a	a	a	1	3	a	a
376	33	10	24	a	10	21	-60	107	14	17	45	15	10	20	-54	45
381	1	a	16	a	0	16	a	a	a	15	a	a	-1	17	a	7
382	66	a	-3	88	a	-3	a	a	a	a	a	a	a	-3	a	a
383	52	65	a	a	63	a	a	a	67	a	a	a	65	10	a	a
384	3	a	3	a	3	a	-62	132	4	a	-40	56	3	a	a	a
385	-10	-3	a	a	-2	a	-50	90	-2	a	a	4	-2	1	a	a
386	7	1	2	a	a	a	a	a	-1	a	a	9	a	1	a	a
Average	51	9	11	10	9	9	-5	31	9	6	2	12	10	9	-18	34

K = capital in horsepower G_1 = cumulative value added per employee
L = labor in workers G_2 = cumulative value added per plant
T = time G_4 = average age of establishment
a = No estimate made, because corresponding coefficient in Table 4.5 was not significant at the .05 level.

FIGURE 4.1

LEARNING AND TOTAL FACTOR PRODUCTIVITY

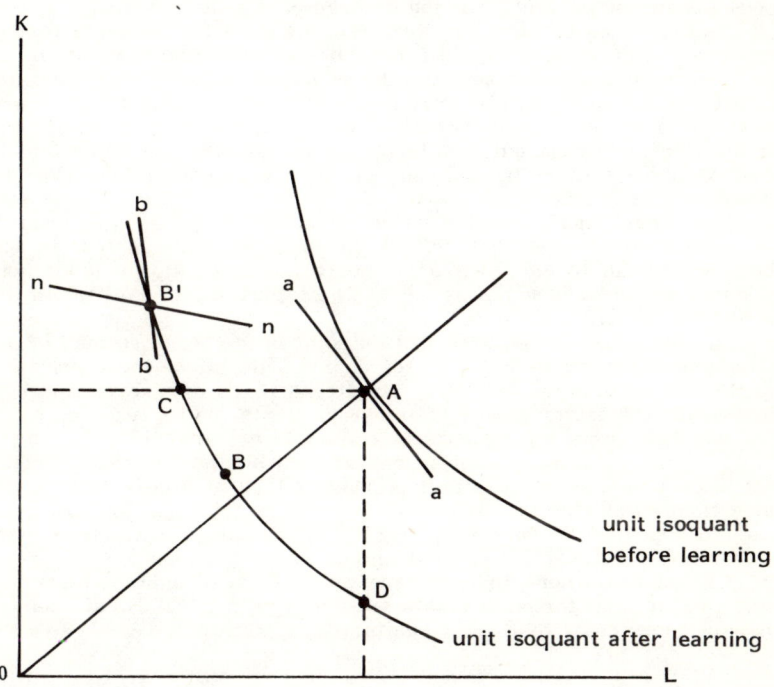

isoquant than the former, but has a higher capital/labor ratio due to a substantial increase in the wage/rental ratio, from aa to bb. At any point along CD, the social product would clearly be greater regardless of the factor/price ratio. But at B', outside this range, the social product may be lower. This would be true, for example, if the equilibrium factor/price ratio for the economy were as represented by nn, as a result of high unemployment. In this case the loss due to factor-market distortions would offset the gains due to an inward shift of the isoquant.

One way to answer this question is to compare value added per unit of capital and labor in large plants of fifty employees or more with that in small plants of under fifty employees.[15] If horsepower is used as a measure of capital the results are quite clear. The ratio of value added per horsepower in large plants to that in small plants in metal products in 1966 is 1.48, the corresponding ratio for value added per worker is 1.82. Thus if point A in Figure 4.1 represents the small plant, the large plant would be represented by a point such as B between C and D. Social product is evidently higher in large plants than in small.

As mentioned earlier, however, reasons exist for believing that the horsepower figures may be misleading if used to compare plants of different sizes at a given time. Todd's estimates in Table 4.3 show that the ratio of his measure of capital to horsepower is substantially higher for the larger plants than for the smaller. In fact, if his coefficients for the whole of Colombian manufacturing in 1966 may be applied to the metal-products sector, it would appear that large plants have a capital/horsepower ratio twice that of small plants.

How would this correction affect the discussion of total product? The ratio of value added per unit capital in large plants to that in small plants would fall to 0.74, while the corresponding ratio for labor would of course remain unchanged at 1.82. The typical large plant would then be represented by a point such as B'.

Ideally, what is required at this point is the set of socially optimal factor prices, as represented by the slope of nn. Since these prices are for obvious reasons not available, an alternative is to evaluate the large plants with the factor prices of the small plants, as represented by aa. With horsepower as the measure of capital (i.e., the point B) and all plants evaluated at the factor prices of small plants, we would conclude that large plants produce a unit of value added at a cost 37.5 percent lower than small plants. With Todd's estimates as a measure of capital, (i.e., the point B'), and with small-plant factor prices, large plants would have costs only 3.4 percent higher than small ones.

On balance, then, the evidence would seem to indicate that in the metal-products sector large plants are not significantly less efficient, in terms of social cost, than small plants.

PART IV

TYPES OF LEARNING

Nothing has yet been said about the second and third hypotheses, which refer to the characteristics of the learning process in metal products. Hypothesis two stated that it might be possible to distinguish between two types of learning, one dependent upon cumulative output and the other upon elapsed time. Hypothesis three stated that it might be possible to distinguish between two types of learners—firms and their workers.

An intriguing question is whether one may compare the importance of the different types of learning simply by examining the learning effects shown in Table 4.6. Looking at industry 351, for example, can one say that learning is primarily a function of cumulative value added per employee, since the learning effect for this specification (86 percent) is greater than for either of the other two specifications in this industry. The problem with such a procedure is that it almost certainly involves some double-counting of learning. Because of multicollinearity between G_1, G_2, and G_4, the 86 percent corresponding to G_1 will include part of the effects of G_2 and G_4. Similarly the percentages for the two remaining indices will include part of the effect of G_1. While this separate estimation procedure will thus overestimate the *magnitude* of the effect of the three types of learning, it will still leave the *ranking* of any two effects unchanged.[16]

If rankings may be compared in this way, the information in Table 4.6 may be used to distinguish between types of learning-by-activity. Two additional steps are necessary. It was suggested earlier that the total learning effect is a combination of the impact of time and the learning index. In the first steps, therefore, the effects of time and learning from Table 4.6 are added together for the sixteen industries in which one or more of the learning indices produced significant coefficients. These industries may be grouped into four categories, corresponding to the relevant two-digit industries (except that the bicycle industry is grouped with the similar industries of the nonelectrical machinery group).

The second step occurs in Table 4.7. It will be remembered that two of the learning indices were based on cumulative value added. In order to abstract from the effects of the learning agent, these two measures are averaged and presented in column 1. The time-dependent index, average age of establishment, is presented in column 2. In this way, the effect of cumulative value added may be compared with the effect of elapsed time in each of the four groups. In the heterogeneous metal-products group, cumulative value added and elapsed time were both important, although elapsed time had a slight edge. In nonelectrical machinery and bicycles, where metalworking activities are combined with assembly, cumulative value added was still important, as might be expected. But here, elapsed time appears to be the dominant influence on productivity. In contrast, the electrical machinery group, which is predominantly an assembly activity, received only a small productivity increase from elapsed time. Cumulative value added, however, had a major effect on productivity in this group. In repair, cumulative value added also had the more important effect, though this effect was smaller than in the other groups.

These results, though somewhat tenuous, do seem consistent with the second hypothesis. For activities with production and managerial tasks of considerable complexity—as in metalworking—productivity seems to be primarily a function of elapsed time. For simpler production and managerial operations—as in assembly and repair—productivity seems to a great extent to be a function of cumulative value added.

Less illuminating was a similar comparison of learning by workers (using cumulative value added per employee) with learning by firms (using the average of the effects of cumulative value added per establishment) in columns 3 and 4 of Table 4.7. As the third hypothesis suggests, firm learning proved to be important in all branches except repair. Learning by workers was important in all groups—also in accord with the hypothesis. Contrary to expectations, learning by workers was least important in nonelectrical machinery and bicycles, in which the metalworking activity accounts for a large part of total value added.

TABLE 4.7

COMPARISON OF THE EFFECT ON LABOR PRODUCTIVITY OF FOUR TYPES OF LEARNING FOR FOUR COLOMBIAN METAL PRODUCTS GROUPS, 1959-66

Group	Estimated Percent Change in Productivity Due To:			
	Cumulative Value Added (1)	Elapsed Time (2)	Learning by Workers (3)	Learning by Firms (4)
Metal products	26	38	37	26
Nonelectrical machinery, bicycles	22	48	18	37
Electrical machinery	34	5	35	19
Repair	14	0	20	4

The relative unimportance of labor-embodied learning in nonelectrical machinery may perhaps be explained by a failure to obtain significant results for the labor-experience version of the learning model. Part II argued that worker learning in metalworking would be primarily a function of time, due to the complexity of the production tasks. Since the variable measuring average years of experience per employee did not prove significant, the calculations of Table 4.7 make no allowance for labor-embodied learning.[17]

Thus the empirical results appear consistent with both the second and third hypotheses. Both the nature of the learning process and the learning agent differ between production activities.

PART V

PRODUCTIVITY AND EMPLOYMENT

The discussion to this point has focused primarily upon the effect of learning on productivity. However, government objectives are not confined exclusively to increasing output. One might be particularly interested in examining the extent to which productivity increases from learning were incompatible with increases in employment.

It should be mentioned first that increases in labor productivity due to learning are likely to have less of an effect on employment than two other types of labor productivity increase. One of these is an increase in the capital/labor ratio with a given technology due to a rise in the relative price of labor. Since capital will be substituted for labor, employment will necessarily fall. Another case is that of purely labor-saving technological change where, if factor prices remain constant, employment will once again fall while productivity increases. With learning from experience, the productivities of capital and labor will both rise as the increase in the productivity of capital cushions the impact on employment. Indeed, with a Cobb-Douglas production function (as in the present case) and constant relative factor prices, the capital and labor required to produce a given output will both fall in the same proportion.

Even with learning-by-doing the conflict between increases in productivity and employment is not so self-evident as might at first appear. Obviously, if a fixed quantity of output is to be produced, then employment generated will vary inversely with productivity. If the amount to be produced varies, for example, as a function of the price, this relation may not hold. If demand is quite price-elastic, a price decrease made possible by productivity gains may stimulate a large increase in the quantity demanded and hence in employment. Moreover, if the product in question is a tradeable good, as in the present case, the increase in demand will come primarily at the expense of imports, so that employment in other domestic industries will not necessarily be seriously affected.

This second explanation of the relationship between employment and productivity seems to be the one more consistent with the record of Colombian metal products. As shown in Table 4.8, both productivity and employment increased by 6 percent annually during the period under study. Even more striking is the positive relationship between productivity growth and employment growth that appears at the two-digit level. The electrical machinery industry had the highest productivity growth and the highest employment growth, while the transportation equipment industry had the lowest growth rate for both indices.

At the very least we may conclude that in the present case rapid increases in productivity do not seem to have been inconsistent with equally rapid increases in employment.

TABLE 4.8

AVERAGE ANNUAL CHANGE IN LABOR PRODUCTIVITY AND IN EMPLOYMENT FOR FOUR COLOMBIAN METAL PRODUCTS GROUPS, 1959-66

Group	Average Annual Percent Change In:	
	Output per unit labor	Employment
Metal products	5.5	3.2
Nonelectrical machinery	6.4	6.8
Electrical machinery	6.8	9.4
Transportation equipment	3.1	1.9
Total	6.0	6.1

PART VI

CONCLUSIONS

The implications of the learning version of industrial development differ substantially from those of the versions emphasizing capital, scale, or technology. These more conventional versions all imply the need for a developing economy to remain open, welcoming foreign investment and foreign aid, and thriving in the rigors of international competition. Such a policy, the learning version implies, may delay or deter the country's workers and firms from acquiring the experience necessary to reach high levels of productivity. But indiscriminate protection of metal-products industries is also likely to founder because of shortages of precisely those skills it might be thought to create. Such a policy is not the answer.

This study implies that the import-substitution barrier in metal products may be breached—at a price. The learning process in metal products requires both time and production experience to enable firms and their workers to acquire the necessary production and managerial skills. If, as has been argued, firms fail to internalize a significant part of the benefits of learning, they should be subsidized during the learning period. The results of this study offer some guidelines for an optimal strategy of subsidization in metal products. The relevant questions are whom, how, and how long to subsidize. Answers to these questions depend upon the level of development of the metal-products sector in the country under consideration, but the following remarks are probably relevant for countries such as Colombia at an intermediate stage of industrialization.

With regard to the first question of whom to subsidize, metalworking and, to a lesser extent, casting, forging, and stamping are the principal candidates, since external economies from learning are probably highest in these activities. Contrary to practice as of the early seventies, heavy protection is less desirable in assembly, where externalities are probably lower. Without an assembly sector, little demand is likely to exist for components produced by domestic metalworking, casting, forging, and stamping firms.

As for the question of how to subsidize, subsidies are theoretically preferable to tariffs, since they do not distort the structure of market prices. This study has suggested that time and cumulative output are equally important for learning—especially in industries such as metalworking, where the production process is complex. If so, these subsidies should not be designed solely to encourage a high volume of output in as short a time as possible; production should be spread over time. One means of subsidizing experience, in terms both of time and of cumulative output, might be per-unit subsidies up to a certain volume of output per year, with no subsidies beyond this level. The level of subsidized output could be gradually increased over time.

This study has also suggested that learning by firms (in the sense of the development of a system for controlling production and nonproduction activities) may be as important as learning by workers. If so, the learning process might be speeded by engaging in joint ventures with foreign capital or by borrowing foreign technical assistance.

The question of how long to reinforce the learning process is the most difficult to answer. This study refers to a given seven-year period during which learning explained roughly one-half of the total increase in productivity. If one were forced to choose a measure of the duration of the learning process, years would appear to be more appropriate than months. When further years of observation become available, it would be helpful to examine how rates of learning change over time.

Finally, it is worthwhile noting that in the case under study no conflict between increases in productivity though learning and increases in employment was apparent. Rather the sectors with the highest rates of increase in labor productivity also had the highest rates of increase in employment.

APPENDIX TABLE A.1
A TEST OF STRUCTURAL DUALISM IN COLOMBIAN METAL PRODUCTS, 1959-66

No. Industry	No Learning (1)	Cum. Value Added Per Employee (2)	With Learning — Cum. Value Added Per Establishment (3)	Average Age of Establishment (4)
		F-statistic		
35 Metal Products				
351 Tinware products	5.2*	5.3*	2.8**	3.1**
352 Tools	3.2**	2.3	2.5**	1.9
353 Cutlery	6.7*	4.7*	5.0*	5.8*
354 Nonelectric kitchen appliances	1.7	1.4	1.2	1.3
355 Aluminum products	12.5*	6.2*	5.8*	3.0**
356 Wire products	0.9	1.0	0.6	0.5
357 Foundries	6.2*	4.2*	3.7*	5.9*
358 Machine shops	12.2*	6.8*	4.2*	5.8*
359 Other metal products	7.1*	6.7*	8.4*	5.7*
36 Nonelectrical Machinery				
361 Turbines	11.2*	8.7*	7.9*	4.2*
362 Agricultural machinery	8.6*	6.0*	1.3	3.5*
363 Industrial machinery	0.4	0.4	0.3	0.4
364 Machinery parts	7.5*	5.8*	2.6**	4.5*
37 Electrical Products				
371 Electrical machinery	4.7*	2.9**	1.6	2.1
372 Radio and television	0.8	2.5**	3.2**	2.2
373 Electrical appliances	6.2*	4.7*	5.3*	3.3**
374 Electric wire	1.9	1.8	0.5	2.4
375 Light bulbs	2.0	1.7	1.6	1.9
376 Electrical installations	4.1*	2.4**	2.1	2.0
38 Transportation Equipment				
381 Naval repair	1.5	1.4	1.4	1.2
382 Railway repair	a	a	a	a
383 Automobiles	9.9*	8.0*	7.5*	7.8*
384 Bicycles	6.2*	2.7**	0.8	4.7*
385 Automobile repair	5.0*	3.5*	3.5*	4.5*
386 Aircraft repair	1.2	1.1	0.4	0.5
Average	(5.3)	(3.8)	(3.1)	(3.3)

* Reject hypothesis of same production function at .01 level. ** Reject hypothesis of same production function at .05 level.
a = no small firms; test not applicable.

ENDNOTES FOR CHAPTER 4

1. R. M. Solow, "Technical Change and the Aggregate Production Function," *Review of Economics and Statistics* XXXIX (August 1957): 312-320.

2. Richard R. Nelson, "A Diffusion Model of International Productivity Differences in Manufacturing Industry," *American Economic Review* LVIII, Part 1, (December 1968): 1219-1248.

3. Note that this technological dualism, characterized by *different production functions* for large and small firms is different from the type of dualism that can occur under the neoclassical version if small and large firms have the same production function but face different factor prices.

4. E. Mansfield and Richard R. Nelson, *Production Functions for a Dual Industrial Structure—Colombian Manufacturing* (Santa Monica, California: The RAND Corporation, 1968); Karsten Laursen and Lester D. Taylor, "Unemployment, Productivity and Growth in Colombia" (Bogotá 1968), mimeographed. Both of these works have used this method to explain productivity differences between small and large firms for Colombian two-digit industries.

5. Various measures of G have been suggested. A relationship between productivity and cumulative investment was proposed by Kenneth Arrow in "The Economic Implications of Learning by Doing," *Review of Economic Studies* 39 (June 1962): 155-73, and tested by E. Sheshinski, "Tests of the Learning by Doing Hypothesis," *Review of Economics and Statistics* 47 (February 1965): 81-86. A simple relationship between productivity and time was proposed by W. Fellner in "Specific Interpretations of Learning by Doing," *Journal of Economic Theory*, 1, 1969: 119-144, with empirical support from Paul David, "Learning by Doing and Tariff Protection: A Reconsideration of the Case of the Antebellum U.S. Cotton Textile Industry," *Journal of Economic History* 30 (September 1970): 521-601. However, the most commonly used measure of this production experience is cumulative output. Studies of various metal-products industries by H. Asher "Cost-Quantity Relationships in the Airframe Industry" (Santa Monica: The RAND Corporation, 1956), W. Z. Hirsch "Firm Progress Ratios," *Econometrica* 24 (April 1956): 136-43, and L. Rapping "Learning in World War II Production Functions," *Review of Economics and Statistics* 47 (February 1965): 81-86 have indicated that a doubling of cumulative output may yield a productivity increase of from 10 to 30 percent, most of the gain coming from a reduction in unit labor requirements.

6. These questions are asked in a slightly different context by Richard R. Nelson and Sydney G. Winter in "Production Theory, Learning Processes and Dynamic Competition," (New Haven 1970), mimeographed.

7. For more on the learning curve and references to industrial case studies, see Thomas Arthur Ryan and Patricia Cain Smith, *Principles of Industrial Psychology* (New York: The Ronald Press Company, 1954), p. 436.

8. Hirsch in "Firm Progress Ratios" has offered evidence which indicates that two types of learning may be occurring. On a particular metal-products job, production of a certain type of lathe, Hirsch observed a "progress ratio" of 18; that is, an 18 percent decline in unit labor requirements associated with a doubling of cumulative output. However, this rate of productivity change itself rose with production experience. The next job, producing lathes of a different type, had an associated progress ratio of 25. Thus, in addition to a simple learning process to explain productivity change on a single job, a separate learning-to-learn process may explain an increase in the progress ratio between jobs.

    Of equal interest is the apparent difference in the relative importance of these two types of learning in assembly and machining. Assembly, characterized by operations of only intermediate complexity, had a relatively high initial progress ratio increased only slightly between jobs. In the more complex machining operations, however, the initial progress ratio was relatively low and showed a large increase from one job to the next.

    To distinguish further between these two types of learning may be impossible. Fellner, in his study of Olympic sports "specific Interpretations of Learning by Doing," found that in simpler sports with little change in equipment or rules performance was closely related to cumulative output. In other cases, where strategies were more complex or where rules or equipment had been modified, performance was explained better as a function of time.

9. Gary S. Becker, *Human Capital: A Theoretical and Empirical Analysis with Specific Reference to Education* (New York: Columbia University Press, 1964), p. 12.

10. R. R. Nelson, T. P. Schultz, and R. L. Slighton argue in *Structural Change in a Developing Economy*, (Princeton: Princeton University Press, 1971), p. 83f., that, apparently for fiscal reasons, Colombian firms have a tendency to understate their investment (and profits) in reporting to the national government. No such reason would seem to exist for underreporting in the case of horsepower capacity.

11. John Todd, "Efficiency and Plant Size in Colombian Manufacturing," Unpublished Ph.D. dissertation, Yale University, 1972, pp. 87-93.

12. This phenomenon may perhaps be explained if the production functions are examined in partial equilibrium terms. Consider the version with cumulative output per employee. The coefficient λ gives the effect on productivity of the passage of time when the capital/labor ratio, size of firm, and level of cumulative output per employee are held constant. But if cumulative output per employee is really held constant, this means no production in the last period. Under these circumstances, it is not unreasonable to expect a decline in productivity as workers forget what they have learned previously. A similar argument would explain negative time coefficients in the version with cumulative output per establishment. Note that as might be expected, firm-forgetting is less prevalent than worker-forgetting.

    But what is the meaning of a negative time coefficient associated with the average-age-of-firm variable? In partial terms, if time has passed with no change in the average age of firm, the size class must have had new entrants. A fall in productivity could result only if the lack of experience of these new firms somehow outweighed the increased experience of the original firms that had gotten older. But is it not reasonable that a year of experience would have a greater effect on productivity, the earlier it comes in a firm's life? If so, the negative time coefficient would be a means of taking into consideration the diminishing returns to additional years of experience.

13. Note that estimates were made only for those coefficients of Table 4.5 that were significantly different from zero at the .05 level of significance.

14. See Appendix Table A.1 to this chapter.

15. However, it should be noted that high value added per unit of any factor may be due either to efficiency in production or to monopoly power which permits prices higher than they would be in a competitive equilibrium.

16. Assume that
$$G_1 = X + u$$
$$G_2 = X + Y + u$$
where X and Y are both positive and independently distributed and u is a disturbance. Note that because both learning indices are a function of X, they will have a high multicollinearity between them. Suppose that the true relationship between productivity and learning is an exact one:
$$p = a + \eta (X + Y)$$
Thus G_1 embodies only a part of the total learning effect. The problem is to see whether the resulting estimate of η is smaller than that when G_2, which embodies the whole learning effect, is used. If the relationship that is estimated is
$$p = \hat{a}_1 + \hat{\eta}_1 G_1 + e_1$$
it may be shown that the limiting value to which $\hat{\eta}_1$ tends in probability as the number of observations increases is
$$p \lim \hat{\eta}_1 = \frac{\eta}{1 - \sigma_u^2/\sigma_x^2}$$
Similarly, if the equation is estimated in the form $p = a_2 - \hat{\eta}_2 - e_2$ the corresponding estimate is $p \lim \hat{\eta}_2 = \frac{\eta}{1 - \sigma_u^2/\sigma_{X+Y}^2}$. Since X and Y are independent, $\sigma_{X+Y}^2 = \sigma_X^2 + \sigma_Y^2 > \sigma_X^2$ ∴ $p \lim \hat{\eta}_1 < p \lim \hat{\eta}_2 < \eta$

17. But the results with the labor-experience variable may be interesting precisely because of their nonsignificance. As defined in Part III, this variable would measure average years of experience of employees only if mobility of experienced workers was low. It was assumed in the computation of the index that all additions to the labor force in a size group consist of inexperienced workers. If,

in fact, considerable recruitment of experienced workers took place, the index will underestimate the average experience level of workers. Moreover, if the extent of such recruitment is a function of firm size, the degree of underestimation will not be uniform across size groups. Robert Slighton "Relative Wages, Skill Shortages and Changes in Income Distribution in Colombia" (Santa Monica: The RAND Corporation, October, 1968), pp. 57-58 observed that during this period of oversupply on the labor market, large high-wage firms did in fact try to use their hiring policies to improve the quality of their labor force. If so, the index used would considerably underestimate the experience level of workers in large firms. It is not surprising, therefore, that this variable should be unable to explain the productivity gap between large and small firms. In fact, the nonsignificance of this variable is at least consistent with the existence of significant mobility of experienced workers in metal-products industries.

Chapter 5

Technological Change in the Thermal Electricity Generating Industry
Manuel Ramirez G.

This chapter presents the results of a test for the extent and types of technological change over time in thermal generating plants in Colombia. It attempts to identify domestic sources of technological change which may supplement the increase in technical efficiency embodied in new imported machinery and possibly compensate for the factor biases which such imported machinery incorporates. Since the nature of technological change in any country tends to reflect relative factor prices, imported machinery will be expected to incorporate labor-saving change when developed in the more advanced capital-intensive countries. The results are of particular interest with respect to the possibility of adapting the technology implicit in foreign machinery towards the greater use of the country's most abundant factor, labor.

Generation of electrical energy has been chosen for study because of several favorable characteristics. The product is homogeneous; the technology is simple, and the input structure can be meaningfully reduced to the three basic factors of labor, fuel, and machinery. Further, the industry has received considerable analysis in other countries with special emphasis on technological change, thus opening up the possibility of comparison of results. Finally, data were available in a form which could become useful without undue collection difficulties.

Electricity can be generated in hydroelectric or thermoelectric plants; the technology is completely different in these two cases. This study considers only thermoelectric plants; in Colombia a large percentage of electricity is generated in hydroelectric plants, but the latter are difficult to include in the present sort of analysis due to a variety of complicating factors like topography.

Technological change in the electricity generating industry has been studied on numerous occasions and in various ways.[1] Most analyses have begun by obtaining an expression for the production function to serve as the basis for estimating the technical efficiency of the various observations. The literature approaches this task either by estimating an "average" production function or an "extreme" production function. The latter corresponds to the theoretical concept of production function, expressing the maximum quantity of output which can be obtained from a given amount of inputs.[2] It is applied in this study.

On occasion the method of analyzing changes in the cost structure of the firm and trying to relate them to technological change has been used. The best study along these lines was done by Samuel Hollander in reference to several Dupont rayon plants.[3] In general, however, technological change is very difficult to distinguish from other sources of changed costs of production.

Methodology of the Analysis in Colombia

Data were obtained for fifteen plants using fuel oil and five using natural gas. The data are monthly and cover periods of one to four years (between 1966 and 1969) depending on the plant.[4]

We assume that each observation, corresponding to a month's operation of one plant, represents a technological process in the production of electricity. The output—electrical energy—is measured in kilowatt-hours; the inputs are labor measured in man-hours, fuel in British Thermal Units (BTU), and capital in kilowatts of productive capacity in the plant. This last measure has been adjusted in several ways to provide a better indication of the productive services of the machines: by average utilization, measured by the number of turns during which the machinery is used; by the number of days of use per month; and by a technical factor related to altitude and average temperature of the location of the plant. (This last factor is responsible for variations of up to 28 percent in the productive capacity of plants included in this study.) Energy produced divided by inputs is the output-input coefficient. If we then assume constant returns to scale, these coefficients provide a description of the production function and a very simple measure of efficiency. Figure 5.1 illustrates the idea in a case involving only two inputs; each observation presents the combination of inputs required to produce one unit of output in a given plant in a given month. Under the usual assumptions of activity analysis, a representation of the production function can be obtained by considering only the efficient processes, those characterized by the fact that no other process can generate the same amount of output with the same or less of all factors, and less of at least one of them. In Figure 5.1, processes 1, 2, 3, 4, and 5 are efficient while 7, 8, and 9 are not. A process is basic if it cannot be expressed as a convex combination of other efficient processes. In Figure 5.1, processes 1, 2, 4, and 5 are basic. Process 3 is not basic since it can be expressed as a convex combination of the efficient processes 2 and 4. Knowing the "basic processes" is the same as knowing the production function, since any other process can be expressed as a linear combination with positive coefficients of the basic processes and the slack activities.[5]

Let x_i be the level of operation of activity i; for our present purposes we may equate this to the quantity produced utilizing activity i. Let $a_k = (a_{kj})$ be the vector of unit inputs corresponding to process k; a_{kj} is the quantity of input j necessary to obtain one unit of output using process k. Let $A = [a_{kj}]$ be the matrix of all activities. A constitutes a complete description of the technology. Given a_k, the maximum production obtainable by using the quantity of input specified in a_k can be easily calculated. If process i is operated at a level x_i, x_i units of output are obtained. We use $a_i x_i$ units of the distinct inputs so that the maximum quantity of output which could be obtained from inputs in the quantity a_k is given by the maximum value of

FIGURE 5.1

EFFICIENT AND BASIC PROCESSES

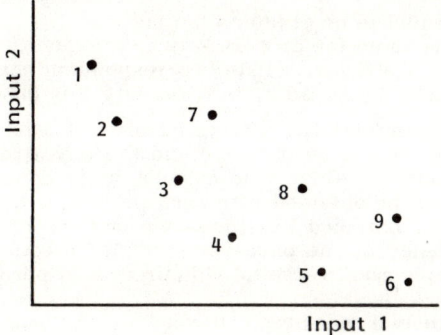

$$\sum_{i=1}^{n} x_i \qquad (1)$$

subject to the restriction that the quantity of an input used be equal to or less than that available:

$$Ax_i \leq a_k \qquad (2)$$

and that no process may be operated at a negative level:

$$x_i \geq 0. \qquad (3)$$

This is, of course, a problem of linear programming. The problem always has a solution since a_k is a column of A. For the same reason the solution is always equal to or greater than one.

If the maximum value for process k is 1, the quantity actually produced, the process is efficient. If the corresponding activity levels are such that $x_j = 0$ for all $j \neq k$ and $x_k = 1$, activity k is basic.

By means of this approach, solving problems 1-3 for each activity, all the basic processes can be obtained and thereby a representation of the production function. Once this calculation is done, the maximum production which can be obtained with each process is known. Dividing the quantity actually obtained by this maximum, one has an estimate of the technical efficiency of the observation.[6] When returns to scale are not constant, a simple modification of this procedure permits us to obtain the desired results.[7]

This type of analysis has been criticized as very sensitive to extreme observations which may contain errors of observation rather than represent feasible technological processes. In order to allow for this objection, we have undertaken a sensitivity analysis in the following way: after obtaining the estimates of technical efficiency as just described, we remove from the data those observations with unit efficiency, and repeat the process, obtaining another set of estimates of technical efficiency. Subsequent analysis indicated no statistically significant differences in the results obtained using the two estimates of efficiency. In what follows we report and use only the results obtained using all the observations.[8]

Overall results are too bulky to be fully presented here. An analysis of these results is presented in what follows and a summary of average observations for the four years is presented in Table 5.1.

Levels of Efficiency and Their Determinants

The most obvious feature of Table 5.1 is the generally low level of the estimates of technical efficiency (E). The plants are producing much less than they could with the same inputs and with activities observed in the sample.[9]

One possible cause of varying efficiency levels is varying capacity utilization. In general this utilization is low in the sample, perhaps due to demand factors. The demand for electricity is not constant during the day, but has more or less well-defined peak periods. Incorporating other causes of underutilization into the analysis would have been interesting, but the information could not be obtained.[10] We will use the relation between actual production and maximum possible production of the specific plant (manufacturer's data on capacity in kilowatts times the temperature and pressure correction factors) to define the variable utilization (U). Average data for this variable are found in Table 5.2.[11]

TABLE 5.1

AVERAGE VALUES OF TECHNICAL EFFICIENCY ESTIMATES, TWENTY THERMOELECTRIC PLANTS

Plant	Method 1[a]	Method 2[b]
1	0.347	0.398
2	0.367	0.448
3	0.674	0.785
4	0.241	0.282
5	0.321	0.368
6	0.295	0.339
7	0.122	0.143
8	0.205	0.243
9	0.148	0.171
10	0.264	0.322
11	0.277	0.336
12	0.289	0.356
13	0.249	0.295
14	0.502	0.602
15	0.457	0.572
16	0.186	0.218
17	0.414	0.510
18	0.347	0.398
19	0.490	0.558
20	0.499	0.572

[a]Method 1 assumes constant returns to scale.

[b]Method 2 does not assume constant returns to scale. Values are the average for each plant; this explains why no plant emerges with unit efficiency.

TABLE 5.2

AVERAGE VALUES OF SOME INDEPENDENT VARIABLES, TWENTY THERMOELECTRIC PLANTS

Plant	Utilization (U)	Maximum Possible Production (MPP)	Year of Installation (A)	Country of Origin (OR)
1	50.9	202,513	1961	Germany
2	51.9	747,075	1960	United States
3	99.7	428,000	1947	England
4	16.9	2,745,383	1954	England
5	37.4	798,668	1961	England
6	28.4	812,119	1959	Germany
7	9.1	22,107	1961	England
8	28.5	26,266	1961	England
9	17.6	95,630	1964	Germany
10	39.6	54,396	1956	United States
11	34.2	48,988	1961	Germany
12	39.1	199,384	1958	Germany
13	44.3	53,944	1966	United States
14	66.1	499,996	1963	England
15	59.6	981,806	1962	England
16	21.3	45,083	1959	United States
17	63.0	113,830	1961	England
18	6.3	317,262	1948	United States
19	82.3	6,654,480	1962	United States
20	78.8	8,186,067	1964	United States

Increasing returns to scale are another cause of differences in measured efficiency that has emerged in some other studies as quite important. They will show up in this study when we use the first method for estimating the technical coefficients. As a measure of plant scale we will use maximum possible production (MPP). Data on this variable are also found in Table 5.2.

Both the technical literature and previous economic studies indicate that new plants are more efficient than old ones due to technological improvements. We expect this to be the case in the present study; accordingly, we define a variable designed to reflect this effect. Technological change is generated by the research in the capital goods industry abroad; since we are not here interested in that industry, we assume as an approximation that change results simply from the passage of time. We use the date of installation of the plant to indicate the vintage of the equipment (data on this variable (A) are found in Table 5.2), and as an approximation, assume an exponential increment of efficiency.

The technical efficiency of machines could differ according to the country in which they were built. A dummy variable, set at one if the machine was manufactured in the United States and zero if it was made in Europe, serve to identify this effect. An additional dummy with value one if the machinery was English and zero if it was not failed to give significant results. Data on origin are presented also in Table 5.2.

Evidence from other studies indicates that the efficiency of an operating plant changes as a result of a learning phenomenon on the part of the operatives.[12] It seems acceptable in this analysis to use accumulated production as a proxy for the learning process; since the plants are of quite different sizes, we use as the independent variable accumulated production divided by maximum possible production (AP/MPP).[13] We introduce two functions of this ratio, both commonly used in this type of study, into our regression equations: a logarithmic one,

$$\log AP/MPP \tag{4}$$

and an inverse function,

$$1/(AP/MPP). \tag{5}$$

The final choice between these two forms is made according to the econometric results.[14] The relationships between log E and the two variables just defined are illustrated by the curves of Figure 5.2. Often the major difference is that the curve relating log E and log AP/MPP (a in Figure 5.2) has no maximum nor asymptotic value, while that relating log E and 1/(AP/MPP) (b in Figure 5.2) does.

In addition to the phenomenon just mentioned, one may find a local inventive process or activity, not directed at the creation of entirely new processes, but aimed at the modification of the imported machinery and processes in order to adjust them better to local conditions. An appropriate measure of this activity would be expenditures on research and development or man-hours dedicated to this activity. Unfortunately, we do not have data of precisely this sort. As an approximation to the variable in question we use accumulated labor on plant maintenance (MA), since it appears that the majority of this activity takes place during the maintenance process.[15] The functional forms used were the same as with the previous variable.

It is to be expected that a plant will not operate in a normal fashion during months in which important repairs are undertaken. In order to take this into account, we will utilize a dummy variable (R) whose value will be one in those months during which important repairs are made and zero in other months.

Following the above considerations, we estimate the following equations:

$$\log E = a + bMPP + c \log MA + d \log AP/MPP + eX + fU$$
$$+ gR + hOR + \Theta \tag{6}$$

$$\log E = a + bMPP + c/MA + d/(AP/MPP) + eA + fU$$
$$+ gE + hOR + \lambda \tag{7}$$

where Θ and λ are residuals; E is technical efficiency of the plant in the month of observation; MPP is the maximum possible production in kilowatt-hours per month; MA is accumulated labor input in maintenance; AP/MPP is accumulated production divided by maximum possible production; A is the year of installation; U is the coefficient of utilization in percent; R is a variable to distinguish months in which important repairs were effected, and OR is a variable to distinguish the place of origin of the machinery.

These equations were estimated for the two sets of calculated technical efficiencies. The results for the group estimated on the assumption of constant returns to scale are:

FIGURE 5.2

ALTERNATIVE FORMS OF LEARNING CURVES

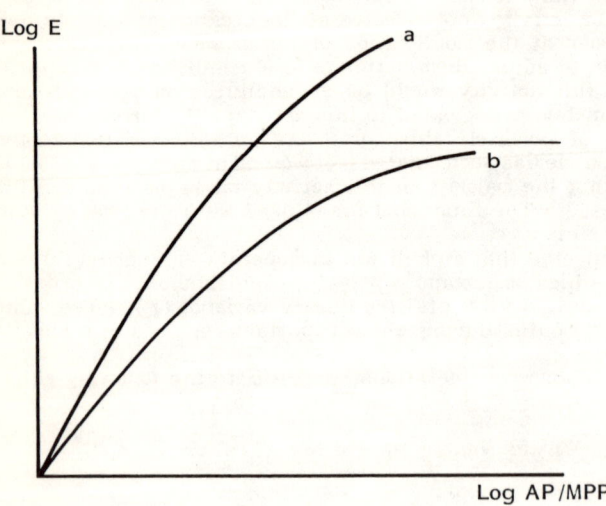

Note: Log E = Log of Technical Efficiency

Log AP/MPP = Log of Accumulated Production Divided by Maximum Possible Production

$$\ln E = 4.546 + 0.0000182 \text{ MPP} + 0.0266 \text{ A} + 0.0105 \text{ U}$$
$$(3.367) \qquad\qquad (8.235) \qquad (16.49)$$

$$- 0.0575 \text{ R} - 0.0320 \text{ OR} - 0.0386 \text{ MA} - 0.1323 \text{ (AP/MPP)}$$
$$(1.806) \quad\; (1.035) \qquad (4.202) \qquad\; (2.011)$$

$$R^2 = 0.822 \tag{8}$$

$$\ln E = 3.449 + 0.00000967 \text{ MPP} + 0.0256 \text{ A} + 0.00905 \text{ U}$$
$$(1.643) \qquad\qquad\; (8.391) \qquad (12.23)$$

$$- 0.0511 \text{ R} - 0.00301 \text{ OR} + 0.0306 \ln \text{MA}$$
$$(1.604) \quad\; (1.026) \qquad\; (3.923)$$

$$+ 0.136 \ln \text{AP/MPP}$$
$$(4.399)$$

$$R^2 = 0.807. \tag{9}$$

The results for the estimates obtained without assuming constant returns to scale are:

$$\ln E = 4.821 + 0.00000231 \text{ MPP} + 0.0272 \text{ A} + 0.0102 \text{ U} - 0.0563 \text{ R}$$
$$(1.223) \qquad\qquad\; (8.424) \qquad (15.12) \qquad\; (1.621)$$

$$- 0.0285 \text{ OR} - 0.0421 \text{ MA} - 0.1452 \text{ (AP/MPP)}$$
$$(1.103) \qquad\; (4.021) \qquad\; (2.123)$$

$$R^2 = 0.792 \tag{10}$$

$$\ln E = 3.642 + 0.00000028 \text{ MPP} + 0.272 \text{ A} + 0.0102 \text{ U} - 0.0563 \text{ R}$$
$$(1.012) \qquad\qquad\; (4.287) \qquad (11.47) \qquad\; (1.421)$$

$$- 0.00276 \text{ OR} + 0.0318 \ln \text{MA} + 0.148 \ln \text{AP/MPP}$$
$$(0.982) \qquad\; (3.852) \qquad\qquad (4.222)$$

$$R^2 = 0.780. \tag{11}$$

The results are quite similar in all these cases. The small effect of increasing returns to scale is a surprising result; as far as the other variables are concerned the differences are not significant. Due to the slightly better results obtained using the first group of technical efficiencies, we decided to use that group in the rest of the analysis, correcting the effect of economies of scale via an independent variable and not by the method of estimating efficiencies.

As between the alternative functional forms of the learning variable, we chose the inverse, equation (8), partly for its slightly better econometric performance and also because it provides a limit to the learning possibilities. The final results should not vary much even if another of the equations were chosen as the base for what follows.

To identify other important factors specific to the plant or to the month, we estimated the equation again adding dummy variables for months and plants. These were not statistically significant either individually or by blocks, showing that all the systematic influences associated with plants or months are already incorporated in the original equation. No indication of multicollinearity appears in the independent variables of the equation, as can be observed in the matrix of partial correlation coefficients (Table 5.3), and in the fact that changes in the coefficients produced by removing some of the variables are quite small.

TABLE 5.3

PARTIAL CORRELATION COEFFICIENTS AMONG INDEPENDENT VARIABLES EMPLOYED: TWENTY THERMOELECTRIC PLANTS

	(MPP)	(A)	(U)	(R)	(OR)	(1/MA)	(1/AP/MPP)
(MPP)	1.0000	0.1831	0.3495	0.1458	0.3746	-0.1592	-0.1915
(A)	0.1831	1.0000	0.0313	0.2282	0.0174	0.1827	-0.4039
(U)	0.3495	0.0313	1.0000	0.1144	0.0828	-0.2168	-0.6250
(R)	0.1458	0.2282	0.1144	1.0000	-0.0060	-0.1996	-0.2104
(OR)	0.3746	0.0174	0.0828	-0.0060	1.0000	-0.2255	0.1221
(1/MA)	-0.1592	0.1827	-0.2168	-0.1996	-0.2255	1.0000	0.0241
(1/AP/MPP)	-0.1915	-0.4039	-0.6250	-0.2104	0.1221	0.0241	1.0000

Observation of the residuals of the individual plants gives evidence of autocorrelation, with a different structure in each plant. In view of this, we adopt an estimating technique that supposes the matrix of variance-covariance of the residuals to be of the form:

$$\Sigma = \begin{bmatrix} \Sigma_{11} & 0 & 0 & \cdots & 0 \\ 0 & \Sigma_{22} & 0 & \cdots & 0 \\ \vdots & \vdots & & & \vdots \\ 0 & 0 & 0 & & \Sigma_{20,20} \end{bmatrix} \qquad (12)$$

in which

$$\Sigma_{ii} = \begin{bmatrix} 1 & \sigma_i & \sigma_i^2 & \cdots & \sigma_i^{t_i-1} \\ \sigma_i & 1 & \sigma_i & \cdots & \sigma_i^{t_i-2} \\ \vdots & \vdots & & & \vdots \\ \sigma_i^{t_i-1} & \sigma_i^{t_i-2} & \cdots & & 1 \end{bmatrix} \qquad (13)$$

and t_i is the number of months observed in plant i.

If the σ_i were known, the equation could be estimated by generalized least squares.[16] Nevertheless, since there are no lagged dependent variables, the σ_i estimated with the residuals of the ordinary least squares are consistent estimators of the true σ_i and the estimates of the parameters of the equation obtained by using generalized least squares with a variance-covariance matrix given by inserting in (12) the estimates of σ_i are also consistent.[17] Since Σ is of the form of (12), its inverse is given by

$$\Sigma^{-1} = \begin{bmatrix} \Sigma_{11}^{-1} & 0 & 0 & \cdots & 0 \\ 0 & \Sigma_{22}^{-1} & 0 & \cdots & 0 \\ 0 & 0 & \cdot & & \\ \cdot & \cdot & & \cdot & \\ \cdot & \cdot & & & \cdot \\ \cdot & \cdot & & & \cdot \\ 0 & 0 & 0 & & \Sigma_{20,20}^{-1} \end{bmatrix} \quad (14)$$

where, as can easily be demonstrated:

$$\Sigma_{ii}^{-1} = \frac{1}{1-\sigma_i^2} \begin{bmatrix} 1 & -\sigma & 0 & \cdots & 0 \\ -\sigma_i & 1-\sigma_i^2 & -\sigma_i & \cdots & 0 \\ 0 & -\sigma_i & 1+\sigma_i^2 & \cdots & 0 \\ \cdot & \cdot & \cdot & & \cdot \\ \cdot & \cdot & \cdot & & \cdot \\ \cdot & \cdot & \cdot & & \cdot \\ 0 & 0 & 0 & & 1 \end{bmatrix} \quad (15)$$

Estimation by generalized least squares with this variance-covariance matrix is equivalent to the use of ordinary least squares with the variables

$w = \pi y$

$Z = \pi X$

in which w is the new dependent variable, Z the matrix of the new independent variables, y the old dependent variable, X the old matrix of independent variables, and π the transformation matrix:

$$\pi = \begin{bmatrix} \pi_1 & 0 & 0 & \cdots & 0 \\ 0 & \pi_2 & 0 & \cdots & 0 \\ 0 & 0 & \pi_3 & \cdots & 0 \\ \vdots & \vdots & \vdots & & \vdots \\ 0 & 0 & 0 & \cdots & \pi_{20} \end{bmatrix} \quad (18)$$

where

$$\pi_i = \sqrt{\frac{1}{1-\sigma_i^2}} \begin{bmatrix} 1-\sigma_i^2 & 0 & 0 & \cdots & 0 \\ -\sigma_i & 1 & 0 & \cdots & 0 \\ 0 & -\sigma_i & 1 & \cdots & 0 \\ \vdots & \vdots & \vdots & & \vdots \\ 0 & 0 & 0 & & 1 \end{bmatrix} \quad (19)$$

The results of applying this procedure to equation (8) were

$$\ln E = 1.366 + \underset{(3.583)}{0.0000231} \text{ MPP} + \underset{(21.985)}{0.0270} \text{ A} + \underset{(16.713)}{0.0106} \text{ U}$$

$$- \underset{(2.868)}{0.0080} \text{ R} + \underset{(3.438)}{0.0194} \text{ OR} - \underset{(3.583)}{0.439} \text{ MA} - \underset{(3.319)}{0.24004} \text{ (AP/MPP)}$$

$$R^2 = 0.871 \quad (20)$$

We accept equation (20) as our best estimate of the relation between the dependent variable E and the group of independent variables previously discussed. In this equation all the coefficients are significant and have the expected signs. The equation explains an important part of the variance in the dependent variable. Technical efficiency is shown to increase with plant size, experience in operation, local inventive activity, the vintage of the equipment, and capacity utilization; efficiency is less if important repairs are made during the month and if the plant was constructed in Europe.

The most important variable in explaining the differences in technical efficiency among plants is the year of installation. According to (20), efficiency has increased by 2.7 percent per year in recently installed plants. A lesser factor is plant size; the difference in efficiency of 6.8 percent between the largest and smallest plant is small in comparison with the difference of 49 percent between the newest plant and the oldest, holding constant the other variables. A plant manufactured in the United States is of almost identical efficiency (0.6 percent more efficient) with one manufactured in Europe.

The utilization-of-the-plant variable explains the greatest part of the variation of technical efficiency within a given plant. A plant increases in efficiency with experience in operation, but these gains decrease with the passage of time. The greatest gain associated with this factor was 0.43 percent in one year; the smallest was 0.05 percent per year. The increases in efficiency associated with the local inventive activity were in general quite small, the greatest was 0.87 percent and the smallest barely noticeable; the largest value is exceptional—it occurred in a very new plant with little accumulated maintenance. This may suggest that the effect associated with this variable is important in recently installed plants, but that all possible benefits are realized rapidly. We must remember that the variable used in the regression is only an approximation of the variable in which we are really interested.[18]

The results are in general the expected ones; the only surprise, perhaps, is the small influence of plant scale on technical efficiency.

The Relation Between Technological Change and Factor Use

How do the various factors which modify the technical efficiency of a plant affect the quantities of each input used in production. For this analysis we will suppose the existence of a production function permitting substitution among factors and changing over time via new processes. Among the various technologies described by this function, one is chosen when a machine is built so as to minimize cost of production at the relative factor prices characterizing the country where it is built. The required factor inputs can then be modified at a certain cost. In the country where the machine is used, these coefficients are probably modified in such a way so as to minimize the total cost of production during the life of the machine, including the cost of modification. Under these conditions it is optimal to modify the machine as quickly as possible, but not up to the point which would have been optimal if the machine had been constructed in the country of use.[19] At each moment the quantity of inputs to be used depends little or not at all on their relative prices; these relative prices act, rather, on the decision to modify or not to modify the machinery at a given point of time and, depending on the conditions under which the activity is realized, how large the modification should be. This process can also depend on experience in the operation of the plant.

Based on this model we estimate functions of the form

$$K/G = g_1(MPP, U, R, OR, MA, AP/MPP, A) \quad (21)$$

$$L/Q = g_2(MPP, U, R, OR, MA, AP/MPP, A) \quad (22)$$

$$F/Q = g_3(MPP, U, R, OR, MA, AP/MPP, A) \quad (23)$$

where K is capital stock, Q output, L labor input, and F fuel input. Prices are not included in these equations for reasons explained above. The independent variables included are the same as used in the "explanation" of technical efficiency.

Average values for the dependent variables are presented in Table 5.4. The equations were estimated by generalized least squares with a

TABLE 5.4

CAPITAL/OUTPUT, LABOR/OUTPUT AND FUEL/OUTPUT RATIOS: TWENTY THERMOELECTRIC PLANTS

Plant	K/Q[a]	L/Q[a]	F/Q[a]
1	1.702	17.870	15.007
2	1.651	11.649	12.011
3	1.386	2.150	5.004
4	5.864	10.501	10.341
5	2.208	6.925	11.820
6	2.767	3.382	14.135
7	4.681	8.306	57.108
8	2.819	2.186	58.897
9	4.677	2.319	59.846
10	2.146	5.350	19.523
11	2.559	1.862	16.193
12	2.148	2.641	15.036
13	3.211	4.627	15.059
14	1.973	0.980	10.883
15	2.122	0.731	11.212
16	4.754	11.690	20.491
17	1.332	2.695	12.222
18	15.762	12.641	14.204
19	1.724	1.075	15.105
20	1.597	0.761	18.441

[a]These are average values for each plant.
K/Q is given in kilowatts of capacity per kilowatt-hour,
L/Q in man-hours per kilowatt-hour, and
P/Q in KBTU per kilowatt-hour.

---

structure of residuals similar to that in the preceding case. The results are as follows:

$$\ln K/Q = 4.3051 + 0.0000276 \text{ MPP} - 0.0202 \text{ A} - 0.0127 \text{ U}$$
$$(3.855) \quad\quad (17.36) \quad\quad (20.27)$$

$$+ 0.0158 \text{ R} + 0.156 \text{ OR} + 0.0317 \text{ MA}$$
$$(0.537)^* \quad (3.336) \quad\quad (2.748)$$

$$+ 0.7912 \text{ (AP/MPP)}$$
$$(10.521)$$

$$R^2 = 0.913 \tag{24}$$

$$\ln L/Q = 5.5683 - 0.000113 \text{ MPP} - 0.0313 \text{ A} = 0.0224 \text{ U}$$
$$(5.081) \quad\quad (11.15) \quad\quad (14.289)$$

$$+ 0.00027 \text{ R} - 0.3394 \text{ OR} - 0.153 \text{ MA} - 1.5256 \text{ (AP/MPP)}$$
$$(0.003)^* \quad (3.280) \quad\quad (5.009) \quad\quad (9.538)$$

$$R^2 = 0.817 \tag{25}$$

$$\ln F/Q = 4.4785 + 0.00000008 \text{ MPP} - 0.0266 \text{ A} - 0.00796 \text{ U}$$
$$(0.0075)* \qquad (17.999) \qquad (8.902)$$

$$+ 0.02917 \text{ R} + 0.1930 \text{ OR} + 0.2077 \text{ MA}$$
$$(1.089)* \qquad (3.080) \qquad (7.240)$$

$$+ 0.4299 \text{ (AP/MPP)}$$
$$(3.949)$$

$$R^2 = 0.882 \tag{26}$$

As in the previous case, the equations explain the majority of the variance of the independent variables; all the coefficients are significant at the 99 percent level (except those marked with an asterisk), and have the expected signs in accord with the model or with previous studies.

The variables operate in quite a distinct form on each of the inputs. The scale variable increases the use of capital slightly, diminishes the use of labor, and has no significant effect on the use of fuel. The difference in the use of capital between the smallest plant and the largest is 0.306 kilowatts of capacity per kilowatt-hour generated (9.12 percent of the average use of capital); in the use of labor it is 2.10 man-hours per kilowatt-hour (38 percent of average use), and in the use of fuel it is a very small 0.01 mega-British Thermal Units (MBTU) per kilowatt-hour (0.048 percent of average use).

The vintage effect leads to a reduction in the quantities of all three factors used. The reduction is of about 2 percent per year for capital, 3.1 percent per year for labor, and 2.6 percent per year for fuel; as expected, the technological change in the country of origin is labor saving, and capacity utilization is an important factor especially in reference to labor and capital. For the average value of the independent variables, an increase of 10 percent in utilization implies a reduction of 5.5 percent in capital, 9.6 percent in labor, and 3.4 percent in fuel. Naturally these results are different in each of the plants.

Requirements of labor, fuel, and capital differ according to the origin of the plant; those manufactured in the United States use less labor but more capital and fuel than the European ones. Origin has a much more important effect on factor proportions than on technical efficiency.

The variable reflecting learning (accumulated production) has more effect on factor use than on technical efficiency, its effect being of the same order of magnitude as that of vintage. The effect of the maintenance variable is smaller, diminishing the quantities of capital and fuel while increasing that of labor, as was to be expected.

The effect of the last three variables, and to a certain degree of the scale variable, is more important in the explanation of the intensity of factor use than in that of technical efficiency. The dummy for month in which repairs are taking place is not important in this case. The other variables are important in both cases.

Comparisons and Implications of These Results

These results are generally in accord with what is known about the industry. The study finds that differences in technical efficiency among plants (relative to the best practice within the sample) and in a given plant at different points of time are related to a number of variables, the most important being capacity utilization. Increases in this variable are associated with decreases in the use of all three inputs per unit of output. The effect is greatest for capital, followed by labor, and finally fuel. This is in complete accord with the study by Y. Barzel, the only one to analyze the effect of capacity utilization.

> Besides economies of scale there are substantial economies in the intensive use of available equipment; these are obvious in the case of capital. They are quite important for labour which is almost a fixed factor after the plant is installed. Even fuel can be saved by operating the plant more intensively.[20]

Economies of scale were found here, but they were less important than in other studies; their effect is important for labor utilization, less important for capital, and not statistically significant for fuel. This ranking is the same as that found by Barzel, R. Komiya, and others, but the value of the scale elasticity for the three factors is much less in our study than in the others.

Shifts of the production function, represented here by the coefficient of the year in which the plant was built, are very important in this study; they represent an average 2.7 percent per year increase in technical efficiency. The effect on the input use is a reduction for all, with that of labor at 3.1 percent per year and fuel at 2.7 percent per year being greater than the 2.0 percent per year for capital. Other studies examine this effect with dummy variables or estimate different production functions for different periods. The movements are not uniform during the periods under consideration, but the general tendency is the same as that found here. The average value of the reduction in input use is of the same magnitude (about 2.5 percent per year), and the differences in the input savings follow the same pattern found in this study.

Barzel used accumulated hours in operation, a variable which he takes as an index of depreciation, to predict labor and fuel use. The coefficient for the labor equation was not significant; for the fuel equation it was significant but of incorrect sign according to his interpretation. Under our interpretation this variable would be associated with learning and the result would corroborate the hypothesis that such an effect exists.

In our study, the learning variable (accumulated production/maximum possible production) was significant; the efficiency of the plant increases in a small but significant way as this variable increases. The variable is quite important in the equations which explain the use of inputs; capital and fuel diminish while labor increases as the variable increases, suggesting that experience permits a substitution of labor for capital and fuel. The same arguments apply to the variable "accumulated maintenance," but its effect is much smaller; it is only an approximation for the variable "expenditures to alter the plant" so it is to be expected that with information on that variable directly, the effect could be distinguished better. These expenditures may be what permit the incorporation of experience into the modifications of the plant.

Over a period of five years of average operation, the combined effect of these two variables is a reduction of 0.3985 kilowatts capacity per kilowatt-hour (11.88 percent) in the use of capital, a reduction of 3.63 kilo-British Thermal Units (kBTU) per kilowatt-hour (17.68 percent) in that of fuel, and an increase of 2.27 man-hours per kilowatt-hour (41.07 percent) in labor. These values are estimated at the average values of the other variables. These reductions and increases are equivalent to a reduction of 37.20 pesos per kilowatt hour or 17.7 percent in cost, at factor prices of 5.92 pesos per man-hour, 11.95 pesos per BTU, and 18.22 pesos per kilowatt of monthly capacity, the averages for the period.

The other two variables included in the study were origin of the plant and a dummy to distinguish months in which the plant did not operate under normal conditions. The European plants are slightly more efficient than the American ones. They use less capital and fuel and more labor. Taking into account these effects one megawatt-hour (Mwh) generated by a European plant turns out to be $6.16 cheaper (2.93 percent) than one generated by an American plant; the difference is quite small and probably not significant given all the sources of error in the information. This would explain the presence of plants of varying origins.

The importance of the variables is not the same for all plants; those which represent learning and local inventive activity are much more important in new plants, suggesting that the greater part of these effects occurs during the first years of operation of a plant. Unfortunately, we have relatively little data corresponding to these first years, so it was not possible to fully analyze this phenomenon.

The studies of S. Hollander and J. Katz on technical change in other industries are of interest. Hollander found that a large part of the technical improvements in the Dupont rayon plants are associated with what he calls "small technical change" generally produced within the plants. (Small is defined as "having had a relatively simple development.") The contribution of these "small" changes was around 80 percent of total change in the four plants studied. These changes required investment in plant and equipment, but in the majority of the cases the investment involved replacement of equipment—necessary even in the absence of the changes—rather than net additions to capital formation. Katz estimated technological change in various Argentine industries and related this change to various variables measuring payments for imported technology and local inventive activity. The main results showed that:

> 90 percent of the variance among industries in technological change is (explained) statistically by the interindustrial variance of two variables: 1) the rate of increase in physical volume of production, and 2) accumulated research and development expenditures carried out locally in order to adapt to local conditions, and/or to improve marginally a design or product and/or process obtained previously by importation.

Our conclusions are thus reinforced by this multi-industry analysis in another Latin American country.

Our study shows that technological change in the electrical energy generating industry comes principally from abroad, incorporated in the generating equipment. It has for the most part the same characteristics as technological change in the same industry in the United States and Europe. Along with this imported change, one finds an internal learning and adaptation process which modifies the imported technology to the local context by means of changes in factor proportions.

ENDNOTES FOR CHAPTER 5

1. R. Komiya estimated Cobb-Douglas and limitational production functions for a sample of 235 new plants constructed between 1930 and 1956; his objective was to estimate the *ex ante* production function, not considering changes subsequent to the installation of the machinery. He found a tendency for fuel use to decrease and capital to increase, strong economies of scale, and an important reduction in labor requirements over time. See R. Komiya, "Technological Progress in the Production Function in the United States Steam Power Industry," *Review of Economics and Statistics* Vol 44, (1962). In this study, and other similar ones, a substitutional production function of Cobb-Douglas or constant elasticity of substitution type did not give completely satisfactory results as a description of the technology.
    W. R. Hughes found the orientation of technological change in the industry to be toward the construction of larger plants and the substitution of capital for fuel through greater thermic efficiency. See W. R. Hughes, "Scale Frontiers and Electric Power," in W. N. Capron, *Technological Change in Regulated Industries* (Washington: Brookings Institution, 1971).

2. The origin of studies using the "extreme" production function approach was the development of activity analysis and mathematical programming techniques. See, for example, T. C. Koopmans, "Analysis of Production as an Efficient Combination of Activities" Chapter 3 in T. C. Koopmans, ed., *Activity Analysis of Production and Allocation*, Cowles Commission Monograph 13, (New York: Wiley, 1951). It was used for the first time by M. J. Farrell in an analysis of American agriculture. See M. J. Farrell, "The Measurement of Productive Efficiency," *Journal of the Royal Statistical Society*, series A, part 3, Vol. 120 (1957). Farrell and M. Fieldhouse subsequently generalized the method in order to permit consideration of increasing returns to scale and used this generalization in an analysis of British agriculture. See M. J. Farrell and M. Fieldhouse, "Estimating Efficient Production Functions Under Increasing Returns to Scale," *Journal of the Royal Statistical Society*, series A, part 2, Vol 125 (1962). D. G. Aigner and S. F. Chu elaborated a logarithmic version of the method and estimated a Cobb-Douglas version for some industrial sectors in the United States, using data of G. Hildebrand and T. Liu. See D. G. Aigner and S. F. Chu, "On Estimating the Industry Production Function," *American Economic Review* Vol. 58 (1968); G. Hildebrand and T. Liu, *Manufacturing Production Functions in the United States, 1957* (Ithaca: Cornell University Press, 1965).
    Most of the studies using this focus seem to have involved the agricultural sector and in many cases the data used were at a high level of aggregation, with inputs and outputs in monetary units, thus introducing many of the estimation and interpretation problems found in the use of aggregate production functions.

3. S. Hollander, *The Sources of Increased Productivity: A Study of Dupont Rayon Plants* (Cambridge, Massachusetts: M.I.T. Press, 1965).

4. The plants present this monthly information to the Instituto Colombiano de Energia Electrica (ICEL). They are presented in a more complete form in M. Ramirez, "Technological Change in the Colombian Electric Power Industry" (Ph.D. dissertation, Yale, 1974).

5. For a thorough discussion of this, see Koopmans, *Activity Analysis of Production and Allocation*, Chapter 3.

6. In this study we analyze only technical efficiency (the relation between the quantity of output obtained and the maximum which could have been obtained with the same quantities of inputs), and not price efficiency (the relation between the amount of money spent in production and the minimum quantity which could have been spent to achieve the same level of output, given the efficient activities and factor prices). This is logical since our prime interest is technological change.

7. See Ramirez, "Technological Change," pp. 27-34 for the details of this process.

8. To see the full results, see Ibid.

9. Conceivably more efficient activities not observed in this sample could exist.

10. For discussion of some of these, see Chapter 7 of this volume by Francisco Thoumi.

11. For complete data, see Ramirez, "Technological Change," Appendix.

12. See, for example, A. A. Alchian, "Reliability of Progress Curves in Airframe Production," *Econometrica* Vol. 31 (1963); W. Z. Hirsch, "Manufacturing Progress Functions," *Review of Economics and Statistics* Vol. 34 (1952), and others.

13. Data for this variable are found in Ramirez, "Technological Change," Appendix.

14. A positive relation between efficiency and accumulated production is reflected as a positive coefficient in equation (6) and a negative one in equation (7).

15. A similar idea is found in a recent study by Jorge Katz on Argentine industry. See J. Katz, *Importación de Tecnología, Aprendizaje Local y Industrialización Dependiente* (Buenos Aires: Instituto Torcuato di Tella, 1972), mimeographed. He found a significant relationship between technological change in an industry and the accumulated value of research and development expenditures and between technological change and the accumulated value of research and development expenditures plus other technical expenditures (which includes maintenance, quality control, and technical management). The sort of research and development which he finds in Argentina is described as follows: "A significant proportion of local inventive activity is at this time dedicated to adaptation and to marginal improvements of processes and/or products whose technology was previously obtained through importation."

16. See, for example, H. Theil, *Principles of Econometrics* (New York: Wiley, 1971).

17. See P. Balestra and M. Nerlove, "Pooling Cross-Section and Time Series Data in the Estimation of a Dynamic Model: The Demand for Natural Gas," *Econometrica* Vol. 34 (1966), or Theil, *Principles of Econometrics*, for some of the problems which appear in this case and some methods of estimation.

18. For a more detailed analysis, see Ramirez, "Technological Change," pp. 71-73.

19. For a mathematical model which includes these assumptions and generates these results, see Ibid., pp. 54-60.

20. Y. Barzel, "The Production Function and Technical Change in the Steam Power Industry," *Journal of Political Economy* Vol. 72 (1964).

Chapter 6

Plant Size, Factor Proportions, and Efficiency in Colombian Industry
John Todd

An area of substantial controversy among policy makers in the developing countries is whether large-scale manufacturing enterprises are more efficient from a social point of view (i.e., have higher total factor productivity) than small and medium size establishments. A few quotations will help to illustrate. (Note the high correlation between size and capital intensity shown in Table 6.1 below.)

> "for most industries . . . capital intensive modern production methods are so much more economic than labor intensive ones that the opportunities for the substitution of labor for capital are extremely limited."[1]

> "In the first place, capital-output ratios tend to be lower in small industries . . . ."[2]

> "It is worth noting in this connection that large scale modern industry is usually much less profitable than the small craft-type industries, in addition to being more costly in terms of capital and creating less employment."[3]

> "For almost any factor prices and in almost any industry, efficiently operated modern technology is more productive than craft production . . . ."[4]

These quotations and others like them leave two impressions. First, all the authors are surprisingly sure of their judgments. Second, the absence of any agreed-upon common statistic makes many such statements difficult to prove or disprove.

This chapter discusses differences in the economic characteristics and performance of Colombian manufacturing firms by size of plant, compares the social efficiency of small and large plants in Colombia as of the mid-sixties, and comments on various governmental policies in this area. Part I deals with issues of methodology and theory. Part II presents our estimates of social efficiency by size of plant, and explains the rationale and limitations of the index used. Large plants were generally found to be less efficient than smaller ones. Part III discusses several possible explanations for this result, and Part IV deals with policy implications.

TABLE 6.1

INDICATORS OF THE CAPITAL/LABOR RATIO,
BY GROUPED SIZE CLASSES, 1966

Plant Size (number of employees)	Very Small (less than 15)	Small (15-49)	Medium (50-199)	Large (200 or more)
Indicator				
$\dfrac{\text{Horsepower}^a}{\text{Total Employment}^b}$	1.75	3.14	3.07	4.76
$\dfrac{\text{Value of Fixed Assets}^c}{\text{Horsepower}}$	2.6	2.8	5.2	5.6
$\dfrac{\text{Value of Fixed Assets}^c}{\text{Total Employment}}$	4.6	8.8	16.0	26.7
$\dfrac{\text{Value of Fixed Assets}}{\text{Total Employment}}$ (index: Large plants = 100)	17.0	33.0	60.0	100.0

Source: Departamento Administrativo Nacional de Estadística (DANE), *Anuario General de Estadística,* 1966-1967, Tomo IV.

[a] Installed horsepower capacity (excluding in-plant electrical generators) ready to use.

[b] Paid and unpaid workers as of November 31, 1966.

[c] Estimated based on DANE investment data and explained in Part II under section entitled "Value Added/Fixed Capital Ratios by Size of Plant." The unit in which this ratio is defined (thousands of 1958 pesos per horsepower) is not very meaningful for reasons explained below.

PART I

THEORY AND METHODOLOGY

Importance of Firm Size

Colombia's manufacturing sector, like that in most developing countries, is comprised of a wide range of firm and plant sizes.[5] Available data indicate a strong correlation between size and capital/labor ratios (see Table 6.1). Although quantitative evidence is not available, most observers would agree that size is also highly correlated with more modern production methods, percentage of capital equipment which is imported, and political and economic influence. Therefore, economic characteristics related to firm or plant size are likely to be related to these other variables as well.

Size of firm is a useful variable in economic analysis both because it may be a proxy for other important variables like factor proportions on which little statistical information is directly available, and because it is an important dimension in its own right. Many economic policies and circumstances have, or are alleged to have, their impact by size of firm. For example, access to cheap credit and foreign exchange and ability to deal with red tape are all alleged to vary with size of firm. Furthermore, many developing nations have instituted measures specifically designed to assist smaller firms. To evaluate these circumstances and policies, comparative analysis by size of firm is necessary. Practically speaking, analysis is feasible since data are reasonably available by size of firm; and from a policy point of view, size is a more easily useable variable than many others (e.g., modernity of technology).

Plant Size and Firm Size

Although much theory postulates economic differences by size of firm, almost all of the manufacturing statistics available in Colombia refer to plants. This difference can be important. Economies of scale, for example, are partially related to size of plant (particularly in production technology) and partially related to size of firm (in marketing and management services). It seems reasonable to assume that some of the differences in wage rates and perhaps most of the differences in access to capital and foreign exchange are related basically to size of firm and not to size of plant. In interpreting the empirical results of this study, it is important to remember that, strictly speaking, they pertain only to size of plant; until we know the relative importance and special characteristics of multi-plant firms, they must be interpreted with care.

Choosing an Index of Social Efficiency

The private rate of return becomes an interesting guide to resource allocation when prices of inputs are close to the marginal social opportunity cost and output prices reflect the opportunity cost of factors used in producing the marginal unit. (The term "social efficiency" is used to reflect this valuation of inputs and outputs at their social opportunity cost). But it seems unlikely that these conditions were approximated in mid-sixties' Colombia. Robert L. Slighton presents persuasive evidence that the wage differential between large and small plants was considerably greater than scarcity criteria would suggest to be necessary.[6] Furthermore, given the apparently substantial unemployment and/or underemployment, it may even have been that most plants paid wages above the marginal social opportunity cost of labor, with the larger plants farther above. While less evidence exists, most experts agree that much capital was underpriced in Colombia and that larger firms had easier access to it.[7] Similar arguments exist regarding access to imported raw materials. In short, the profit rate is not likely to be a very helpful index for our purposes. (In any case, data on profits by firm or plant size do not exist.)

In principle, a measure of social efficiency should take into account externalities, dynamic effects, and distributional impact, but here, due to data limitations, we try simply to measure the impact of a plant on current national income.[8] Of two possible indicators, the benefit/cost ratio and the net benefit/unit constraint ratio,[9] which given all the relevant information and a large computer would be identical,[10] the latter is more attractive for our purposes. It concentrates on capital, presumably the main constraint, and thus facilitates an intuitive understanding of the issue.[11] More important, with only capital in the denominator, its absolute cost—on which no good data are available—becomes unimportant; only the relative value across size classes matters. This is not the case with the benefit/cost ratio. The proxy for capital stock used here is based on installed horsepower capacity adjusted by investment data. Minor adjustments for labor or foreign exchange usage are, as needed, done in the numerator.[12] The specific measure of social efficiency used is thus "value added minus any non-capital scarce factor costs per unit of capital," i.e.,

$$[VA - \sum_{i=1}^{n} (QSF_i \cdot PSF_i)]/K,$$

where QSF and PSF are the quantity and price of the n scarce factors other than capital. It is interesting and feasible to make adjustments to value added because of probable differences between the social and private costs for labor and imported raw materials. As it turns out, neither adjustment significantly affects the relative values of the index across plant sizes, so in practice the output/capital ratio becomes an acceptable indicator of social efficiency.

The Output/Capital Ratio by Size of Plant—Some Theoretical Context

Before further discussing the data, it is useful to consider what sets of conditions are consistent with the strong correlation observed between size and capital/labor ratio. We first consider this question with a very simple model, then gradually relax the assumptions.

Assume the private objective of profit maximization and the existence of two inputs—capital and labor. With smooth, convex isoquants, constant returns to scale (CRTS) throughout, and factor prices equal for all scales of operation, the privately optimal capital/labor ratio is the same for all scales of operation (Figure 6.1). Both Q/K and private efficiency—defined by maximization of (Q-WL)/K, where Q is value added, K capital, L labor, and W wage rate—will be equal for all sizes of firm (points A, B, and C in Figure 6.1 are examples). The capital/labor ratio utilized at each scale is identical. Thus no unique optimal scale of operations exists from either a private or a social point of view, and market structure is undetermined.[13]

Under increasing returns to scale (IRTS) over a certain range and decreasing returns thereafter, there is a privately optimal scale where decreasing returns set in, and a maximum value of (Q-WL)/K. Suppose it is point C in Figure 6.2. Since the optimal capital/labor ratio at each scale is again the same, the scale (here output C) which maximizes (Q-WL)/K also maximizes Q/K, since WL/K is equal along any ray.[14] Thus if, due to segmented markets, we observe points A, C, and F in operation, we know that point C has both a higher profit rate and a higher output/capital ratio than points A and F. Of course a point like G would have a still higher output/capital ratio.

In reality, the less developed countries show a strong tendency for larger firms and plants to have a higher capital/labor ratio.[15] Two explanations are the most plausible. First, production functions may not be homothetic;[16] there may be greater IRTS along the more capital intensive rays, as exemplified in Figure 6.3.[17] Second, the price of labor in

FIGURE 6.1

FACTOR PROPORTIONS AND LEVEL OF PRODUCTION UNDER CONSTANT RETURNS TO SCALE AND EQUAL FACTOR PRICE RATIOS

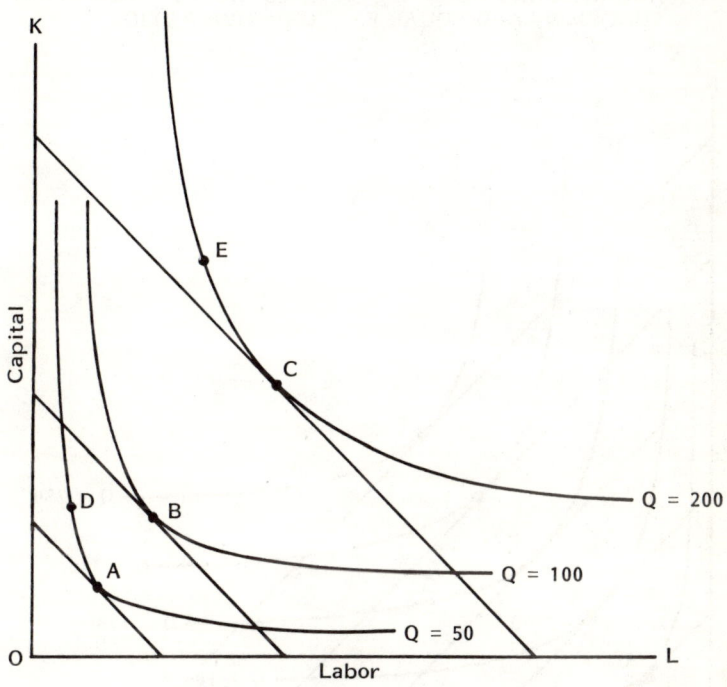

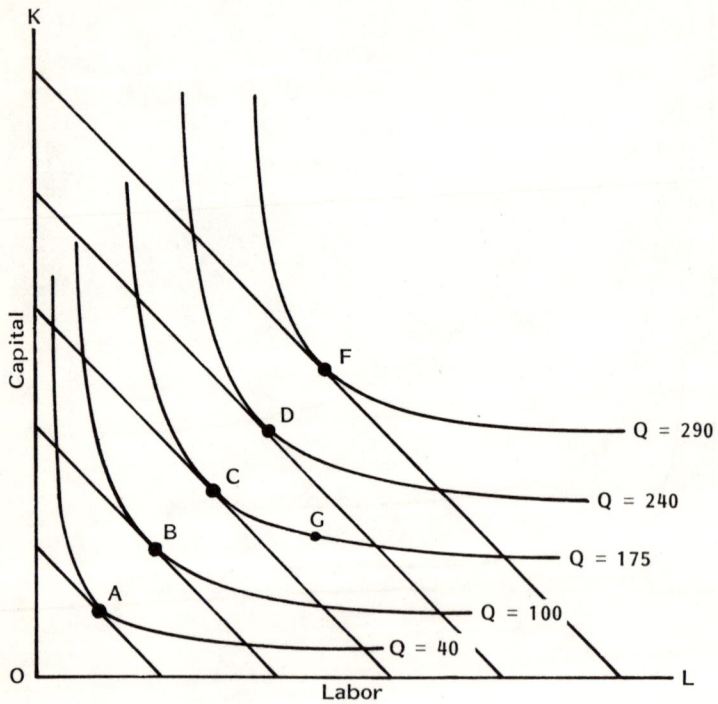

FIGURE 6.2

FACTOR PROPORTIONS AND LEVEL OF PRODUCTION UNDER INCREASING RETURNS TO SCALE, A HOMOTHETIC PRODUCTION FUNCTION, AND EQUAL FACTOR PRICE RATIOS

FIGURE 6.3

FACTOR PROPORTIONS AND SIZE UNDER INCREASING RETURNS TO SCALE, A NON-HOMOTHETIC PRODUCTION FUNCTION, AND EQUAL FACTOR PRICE RATIOS

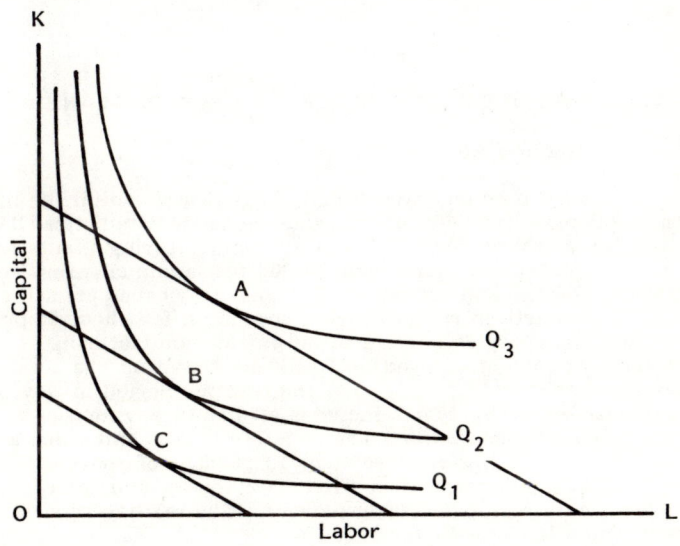

larger firms (plants) may be higher and/or the price of capital may be lower.[18] A combination of both effects is shown in Figure 6.4.

With two forces affecting the output/capital ratio by size of firm (plant)—the differential returns to scale along rays of different capital intensity and the different relative factor prices by size of the production unit—no generalization is possible as to which size of firm (plant) will have the larger $(Q-WL)/K$ or Q/K, nor even the higher K/L. If returns to scale are more important for the more capital-intensive technologies *and* the relative price of labor is higher for larger firms (plants)— a logical set of assumptions—then large firms (plants) would be expected to have higher K/L ratios.[19] Still, even if equal profit rates across size are assumed, it is not possible to deduce which scale or which capital/labor ratio will have the highest output/capital ratio. *A fortiori*, if equal profit rates are not assumed, then even given equal factor prices, no generalization can be made as to which scale or which K/L will imply a higher Q/K. In short, unless equal profit rates *plus* either homothetic isoquants or equal factor prices are assumed, then output/capital ratios must be measured directly if cross-size comparisons are to be made.

PART II

ESTIMATING NET SOCIAL BENEFIT BY SIZE OF PLANT

Description of Data and Adjustments

The data used here on value added, wages, and capital (or proxy) come from the Departmento Administrativo Nacional de Estadística (DANE). They cover (or are intended to cover) all manufacturing plants having five or more employees or more than 24,000 pesos annual gross output (U.S. $1500 in 1968),[20] and exclude what is generally called artisan manufacturing. In 1964 artisan manufacturing accounted for about 55 percent of employment and about 20 percent of output in manufacturing.

The ten size categories used by DANE are based on the total number of workers (paid and unpaid) as of the last pay period in November. The largest size class (9), which includes all plants having 200 or more employees, accounts for a high share of total workers and value added. (Tables 6.2 and 6.3.) In 1967 less than 10 percent of the value added came from plants having less than fifteen employees and more than 50 percent from plants with over 200 employees. The relative importance of the largest plants increased over 1956-67.

Statistics collected by DANE include employment, wages, fringe benefits, value of gross production, purchase of raw materials and power, purchase of fixed capital, and installed horsepower capacity. Among the various weaknesses in DANE's data is an overestimation of value added due to failure to subtract out certain purchased inputs.[21] Although we have no breakdown of these figures by size of plant, it would appear almost certain that the costs in question are more important in the larger firms and therefore in the larger plants as well; large-firm value added is probably overestimated by a greater percentage than that of small firms.

Another problem relates to plants with less than fifteen employees and to the period after 1962. Prior to that year, the sample of the plants with less than fifteen workers was assumed to be representative of its size class and sector, and the nonsample was blown up accordingly; this probably gave roughly accurate results.[22] After 1962 (as computers became more prevalent) the statistics from the last year in which a nonsampled plant had reported (often as far back as 1962) were simply

FIGURE 6.4

FACTOR PROPORTIONS AND SIZE UNDER INCREASING RETURNS TO SCALE, A NON-HOMOTHETIC PRODUCTION FUNCTION, AND A HIGHER RELATIVE PRICE OF CAPITAL FOR SMALL FIRMS

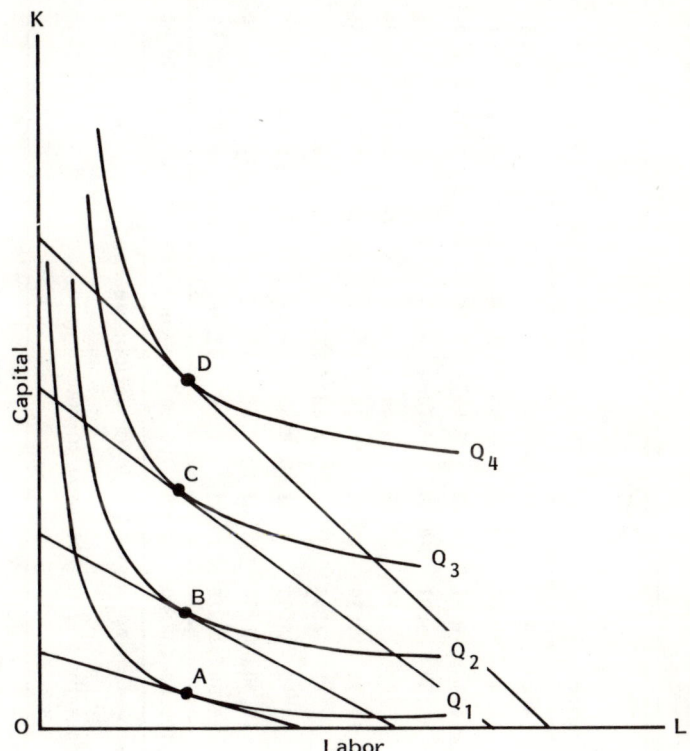

TABLE 6.2

PERCENT DISTRIBUTION OF TOTAL EMPLOYMENT BY SIZE CLASS, 1956-67[a]

Size Class	Number of Workers	1956	1957	1958	1959	1960	1961	1962	1963	1964	1965	1966	1967
0	Less than 5	4.24	4.20	4.27	3.71	3.68	3.51	3.65	3.65	3.75	3.66	3.62	3.73
1	5-9	10.41	10.43	9.47	8.73	8.18	8.20	8.22	8.19	8.49	8.52	8.05	6.95
2	10-14	6.10	6.31	6.23	5.69	5.34	5.12	5.34	6.46	7.07	7.33	6.83	4.64
3	15-19	4.54	4.97	4.89	4.70	4.43	4.41	4.27	3.08	2.68	2.20	2.16	3.34
4	20-24	3.48	3.71	3.99	3.54	3.17	3.28	3.49	2.94	2.63	2.77	2.66	3.16
5	25-49	12.18	12.30	11.91	11.64	11.56	11.55	11.26	10.35	10.35	10.51	10.08	10.69
6	50-74	7.21	7.08	7.43	7.68	7.22	7.16	6.96	7.29	6.48	6.51	6.29	7.12
7	75-99	4.95	4.68	4.38	4.46	4.31	4.65	4.62	4.75	5.18	5.01	5.36	5.30
8	100-199	12.30	11.51	11.85	12.59	12.27	12.01	12.48	12.70	12.73	12.26	12.91	13.27
9	More than 200	34.54	34.75	35.52	37.22	39.76	40.03	39.67	40.54	40.59	41.18	41.99	41.78
10	Total	100.00	100.00	100.00	100.00	100.00	100.00	100.00	100.00	100.00	100.00	100.00	100.00

Source: DANE, *Anuario General de Estadística*, various years.

[a] Columns do not necessarily add to 100, due to rounding.

TABLE 6.3

PERCENT DISTRIBUTION OF VALUE ADDED BY SIZE CLASS, 1956-67[a]

Size Class	1956	1957	1958	1959	1960	1961	1962	1963	1964	1965	1966	1967
0	1.82	1.84	1.88	1.42	1.55	1.37	1.54	1.17	1.20	1.15	1.11 (1.6)	1.31
1	4.49	4.25	3.94	3.45	3.25	3.18	3.20	2.59	2.54	2.46	2.49 (3.8)	2.34
2	2.45	3.12	3.06	2.82	2.75	2.48	2.58	2.72	2.82	2.79	2.58 (4.2)	2.12
3	2.47	2.44	2.39	2.31	2.22	2.40	2.31	1.68	1.57	1.22	1.12 (1.1)	1.65
4	1.98	2.30	2.43	1.87	1.74	1.73	1.84	1.81	1.74	1.63	1.64 (1.6)	1.85
5	8.96	8.97	9.25	5.85	8.43	8.68	8.37	7.18	7.57	8.15	8.09 (7.8)	7.84
6	6.68	7.18	7.25	6.94	6.15	5.81	5.48	5.92	6.30	5.95	5.29 (5.1)	5.93
7	7.40	5.39	3.86	4.07	4.24	5.55	4.39	4.48	4.47	4.54	4.9 (4.8)	5.52
8	14.41	15.58	16.78	18.09	17.25	17.25	18.06	18.64	18.22	19.20	18.36 (17.7)	18.35
9	48.79	48.88	49.10	50.12	52.38	51.51	52.17	53.79	53.52	52.83	54.32 (52.3)	53.09
10	100.00	100.00	100.00	100.00	100.00	100.00	100.00	100.00	100.00	100.00	100.00 (100.00)	100.00

Source: DANE, *Anuario General de Estadística*, various years.

[a] Columns do not necessarily add to 100, due to rounding.
( ) = Figures based on the simple correction methodology of Table 6.4 as explained below. They are our best estimate.

reused. This imparted a downward bias to all monetary figures and a potential bias to the employee and horsepower figures as well. To estimate the extent to this bias, the original printouts of each plant's basic data for 1962 and 1966 were obtained. The reporting plants in 1966 were assumed identical to the nonreporting plants in the same size class, permitting an adjustment to the value added figures in the nonreporting plants.[23] Unfortunately, the horsepower figures had to be accepted as given since the 1966 data covered only employment and output figures; bias here is not likely to be too serious since the horsepower figures are not affected by inflation. As a result of this adjustment (see Table 6.4), the relative value added per worker of the smallest plants improves after 1962 rather than deteriorating.[24]

Although used by some analysts, DANE's installed horsepower capacity figures are not a good proxy for capital stock for two reasons. First, machinery as a percentage of capital stock varies over time, among sectors, and among size classes; second, even for machinery, the ratio of horsepower to constant peso value of capital varies over time, among sectors, and among size classes.[25] Accordingly, we use both horsepower and an estimate of capital based on a firm's reported investment (accumulated over time), and we check for consistency between the two.

DANE's gross investment figures (labelled "net" but in fact net of sales rather than depreciation, so really gross) are annual flows and may be expected to bear some relation to changes in installed horsepower, after allowance for depreciation. To check the consistency of the investment and horsepower statistics, the following linear relationship[26] was tested on a variety of data and with various options:[27]

$$IN_t/PIN_t = B_o + B_1 HP_{t-1} + B_2 DHP + e$$

where:

IN_t = net investment in fixed capital in year t,
PIN_t = manufactured products price index in year t,
HP_{t-1} = installed horsepower at the end of year t-1, and
$DHP = HP_t - HP_{t-1}$.

Briefly, the results do not show a strong relationship, either time-series or cross-section, between the investment figures and changes in horsepower. The accuracy of the investment figures is suspect, however. Slighton argues, for example,[28] that to avoid taxes companies often underreport their investment to balance their accounts. Furthermore, some firms may not understand that replacement investment is to be reported. The low correlations for annual time-series data do not rule out the possibility of a significant underlying relationship, even allowing for the possible inadequacies of the investment data mentioned above. The long gestation of some investments, some intersize class movement of plants, and the erratic reporting procedures (a high percentage of plants reporting to DANE in any one year show net investment equal to zero), all of which weaken any short-run relationship, do not preclude a long-run tie being reasonably well reflected in the data.

Our basic concern here is whether the peso value of an installed horsepower (referred to hereafter as K/HP) varies systematically with size of plant. To test this, plants have been grouped into four size classes.[29] Notice first that over the period 1956-1967 the large plants increased their percentage of fixed investment from 50 percent to nearly 70 percent (Table 6.5), while their percentage of the change in horse-

TABLE 6.4

VALUE ADDED PER WORKER, BY SIZE CLASS, SELECTED YEARS

(Thousands of 1952 Pesos)

Size Class	1957	1962	1966[a]	1966[b]	1967	$\frac{1962}{1957}$	$\frac{1966^a}{1962}$	$\frac{1966^b}{1962}$	$\frac{1962}{1957}$	$\frac{1966^a}{1962}$	$\frac{1966^b}{1962}$
0	351	441	335	509	397	1.26	0.76	1.15			
1	325	406	336	542	381	1.25	0.83	1.33	1.26	0.80	1.39
2	395	503	410	699	519	1.27	0.82	1.70			
3	392	565	564		561	1.44	1.00				
4	495	551	672		663	1.11	1.22		1.29	1.12	
5	582	774	873		830	1.33	1.13				
6	810	820	914		944	1.01	1.01				
7	919	989	1,006		1,181	1.08	1.02				
8	1,080	1,507	1,545		1,566	1.40	1.03		1.02	1.03	
9	1,123	1,370	1,405		1,440	1.22	1.03				
10	798	1,042	1,087		1,132	1.31	1.04				

Source: DANE, *Anuario General de Estadística*, various years, except for 1966[b], the methodology for which is explained in Part II under the section entitled "Description of Data and Adjustments."

[a] Published by DANE.

[b] My calculation.

TABLE 6.5

PERCENT DISTRIBUTION OF FIXED INVESTMENT AND HORSEPOWER, BY GROUPED SIZE CLASSES, 1956-67

Plant Size Class	1956	1957	1958	1959	1960	1961	1962	1963	1964	1965	1966	1967
Investment in Fixed Capital (IN)												
Very Small[a]		5.7	4.3	5.1	3.9	3.7	3.4	5.4	4.3	4.1	3.6	2.4
Small[b]		12.9	9.9	11.5	11.9	12.2	8.9	10.6	8.6	10.1	8.4	7.0
Medium[c]		31.3	27.6	37.6	26.5	22.8	22.0	30.5	19.2	18.8	18.3	21.8
Large[d]		50.2	58.2	45.8	57.7	61.3	65.7	53.5	67.9	66.9	69.7	68.2
Horsepower (HP)												
Very Small	9.1	8.9	8.7	8.3	8.1	7.7	8.1	8.5	8.8	9.1	9.2	7.3
Small	11.5	11.7	12.3	11.2	12.0	12.4	12.3	12.9	12.9	13.4	13.2	17.9
Medium	19.0	19.0	18.7	20.7	19.6	20.4	20.8	20.4	19.8	19.7	21.3	22.6
Large	60.5	60.4	60.2	59.8	60.4	59.5	58.8	58.1	58.7	57.8	56.4	52.2
Change in Horsepower (DHP)[e]												
Very Small		8.0	-4.5	5.3	-3.8	0.2	14.2	11.9	12.9	16.6	11.2	-2.8
Small		13.3	47.4	1.5	46.5	22.3	10.2	18.8	12.5	25.1	7.6	42.6
Medium		19.0	4.5	37.4	-32.1	38.6	27.1	17.1	9.7	17.0	67.3	29.9
Large		59.7	52.6	55.8	89.5	38.9	48.6	52.1	68.1	36.7	13.9	30.3

Source: DANE, *Anuario General de Estadística*, various years.

[a] class sizes 0, 1, 2
[b] class sizes 3, 4, 5
[c] class sizes 6, 7, 8
[d] class size 9
[e] $DHP_t = HP_t - HP_{t-1}$

power varied widely around an average of about 50 percent until falling sharply after 1964. Over the entire period, the large plants accounted for 61 percent of the fixed investment and only 46 percent of the change in horsepower. Their share of total installed horsepower capacity fell from 60 percent in 1956 to 56 percent in 1966 and 52 percent in 1967.

The various assumptions which could be made about depreciation and initial (1956) fixed capital stock lead to different estimates of K/HP. [30] One alternative is to assume that accumulated gross investment since 1956 equals the present value of the fixed capital stock (i.e., that the value of fixed capital in 1956 is equal to the depreciation during 1956-67); the resulting statistic is shown as INR/HP67 in Table 6.6. Toward the other extreme, we could assume zero depreciation (or that depreciation was equal to underreporting of investment), so that accumulated investment since 1956 gives the net fixed capital formation over the period; the resulting ratio is shown as INR/DHP in Table 6.6. Both alternatives show a higher ratio for the large plants than for the rest by a ratio of almost two to one, but with somewhat different patterns among the four size groups. A fully satisfactory statistic should include an estimate of depreciation; otherwise groups with high initial fixed capital stocks will have an upward biased estimate of K/HP relative to other groups. Two such calculations (Y5 percent and Y10 percent of Table 6.6) also show a fixed capital/horsepower ratio of twice as high for the large firms as for the small ones. Though there is considerable variation in the pattern across three digit industries, the most frequent one is that which emerges from the aggregate statistics, indicating that the overall pattern is not due to an aggregation bias. [31] (Table 6.7.)

There appears to have been a relative increase over time in the fixed capital/horsepower ratio (K/HP) of the larger plants. Note, for example, the positive trend in the annual investment to change in horsepower ratio for large firms, YL_t, compared to the relatively stable values of YVS_t, YS_t, and YM_t. Part of this trend may be artificial and attributable to a decrease in the number of medium size plants moving into the large-plant category. In this case the later year estimates will be more accurate. [32]

The fixed capital/horsepower ratio used in the rest of this chapter is Y10 percent. It makes an explicit allowance for depreciation; since as between Y5 percent and Y10 percent the largest plants come off better with Y10 percent, we follow the usual custom of choosing the option which least favors our eventual conclusions.

Value Added/Fixed Capital Ratios by Size of Plant

Our best estimate of value added/fixed capital by size of plant is presented in Table 6.8. Many further adjustments would be desirable to produce a more accurate indicator of social efficiency; lack of appropriate data restricts our attention to two such possible adjustments. These are a nonzero social opportunity cost of labor and shadow pricing of the underpriced foreign exchange used to import raw materials. While neither adjustment affects the basic conclusion that large plants are much less efficient than small ones, the exercise does help to broaden our information about the different plant sizes.

The sensitivity of the relative net social benefit/fixed capital ratios to different assumptions about the marginal social cost of labor (MSC_L) is explored using two alternatives to the value of zero assumed in Table 6.8. [33] One is MSC_L equal to the actual wage paid (see Table 6.9), and the other is MSC_L equal to the average wage paid in the three smallest

TABLE 6.6

ESTIMATES OF THE FIXED CAPITAL/HORSEPOWER RATIO, BY GROUPED SIZE CLASSES, 1957-67

							Year (t)					
		1957	1958	1959	1960	1961	1962	1963	1964	1965	1966	1967
Gross investment/ Change in Horse-power, by Year, 1956-67 (Y_t)	YVS_t Very Small	3.5	3.1	2.0	3.3	3.5	2.1	1.6	2.5	2.4	2.4	5.6
	YS_t Small	5.3	2.9	4.7	3.5	4.3	5.0	2.0	3.9	4.0	4.7	0.7
	YM_t Medium	8.6	8.1	3.4	12.6	4.8	6.0	4.9	6.8	6.5	3.8	2.5
	YL_t Large	4.4	4.9	2.1	4.6	6.1	7.6	2.9	6.3	8.3	9.9	5.3
		$\Sigma INR/HP_{67}$			$\Sigma INR/DHP$				$Y10\%$			
Alternative Estimates of the Ratio Fixed Capital/Horsepower, 1967.	Very Small	3.7			8.1		$Y5\%$		2.6			
	Small	3.7			5.2		4.0		2.8			
	Medium	7.1			11.2		3.6		5.2			
	Large	7.8			15.8		7.1		5.6			
							8.2					

Source: Based on data from DANE, *Anuario General de Estadística*, various years.

ΣINR = sum of deflated investment 1956-67

$DHP = HP_{67} - HP_{56}$

$Y_t = \dfrac{INR_t}{\overline{(.10 \cdot HP_{t-1}) + (HP_t - HP_{t-1})}}$ (10% depreciation rate)

$Y5\% = \dfrac{\Sigma INR}{\overline{(.05 \cdot HP) + (HP_{67} - HP_{56})}}$ (5% depreciation rate)

$Y10\% = \dfrac{\Sigma INR}{\overline{(.10 \cdot HP) + (HP_{67} - HP_{56})}}$ (10% depreciation rate)

HP = sum of annual, horsepower stock 1956-67, or $\sum_i HP_i$ where i runs from 1956 to 1967

TABLE 6.7

ALTERNATIVE ESTIMATES OF THE FIXED CAPITAL/ HORSEPOWER RATIO, BY GROUPED SIZE CLASSES,[a] 1967
(Selected Three-digit Sectors)

Sector		Size Class	$\Sigma INR/HP_{67}$	$\Sigma INR/DHP$	Y5%	Y10%
206	Bread Products	Very Small	3.6	6.5	3.9	2.8
		Small	15.3	-3,368.2	32.6	16.2
		Medium	14.1	23.8	16.3	12.3
		Large	8.6	-21.5	99.9	15.0
241	Shoes	Very Small	4.3	13.7	6.1	3.9
		Small	4.5	14.0	6.6	4.3
		Medium	4.6	22.5	8.0	4.8
		Large	17.0	160.5	28.5	15.6
261	Furniture	Very Small	1.5	-20.7	3.5	1.6
		Small	2.2	4.9	3.0	2.1
		Medium	4.0	9.6	5.0	3.4
		Large	3.6	10.7	5.0	3.3
311	Basic Chemicals (Not Oil)	Very Small	6.1	8.7	6.6	5.3
		Small	1.9	2.1	1.6	1.4
		Medium	10.2	11.2	9.5	8.3
		Large	8.0	10.1	7.6	6.1
331	Bricks	Very Small	1.2	29.5	2.4	1.3
		Small	2.1	7.2	2.9	1.8
		Medium	3.6	8.7	4.8	3.3
		Large	7.2	-123.7	7.5	3.7
355	Aluminum Products	Very Small	-1.1	-2.6	-0.8	-1.3
		Small	2.1	2.8	1.7	2.2
		Medium	5.5	-62.7	6.3	14.1
		Large	0.9	2.4	0.8	1.2

Source: DANE, *Anuario General de Estadística*, various years.

[a] Definitions are the same as in Table 6.6 except that the period covered is 1959-67, since data at this level of aggregation were not available before 1959.

TABLE 6.8

OUTPUT/FIXED CAPITAL RATIOS,[a] BY GROUPED SIZE CLASSES,
1956-67 AVERAGE

	Plant Size (number of workers)			
	Very Small (less than 15)	Small (15-49)	Medium (50-199)	Large (200 or more)
VA/Fixed Capital	1.01 (1.17)[b]	1.06	0.83	0.48
Index: Large plants = 100	210 (243)[b]	221	173	100

Source: VA and HP data from DANE, *Anuario General de Estadística*, various years. The estimates of Y10% from Table 6.6.

[a]Defined as: $\frac{VA}{HP \cdot Y10\%}$ (i.e., with fixed capital defined by HP·Y10%).

[b]Reflects my adjustment to value added as explained in Part II under the section entitled "Description of Data and Adjustments" and detailed in Table 6.4.

TABLE 6.9

VALUE ADDED - (PAID + IMPUTED WAGES)[a], BY SIZE CLASS, 1956-67
HORSEPOWER

Size Class	Number of Workers	1956	1957	1958	1959	1960	1961	1962	1963	1964	1965	1966	1967
0	Less than 5	1.69	1.60	1.56	1.05	1.61	1.57	1.85	1.46 (1.70)	1.47 (1.95)	1.54 (2.30)	1.26 (1.89)	1.23 (1.06)
1	5-9	1.98	1.62	1.69	1.47	1.56	1.69	1.78	1.45 (1.68)	1.31 (1.73)	1.30 (1.92)	1.31 (2.06)	1.25 (1.67)
2	10-14	1.96	1.97	1.59	1.54	1.88	1.83	1.85	1.51 (1.80)	1.42 (1.82)	1.35 (1.94)	1.32 (2.24)	1.40 (1.83)
3	15-19	1.96	1.77	1.19	1.67	2.06	1.96	2.37	1.93	1.87	1.45	1.36	1.56
4	20-24	2.02	2.07	2.02	1.68	2.08	1.66	1.99	2.16	2.14	1.82	1.97	2.13
5	25-49	2.54	2.09	2.03	2.05	1.90	2.21	2.24	1.55	1.53	1.69	1.72	0.93
6	50-74	2.95	3.28	2.94	2.57	2.67	2.27	2.17	2.31	2.87	2.93	2.78	1.38
7	75-99	4.74	2.42	2.07	2.45	2.78	2.94	3.36	3.26	2.80	2.54	2.58	2.43
8	100-199	3.34	3.33	3.14	2.79	3.25	3.70	3.72	3.78	3.30	3.82	3.03	3.16
9	200 or more	1.86	1.63	1.50	1.54	1.79	1.82	2.05	2.06	1.83	1.84	1.71	1.68
10	Total	2.22	1.95	1.81	1.79	2.03	2.10	2.28	2.20	2.00	2.06	2.01	1.70

Source: Same as Table 6.8.

( ) = Figures that reflect the adjustment to value added explained in "Description of Data and Adjustments," Part II.

[a] i.e., $\dfrac{VA - [(SS + PS) \cdot TO/TR]}{HP}$, where SS is wages and salaries; PS is fringe benefits; TO is total numbers of workers; TR is total number of paid workers.

size classes, referred to as the craft wage (see Table 6.10).[34] In Tables 6.8 to 6.15, my adjusted figures for 1966 are shown in parentheses. In Table 6.11 the average value (over 1956-67) of each measure is shown with firms grouped into four size classes.[35] Horsepower is used without adjustment as the proxy for capital stock; this enables us to use all ten size categories and all twelve years, and does not affect our conclusions about the impact of this adjustment, which depends on how the numerator reacts to varying assumptions about the MSC of labor.

In general, when MSC_L is assumed to equal the actual wage paid (Table 6.9) its inclusion in our measure of social efficiency does not much affect relative efficiency.[36] The relative value for size class 8 is slightly higher in Table 6.9 than in Table 6.8, and those for the smallest plants before 1962 slightly lower. Wage differences across size classes are, however, quite large, and when MSC_L is assumed equal to the average wage paid in the three smallest size classes, the relative positions of the largest plants improve a great deal, particularly in relation to the smallest ones (Table 6.10). The largest plants now have a higher benefit/horsepower ratio than the smallest though if we apply our K/HP estimates (see Table 6.15), they are again lower in terms of social benefit/capital stock. The relative position of size class 9 is improved somewhat, but classes 6, 7, and 8 still show generally higher values.

Application of a shadow price to imported raw materials is appropriate when the currency is overvalued, so that the peso price of an imported intermediate good does not reflect its social cost. Several attempts have been made to estimate the equilibrium exchange rate for Colombia around the mid-sixties. The difference of relevance to us here is not that between actual and equilibrium exchange rates but that between the present monetary cost and the present marginal social benefit of imports. In terms of Figure 6.5, we need BE/AB, not BC/AB. Suppose this percentage averaged 50 percent over the period 1956-67 (perhaps a little higher than most other estimates but within the usual range). We can then compute the net social benefit/horsepower ratio as:[37]

$$[VA - (.5 \cdot MP \cdot \%MPF)]/HP$$

where:

  VA = value added,
  MP = total intermediate inputs,
  %MPF = percentage of MP imported by that size class, and
  HP = horsepower.

Despite the substantially higher share of inputs imported by larger firms (see Table 6.13), this adjustment makes little difference to the estimated relative efficiency of size classes. (Compare Table 6.14 with 6.8.) Although the percentage of imported, intermediate inputs grows significantly with size of plant, intermediate inputs as a percentage of value added decrease (larger plants are more vertically integrated), and this partially offsets the former tendency. As a result, the degree of overvaluation is not an important parameter in our calculations. Lack of information prevents the effecting of another adjustment for importation of capital goods. With the higher K/O ratio of large plants and the probability that a higher share of their capital is imported, this factor might be significant, lowering their relative performance. On the other hand, the evidence presented by Carlos F. Díaz-Alejandro in Chapter 8 indicates that large firms (and presumably large plants) account for most of

TABLE 6.10
VALUE ADDED − (LABOR FORCE × CRAFT WAGE), BY SIZE CLASS, 1956-67
HORSEPOWER

Size Class	Number of Workers	1956	1957	1958	1959	1960	1961	1962	1963	1964	1965	1966	1967
0	Less than 5	1.69	1.60	1.56	1.05	1.61	1.57	1.85	1.41 (1.70)	1.47 (1.95)	1.54 (2.30)	1.26 (1.89)	1.23 (1.66)
1	5-9	1.98	1.51	1.69	1.47	1.56	1.69	1.78	1.45 (1.68)	1.31 (1.73)	1.49 (2.20)	1.31 (2.06)	1.25 (1.67)
2	10-14	1.96	1.99	1.59	1.54	1.88	1.83	1.85	1.57 (1.80)	1.42 (1.82)	1.35 (1.94)	1.32 (2.24)	1.42 (1.83)
3	15-19	2.21	1.99	1.72	1.91	2.31	2.23	2.64	2.41	2.31	1.90	1.67	1.80
4	20-24	2.34	2.50	2.37	1.97	2.44	1.95	2.32	2.71	2.63	2.40	2.44	2.52
5	25-49	2.97	2.46	2.41	2.39	2.23	2.60	2.64	1.99	1.97	2.16	2.11	1.12
6	50-74	3.44	3.77	3.42	3.00	3.24	2.84	2.71	3.07	3.72	3.86	3.60	1.72
7	75-99	5.32	2.85	2.74	3.14	3.47	3.53	4.23	4.19	3.75	3.43	3.41	3.07
8	100-199	3.91	3.86	3.64	3.24	3.78	4.35	4.37	4.58	4.13	4.70	3.80	3.90
9	200 or more	2.26	2.01	1.93	1.94	2.26	2.37	2.65	2.73	2.51	2.61	2.67	2.37
10	Total	2.63	2.33	2.23	2.18	2.48	2.62	2.84	2.84	2.26	2.77	2.69	2.25

Source: Same as Table 6.8

( ) = Figures that reflect the adjustment to value added explained in "Description of Data and Adjustments," Part II.

Craft Wage = average wage paid in plants having less than fifteen employees

TABLE 6.11

COMPARISON OF INDICATORS OF EFFICIENCY FROM TABLES 6.8, 6.9 and 6.10, BY SIZE CLASS

Size Class	Number of Workers	VA/HP Absolute Level	VA/HP Index[a]	$VA - (TO \cdot AW)$/HP Absolute Level	$VA - (TO \cdot AW)$/HP Index[a]	$VA - (TO \cdot CW)$/HP Absolute Level	$VA - (TO \cdot CW)$/HP Index[a]
0	Less than 5	2.35 (2.7)				1.48 (1.67)	
1	5-9	2.66 (3.0)	98 (110)	1.53 (1.73)	86 (97)	1.54 (1.76)	66 (76)
2	10-14	2.78 (3.12)		1.64 (1.86)		1.64 (1.85)	
3	15-19	3.04		1.78		2.09	
4	20-24	3.30	110	1.98	1.87	2.38	2.24 95
5	25-49	2.9		1.87		2.25	
6	50-74	3.9		2.6		3.2	
7	75-99	4.26	161	2.87	3.09 171	3.6	3.75 159
8	100-199	4.54		3.36		4.02	
9	200 or more	2.68	100	1.8	100	2.35	100
10	Total	3.02		2.01		2.51	

Source: Same as Table 6.8

( ) = Figures that reflect the adjustments to value added explained in "Descriptions of Data and Adjustments," Part II.

VA = value added
HP = installed horsepower capacity
TO = total employment
AW = average wage paid = $(SS+PS)/TR$
CW = craft wage (average wage paid in small plants)

[a] Size class 9 = 100

FIGURE 6.5

THE FOREIGN EXCHANGE MARKET

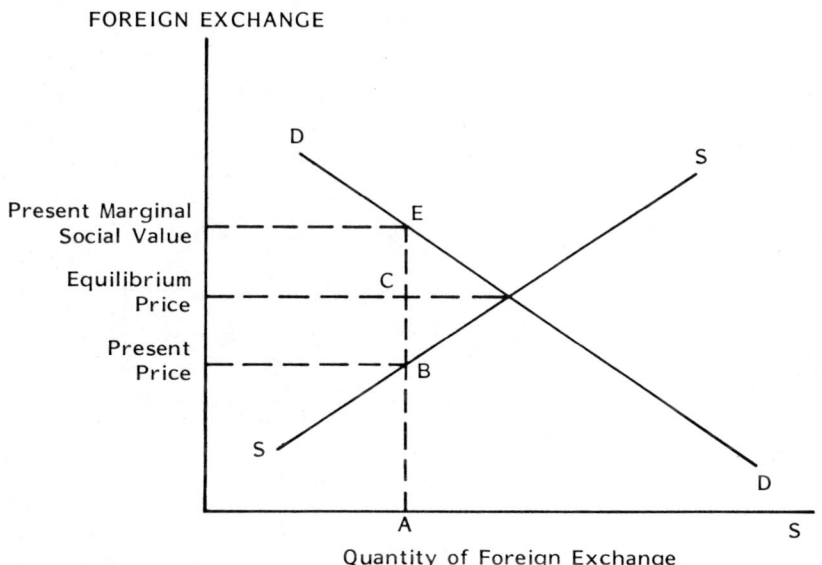

TABLE 6.12

WAGES AND FRINGE BENEFITS (PAID & IMPUTED), AS A PERCENTAGE OF VALUE ADDED[a], BY SIZE CLASS, 1956-67

Size Class	Number of Workers	1956	1957	1958	1959	1960	1961	1962	1963	1964	1965	1966	1967	Average 1956-67
0	Less than 5	40	38	38	42	36	37	35	35	33	31	34	38	36
1	5-9	43	44	44	45	43	42	44	42	41	40	37	39	42
2	10-14	44	41	43	43	41	41	42	40	40	39	38	37	41
3	15-19	42	45	46	45	43	39	39	41	37	39	38	39	41
4	20-24	42	41	41	44	42	42	42	38	35	39	35	36	40
5	25-49	36	37	36	35	36	34	35	38	36	34	31	33	35
6	50-74	32	29	31	32	35	37	38	38	33	33	34	33	34
7	75-99	22	29	38	38	34	28	35	34	37	35	34	32	33
8	100-199	28	26	25	25	25	25	25	25	27	25	27	27	26
9	200 or more	29	30	33	32	31	33	33	33	34	36	35	37	33
10	Total	32	32	34	33	33	33	34	33	34	34	34	35	33

Source: DANE, *Anuario de Estadística General*, various years.

[a] $\dfrac{(SS+PS) \cdot TO/TR}{VA}$

TABLE 6.13

PERCENT OF INTERMEDIATE INPUTS IMPORTED,
BY SIZE CLASS, 1964

Size Class	% MFP	Size Class	% MFP
0	.077	6	.182
1	.108	7	.248
2	.105	8	.233
3	.096	9	.257
4	.170	Total	.205
5	.147		

Source: Unpublished DANE data obtained by R. R. Nelson.
% MFP = Percentage of intermediate inputs imported.

TABLE 6.14
VALUE ADDED - ONE HALF OF IMPORTED RAW MATERIALS[a], BY SIZE CLASS, 1956-67
HORSEPOWER
(Thousands of 1952 Pesos)

Size Class	Number of Workers	1956	1957	1958	1959	1960	1961	1962	1963	1964	1965	1966	1967
0	Less than 5	2.46	2.31	2.24	1.62	2.26	2.25	2.63	2.09 (2.36)	2.01 (2.53)	2.04 (2.83)	1.72 (2.61)	1.81 (2.46)
1	5-9	2.94	2.50	2.56	2.32	2.34	2.53	2.76	2.18 (2.51)	1.96 (2.56)	1.92 (2.80)	1.75 (2.82)	1.70 (2.43)
2	10-14	2.96	2.86	2.30	2.15	2.66	2.60	3.78	2.24 (2.63)	2.04 (2.75)	1.92 (2.93)	1.72 (2.93)	1.87 (2.77)
3	15-19	2.20	2.74	1.88	2.70	3.15	2.82	3.40	2.87	2.54	2.07	1.83	2.22
4	20-24	2.56	2.88	2.67	2.47	2.77	2.15	2.82	2.81	2.50	2.30	2.20	2.59
5	25-49	2.90	2.34	2.31	2.43	2.31	2.58	2.75	2.12	1.98	2.13	1.96	1.14
6	50-74	2.43	2.92	2.98	2.79	2.97	2.90	2.87	3.16	3.51	3.58	3.30	1.72
7	75-99	4.61	2.38	2.54	2.70	3.33	3.48	4.08	3.96	3.65	3.23	3.04	2.80
8	100-199	4.04	3.62	3.32	3.05	3.64	4.21	4.28	4.41	3.95	4.51	3.46	3.71
9	200 or more	2.22	1.92	1.74	1.83	2.16	2.27	2.59	2.65	2.42	2.47	2.45	2.29
10	Total	2.59	2.27	2.12	2.15	2.47	2.61	2.90	2.85	2.62	2.70	2.53	2.22

Source: Same as Table 6.8. Data for % MPF (percentage of raw materials imported) were obtained by R. R. Nelson from DANE.

( ) = Data reflect the adjustment to value added explained in "Description of Data and Adjustments," Part II.

[a] $VA - (.5 \cdot MP \cdot \frac{\% MPF}{HP})$

the exports of manufactured goods. This partially offsets the higher imports of intermediate and (probably) of capital goods by large plants. The net balance-of-payments impact of the large plants in Diaz's study (referring to 1970) was substantially negative, however, so consideration of all these balance-of-payments factors jointly would still work against the larger firms (see Chapter 8, Table 8.3, p. 268.)

Our measures of net social benefit/capital are summarized in Table 6.15. Accepting my estimates of the capital stock/horsepower ratio (i.e., the last four indexes), the basic conclusion is clear; the large plants are considerably less efficient than those of smaller size. Only if horsepower is accepted as the proxy for capital stock and the craft wage as the measure of MSC_L, do the large plants look significantly more efficient than the very small ones. Even in this case, the small plants are almost equal and the medium sized ones remain considerably above the large plants.[38]

Two other factors, neglected here for lack of concrete data, would probably further lower the relative position of the large plants. First, the costs ignored by DANE in computing value added (see endnote 21) are likely to be more important in the large plants. Second, price distortion by high tariffs is more likely to affect prices of the products of the large plants.[39]

There are, of course, other considerations on which no information is available. For example, large plants may generate more or less positive externalities such as technological spin-offs or increases in the stock of human capital and more or less negative externalities, such as pollution than smaller plants. Finally, if the social efficiency of large plants tends to increase over their life span (while that of smaller plants does not) and there are many young, large plants, then our static efficiency ratios would not adequately reflect long-term social efficiency.[40]

In addition to the problems just cited, the inadequacies and inaccuracies of the data used remain. The weakest are the capital stock data; the DANE investment series used to construct the capital/horsepower ratios is considered particularly doubtful; in addition, it includes only investment in fixed capital, ignoring working capital completely. Finally, investment at market prices may not reflect the marginal social cost of the new capital due to differential tariff rates, the overvalued exchange rate, complicated tax breaks, depreciation policies, and differences in the costs of new and used capital. Empirical results using this data should perhaps be referred to as informed guesses. Nonetheless our best guess is that the large plants are less efficient than smaller ones in translating scarce resources into manufactured goods.

Relevant to the distribution of income, Table 6.12 indicates no major differences in labor's share across plant sizes. Smaller plants would appear to contribute toward a greater income equality within the working class, in that they generate more employment per unit of capital than large plants, at a wage lower than that in large plants but closer to that in the nonmanufacturing sector, and in that their capital income is spread among more entrepreneurs.[41]

PART III

EXPLANATION OF DIFFERENCES IN EFFICIENCY BY PLANT SIZE

How can the lower output/capital ratios in the large plants be explained, given that large firms pay much higher wage rates and are reported to have very high profit rates? Three points come to mind.

TABLE 6.15

ESTIMATES OF THE RATIO OF NET SOCIAL BENEFIT TO FIXED CAPITAL[a], BY SIZE CLASS, 1956-67
(Values Averaged over 1956-67)

	Very Small[b]	Small[c]	Medium[d]	Large[e]
1. VA/HP	2.63 (3.06)	2.97	4.33	2.69
2. $\frac{VA-[(SS+PS) \cdot TO/TR]}{HP}$	1.56 (1.79)	1.87	3.09	1.80
3. $\frac{VA-(TO \cdot Craft\ Wage)}{HP}$	1.56 (1.79)	2.24	3.75	2.35
4. $\frac{VA-(.5 \cdot MP \cdot \%MPF)}{HP}$	2.26 (2.56)	2.34	3.53	2.25
5. (VA/HP)/Y10%	1.01 (1.17)	1.06	0.83	0.48
6. $\frac{[VA-([SS+PS] \cdot TO/TR)]/Y10\%}{HP}$	0.60 (0.68)	0.66	0.59	0.32
7. $\frac{[VA-(TO \cdot Craft\ Wage)]/Y10\%}{HP}$	0.60 (0.68)	0.80	0.72	0.42
8. $\frac{[VA-(.5 \cdot MP \cdot \%MPF)]/Y10\%}{HP}$	0.87 (0.98)	0.83	0.67	0.40
	Indices[f]			
1. VA/HP	98 (114)	110	161	100
2. $\frac{VA-[(SS+PS) \cdot TO/TR]}{HP}$	86 (99)	103	171	100
3. $\frac{VA-(TO \cdot Craft\ Wage)}{HP}$	66 (76)	95	159	100
4. $\frac{VA-(.5 \cdot MP \cdot \%MPF)}{HP}$	100 (113)	104	156	100
5. (VA/HP)/Y10%	210 (243)	221	173	100
6. $\frac{[VA-([SS+PS] \cdot TO/TR)]/Y10\%}{HP}$	187 (212)	206	184	100
7. $\frac{[VA-(TO \cdot Craft\ Wage)]/Y10\%}{HP}$	142 (162)	190	171	100
8. $\frac{[VA-(.5 \cdot MP \cdot \%MPF)]/Y10\%}{HP}$	217 (245)	207	167	100

Sources: The data for row 1 are from DANE, *Anuario General de Estadística*, various years. Row 2 is from Table 6.9, Row 3 from 6.10, Row 4 from Table 6.14, Row 5 from Table 6.6.

( ) = Figures reflect my adjustments to value added explained in "Value Added/Fixed Capital Ratios by Size of Plant," Part II.

[a] The variable Y10% is used to measure the ratio of fixed capital to installed horsepower.
[b] Size classes 0,1,2
[c] Size classes 3,4,5
[d] Size classes 6,7,8
[e] Size class 9
[f] Size class 9 = 100

First, the actual wage discrimination faced by the large plants is undoubtedly much less than the difference in average wage rates; greater experience, skills, and stability of the work force undoubtedly account for much (some would say most) of the difference. Second, profit rates of the small and medium size firms may also be quite high (remember we are excluding the artisan sector). Third and most important, the large plants appear to have numerous advantages in the acquisition of capital and foreign exchange and in capacity to deal (in several senses of that term) with the government. Thus our result is not necessarily inconsistent with higher average wage rates and high profits in the large plants.

I believe the most important explanation for the difference in output/capital ratios (or net social benefit/capital ratios when adjustment is made for labor and/or imported raw material use) is the different capital/labor ratios of the different sizes of plants (see Table 6.1). Of course, other possibilities exist. One is decreasing returns to scale, but this is unlikely to be important at the plant level, given the possibilities for multiplant operations. Another possible explanation is dominance of the craft technology in a two technology system; even at equal capital/labor ratios small plant technologies use less labor and less capital per unit of output. This is basically a reverse of R. R. Nelson's technological dualism argument;[42] it seems implausible because it makes the introduction of so much modern technology into Colombia hard to explain. A slightly altered but more plausible version of this last explanation states that different plant sizes produce different products, and that the small-plant products (in general more traditional products) can, at all sizes and at all capital/labor ratios, be produced more efficiently than the typically large-plant products (generally new and more modern).

The main explanation would seem to be the different capital/labor ratios employed by the different sizes of plants. As discussed earlier, these differences could be due to large and small plants facing different factor prices, and/or different production functions, such as nonhomogeneous production functions for similar or identical goods, separate production functions for similar goods (technological dualism), or separate production functions for different goods. Many combinations are possible.[43]

Distinguishing among these explanations is important in the selection of appropriate policy steps. Some data and considerable opinion suggest strong differences in factor prices by size of plant. Table 6.16 shows an average wage about three times as high in the large plants as in the small plants, but part of this gap is undoubtedly due to higher skills, greater experience, and lower turnover rates in the larger plants' work force. Even if the higher wage rates for a given type of worker have been partially forced on the large firms, they have been used to purchase a superior labor force. Slighton attempted to hold some of these elements of labor quality constant and still found a ratio of about two to one in the average wage of equivalent workers.[44] Though he may not have been able to normalize for all relevant differences, the wage differential which remains is substantial, and supports the widely shared opinion that wage rates in the large plants are higher than needed to attract and keep the existing labor force.

Very little concrete evidence is available to support the plausible belief that credit is more difficult to obtain and more costly for smaller plants.[45] One Planeación source indicates that "it is unlikely that the small and medium firms receive more than one third as much credit per peso of value added as do the large firms." But this result is difficult to interpret since large firms appear to extend considerable net credit to smaller ones.[46] Nonetheless, in situations where large and small firms are in competition, the credit problems of the latter are likely to be par-

TABLE 6.16
WAGES AND FRINGE BENEFITS PER PAID WORKER, BY SIZE CLASS, 1956-67
(Thousands of 1952 Pesos)

Size Class	Number of Workers	1956	1957	1958	1959	1960	1961	1962	1963	1964	1965	1966	1967
0	Less than 5	1.45	1.34	1.26	1.28	1.34	1.33	1.54	1.24	1.14	1.09	1.15	1.52
1	5-9	1.57	1.43	1.37	1.41	1.50	1.52	1.77	1.46	1.31	1.28	1.23	1.47
2	10-14	1.79	1.60	1.59	1.68	1.88	1.84	2.11	1.85	1.69	1.64	1.55	1.99
3	15-19	1.94	1.76	1.72	1.76	1.88	1.99	2.19	2.42	2.30	2.37	2.11	2.17
4	20-24	2.04	2.05	1.88	1.85	2.06	2.08	2.32	2.59	2.44	2.49	2.36	2.40
5	25-49	2.26	2.16	2.10	2.11	2.30	2.38	2.70	2.85	2.80	2.85	2.70	2.76
6	50-74	2.50	2.35	2.26	2.27	2.63	2.77	3.08	3.37	3.41	3.34	3.08	3.16
7	75-99	2.80	2.65	2.51	2.70	3.01	3.14	3.46	3.19	3.36	3.49	3.43	3.74
8	100-199	2.82	2.78	2.69	2.83	3.13	3.34	3.78	4.09	4.17	4.21	4.16	4.29
9	200 or more	3.43	3.34	3.46	3.34	3.66	3.97	4.49	4.77	4.81	5.00	4.94	5.34
10	Total	2.67	2.57	2.57	2.60	2.90	3.09	3.49	3.68	3.66	3.75	3.70	4.00

Source: DANE, *Anuario General de Estadística*, various issues.

ticularly severe. Overall, a difference in access to credit doubtless exists, due in part to market distortions (favored treatment for large firms by banks and government) and in part to "real" economic considerations.[47] With even more certainty, substantial differences in relative factor prices do exist.

Differences in factor prices can explain differences in capital/labor ratios only if significant substitutability exists between capital and labor.[48] I believe such substitutability does exist. Gordon Winston has noted[49] the considerable confusion to be found among the various possible definitions of the elasticity of substitution. While personal observation may sometimes suggest that the *ex post* elasticity of substitution of labor services for capital services is not great, this is not the relevant elasticity in estimating the long-run effects of factor price changes on factor use. First, *ex ante* elasticity of substitution will certainly be greater. Second, the elasticity of substitution of labor services for capital stock will be greater, due to the responsiveness of capacity utilization to factor prices. Finally, as the next section points out, changes may also occur in the mix of plants producing various products or in the product mix itself. Thus it would seem (and recent empirical estimates bear this out)[50] that the macro, *ex ante* elasticity between labor flows and capital stock is substantial.

Data by size of plant and by legal status of firm provide a further piece of circumstantial evidence on this point in Colombia (see Table 6.17). Note that the capital/labor ratio varies substantially by organizational form even for the smallest plants. Value added/horsepower, however, bears no systematic relation to organizational form. Horsepower/worker rises with size only for proprietorships, not for corporations. One possible interpretation of these facts is that the small plants listed as corporations are frequently in multi-plant situations. This would suggest that access to cheap capital and imports may cause high capital/labor ratios even at small scales of operation.

In short, while differences in production functions by plant size no doubt play a role in explaining the difference in capital intensities, there is also considerable evidence that differences in relative factor prices are important.

PART IV

POLICY IMPLICATIONS

The most obvious implication of the results presented above is that existing policies or circumstances which divert resources and markets from smaller to larger firms run a serious risk of lowering both output and employment.[51] The belief that larger firms are socially more efficient must clearly be reexamined. As to desirable future policies, the results can only suggest some possible fruitful directions; many considerations are involved and many uncertainties exist as to the direct applicability of such results. Many policies do (or would) differentiate by size of firm and not size of plant. Although I believe that factor proportions and factor productivity would differ by firm size very much as they do by plant size, no solid evidence for this exists. It is consistent with the fact, noted in the previous section, that small plants which are part of multi-plant firms appear to have higher capital/labor ratios and higher value added per worker than small proprietorships.

Another problem involves the difference between average and marginal ratios. To evaluate policies affecting the share of output from the small and medium size plants, the most relevant data are the marginal

TABLE 6.17

HORSEPOWER/TOTAL EMPLOYMENT AND VALUE ADDED/HORSEPOWER, BY ORGANIZATIONAL FORM AND SIZE CLASS, 1966

Organizational Form	Size Class										Total
	0	1	2	3	4	5	6	7	8	9	
	Horsepower/Total Employment, 1966										
Proprietorship	1.40	1.10	1.21	1.66	1.21	1.45	1.16	1.25	2.34	2.11	1.30
Limited Partnership	4.87	3.41	2.36	2.88	2.39	2.54	1.75	1.89	2.39	3.43	2.57
Corporation	14.15	7.97	6.67	8.77	5.50	13.78	4.36	4.93	5.44	5.23	5.47
	Value Added[a]/Horsepower, 1966 (thousands of 1952 pesos)										
Proprietorship	1.8	2.3	2.4	2.8	3.3	3.4	3.6	4.7	2.5	3.1	2.6
Limited Partnership	1.6	1.7	2.2	1.9	3.2	2.8	4.2	3.6	3.6	2.8	3.0
Corporation	4.0	2.8	1.5	1.9	2.6	1.8	4.1	4.0	3.6	2.8	2.9

Source: DANE, *Anuario General de Estadística*, 1966–67, Tomo IV.

[a]Value added figures are not corrected for methodology error affecting small plants after 1962, as discussed in "Description of Data and Adjustments," Part 2.

output/capital and labor/capital ratios, not the corresponding average ratios. (The relevance of marginal ratios depends upon the policy under consideration.) To use the (average) figures presented earlier, we must assume some fixed relationship between the marginal and the average social efficiency ratios, clearly an arbitrary assumption.

A possible objection to increasing the share of output produced in the small and medium size plants is that, even if the present percentage is below that which would have resulted from optimal policies in the past, it may not be worth the effort to crank up special inducements to this sector if, as development proceeds, its optimal share can be expected to decline. Available evidence [52] suggests that the development process is not necessarily associated with a rapid decline in the relative (and certainly not the absolute) importance of small and medium size plants (remember that we are excluding the very small artisan operations). [53]

A final issue, on which some evidence can be presented, concerns the flexibility of the manufacturing sector in terms of plant size. The difference in average, static social efficiency by size of plant demonstrated earlier is a snapshot view at a point of time. Whether or not significant gains could be realized from a reallocation of resources toward small plants depends upon the substitutability between the output of the smaller plants and that of the large plants; if it is low, the relative net social benefit/capital ratios would move towards equality very quickly as the reallocations occurred so, though beneficial, it would be relatively unimportant. Insofar as small and large plants produce similar products, the substitution should be an easy matter, since the structure of demand would not need to change.

To determine the extent of intrasectoral coexistence of various plant sizes, we have divided 1960 and 1965 four-digit sectors (the finest distinction made in the manufacturing data) into three types: M = dominated by (more than 80 percent of value added produced by) large plants, C = dominated by small plants, and O = all other sectors (Table 6.18). While all plants in a four-digit sector do not necessarily produce the same products, it seems likely that the products are at least good substitutes; if not, the capacity to produce very close substitutes probably exists. For example, the small plants in the brick sector produce a cruder, more uneven product than large plants. While not a good substitute for every use, these bricks could substitute for the products of the larger plants in many uses. Five sets of definitions of large and small are used, referred to as versions 1 through 5.

Looking at the total value added in O, M, and C-type sectors, we see that when large is defined as "more than 200 employees," only about 30 percent of value added in manufacturing came from sectors dominated by these plants, as of the early sixties. In all other four-digit sectors, smaller plants contribute more than 20 percent of value added. This suggests considerable scope for the relative expansion of the small and medium size plants, even without shifts in the sectoral distribution of production.

Further, efficiency may show additional induced improvements when sectors become more size diversified. Value added/horsepower ratios (VA/HP) are highest in sectors where output is more evenly spread across size classes (O-type), and lowest in sectors dominated by large plants (M-type) (Table 6.19). This superiority of the more size diversified sectors also holds within the individual size classes. In size class 9 for example, VA/HP is uniformly higher[54] by a wide margin in O sectors than in M sectors for both 1960 and 1965. Furthermore, comparing size class 9 in the M-type sectors, its VA/HP ratio is higher in those M-type sectors defining large to include more of the medium size plants (version 3) than in those defining large only as size class 9 (versions 1 and 5).

TABLE 6.18

PERCENT DISTRIBUTION OF VALUE ADDED AMONG FOUR-DIGIT INDUSTRIES CLASSIFIED BY WHETHER DOMINATED BY LARGE PLANTS, SMALL PLANTS OR NEITHER, 1960-65

Version	Sectors	1960	1965	Definition of Large (Number of workers)	Definition of Small (Number of workers)
1	O	67	71	200 or more	Less than 25
	M	30	27		
	C	3	2		
2	O	35	35	100 or more	Less than 50
	M	57	38		
	C	8	8		
3	O	20	18	50 or more	Less than 50
	M	72	75		
	C	8	8		
4	O	25	27	100 or more	Less than 100
	M	57	58		
	C	18	15		
5	O	45	49	200 or more	Less than 200
	M	30	27		
	C	25	24		

Source: Unpublished DANE data.

M = dominated by large plants
C = dominated by small plants
O = dominated by neither

TABLE 6.19

VALUE ADDED/HORSEPOWER BY SIZE CLASS AND BY WHETHER FOUR-DIGIT INDUSTRY DOMINATED BY LARGE OR SMALL PLANTS, 1960 AND 1965
(Current Pesos)

Version:[a]	1			2			3			4			5		
						Type of Four-Digit Sector									
Size Class	O	C	M	O	C	M	O	C	M	O	C	M	O	C	M
1965															
0	10.0	10.0	---	16.0	8.0	---	16.0	8.0	---	11.0	10.0	---	9.0	10.0	---
1	8.0	7.0	---	9.0	7.0	---	8.0	7.0	---	9.0	8.0	---	11.0	7.0	---
2	9.0	7.0	---	10.0	7.0	---	10.0	7.0	---	9.0	8.0	---	11.0	8.0	---
3	8.0	6.0	---	9.0	7.0	---	9.0	7.0	---	8.0	8.0	---	9.0	8.0	---
4	12.0	7.0	---	12.0	9.0	---	11.0	9.0	---	10.0	10.0	---	14.0	10.0	---
5	10.0	4.0	---	9.0	11.0	---	8.0	11.0	---	7.0	13.0	---	7.0	11.0	---
6	16.0	---	13.0	15.0	---	21.0	14.0	19.0	---	16.0	---	21.0	23.0	---	13.0
7	14.0	---	12.0	15.0	---	9.0	13.0	---	14.0	15.0	---	9.0	15.0	---	12.0
8	21.0	---	4.0	19.0	---	18.0	12.0	---	20.0	19.0	---	18.0	26.0	---	7.0
9	18.3	---	7.1	13.5	---	9.8	9.8	---	10.4	13.5	17.0	9.8	18.4	12.8	7.0
Total	15.2	7.7	7.0	13.2	9.0	10.8	10.3	9.0	12.0	13.0	11.0	10.8	18.0	11.0	7.0
1960															
0	6.0	3.0	---	7.0	4.0	---	8.0	4.0	---	9.0	4.0	---	10.0	4.0	---
1	6.0	5.0	---	6.0	6.0	---	6.0	6.0	---	7.0	6.0	---	10.0	5.0	---
2	7.0	4.0	---	8.0	6.0	---	7.0	6.0	---	8.0	6.0	---	10.0	6.0	---
3	8.0	6.0	---	8.0	7.0	---	8.0	7.0	---	8.0	7.0	---	10.0	7.0	---
4	7.0	8.0	---	8.0	8.0	---	7.0	8.0	---	8.0	7.0	---	8.0	7.0	---
5	7.0	6.0	---	6.0	6.0	---	6.0	6.0	---	6.0	6.0	---	10.0	6.0	---
6	9.0	---	5.0	8.0	---	15.0	8.0	---	11.0	10.0	---	15.0	12.0	---	5.0
7	9.0	---	9.0	9.0	---	7.0	6.0	---	11.0	12.0	---	7.0	10.0	---	9.0
8	10.0	---	3.0	13.0	---	8.0	9.0	---	9.0	14.0	---	8.0	11.0	---	3.0
9	9.0	---	4.0	10.5	---	5.0	10.6	---	5.2	10.7	3.9	4.9	9.1	7.0	4.0
Total	8.5	4.6	4.0	13.2	9.0	10.8	7.5	5.8	6.0	10.0	6.2	5.3	9.7	6.3	3.9

Source: Unpublished DANE data.

[a]For definitions, see Table 6.18.

One possible explanation for this interesting result is that the competitive pressure of the smaller plants keeps the larger ones more efficient. Also, a technologically based correlation may exist between capital intensity and economies of scale; in other words, domination by large plants (very little size diversity in a sector) may be a result of significant economies of scale, which are in turn associated with high capital intensity. Or both of these may be particularly characteristic of those new and highly protected sectors often characterized by lack of experienced workers and management and by initial excess capacity.

Potential substitution of the output of small plants for that of large ones depends not only on intrasectoral but also on intersectoral substitution; the sectoral structure of production always has some flexibility, both because changes in relative prices will have an effect on the structure of domestic demand and because the existence of foreign trade means that the structure of production need not be identical to the structure of domestic demand. The potential for raising the share of smaller plants in manufacturing output through changes in the product mix would be lessened if small and medium size plants with particularly high relative social efficiencies are concentrated in only a few sectors or departments. In fact, sectors so characterized are widely distributed throughout the economy; Table 6.20 lists three-digit sectors in which large plants of class 9 have a VA/HP ratio either 50 percent higher or lower than the other plants. Data by department and size of plant were available only for 1958. The three largest departments (Cundinamarca, Antioquia and Valle) accounted for approximately 70 percent of the value added in that year (Table 6.21). Only for Antioquia, a textile center, was the share of output in the largest plants significantly above average. In Table 6.22 our basic statistics (VA/TO, HP/TO, and VA/HP) show broadly similar patterns in these three departments as for the nation;[55] three smaller departments are also shown for comparison.[56] In all departments, VA/HP is lower for size class 9 than for the other classes. The data suggest, then, that a redistribution of output away from the large plants (with their lower output/capital ratios) would not be seriously impeded by either sectoral or regional bottlenecks.[57] In summary, the evidence suggests a considerable scope for the relative expansion of small and medium sized plants. In some lines they produce nearly identical products to those of large plants. In other cases, they produce or could produce close substitutes. Furthermore, changes in relative prices and availabilities could change the structure of domestic and/or foreign demand. While further research into the extent of substitution and complementarity between small and large firms and plants is necessary, the information discussed above creates a presumption that such a shift would be both feasible and beneficial.

Given the higher average net social benefit/capital ratios in the small and medium size plants and the apparent flexibility in the composition of the manufacturing sector by size of plant, economic policies which tended to equalize the opportunities of the smaller and larger plants (without adversely affecting the efficiency of either group) should attract more of the constraining factor(s) to the small and medium plants and thereby raise both employment and output in manufacturing. The higher output share of smaller plants would be a key factor; improved efficiency, especially of the large plants, could also play a role.

Obviously this strategy has limits. First, smaller plants should probably not be put in a significantly more advantageous position overall because of the presumably adverse effect on the incentive to grow. Second, since flexibility by size is limited (for many products large plants are far more efficient and the substitutability between their output and the products of the smaller plants is not very high), the "ideal"

TABLE 6.20
RELATIVE VALUE ADDED/HORSEPOWER (R), PLANTS OF SIZE CLASSES 0-8 COMPARED TO PLANTS OF SIZE CLASS 9, SELECTED FOUR-DIGIT INDUSTRIES, 1966[a]

Four-Digit Industry Number	Industries with R > 1.5
2030	Fruits and Vegetables
2060	Bread
2320	Knitted Fabrics
2360	Silk
2440	Women's Clothing
2460	Hats
2710	Wood Pulp and Paper
3110	Chemicals
3140	Soap
3180	Waterproofing and Adhesives
3320	Glass and Glass Products
3330	Ceramics
3340	Cement
3410	Iron
3530	Cutlery
3540	Nonelectric Stoves
3550	Aluminum Products
3630	Industrial Machinery
3710	Electrical Machinery
3810	Boats and Boat Repair
3830	Auto Assembly
Number	Industries with R < .67
2020	Milk Products
2050	Milled Products
2080	Candy and Chocolate
2090	Other Food
2130	Beer
2140	Soft Drinks
2510	Wood
2810	Printing
2910	Leather
3020	Rubber Products for Home Use
3210	Oil Refining
3350	Cement Products
3440	Nonferrous Metals
3520	Hand-tools and Hardware
3730	Electro-Mechanical Equipment
3740	Wire and Cable
3760	Electrical Installation Equipment
3850	Automobile Repairs
3860	Airplane Repairs

Source: DANE, unpublished data.

[a] $R = \dfrac{VA/HP\ (T = 0\ to\ 8)}{VA/HP\ (T = 9)}$ (T = Size Class)

TABLE 6.21

PERCENT DISTRIBUTION OF VALUE ADDED, BY SIZE CLASS, SELECTED DEPARTMENTS, 1958

Department	Size Class										Percent of National Total
	0	1	2	3	4	5	6	7	8	9	
Cundinamarca	1.4	4.5	3.7	3.4	3.5	11.8	7.4	5.7	14.5	43.7	27.0
Antioquia	1.0	1.9	1.6	1.5	1.3	4.8	4.9	2.3	8.8	71.4	25.0
Valle	1.7	2.9	2.2	1.7	2.4	10.1	5.8	3.1	18.8	50.8	18.5
Bolivar	2.7	7.2	5.6	1.8	2.2	16.4	5.1	1.3	27.2	29.9	2.7
Boyaca	2.9	4.1	1.8	0.2	0.6	1.8	8.8	0.0	23.9	55.4	2.3
Caldas	3.0	6.0	4.0	1.8	1.3	12.9	14.0	3.4	38.0	15.1	5.2
Colombia	1.9	3.9	3.1	2.4	2.4	9.3	7.3	3.9	16.8	49.1	100.0

Source: DANE, unpublished data.

TABLE 6.22

VALUE ADDED PER HORSEPOWER, VALUE ADDED PER WORKER, AND HORSEPOWER PER WORKER, BY DEPARTMENT AND SIZE CLASS, 1958

Department	0	1	2	3	4	5	6	7	8	9	10
					VA/HP (thousands of 1952 pesos)						
Cundinimarca	3.60	3.92	3.74	3.55	4.46	4.00	3.97	3.95	4.30	2.24	3.06
Antioquia	2.83	4.27	4.79	3.48	3.13	3.44	3.90	2.15	3.94	2.57	2.79
Valle	3.88	2.93	2.15	2.47	3.28	3.53	4.60	6.38	3.09	2.72	3.00
Bolivar	1.78	2.62	1.90	2.34	4.58	2.58	1.96	7.45	28.40	0.65	1.55
Boyaca	4.71	3.90	4.61	1.22	1.36	2.40	5.66	0.00	2.72	0.83	1.24
Caldas	2.50	3.13	3.45	3.75	3.96	3.40	3.75	3.97	8.03	2.52	4.11
Colombia	2.50	3.00	2.80	2.80	3.40	3.20	4.20	3.50	4.20	2.20	2.80
					VA/TO (thousands of 1952 pesos)						
Cundinamarca	3.14	3.14	3.62	4.00	4.08	5.72	6.04	6.87	7.90	11.53	6.92
Antioquia	3.11	2.66	3.35	3.25	4.15	4.78	5.64	5.06	8.81	9.85	7.70
Valle	4.53	3.54	3.70	3.66	6.52	7.44	8.35	6.50	11.10	11.82	8.90
Bolivar	3.91	4.57	4.76	4.94	5.72	6.33	5.67	4.10	61.90	14.85	9.47
Boyaca	2.00	1.87	2.68	3.47	7.00	4.51	17.06	0.00	15.01	6.57	6.44
Caldas	3.40	3.70	4.98	2.70	4.31	8.01	9.90	7.63	18.30	5.76	7.97
Colombia	3.30	3.10	3.70	3.70	4.60	5.90	7.40	6.70	10.70	10.50	7.60
					HP/TO						
Cundinamarca	1.02	0.80	0.96	1.10	0.91	1.43	1.52	1.73	1.83	5.13	2.26
Antioquia	1.09	0.62	0.70	0.93	1.32	1.38	1.45	2.35	2.23	3.82	2.75
Valle	1.16	1.20	1.71	1.48	1.98	2.10	1.81	1.01	3.60	4.33	1.96
Bolivar	2.19	1.74	2.51	2.11	1.24	2.45	2.90	0.55	2.18	22.70	6.10
Boyaca	0.42	0.48	0.58	2.83	5.14	1.90	3.01	0.00	5.50	7.90	5.18
Caldas	1.35	1.17	1.44	0.71	1.09	2.35	2.63	1.92	2.27	2.30	1.93
Colombia	1.30	1.00	1.30	1.30	1.40	1.90	1.70	1.90	2.60	4.70	2.80

Source: DANE, unpublished data.

increase in the relative share of small and medium size plants may not be great. Third, due to transition costs and sunk investment, the decrease in share of large firms should not be abrupt and should generally not entail shutting down existing facilities, unless their use of scarce factors other than fixed capital is very high. What remains is a relatively modest proposal: the economy would probably benefit from intelligently induced marginal shifts in the composition of output from the large to the small and medium size plants in the manufacturing sector.

How should such a change be induced? The following discussion is not intended to pinpoint specific proposals, but to indicate the range of policy options available and to suggest some useful classifications of such policies. Nonetheless, some general guidelines do emerge as to which types of policies are likely to be most helpful. One two-way classification of policies distinguishes between those aimed at reducing or eliminating current disadvantages of smaller plants relative to larger ones, and those providing new services of special benefit to the smaller plants (though available to all plants). Examples of the former would be equalization of the price and availability of capital or foreign exchange and a decrease in red tape and political influence in the dealings of business with government.[58] The most common suggestion is to reduce or eliminate differences in factor prices due to factor market distortions, e.g., to lower the price of capital for small firms or to lower the wage rate for large firms. If all factor prices could be made equal to marginal social opportunity cost, output and employment would be maximized.[59] When only some factor prices can be affected, however, the outcome is more complicated. Narrowing an existing factor price differential has two effects; it changes the gap in output/capital ratios by changing the gap in capital/labor ratios, but it also affects the relative profit positions and hence the relative expansion of the different size of firms. Assume, for example, that the prices of capital and labor for the small firms are equal to their marginal social costs, while the price of capital to large firms is below marginal social cost and the price of labor above. Assume also that the output/capital ratio is generally higher in the small firms. An increase in the price of capital to large firms would both lower their capital/labor ratio and lower their share of total output; both of these changes would be beneficial. A decrease in the price of capital to the smaller firms, however, would increase their relative share (which is good), but it would also increase their capital/labor ratio (which is bad). If it is not possible to raise the price of capital to the large firms, so that the alternatives are lowering the price of capital to the small firms or doing nothing, then the former *may* be a second best solution, depending on the relative strength of the two effects mentioned above. Similarly, lowering the wage rate for the large firms would lower their capital/labor ratio (good), but increase their relative share (bad); again the net effect is indeterminate. Sometimes a given imperfection should not be removed unless another one can be removed at the same time.

Since some imperfections may be difficult to remove, such as the low price of capital to the large firms, complicated second best situations are probable. It would seem wise, where possible, to move factor prices in the right direction (i.e., towards the ideal in a system with no imperfections) without improving the relative profit position of the group with lower social efficiency.[60]

The second type of policy, provision of new services, might permit an increase in the relative share of the smaller firms without lowering their social efficiency by raising their K/L ratio.[61] It might be particularly attractive when political considerations preclude raising the price of capital to the large firms.[62] A public or semipublic agency providing information on available technologies, somewhat in the manner of an agricultural extension service, could be helpful. Another possibility would be stimulation of commercial middlemen to handle the difficult standardization, marketing, and distribution processes (where economies of scale probably do exist) while leaving the manufacturing processes in the hands of smaller units. Japan and Hong Kong both appear to have benefited considerably from this type of specialization.

Some existing policies or practices clearly have their differential impact by size of plant and must be evaluated accordingly; when designing new policies, however, size is not always a good variable to focus on. The fact that group A of manufacturing plants is socially more efficient than group B does not mean that the A versus B classification is a good one in the planning of new policies. High efficiency may be due to a characteristic common to group X firms (and absent in group Y) and our results due simply to the fact that most of the plants in group X fall also in group A. In such a case, policy should be oriented towards plants in group X, regardless of any other characteristic like size. To be more concrete, some types of small and medium size plants may merit encouragement more than others. If this were the case, policy might better be focused on these plants. Keeping the marginal (in terms of profitability) small firm in business is especially likely to be detrimental to total output, despite the higher average social efficiency of small plants, if the dispersion of efficiencies among small firms is higher than among large firms. In any case, a better policy would relieve constraints on more efficient small firms otherwise thwarted in their efforts for modest expansion of a capital-extensive nature (i.e., retaining a low capital/labor ratio).

Drawing conclusions from static factor productivity averages involves many possible pitfalls and requires careful qualification. But the available data suggest substantially higher average social efficiency in the small and medium size plants, and it would therefore appear that equalizing opportunities across sizes of manufacturing enterprises would raise both output and employment by changing the relative output shares by size and possibly by raising efficiency, particularly in the large plants, via greater competition from smaller units and a higher price of capital. The qualifications mentioned should, however, encourage moderation in any such change of policies. Changes should be carefully monitored and research (particularly of a micro nature) should be conducted on the relative effects of the various policy options outlined above.

ENDNOTES FOR CHAPTER 6

1. Helen Hughes, "Industrialization, Employment, and Urbanization," *Finance and Development* Vol. 8 (1971): 42.

2. International Labour Office, *Towards Full Employment, A Programme for Colombia* (Geneva: International Labour Office, 1970), p. 118.

3. Ian Little, Tibor Scitovsky, and Maurice Scott, *Industry and Trade in Some Developing Countries* (London: Oxford University Press, 1970), p. 91.

4. R. R. Nelson, T. P. Schultz, and R. L. Slighton, *Structural Change in a Developing Economy* (Princeton: Princeton University Press, 1971), p. 368.

5. The distinction between firm size and plant size is discussed in the next section of Part I.

6. Robert L. Slighton, "Relative Wages, Skill Shortages, and Changes in Income Distribution in Colombia," Rand Corporation Research Memorandum No. 5651, (Santa Monica: Rand Corporation, 1968).

7. R. Albert Berry, "The Relevance and Prospects of Small Scale Industry in Colombia," Discussion Paper, Economic Growth Center, Yale University, (April 1971). These issues are discussed further in Part III.

8. As opposed to present value of the national income stream over time.

9. For definitions, see below.

10. All constraining inputs would be weighted by their dual prices.

11. Concern about choices of scale and technology, particularly as they relate to the unemployment problem, imply concern about some scarce (or scarcest) factor (i.e., price so low it must be rationed, or the short factor in a fixed coefficients model). This factor is usually assumed to be capital; the other possible contenders are foreign exchange and skilled labor. We deal with foreign exchange explicitly later in this chapter; data on skilled labor are inadequate to permit analysis.

12. Necessary where social opportunity cost is not equal to market price.

13. Note that, in comparing two points on the same isoquant (e.g., A and D), the one with the higher K/L will always have a lower Q/K as long as some factor substitutability exists. In comparing any two points (e.g., A and E), the one with the higher K/L will have a lower Q/K since CRTS are found throughout.

14. On each isoquant the point of tangency with an iso-factor cost line maximizes $Q/(WL + rK)$ where r is the price of capital. Since W and r are equal for all firms and Q equals value added, this also maximizes $(Q-WL)/K$.

15. For the data on Colombia, see Table 6.1.

16. A homothetic production function is one which is homogeneous of any degree.

17. Roughly similar results obtain in the more complicated case of two separate sets of isoquants, one representing traditional technology and the other a newer, imported technology which, for any given set of factor prices, has a larger optimum scale and a higher optimum capital/labor ratio. We could observe both technologies in operation if each had the same profit rate, or if the capital market was not perfect. As in the case illustrated in Figure 6.3, larger firms would have higher capital/labor ratios even with equal factor prices.

18. Another possible cause of differences in output/capital ratios by size of firm is the rate of capacity utilization. Knowing the rates of capacity utilization by size of firm would not change the measurements of social efficiency used here, but it could help to explain them, and to provide circumstantial evidence on the potential for increases in social efficiency for the various firm sizes. In this connection, see Chapter 7.

19. Given equal factor prices for all firms but nonhomothetic isoquants (e.g., greater economies of scale along the more capital-intensive rays), and equal profit rates for the marginal firm of each size, then if more than one scale is observed operating, it must be true that the one with higher capital/labor ratio has a lower output/capital ratio. With equal profit rates (i.e., (Q-WL)/K equal) and equal W, then a lower L/K implies a lower Q/K. With CRTS throughout but different factor prices by size of firm, then by the reasoning on page 9, the firm with higher K/L will again have lower Q/K.

20. All plants of fifteen or more employees are to submit their data every year, but only a sample of the smaller plants is asked to report each year. Field offices are to check on births and deaths of plants. Since the data are collected and collated on the basis of plants and not firms, Bavaria, the large beer trust, has fourteen different plants all reporting separately to DANE and all counted as separate establishments in the published data.

21. Its calculation of value added ignores many expenses, particularly those of a service nature. The Superintendencia de Sociedades Anónimas has estimated that as a result DANE overestimates value added by 13 percent. This figure is used by the Central Bank in preparing the national accounts.

22. In 1962 a full census was taken and the reported figures for these smaller plants exhibited no unusual change, giving circumstantial support to the rough accuracy of the pre-1962 methodology.

23. One check as to the representativeness of the sample (the plants which reported in 1966) was possible. From the 1966 printout of the individual plant data, the data on value added per worker (VA/TO) and value added per plant (VA/EST) for those plants which last reported in 1962 (i.e., were never sampled over this period) were compared to all the plants in the 1962 printout. It appears that the sample bias is well under 5 percent.

24. The value added figures could possibly have been adjusted also for product price differences by size of plant. Available data were inconclusive on this point so no such adjustment is made. For a fuller discussion see John Todd, "Efficiency and Plant Size in Colombian Manufacturing" (Ph.D. dissertation, Yale University, 1972), Chapter II, Section G.

25. One guess could be that, due to a growing sophistication of machinery, the constant peso value of one horsepower of machinery tends to increase over time. Second, due to a difference in quality and sophistication of machinery the smaller plants would at any given time have a lower constant peso value of one horsepower of machinery. Finally, the smaller plants might have a higher ratio of machinery to total capital stock, due to their less sophisticated storage and processing equipment and their generally smaller percentage of capital stock in buildings and land. It is often stated that the electric motor is the heart of the traditional sector's capital stock.

26. The term HP_{t-1} is meant to reflect depreciation and DHP new investment. Ideally, the first term should contain some weighting by age of horsepower stock, but such a measure is impossible since reasonable data are only available from 1956.

    This specification assumes a constant percentage of investment taking place in machinery and an unchanging constant peso equivalent of new horsepower, contrary to our expectation that the constant peso equivalent of a horsepower has been increasing due to the increasing sophistication of machinery. Note, however, that if the price of machinery is falling over time (true for some products from the United States and Europe), this expectation may be less appropriate and the rationale for these regressions strengthened. The specification also suffers from the fact that plants move in and out of any particular category for which the regression is tested. Previously established plants moving into a category (e.g., a size category) bring all of their horsepower but only that year's investment. A good fit could only be expected in a category sufficiently homogeneous so that plants have a similar relationship between horsepower and investment (i.e., roughly similar technology) but not so narrow that it suffers from a changing set of plants.

27. A detailed discussion of these regressions can be found in Appendix One of my dissertation.

28. Nelson, Schultz, and Slighton, *Structural Change*, p. 83 f.

29. This eliminates some of the intersize class movement. The grouping is as follows: DANE's classes 0, 1, and 2 = very small (VS); 3, 4, and 5 = small (S); 6, 7, and 8 = medium (M); and size class 9 = large (L).

30. The capital figure estimated here includes only physical assets. Total capital, including working capital is more relevant. While very little data are available on working capital, most observers feel that the ratio of working capital to total capital is higher for the large firms. Thus the figures used in this chapter may underestimate the large plants' proportion of the capital stock.

Plant Size - 235

31. Well behaved aggregate statistics are often composites of wildly scrambled and fluctuating sectoral or regional statistics. It is comforting to note that, for six three-digit sectors with enough consecutive observations, these statistics, particularly Y5 percent and Y10 percent, are relatively well behaved.

32. The increase in plants was much faster up to 1962 than after.

Number of Plants in Size Class 9

Years	56	57	58	59	60	61	62	63	64	65	66	67
No. of Plants	134	157	163	181	198	204	217	217	223	240	248	244

Our only data on the number of new plants in size category 9 are two in 1962 and five in 1966. The period 1956-62 saw an increase of eighty-three large plants while 1962-67 saw only an increase of twenty-seven; many more existing plants must therefore have moved up into size class 9 before 1962 rather than after, unless 1962 and 1966 both had an unusually small number of new plants in size class 9. When plants move to a different size class, they take with them all of their horsepower but only that year's investment. Thus when there is significant movement of plants into size class 9, our estimates of K/HP for large plants will be downward biased and those for medium plants upward biased. Thus the figures after 1962, with less such movement, should be more accurate, and the time trend of K/HP for the large plants less than indicated by the time trend of YL_t.

33. This does not necessarily imply that the marginal product of employed labor is zero; rather that, because of the high rate of unemployment, the present dual price of labor (its marginal social cost) is zero.

34. Unpaid labor is assumed identical to paid labor in both its actual wage (imputed) and its MSC_L. This simplifies our calculations.

Available data (see Table below) show that the majority of unpaid workers are employers; both their earnings and their MSC are probably a little above those of paid workers in the same size class. Many of the rest are members of the employer's family, probably

DISTRIBUTION OF DANE MANUFACTURING EMPLOYMENT, 1964

Total	Paid		Unpaid	
	White-Collar	Blue-Collar	Employers	Family Workers
283,571	50,842	221,346	9,241	2,142

Source: DANE

women and children whose imputed wage and MSC are presumably lower than those of the average paid worker in the same size class. Thus it is unclear whether, on average, unpaid workers have higher or lower earnings and MSC than the average paid worker. In any case, their importance is not large, except for the bottom size classes (35 percent for 0, 19 percent for 1, 9 percent for 2, and falling off rapidly).

35. It could be argued that we should include the assumption of a negative opportunity cost of labor (i.e., value employment independently of output). Possible justifications might be:

   a) learning by doing—just by being employed, workers enjoy gains in their productivity not immediately capturable by the firm and therefore best thought of as a positive externality of employment;

   b) distribution of income—the higher is the level of employment the more equal the distribution of income;

   c) political stability.

   Aside from the practical matter that it would be difficult to make a plausible monetary estimate of the value of additional employment independent of output, there are also some theoretical objections. Perhaps most important, not all forms of labor are in excess supply, (e.g., certain industrial skills). One of the commonly heard reasons for the low frequency of multiple shift operations in Colombia is the shortage of reliable supervisory personnel.

36. This is implicit also in the fact that the wage share is remarkably stable across size classes and over time. Table 6.14 shows total wages (including fringe benefits and assuming unpaid workers receive the same as paid workers) as a percentage of value added.

37. Horsepower is used again as a convenience to permit all years and size categories to be shown. Estimates with the appropriate capital stock adjustments are shown in Table 6.15.

38. These results differ strikingly from those of Nelson et al., *Structural Change*. Like them, we conclude that labor productivity is an increasing function of plant size. But our estimates of output/capital ratios and total factor productivity imply that the largest firms are relatively inefficient. These different conclusions stem from two major sources. First, Nelson et al. were unaware of the downward bias in DANE statistics, especially monetary values, for the smaller size categories. Second, they used horsepower as a proxy for capital; our analysis has suggested that the ratio horsepower/fixed assets is much lower for large plants than for small ones.

39. Of course, if this higher protection is a valid application of the infant industry argument, then the higher prices are accurate measures of social benefit in the long run.

40. The period of most rapid increase in the manufacturing sector (particularly for large plants) occurred during the coffee boom of the early fifties. Another mild increase occurred in the very early sixties. It seems unlikely that the average age of large plants is at present particularly young vis-à-vis the average age at some future date.

41. For corporations, however, some of the capital income goes to small stockholders, who may not be high in the income distribution.

42. R. R. Nelson, "A Diffusion Model of International Productivity Differences in Manufacturing Industry," *American Economic Review* LVIII (December 1968): 1219-1248.

43. These two major explanations are also interrelated through the learning by doing process. If technology is originally homogeneous but factor price differences induce large plants to adopt and improve the more capital intensive technologies, then the observed technology map will eventually display greater economies of scale along the capital-intensive rays.

44. Slighton, "Relative Wages, Skill Shortages and Changes in Income Distribution in Colombia," p. 27.

45. One study in Japan found an interest rate differential of 11.5 percent to 17.4 percent as between corporations with capital over 100 million yen and ones with capital below 2 million yen. This study is referred to in B. Hoselitz, ed., *Role of Small Industry in the Process of Economic Growth* (New York: Humanities Press, Inc., 1968), p. 52. Such estimates are few, however, and much of the difference in nominal interest rates is surely attributable to differences in risk. The mortality rates for small firms far exceed those of large firms, and one would expect a rational credit distributor to take this into account.

46. It is also unclear whether this reflects unequal treatment, which might be a cause of different capital/labor ratios, or whether it is a natural result of small firms having lower capital/labor ratios.

47. It is worth noting that no automatic reason exists for giving first priority to elimination of factor price differences due to distortions as opposed to differences due to "real economic considerations." The political and social costs of removing a distortion might be quite high (e.g., repealing a bad law) while the benefit/cost ratio of eliminating differences based on "real economic considerations" (e.g., improving interworker communication on the job market) might be very high.

48. In a dual technology system, differences in factor prices could explain the existence of different size firms with different capital/labor ratios even if the individual production functions had very little substitutability.

49. Gordon Winston, "On the Inevitability of Factor Substitution," Williams College Research Memorandum No. 46, (April 1972).

50. Henry Bruton, "The Elasticity of Substitution in Developing Countries," Williams College Research Memorandum No. 45, (March 1972).

51. Unless dynamic considerations outweigh our static results.

52. Berry, "The Relevance and Prospects," pp. 40-42.

53. Although as Staley and Morse have pointed out, considerable changes may be found in the sectoral composition of the smaller plants as development proceeds. Eugene Staley and Richard Morse, *Modern Small Industry for Developing Countries* (New York: McGraw-Hill, 1965).

54. Remember that, within size classes, adjusting for capital/horsepower ratios has no effect.

55. Not surprising since they account for such a high share of national activity.

56. In retrospect, these smaller departments were not well chosen since Bolivar has a significant petroleum industry and Boyaca contains the Paz del Rio steel plant.

57. Table 6.22 does indicate, however, that an increase in the relative importance of the smaller plants may help the less industrialized (and poorer) regions somewhat more, a positive side effect.

58. The extent and the exact form of such differentials naturally varies from country to country. In Colombia, I had the distinct impression that larger plants had a considerable advantage in all these respects, due not only to their greater political influence and personalities but also to the belief, common among planners, bankers, and bureaucrats in Colombia, that large, modern plants constitute the best path to development. It would be implausible to argue that the Colombian government is powerless to reduce or partially compensate for these disparities.

59. Abstracting from short-run considerations such as transition costs and the running down of fixed capital.

60. Remember also that the effect of a particular policy such as raising the price of capital to the large firms may be more beneficial via its impact on the efficiency of those firms than in its impact on the relative importance of large and small firms.

61. Hopefully the service in question would, *ceteris paribus* raise their efficiency; some services induce firms to grow, which would raise their K/L ratio and work towards lowering their efficiency.

62. Note that policies in the first group, such as improving the capital market, will be beneficial even if the output/capital ratios are not higher in the small and medium size plants. Policies in the second group, however, insofar as they only change the relative expansion rates without improving the efficiency within size classes, could be counterproductive if the smaller plants are not socially more efficient.

LIST OF ABBREVIATIONS

DANE	= Departmento Administrativo Nacional de Estadística (Department of National Statistics)
EST	= number of establishments (plants)
TO	= total number of workers
TR	= paid workers
SS	= wages and salaries
PS	= fringe benefits
PB	= value of gross product
MP	= purchased raw materials and electric power
VA	= value added
IN	= purchases of fixed capital
HP	= installed horsepower capacity (excluding electrical generating equipment)
M type sector	= a four-digit sector at least 80 percent of whose output is produced in large plants
C type sector	= a four-digit sector at least 80 percent of whose output is produced in small plants
O type sector	= all other four-digit sectors
MSC_L	= marginal social cost of labor
AW	= average annual wage [(SS + PS)/TR]
CW	= average annual wage in the smallest plants (< 15 employees)
%MPF	= percentage of raw materials imported
HP_{t-1}	= horsepower capacity in the preceding period
DHP_t	= change in horsepower capacity ($HP_t - HP_{t-1}$)
K	= value of fixed capital
INR	= investment in fixed capital deflated by the price index for manufactured goods
Y10%	= an estimate of the ratio of value of fixed capital to horsepower capacity (K/HP)
NSB	= net social benefit

Chapter 7

The Utilization of Fixed Industrial Capital in Colombia: Some Empirical Findings
Francisco Thoumi

Introduction

As indicated in the introduction, one of the major unresolved dilemmas in the industrialization process of many developing countries has been the persistent observation of excess capacity. Since the phenomenon has not yet been adequately explained, due to a lack of both theoretical conceptualization and empirical work, it is no surprise that little if any progress has been made in resolving the problem.

This chapter studies some of the issues related to the utilization of machinery and equipment in the Colombian industrial sector and attempts to determine which factors or causes affect such utilization.

The phenomenon of capacity utilization must be viewed in the overall context of a country's industrial sector. Of particular interest here are the possible interrelationships between the phenomenon itself, the process of learning-by-doing, and plant size (it is a possible component in the factor productivity/establishment size relationships discussed in Chapter 6). Is underutilization of capacity an aspect of the early stage inefficiency likely to characterize any firm? Is learning how to organize more efficient use of capacity over the day and over the year an important component of learning-by-doing? Does the tendency of large firms to have low output/capital ratios reflect in part the fact that they have low rates of capacity utilization, induced partly by the low price at which they can get capital? Does the opportunity to export resolve the capacity utilization problem, as suggested in some versions which relate it primarily to lack of domestic demand? All these are legitimate questions to ask about the possible interrelations between fixed capital utilization and the issues explored in other chapters.

The present study is based on direct interviews taken in late 1970 and early 1971 and quantitative data from 290 industrial firms.[1] The analysis therefore combines statistical techniques with the often qualitative results of the interviews.

The Issue of Capital Utilization

The utilization of fixed industrial capital appeared as an issue among theoretical economists during the Great Depression, as it was self-evident that the level of capital utilization at the time was not socially optimal.

Those theoretical references to capital utilization were made in the context of imperfect competition and tried to establish a relationship between the level of utilization of capital and the market environment in which the firm was selling. In particular, it was determined that the level of capital utilization was "higher" under perfectly competitive than in monopolistic markets; that is, in short-run equilibrium, a monopolist firm would use a higher capital/labor ratio than a firm selling its product in a perfectly competitive market.[2]

The traditional theory of the firm defines the level of each variable, such as fixed cost or production, "per unit of time" but it does not explain what actually happens within that unit of time. For example, if the time unit is a day, the theory does not say how many hours a day the plant is actually working. This characteristic makes the theory quite inadequate to handle issues of utilization within a day, hour, or whatever. Comparisons over time almost invariably assume implicitly that what happens in the unit of time remains unchanged; for example, the textbook case interprets the downward shift of an isoquant as resulting from technological improvement rather than from an increase in the number of hours worked per day.[3] With such an assumption, it is not surprising that utilization theory is underdeveloped.

Only recently R. Marris, G. Winston, and G. Winston and O. McCoy developed theoretical frameworks including a time dimension "within the unit of time" in which the usual functions are defined.[4] These models explain how, given input price variations over whatever time unit is used, a plant in equilibrium could be closed part of the time unit. In order for a firm to work a night shift, it is not sufficient that the shift be "profitable"; in addition the average cost of a multiple-shift operation must be less than that of a single-shift operation. In more intuitive terms, the decision to work one, two, or three daily shifts is based on a comparison between the lower capital costs per unit of output that result from using the fixed capital during more hours per day and the increase in costs per unit of output which result from higher labor, managerial, and other costs of working at night.

Given input price variation over the course of the day, the firm makes a long-run decision to work a certain number of hours per day. In the "real" world, labor costs differ systematically and often significantly between day and night (or among shifts); the number of shifts a plant works should depend largely on these long-run factors. In the short-run, it would be expected to adjust output to specific demand and supply conditions by modifying the amount produced within a shift. The indivisibility caused by the legal or institutional practice of hiring laborers "by the day" limits the flexibility of the firm to respond to short-run fluctuations, making it impossible to "shrink" a shift to less than the normal shift hours and limiting the "stretching" possibilities to a few overtime hours.

Empirical work on excess capacity, like the theoretical effort, has been limited. During their studies and travels, development economists have, however, very frequently pointed out the surprisingly low level of "capacity utilization" in less developed countries, and have advanced a series of possible causes for the idleness or bad use of capital. Some of these possibilities are uncertainties of demand resulting in overinvestment;[5] the tendency of small oligopolistic protected markets in poor countries to create "excess capacity" when firms overinvest and adopt new technologies with large indivisibilities in production to improve their competitive position;[6] and a scarcity of raw materials leading possibly to underutilization of capital in a country following import substitution industrialization policies and bumping up against a foreign exchange constraint. Night wage premiums can cause capital to lie idle at night if the process of production is labor intensive; a lack of qualified manpower required by modern technology is another possible cause as the number of workers with the required skills may permit only one shift.[7] A lack of foremen willing to work the night shift,[8] and a lack of financial capital in countries where capital market conditions force firms to finance sales and/or purchases of inputs are still other possible causes.[9] Import-licensing policies in less developed countries (LDCs) can also cause over-investment for two reasons. First, when a firm applies for a license, it tends to ask for a larger than necessary allowance because the license might be granted for a smaller amount than that applied for, and because the firm is uncertain about the possibility of obtaining another license in the future when more fixed capital might be needed. Second, one of the criteria usually applied in deciding whether to grant a license is the "ability of the country to satisfy its own needs." In practice, this often means that if a firm can demonstrate its ability to satisfy the domestic demand for a product within a "reasonable" time horizon, it can prevent the granting of import licenses to new firms wishing to get established. Thus a monopolist can protect his market by showing an excess capacity with which to satisfy the future needs of the country. It has also been argued that cheap domestic and international loans can lead to excess capacity when the private investors end up paying a negative interest rate, having received a loan in domestic currency and used it to import a specific capital item under conditions of international inflation and domestic devaluation.[10]

In spite of the many references to "excess capacity" and its various possible causes in poor countries, only two nonimpressionistic studies on the subject exist. One is Winston's study of Pakistan and the other is C. K. Kim and J. K. Kwon's study of Korea.[11]

Winston's pioneering work used aggregate cross-section data for twenty-six groups of industrial firms, most of which coincided with standard two-digit industries while the rest coincided with three- and four-digit industries. Multiple regression was used to explain industrial capital utilization measured as hours of capital use per week as a percentage of a two and a half shift day (a 100-hour week).[12] Winston's results were surprisingly "good" as 80 percent of the variation in capital utilization was explained by four variables: competing imports measured as a percentage of total supply; export sales measured as a proportion of total domestic production; the capital/income ratio, which reflects the capital intensiveness of the production process; and the average firm size measured as annual production of the reporting firms in each industrial group.[13]

Kim and Kwon's recent study was based on data for thirty industrial sectors during the 1962-71 period. The utilization measure was the ratio of actual to maximum possible electricity consumption. A proxy of capital intensity was the most important determinant of utilization; a measure of industrial concentration was inversely related to it, while a ratio of total bank borrowings and foreign loans to either liabilities or net worth[14] was positively related to utilization. Less important determinants were sectoral exports (positive), imported inputs (negative), and imports competing with the plant's final products (negative). A very important finding was the tendency towards increasing utilization; the level rose by more than 100 percent during the ten-year period considered. Although more extreme, this tendency is similar to the one observed by M. R. Foss in the United States.[15]

These two studies found capital utilization in Pakistan and Korea to be significantly lower than the levels reported by Foss for the United States; both suggested the possibility of a positive relationship between economic development and industrial capital utilization.[16]

Capacity Utilization in Colombia: The Study

Many studies have mentioned the low level of capital utilization in Colombia; this also became an important assumption in the 1972 development plan,[17] which called for heavy expenditure in the construction sector with the expectation of generating multiplier effects in the industrial sector such that its output would increase with little new investment because of the existence of "excess capacity."

This chapter analyzes the extent and meaning of the "low level" of industrial capital utilization in Colombia, the most important determinants of capital utilization, and possible policy measures for its modification.

In late 1970 and early 1971 interviews were carried out with 290 firms to determine their level of capital utilization and their main problems.[18] Quantitative information on these firms was obtained from the Ministry of Development and the National Planning Department.[19] Stepwise regression analysis was then used to determine which variables were important in "explaining" the variation in utilization across firms. Impressionistic information obtained during the interviews provides a complementary input to the analysis.

The study differs in various ways from those of Winston and Kim and Kwon. First, the data were collected at the level of the firm, eliminating some of the problems inherent in aggregative analysis. Second, being based on interviews, it could draw on the experience and opinions of the managers, possibly quite important albeit subjective. Third, the level of disaggregation allows the introduction of variables which would disappear in more aggregative analysis, such as the location and age of the plants.

The measures of capital utilization used were designed to reflect the theory developed (see below). The main input price variation is thought to be among various daily shifts. Therefore, one measure used was the number of hours actually worked in a day (h) divided by the maximum possible number of daily hours (usually twenty-four) that the plant could work under ideal conditions (H).[20] Another was the output obtained during the hours worked as a percentage of the maximum output obtainable during this time (u).[21] As suggested earlier, it seems plausible that the percentage of hours worked during a day would tend to be determined by a long-run equilibrium decision, while the firm would adjust to short-run fluctuations by modifying u, the "intensity of use," during working time. Besides these two measures, a combination $U = \frac{h \cdot u}{H}$ was also used.

Entrepreneurs were also asked the maximum hours per day (H_e) their plant should work; a measure of utilization U_e, defined as

$$U_e = \frac{h \cdot u}{H_e},$$

was also used as a dependent variable.

These measures of capital utilization were further refined to reflect certain technological characteristics of production. In cases of unbalanced production processes, capital utilization was defined by the utilization of the bottleneck process. In cases of plants with continuous and noncontinuous processes, the measures were based on the noncontinuous process, as long as the continuous process did not constitute a bottleneck.[22]

Under the assumption of constant returns between day and night shifts and given the stock of capital, U measures the ratio of actual daily output to maximum potential daily output,[23] and U_e measures the ratio of actual daily output to maximum daily output obtained during the maximum number of hours that the entrepreneur would consider keeping the plant open.

The explanatory variables were chosen to aid in quantifying the importance of the different proposed explanations of capital underutilization in poor countries. It was impossible, however, to obtain all the variables needed by one or another of the different explanations; the lack of a simple one-to-one relation between sets of variables and explanations inevitably blurs the results.

The explanatory variables are:

(1) A proxy for the capital/labor ratio (needed since no data on capital is available), HP/L, horsepower installed divided by the number of blue-collar workers.

(2) The market share (MS) of each firm, used to test the importance of market structure upon capacity utilization, and defined as the gross output of the firm divided by the gross output of the competing sector.[24]

(3) Age of the firm (A). This variable can reflect the advantages of older firms where the learning-by-doing process is important, or because many industrial sectors of Colombia are new and therefore mistakes of overinvestment fade out with time as the economy grows.

(4) Yearly value added (VA), a measure of size; this could be important as an explanatory variable since it is believed that large firms have easier access to loans, good management, and import licenses.

(5) The ratio of imported to total raw materials and intermediate goods (M), was used to test whether imported raw materials made a difference in capital utilization.[25]

(6) The national and regional origin of the entrepreneur (E), introduced by using a dummy variable:[26] $\underline{1}$ was assigned to firms in which the manager was a foreigner or a Colombian of Antioqueño, or foreign descent; $\underline{0}$ was assigned to the rest of the firms.

(7) The quality of having any foreign capital (FC) was introduced as a dummy variable, since foreign capital is associated with know-how.

(8) The quality of having received a loan from a credit line of AID, the World Bank or the Interamerican Development Bank (IDB) was introduced as a dummy variable (AID), to test the importance of cheap loans.

(9) A location dummy (BM) was introduced because of complaints in Colombia about the centralization of economic and political power. The value $\underline{1}$ was assigned to firms located in Bogotá or Medellín and the value $\underline{0}$ to firms located in Cali, Barranquilla, Pereira, or Manizales.

(10) A dummy variable (SA) separating corporations from the rest of the firms was introduced, since managerial professionalism and ownership-management separation could be an important determinant of utilization.

(11) Another dummy (PF) separating the firms with products subject to government-created price controls from the other firms was used to test the importance of the price fixing policies followed by the government during the last decade.

The Study Results: Utilization Levels

Table 7.1 shows the unweighted mean, standard deviation, and minimum and maximum values of the utilization measures U, U_e, h/H, and u.

TABLE 7.1

GENERAL UTILIZATION PARAMETERS, 1970

Utilization Measure	Mean	Standard Deviation	Minimum Value	Maximum Value
U	.508	.274	.04	1.00
U_e	.691	.248	.06	1.00
h/H	.638	.285	.33	1.00
u	.779	.197	.12	1.00

The mean utilization values might at first sight appear "low," but compared to the results of other studies, they are high. Winston's findings, based on a 100-hour week, show that Pakistan's (1965) plants work only 33 percent of the time and his modification of Foss's estimates shows a level of 51.8 percent in the United States (1959).[27] Modifying the measure h/H used in this study to make it comparable to these estimates one concludes that at the end of 1970 Colombian firms were operating at least 45.6 percent of the time and very likely more.[28]

These estimates lead us to question the existence of a positive relationship between economic development and industrial capital utilization. Economists have found the low levels of utilization in poor countries surprising, since an idle machine in a poor country is more expensive than in a rich country because of the former's higher rates of interest and lower wages. But this is not the only determinant of relative utilization; poor and rich countries do not necessarily have identical machines, industrial structures, or input price fluctuations. If the rich countries have more capital-intensive or bigger machines or are, in general, more capital intensive, or have a lower natural night wage differential reflecting people's preferences, then it is possible for their "optimum" average utilization levels to be higher than in poor ones. One should not therefore expect a priori any specific relationship between the degree of economic development and capital utilization levels; any difference would depend not only upon differences in interest/wage ratios but also upon differences in capital/labor ratios, in type of machine, and in people's preferences.

Fixed Industrial Capital - 247

Table 7.1 also shows a large variation in utilization levels among Colombian firms. As expected, some firms work twenty-four hours a day at "full capacity," while others work only one shift at very low capital utilization levels. The interviews showed three-shift operations to be widespread in Colombia and strong labor opposition to either night work or rotating shifts to be almost nonexistent among workers.[29] Table 7.2 shows utilization levels for ten selected sectors containing at least eight firms in the sample taken. It is apparent that the textile, fertilizer, and cement sectors are working at very high utilization rates. The same is true of the glass, paper, tire, and steel factories visited. At the other extreme, the clothing and shoe sectors have very low utilization rates, unless utilization is measured by the maximum number of shifts the entrepreneur is willing to work (U_e). Consideration of the ratio U/U_e indicates that in the low utilization sectors the entrepreneurs consider the number of shifts they are working to be normal and therefore do not think of full capital utilization as operating the fixed capital stock twenty-four hours a day (Table 7.3).

A comparison of Tables 7.1 and 7.2 shows a tendency for utilization standard deviations to be smaller within subsectors than for the industrial sector as a whole. This tendency is stronger for the measures U and h/H and for sectors where the technology is very labor intensive (shoes, clothes) or very capital intensive (fertilizers, cement).

The four utilization measures were not, in general, highly correlated with each other (see Table 7.4). The relatively low correlations between h/H and u (.235) and between h/H and U_e (.438) indicate the lack of a clear relationship between the number of hours worked and the intensity of use of capital when in operation. A number of firms following multiple-shift patterns were working well below "capacity."[30] Clearly, studies asking entrepreneurs about the utilization of "capacity" will not elicit answers reflecting the utilization pattern of capital equipment through the twenty-four hours of a day. The higher correlation coefficient between U and h/H is, of course, expected by definition.

Determinants of Utilization

Linear, stepwise, repression analysis, applied to the whole sample, gave the following results for the independent variable U:

$$U = 40 + 8.9 \text{ SA} + .69 \frac{\text{HP}}{\text{L}} + 13.9 \text{ AID} + 0.00000074 \text{ VA}$$
$$(.4001) \quad (.4901) \quad (.5505) \quad (.5815)$$

$$+ .14 \text{ MS} + 5.6 \text{ E} \tag{1}$$
$$(.5907) \quad (.5989)$$

where the figures in brackets show the coefficients of multiple correlation at each step (r). The coefficients of SA, $\frac{\text{HP}}{\text{L}}$, AID, and VA are significant at the 999 percent level, the coefficient of MS is significant at the 97 percent level and that of E at the 96 percent level.

Surprisingly, the most important variable in explaining the composite utilization measure is the dummy which differentiates corporations from other firms. This variable, together with the capital-labor measure, the dummy for a foreign loan, and the variable of size "explain" 34 percent of the variation in U. The market share and the entrepreneur's origin, while statistically significant, do not add much to the coefficient.

TABLE 7.2

ALTERNATIVE UTILIZATION PARAMETERS, BY INDUSTRY, 1970

Sector and International Standard Industrial Classification (ISIC)	Number of Observations	Utilization Measure	Mean	Standard Deviation
Textiles 23	18	U	.852	.178
		U_e	.868	.145
		h/H	.972	.086
		u	.868	.145
Leather Shoes 2411	8	U	.260	.073
		U_e	.675	.093
		h/H	.375	.077
		u	.675	.093
Clothes 2431 to 2448	29	U	.262	.077
		U_e	.730	.200
		h/H	.339	.031
		u	.766	.193
Printing 2811 2813	9	U	.502	.136
		U_e	.735	.215
		h/H	.592	.206
		u	.883	.177
Fertilizers and Nonedible oils and fats 3111 to 3122	9	U	.800	.194
		U_e	.800	.194
		h/H	1.000	.000
		u	.800	.194
Soaps and Toothpaste 3141 to 3147	10	U	.524	.268
		U_e	.723	.308
		h/H	.633	.246
		u	.788	.241
Bricks 3311	13	U	.521	.268
		U_e	.642	.306
		h/H	.551	.239
		u	.915	.167
Cement 3341	8	U	.900	.134
		U_e	.900	.134
		h/H	1.000	.000
		u	.900	.134
Cement Manufactures 3352, 3357 3354, 3356 and 3357	10	U	.397	.255
		U_e	.660	.239
		h/H	.516	.254
		u	.800	.194
Household Appliances 3543, 3717 and 3732	15	U	.323	.199
		U_e	.409	.253
		h/H	.422	.153
		u	.734	.294

TABLE 7.3

SHARE OF MAXIMUM POSSIBLE HOURS WHICH ENTREPRENEURS BELIEVE THEIR PLANT SHOULD WORK (U/U_e), AVERAGE BY INDUSTRY, 1970

Textiles	.981	Soap	.724
Shoes	.391	Bricks	.811
Clothes	.359	Cement	1.000
Printing	.683	Cement Manufactures	.601
Fertilizers	1.000	Household Appliances	.789

TABLE 7.4

CORRELATION MATRIX OF UTILIZATION MEASURES

	h/H	U_e	u	U
h/H	1.000	.438	.235	.896
U_e		1.000	.718	.646
u			1.000	.574
U				1.000

None of the other variables was statistically significant at the 90 percent level and no multicollinearity problems were apparent.[31]

Why the significance of the corporate firm as a determinant of utilization? Colombian corporations differ from other firms because the separation of management from ownership allows for more "professionalism" in management; it also eliminates some of the obstacles to multiple shifting in noncorporations resulting from the tendency not to hire people to supervise production during the night shifts. This conclusion is strongly supported by the impressionistic evidence of the interviews; they showed the main obstacles to a night shift to be the high implicit price of the manager's leisure time at night and the "very high cost" of hiring a good night supervisor. Seemingly, the concentration in these firms of the supervising, advertising, financing, and other tasks in the head of one person makes the supervising services part of a "joint product"; this raises the cost of night-shift supervising a great deal, as the night plant manager would not have the other tasks.

Horsepower per blue-collar worker (a proxy for the capital/labor ratio) came out second to the corporation dummy in its effect on utilization; it appears to be important in determining utilization when night wage surcharges are an important addition to costs. This confirms the impression from the interviews, where the higher night wages were mentioned as an obstacle to multiple shifting only in the most labor-intensive sectors like clothes, shoes, and furniture. The entrepreneurs in these sectors also mentioned other labor problems which complicate the use of multiple shifts. These include the workers' desire to produce a complete item by themselves (the cases of furniture and clothes), and the need to adjust machine speed and height to each worker (shoes).

Industrial loans from international sources tend to go to established firms. [32] The relationship mentioned by Hirschman between foreign loans and underutilization due to overestimation of demand and lack of familiarity with the technology used does not seem to exist in Colombia. [33] These loans have been conditional on feasibility studies and good organization and management performance by the recipient firms. Such characteristics would probably account for the higher utilization levels observed. The direction of the causality relationship is, however, an open question. Are the firms selected on the basis of better organization, or does their organization improve with the granting of the loan and the conditions it requires?

As mentioned before, the market share and the origin of the entrepreneur do appear as statistically significant explanatory variables; however, given the small increase in the multiple correlation coefficient due to their inclusion, these variables cannot be considered important determinants of utilization. Interestingly, the sign of the MS coefficient is positive, suggesting that monopolistic firms tend to use capital more intensively than oligopolistic ones. [34]

Several variables had no observable impact on utilization levels. Among these were age of firm, the percent of imported inputs, and the dummy variables for location, foreign capital ownership, and official price setting. The unimportance of age of firm suggests that firms reach their normal level of utilization fairly rapidly, after which the variable has no effect; possibly low utilization levels during the first two or three years do not show up in a cross-section analysis as new firms are a small part of the sample and as some of the firms are up to sixty years old; the measured age-utilization relationship therefore reflects a long-run tendency, and not the gestation period. The lack of significance of the percentage of inputs imported may be the result of the improved balance-of-payments situation during 1970, and possibly also of the suspected policy of granting licenses to firms which had obtained them in the past. [35] Foreign capital and the centralization of governmental activities in Bogotá do not appear to affect utilization while the entrepreneur's national and regional origin could have a slight effect on utilization.

A regression with h/H as the dependent variable was similar to equation (1), although it had a higher correlation coefficient (.64):

$$h/H = 40.2 + 12.3\ SA + 14.58\ AID + .60\ \frac{HP}{L} + .2150\ MS$$
$$(.4657) \quad (.5449) \quad (.6000) \quad (.6211)$$

$$+ 9.12\ PF + 6.60\ E \qquad (2)$$
$$(.6313) \quad (.6409)$$

The failure of value added to appear in this regression, coupled with its low impact on the correlation coefficient of equation (1), seem to indicate that size, as measured by value added, is not strongly related to utilization in Colombia. The appearance of the AID variable as one with positive explanatory effect confirms the impression that AID funds have gone to established and "sound" firms.

The correlation coefficients of .60 and .64 in equations (1) and (2) suggest that some important variables were left out. Since most domestic demand problems could be solved by exports, one would expect exports to be an important determinant of utilization, but the impossibility of obtaining reliable data precluded its use.

The "bunching" of the residuals in some sectors suggested the existence of *ad hoc* sector-specific variables affecting utilization. The residuals were particularly bunched in textile firms, where real utilization is higher than predicted; and in clothing, shoes, wood products, electrical machinery, and transport equipment, where it is lower than predicted. The interviews shed some light on these differences.

(1) *Textiles* - This sector combines all the characteristics affecting capital utilization positively in Colombia. In the common perception, this is the country's "show" industry, characterized by excellent professional management, a few firms with years of experience in their markets, and a highly mechanized and capital-intensive production process compared with textile industries around the world.[36] Furthermore, it is one of few industries which at the time of this study had developed a consistent flow of exports.[37]

(2) *Clothing* - This sector combines all the factors leading to low utilization of capital. Most of the plants visited were managed by their owner, who supervised the production process and was also in charge of the financial aspects of the firm. These plants are probably the most labor-intensive industrial operations and suffer special difficulties in establishing night shifts because of their female labor force.[38]

(3) *Shoes* - This industry has difficulties in obtaining a constant supply of inputs; the Colombian tanneries prefer to export and to sell to the large domestic producers, even when the smaller producers are willing to pay the "current" price. Quality inputs also seem difficult to obtain, as the hides are damaged by the great number of markings (to protect the cattle from thieves) and by the traditional skinning of the cattle with pointed instead of rounded knives. Some firms spoke of the readjustment of machine speed and height for every worker as complicating multiple-shift operations.

(4) *Wood furniture* - Managers expressed three particular problems. One is the difficulty in finding qualified workers; another, the scarcity of wood inputs (in the case of firms not vertically integrated).[39] Finally, the lack of an organized production line complicates any multiple-shift arrangement because as each worker considers himself an artisan and insists on manufacturing the entire piece of furniture, when workers from two shifts work on the same piece of furniture, its quality goes down significantly.

(5) *Electrical machinery* - This sector includes the three broad categories of industrial and agricultural machinery, small household appliances, and large commercial and home appliances. Machinery producers face large, seasonal fluctuations and since many of them produce only to order, a substantial part of their machinery remains idle during an average working day. This last fact showed in larger negative residuals in equation (1) than in equation (2).

The small household appliance producers face very strong foreign competition from contraband imports and from legal imports of small television sets, blenders, and other items priced less than the maximum tariff-free import allowance for travellers to the Colombian free port of the San Andres Islands. Furthermore, they have to sell on credit, making the output of domestically-owned firms very sensitive to changes in credit policies. It appears that the foreign-owned firm with better access to financial capital produces cheaper goods for middle-class consumption, while the domestically-owned firms produce more expensive articles for upper-class consumption as these require less financing. The industry is still affected by the apparent overinvestment of the early sixties when the production of such items as refrigerators and washing machines started. This overinvestment was apparently due to the entrepreneurs' lack of knowledge about the number and size of the firms entering the market; many firms stated that they "had been the first to produce an article and then everybody else came along."[40]

(6) *Transport equipment* - This sector is special because output is controlled by the government, which assigns import and assembly quotas to each producer. One way to get a larger quota is to demonstrate unused fixed capital; this encourages building capital idleness in the system.[41]

The regressions for the dependent variables U_e and u gave "poor" results as their variation was very little "explained" by the independent variables. Equations (3) and (4) show these results:

$$U_e = 61.65 + .187 \text{ MS} + 8.114 \text{ E} \qquad (3)$$
$$(.1968) \quad (.2538)$$

$$u = 77.17 + .000004224 \text{ VA} \qquad (4)$$
$$(.1257)$$

The coefficients of MS and E in (3) are significant at the 99 percent level and that of VA in (4) at the .96 percent level.

The very low correlation coefficients (.25 and .125) indicate that these two utilization variables, which are based on what the entrepreneur considers to be his plant's capacity and the intensity of the plant's use during the period of operation, do not depend on the "structural" variables used in the regressions. This suggests, as expected, that these two utilization measures are dependent on short-run economic conditions not reflected in the variables used. The fact that value added is the only significant variable in equation (4) suggests that large firms are better able to maintain their desired intensity of utilization than small firms, a possible reflection of easier access to short-run funds in the capital market. The significance of MS and E in (3) could indicate that firms with monopolistic power and with the "right" entrepreneurs' achieve capital utilization closer to that desired by management than do other firms.

Most firms interviewed mentioned the "lack of financial capital" as one of their main problems related to utilization.[42] Their repeated insistence led us to study the reasons for such a need. Financial capital in the Colombian industrial sector is used mostly to finance inventories, sales, and suppliers of inputs. Colombian industrial firms work in an environment of oligopolistic competition for their inputs and products and face segmented capital markets. Under these circumstances, a producer who acts as a financial intermediary can, by making credit available on better terms to its suppliers and/or its buyers, increase its output and its utilization rate. In other words, a segmented capital market allows a firm to use credit as a competitive weapon in oligopolistic commodity markets. When this is the main role of financial capital within a firm, an increase in its availability to the firm will have negative effects on competing firms. Consider the case of a firm producing a household durable good. Given the capital market conditions, a family of demand functions for the good would spring up, depending on the credit conditions offered. If, at the outset, this particular producer sells only on cash terms and has a low level of capital utilization, it can increase capacity utilization by obtaining short-term capital to finance sales. But if some of its competitors are already financing sales, their utilization levels will now decrease. In this situation, while additional financial capital helps the recipient firm, it is clear that the industry's utilization level might not be affected by it. In short, until a specific study is made, the relationship between capital utilization and financial capital availability will remain unknown, despite the individual entrepreneur's honest claims.

Conclusions and Recommendations

Despite the imperfect information and the limitations of the research techniques used, it has still been possible to obtain some important, if qualified, conclusions and make some recommendations. First, it does seem that as of the early seventies industrial capital utilization in Colombia was relatively high compared with the few other countries for which information was available.

Second, the hours of machinery and equipment use for a twenty-four hour period are related to long-run "structural" variables, which are very difficult to modify in the short-run. The importance of the corporation dummy and the relative unimportance of the capital-labor proxy variable coupled with the impressionistic evidence produced by the interviews show that night wage surcharges, an obvious policy variable, are important only in the most labor-intensive sectors, while the implicit price of the manager's leisure and tranquility and the *high cost* of night plant management are important factors limiting the number of shifts in a wide range of industries. Capital-intensive sectors like cement, steel, and glass, are producing on a three-shift basis and it is improbable that they could increase output much in the short run.

Third, from a policy point of view, raising long-run capital utilization to a three-shift basis requires a set of measures which make it profitable for the firm to do so. A purely demand-pull policy will fail as it neglects the fact that, given *any* volume of demand, many firms work only one shift in long-run equilibrium. It is true, however, that a large demand pull could induce some firms to increase the number of shifts worked in the short-run. Since one does not know how fast firms move towards long-run equilibrium (one does not know how short is short-run), one cannot predict the impact of such a policy. The interview evidence suggests that in most sectors the adjustment process takes less than a couple of years and that in most labor-intensive sectors working less than three shifts, the entrepreneurs are willing to forego sales rather than increase the number of shifts.

Fourth, this chapter shows the importance in Colombia of an organizational factor as strongly influencing the number of shifts a firm works. Inasmuch as management could be improved through time, one could then expect a secular increase in capital utilization.[43]

Fifth, the validity of the frequently alleged relationship between financial (short-run) capital and utilization in the Colombian environment is questioned, at least pending the presentation of stronger evidence.

The conceptual and empirical difficulties which plague this study limit the validity of its conclusions. Some readers might view these conclusions as being heavily dependent on the author's impressions and interpretations. It is only hoped that further work on this complicated topic will clarify in a better way some of the capital utilization issues.

Postscript

The interviews upon which this study is based were done in late 1970 and early 1971; the paper itself was written in 1973. Subsequently, the author undertook a follow-up study of capital utilization in Colombia under the auspices of the World Bank.[44] This follow-up study confirmed the findings reported herein. In particular, the study confirmed an increase over time in capital utilization, the relatively high level of Colombian utilization, and the more intensive utilization of fixed capital equipment by corporations compared with noncorporations. Therefore, despite the delay in the final publication of this work, its main conclusions have not been invalidated to date.

ENDNOTES FOR CHAPTER 7

1. For a detailed explanation of the data used, see the appendix to this chapter.

2. J. H. Cassels, "Excess Capacity and Monopolistic Competition," *The Quarterly Journal of Economics* LI (May 1937): 426-443, and E. H. Chamberlain, *The Theory of Monopolistic Competition*, 5th ed. (Cambridge: Harvard University Press, 1946) showed that in perfectly competitive markets firms would maximize short-run profits at the minimum point of the average cost curve while monopolistic firms' optimum will be at a point to the left of the minimum point indicating that optimally they would use more capital per unit of other factors than in perfectly competitive markets, i.e., the use of "capacity" would be lower.

3. An excellent discussion of these issues is found in G. Winston, "A Primer on Pure Flow Production Analysis" (Williamstown, Massachusetts: Williams College, January 1973), mimeographed.

4. See Ibid.; R. Marris, *The Economics of Capital Utilization: A Report on Multiple Shift Work* (New York: Cambridge University Press, 1964; and G. Winston and T. O. McCoy, "Investment and the Optimal Idleness of Capital" (Williamstown, Massachusetts: Williams College, June 1972), mimeographed.

5. This argument has been given great importance in explaining underutilization in the Colombian industrial sector. See P. Feldl, *Relación sobre la Situación Actual de la Industria Manufacturera Fabril de Colombia* (Bogotá: Ministerio de Desarrollo Económico, mayo 1970).

6. Professor Merhav has argued along this line in order to explain low capacity utilization in Israel. See M. Merhav, "Excess Capacity—Measurement, Causes and Uses: A Case Study of Industry in Israel," *Industrialization and Productivity*, Bulletin No. 15, (New York: United Nations, 1970), pp. 22-48.

7. For further discussion of these problems, see W. Hogan, "Capacity Creation and Utilization in Pakistan Manufacturing Industry," *Australian Economic Papers* Vol. 7 (June 1968): 28-53.

8. G. Hadley, "Some Characteristics of Colombian Industry" (Bogotá: Centro de Estudios sobre Desarrollo Económico, Universidad de Los Andes, February 1965) mentioned this as an important factor in the Colombian case.

9. This argument has been given great importance in explaining underutilization in the Colombian industrial sector. See P. Feldl, *Relación sobre la Situación Actual de la Industria Manufacturera Fabril de Colombia* (Bogotá: Ministerio de Desarrollo Económico, mayo 1970).

10. For example, in Colombia in 1970 it was possible to obtain a loan in pesos to import capital equipment from the Agency for International Development (AID) or a World Bank credit line at about 15 percent yearly interest. Since the rate of devaluation of the peso was about 10 percent per year, and since international prices were rising at close to 5 percent per year, the actual interest rate was virtually zero. If, on top of this, one adds the tax breaks that the firm got

due to the payment of the 15 percent interest and the accountable depreciation of the machine, the cost of capital equipment to the firms was negative, which implies that the firm could make money importing the machinery even if it did not use it.

11. G. Winston, "Capital Utilization in Economic Development," *Economic Journal*, Vol. 81, 1971, and C. K. Kim and J. K. Kwon, "Capital Utilization in Korean Manufacturing, 1962-71: Its Level, Trend, and Structure," (Washington: Agency for International Development, May 1973), mimeographed.

12. D. M. Schydlowsky, "A Working Note on the Application of Regression Techniques to Capacity Utilization Data," background paper for Conference on Utilization of Capacity in Industry (Lima, 13-16 May 1979), mimeographed, points out certain difficulties in using regression analysis on these data. These problems arise from the structure of causality of the underutilization of capital and the bunching of observations of the dependent variables around the measures of one, two, or three shifts. While it is clear that the regression model mis-specifies the utilization phenomenon because the causes of underutilization are not simultaneously binding, it is also clear that no alternative method of statistical analysis is at this time available. One should then be aware of the qualifications of a literal interpretation of the regression equation and consider it as a weapon more likely to point in the right direction than a simple impressionistic study of the firm's problems.

13. G. Winston, "Capital Utilization in Economic Development," *Economic Journal* Vol. 81, (March 1971): 42, contains the equation:

$$U = 28.99 - 0.358 M + 0.251 X + 3.747 K/Y + 0.305 S$$
$$\quad\quad\quad (0.074) \quad (0.080) \quad\quad (0.774) \quad\quad (0.094)$$

$$R^2 = 0.8152; \; F = 18.6$$

The figures in parentheses are standard errors of the regression coefficients. M = competing imports, X = Export sales, K/Y = capital/income ratio, S = average firm size.

14. Which reflects the government's impact on credit availability to various industrial sectors.

15. M. R. Foss, "The Utilization of Capital Equipment: Postwar Compared with Prewar," *Survey of Current Business*, Vol. 43 (June 1963): 8-16.

16. See Winston, "A Comparison of Capital Utilization in Pakistan" and Kim and Kwon, "Capital Utilization in Korean Manufacturing."

17. The 1972 development plan is summarized in Departmento Nacional de Planeación, *Revista de Planeación y Desarrollo*, Vol. III, no. 4 (diciembre 1971).

18. The utilization measures were determined by the interviewer and the managers, while the problems of the firm are those which the manager perceives as important. A complete summary of those interviews and the questionnaire used was published by the National Planning Department. See Departamento Nacional de Planeación,

"Comentarios Preliminares de los Resultados de la Encuesta sobre Utilización de la Capacidad Instalada en la Industria Manufacturera Fabril Colombiana" (Bogotá: Document Unidad de Estudios Industriales y Agrarios (UELA) 009-D.I., August 10, 1971).

19. The appendix to this essay shows how every quantitative variable was obtained.

20. H was set at twenty-four hours a day except in cases where the machinery required daily maintenance and/or cleaning, when an allowance for those purposes was made and H was reduced accordingly.

21. As perceived by the manager.

22. For example, if a plant included a high oven that would work twenty-four hours, and if the rest of the plant worked less than twenty-four hours, this number of hours was used to estimate the utilization rate, as long as the oven would not create a bottleneck if the rest of the plant also worked twenty-four hours.

23. Notice that these measures do not make any allowance for the days of the year during which capital is totally idle, such as Sundays and holidays.

24. The definition of competing sector was a subjective one. In most cases it was defined as a four-digit sector; however, both finer and more aggregate classifications were used when the author thought they were a better definition of competing sector.

25. This measure does not necessarily indicate the foreign exchange constraint pressure on the balance of payments as it does not need to be correlated to either the ease with each a firm gets an import license, or the essentiality of the imported inputs in the production process.

26. The importance of the Antioqueño and foreign entrepreneurs has been repeatedly mentioned as a very important factor in the Colombian industrial development because of their special hardworking, business-oriented idiosyncrasies. See E. E. Hagen, *On the Theory of Social Change* (Homewood, Illinois: Dorsey Press, Inc., 1962), pp. 353-384; E. Havens, *Tamesis, Estructura y Cambio* (Bogotá: Ediciones Tercer Mundo, 1966), and A. López, *Migración y Cambio Social en Antioquia durante el Siglo Diecinueve* (Bogotá: Centro de Estudios Sobre Desarrollo Económico (CEDE), Universidad de Los Andes, 1970).

27. See Winston, "A Comparison of Capital Utilization in Pakistan" and Foss, "The Utilization of Capital Equipment."

28. Some Colombian firms, especially the ones producing textiles, cement, glass, and fertilizers were working seven days a week. Some firms work at five and a half days as workers are required to put in forty-four hours a week. Under the assumption that no firm worked more than five days, which clearly underestimates utilization, a minimum utilization level of 45.6 percent [.638 x (5/7)] emerges.

29. One hundred thirteen plants (39%) worked at most one full shift, while 104 (35.8%) worked at least two and one half shifts.

30. This is supported by the evidence that U's lowest correlation coefficient is the one with u.

31. See the correlation matrix in the appendix. The correlation coefficients among the eleven explanatory variables which enter the final equations shown do not exceed .48 and all but three are below .31.

32. Some large, new firms have been financed with these loans; however, their number has been small compared to the already established firms which have received loans from those same sources.

33. If the relationship argued in Hirschman, *Development Projects Observed*, operated through another variable, the probable candidates would be the capital/labor ratio and firm size. But both of these also have positive coefficients in equation (1).

34. Given the size of the Colombian market and the import substitution industrialization policies followed in the past, the MS variable compares monopoly with oligopoly and not with perfect competition. The positive relationship between U and MS is then expected and confirms the findings of Merhav in Israel. See Merhav, "Excess Capacity—Measurement."

35. See the discussion in Chapter 8 of this book.

36. Feldl, *Relación sobre la Situación Actual*, pp. 75-76 estimates that the Colombian textile sector is more capital intensive and mechanized than the European one.

37. The combination of the "right" characteristics may produce a higher utilization than the one predicted by a linear equation because of the nonadditivity of the utilization phenomenon and the mis-specifications of the linear model.

38. This has been mentioned as a particular difficulty of the sector in some Colombian areas. See Feldl, *Relación sobre la Situación Actual*, pp. 27-40.

39. Ibid., pp. 41-43.

40. Ibid., pp. 108-113.

41. For example, an automobile assembly plant that was working one shift in the assembly line and two shifts in the painting shop, proceeded to duplicate capacity when their quota was doubled. A more detailed discussion of the sector is found in Departamento Nacional de Planeación, "Comentarios Preliminares de los Resultados," pp. 114-117.

42. Which has also been given great importance by Feldl, *Relación Sobre la Situación Actual*.

43. Like the one which has taken place in the United States and Korea. See Foss, "The Utilization of Capital Equipment" and Kim and Kwon, "Capital Utilization in Korean Manufacturing."

44. F. E. Thoumi, "La utilización del capital fijo en la industria manufacturera de Colombia," *Revista de Planeación y Desarrollo* X (septiembre-deciembre 1979): 11-96.

APPENDIX A

Data Sources

(1) The data on capacity utilization was obtained through personal interviews with either general managers or production managers of 290 firms. These interviews took place during the last three months of 1970 and January of 1971. During the January, 1971 interviews, all questions were in reference to November, 1970; therefore, our measure of capacity utilization is based on utilization rates during the months at which most industries' reach maximum production because of the Christmas sales expansion. The only exception to this high seasonal utilization was found in a few plants in the food industry where output supply follows a different seasonal pattern.

The interviews usually included a visit to the plant, allowing the interviewers to check some of the information provided by the manager. The interviews were made by a team of economists and industrial engineers from the Division of Industry of the National Planning Department (D.N.P.) and the Development Advisory Service of Harvard University. The interviewers had good knowledge of the Colombian industrial sector and were extensively briefed on the subject of excess capacity.

The firms interviewed were selected from the industrial directory published by the National Statistics Department (DANE). The sample was stratified by size of firm and by industrial subsector.

(2) Quantitative information for the 290 firms visited was obtained from the industrial registry kept by the Ministry of Development. These data included yearly gross output, horsepower installed, yearly wages and salaries paid, yearly social security contributions, number of blue-collar and white-collar workers employed, age of the firm (not of the plant or machinery), yearly consumption of domestic and imported raw materials and intermediate goods, and location of the firm. Data for 1970 was impossible to obtain; therefore, it was necessary to use the last complete registry available, the one taken in December, 1968. This difference in time is probably not very important since the production structure of a firm is unlikely to change significantly in a couple of years.

(3) Qualitative information available at the Division of Private Investment of the D.N.P. was also used. This allowed the introduction of dummy variables in the statistical analysis with respect to:

  i. Whether the firm had received a loan originated in AID, the World Bank, or the IDB.

  ii. Whether the firm had any foreign capital.

  iii. The national origin of the firm's manager.

(4) The National Statistics Department's (DANE) published data on the various industrial sectors were used to determine each firm's market shares; DANE data on physical plant location were used to construct the location dummy variables.

TABLE A-1

CORRELATION MATRIX OF THE EXPLANATORY VARIABLES
ENTERED IN FINAL EQUATIONS

	SA	$\frac{HP}{L}$	AID	VA	MS	E	PF
SA	1.000	.226	.309	.180	.476	.201	.096
$\frac{HP}{L}$		1.000	.115	.049	.346	.062	.079
AID			1.000	.145	.230	.035	.118
VA				1.000	.272	.122	.069
MS					1.000	.126	.057
E						1.000	.004
PF							1.000

Chapter 8

Trade and the Import Control System in Colombia: Some Quantifiable Features[1]
Carlos F. Díaz-Alejandro

Colombia is no exception to the general rule that industrialization and trade are tightly linked in developing countries. Most stages in the growth of the factory sector involve replacement of actual or potential imports by domestic production. In early phases, while this process focuses on final consumer goods, the new local production depends heavily on imported inputs and capital goods. Often delayed by policy, the stage of manufacturing exports may arrive, as it now has in Colombia, and then it is the ability to switch from the local market to the vast world market which permits expansion at a much faster rate than the growth of domestic demand. Manufacturing growth is, in the whole sequence, related to changes in trade patterns.

Manufacturing output tends to rely more on produced capital goods than does agriculture, and most economists would probably accept the proposition that as the K/L ratio rises in a country the share of factory manufacturing in output will rise,[2] this more or less regardless of the presence or absence of various possible types of trade barriers. For several reasons economists want to understand both the process of growth and changing trade patterns, given any set of trade barriers or stimuli, and the effect of changes in that set of trade barriers or stimuli. In the latter field, the degree of validity of the infant industry argument for protection has long been a key question. Earlier chapters have presented some evidence consistent with its validity in Colombia. Chapter 2 traced the growth of the textile industry from an often decried white elephant in its first decade or so to a highly competitive industry, one of the prides of Colombian manufacturing. Chapters 4 and 5 measured for learning-by-doing in two separate industries and found it to be significant. This evidence by no means permits us to reach an overall evaluation of Colombian protectionist policies. Even less solid evidence is available for the impact of export-promotion policies on the efficiency of the aided industries.[3] Such analyses are complicated by the fact that import-substituting and exporting activities are frequently carried out by the same firms.

The importance of learning-by-doing is, then, of key importance in the prediction of output effects of trade barriers, or stimuli in the case of new exports. When one turns to the income-distribution impact of trade, a long established body of literature is available to suggest hypotheses. Assuming that trade is based on relative factor abundance, protection of relatively capital-intensive, domestic industries (manufacturing in need of protection in a labor-abundant country presumably fits this category) is predicted to raise the share of capital and to worsen the personal distribution of income; exports of competitive manufactures will presumably be labor intensive, so the activity will raise the labor share and improve income distribution. But these simple Heckscher-Ohlin predictions are obviously open to question and qualification.[4] A most obvious qualification is raised by the fact (see Chapter 6) that factor proportions seem to be as much or more related to firm or plant size as to industry or sector, capital intensity being an increasing function of size. Chapter 6 raises many doubts about the often assumed positive relation between size and efficiency.

Before a persuasive interpretation of the impact of trade in manufacturing products or the quality of trade policy can be evolved, certain detailed types of information are clearly necessary. What types of firms import and export? How does the existing trade control system discriminate, if at all, among these types?

This chapter seeks to shed some light on these questions by analyzing 1970 registered imports according to size of importers. Familiarity with about 500 major private importers allows import control authorities to be reasonably sure about the destination of half of the registered imports. It is not farfetched to suppose that those 500 major importers make up the core of the Colombian socioeconomic system, and that they and the Instituto Colombiano de Comercio Exterior (INCOMEX)[5] authorities know each other fairly well. With half of imports going to 500 companies, and about 20 percent going to the public sector, only 30 percent has to be distributed in retail fashion.

The chapter will also attempt a quantification of some aspects of INCOMEX behavior in accepting or rejecting import requests, as revealed in its handling of a sample of such requests during 1971. The data will also show that a good share of major industrial exporters is to be found among major importers.

Major Colombian Importers in 1970

From a sample of import license requests made in the second semester of 1971, two types of information were obtained: a census-like coverage of all imports, exports, etc., for each company (*not* plant) in 1970, and data on the specific import request for the second semester of 1971 (amount, rejection or acceptance, reasons for rejections, and so on). The former type of information will be discussed first.

Following INCOMEX categories, major private importers can be subdivided into an industrial and a commercial group. Industrial importers use imports in their production process; commercial importers resell the foreign goods to local buyers. While "Resolution 15" forms give no information on the ownership of the company making the import request, a somewhat rough-and-ready separation was also made according to presumed nationality.[6] In general, a company was presumed to be Colombian-owned unless firm evidence to the contrary could be found. Only companies for which foreign ownership was 50 percent or more were placed under the category of foreign-owned; all others were regarded as national. The sample contained relatively few joint ventures. Note that the definition of foreign-owned companies used here is considerably weaker than that used in the Andean code on foreign investment. Lack of reliable and up-to-date data was the major reason for choosing our weaker definition.

Table 8.1 presents a summary of major industrial[7] importers, classified according to their registered imports during 1970, and whether the companies were national or foreign owned. Data on the number of employees, minor exports, and income and sales taxes paid by these companies are also presented. Three subdivisions were created according to size. These were companies importing more than one million dollars in 1970, those importing between half a million and one million, and those with imports ranging between $100,000 and half a million.

The striking degree of concentration shown in Table 8.1 helps explain the relatively smooth operation of the Colombian import control system. Thus, just eighty industrial companies captured in the sample accounted for 30 percent of all 1970 registered imports; these same companies accounted for 21.2 percent of all income and sales taxes paid during 1970 in Colombia, and employed 19.2 percent of all those engaged in manufacturing in the same year.[8] Since, given the way the data were obtained, some large importers may have been missed, the estimates presented in Table 8.1, and those which follow, for import concentration, as well as for degree of foreign control, are *minimum* ones; further, cases of several companies being under the control of a single conglomerate or family group could also exist.

Note that, even neglecting data problems, it would not be easy to interpret the information presented in Table 8.1. Neither comparable cross-section nor time-series data are available for Chenery-like tests of "normality." Even if they were, further analysis involving variables such as industrial structure would be required before establishing whether the degree of concentration shown is more or less than could be expected if import controls did not exist.

Table 8.2 presents parallel data for the commercial category, while Table 8.3 combines information from the previous two tables. At least 100 companies imported more than one million dollars in 1970 (with an average of $3.1 million each), accounting for 34 percent of all registered imports. Fifty-five foreign-owned companies in this group by themselves represented 20 percent of all Colombian registered imports by 1970.

The degree of concentration falls off rapidly once companies with imports of less than one million dollars are considered. Thus, the eighty-eight companies, foreign and national, industrial and commercial, found to import between a half and one million dollars, accounted for only 6 percent of all imports in 1970, while the 312 companies importing between $100,000 and half a million dollars represented an additional 9 percent of the import bill. In round numbers, one can say that 500 companies handled at least half of Colombian imports. The same companies accounted for 37 percent of all income and sales tax payments, and 32 percent of those employed in "modern" commerce and manufacturing.

Given the economic importance of those firms importing more than one million dollars, their names and presumed major activity are given in Annex A. This annex and other data (not shown) indicate the heavy concentration of import-intensive foreign investors in chemicals, pharmaceuticals, and metal-mechanic industries, which are typically associated with fairly recent import substitution. National companies are more spread out among different activities.

At least eighty industrial companies importing more than one million dollars a year in 1970-71 hired an average of 923 employees. An additional sixty-three companies, importing between a half and one million dollars, had each an average of 496 employees. Finally, 177 industrial companies in the third category had an average of 310 employees each.

TABLE 8.1

MAJOR INDUSTRIAL IMPORTERS IN COLOMBIA, BY LEVEL OF IMPORTS AND BY NATIONALITY, 1970

Number of Companies	Classification (imports in US$)	Registered Imports, 1970 (million US$)	Number of Employees (thousand)	Minor Exports, 1970 (million US$)	Income and Sales taxes paid in 1970 (million pesos)
49	Industrial (foreign-owned) more than one million	167.22	25.50	20.02	563.02
31	Industrial (national) more than one million	107.49	48.84	18.98	966.38
80	Total	274.71	73.84	39.00	1,529.40
27	Industrial (foreign-owned) between half and one million	19.76	12.25	3.58	127.92
36	Industrial (national) between half and one million	23.59	19.02[b]	7.23[a]	221.99
63	Total	43.35	31.27	10.81	349.91
58	Industrial (foreign-owned) between $100,000 and half million	15.43	12.73	3.19	127.58
119	Industrial (national) between $100,000 and half million	27.99	42.11	45.90[a]	456.08
177	Total	43.42	54.84	49.09	583.66
134	Total (foreign-owned)	202.41	50.48	26.79	818.72
186	Total (national)	159.07	109.47	72.11	1,644.45
320	Grand Total	361.48	159.95	98.90	2,463.17

Sources and method: See text of the chapter for explanation.

[a] Includes sugar exports. A total of six sugar companies included in this table exported $40 million.
[b] Refers to only thirty-five companies.

TABLE 8.2

MAJOR COMMERCIAL IMPORTERS IN COLOMBIA, BY LEVEL OF IMPORTS AND BY NATIONALITY, 1970

Number of Companies	Classification (imports in US$)	Registered Imports, 1970 (million US$)	Number of Employees (thousand)	Minor Exports, 1970 (million US$)	Income and Sales taxes paid in 1970 (million pesos)
6	Commercial (foreign-owned) more than one million	14.06	0.88	0.67	55.78
14	Commercial (national) more than one million	25.38	9.52[b]	1.05	16.43
20	Total	39.44	10.40	1.72	72.21
5	Commercial (foreign-owned) between half and one million	4.07	0.83	-0-	22.69
20	Commercial (national) between half and one million	13.33	2.02	0.78	25.81
25	Total	17.40	2.85	0.78	48.50
13	Commercial (foreign-owned) between $100,000 and half million	3.30	2.01	0.15	15.64
122	Commercial (national) between $100,000 and half million	25.53	13.04	17.17[a]	56.50
135	Total	28.83	15.05	17.32	72.14
24	Total (foreign-owned)	21.43	3.72	0.82	94.11
166	Total (national)	64.24	24.58	19.00	98.74
180	Grand Total	85.67	28.30	19.82	192.85

Sources and method: See text of the chapter for explanation.

[a] Includes exports of association of banana growers.
[b] Refers to only thirteen companies.

TABLE 8.3

MAJOR COLOMBIAN IMPORTERS, BY LEVEL OF IMPORTS AND BY NATIONALITY, 1970

Number of Companies	Classification	Registered imports, 1970 (million US$)	Share in total registered imports (%)	Share in total income and sales taxes (1970)(%)
100	Imports of more than one million dollars; national and foreign, industrial and commercial	314.15	34.1	22.2
88	Imports of between half and one million dollars; national and foreign, industrial and commercial	60.75	6.6	5.5
312	Imports of between $100,000 and half million dollars; national and foreign, industrial and commercial	72.25	7.8	9.1
153	Total (foreign-owned)	223.84	24.3	12.6
342	Total (national)	223.31	24.3	24.2
500	Grand Total	447.15	48.6	36.8
	Official registered imports under the reimbursable category	145.20	15.8	----

A comparison of these figures with data reported by the Colombian Ministry of Labor and Social Security suggests that the sample succeeded in registering at least the largest Colombian firms, on the assumption that most of the largest firms according to employment are also the largest importers.[9]

Table 8.1 reveals major industrial exporters among the major importers. Registered Colombian manufactured exports (excluding items such as sugar) are estimated[10] to have reached $76.7 million during 1970; the eighty largest importers would thus account for 49 percent of those exports. The 314 largest industrial importers (excluding several sugar mills) would account for 77 percent of manufactured exports.

A ranking of major importers by level of exports permits a more accurate measure of industrial export concentration. The fourteen largest national industrial exporters in the sample (excluding sugar mills) had registered industrial exports of $26.89 million in 1970, while the ten largest foreign-owned exporting industrial companies had $20.41 million of exports in 1970. Thus, twenty-four industrial companies accounted for 62 percent of all (non-sugar) industrial exports. Foreign-owned companies, by themselves, represented at least 27 percent of all Colombian industrial exports in 1970.

Some important characteristics of major industrial importers/exporters are highlighted in Table 8.4. Average wages decline with company size as measured by annual imports, but foreign-owned companies show higher wages for each size category than national firms. For each size category, foreign companies also have higher imports per employee than do national companies, with imports per employee declining with size for both groups. The forty-nine foreign-owned industrial companies importing more than one million dollars each show an astounding level of $6,557 worth of imports per employee, and although their exports per employee are higher than those of national firms in the same import size category, their "trade deficit" remains far superior to that of any other category. As a rule, large foreign-owned companies are more concentrated in Bogotá than large national firms. These characteristics will be reexamined for all companies in the sample in a later section of this paper.

Among the most striking facts about the twenty-four major exporters—ten foreign-owned and fourteen national—are the persistence of a "trade deficit" and the large average size of the companies. (See the last two rows of Table 8.4.) Neither fact fits well with an image of firms producing labor-intensive, manufactured exports; rather, many of the same companies which have benefited, and still are benefiting from import-intensive import substitution, now seem to benefit from the newer export-promotion policies. It is nevertheless encouraging that these companies are less concentrated in Bogotá than other groups shown in the same table.

Income and sales taxes paid per employee, like wages and imports per employee, appear to decline with company size; in contrast to wages and imports, the national companies show higher tax payments per employee in the two smallest size categories. In spite of their large average size, the twenty-four large exporters show relatively small cash tax payments, which may be explained by Colombian export subsidy schemes.

In summary, a picture of substantial concentration emerges from this review of major 1970 private importers. It is impossible to say from the reviewed data whether such concentration is higher or lower than in other countries, nor whether or not it is encouraged or discouraged by the import control system. (More on this below.) But the data help explain why the management of import controls is not as impossible a task as it appears at first sight when one is told that a handful of authorities decide on about 150,000 import applications per year. Some 500 private

TABLE 8.4

SOME CHARACTERISTICS OF MAJOR INDUSTRIAL IMPORTERS, BY LEVEL OF IMPORTS AND BY NATIONALITY, 1970

Classification (Imports in US$)	Wages per employee (pesos)	Imports per employee (US$)	Percent of companies in Bogotá	Percent of companies in Medellín	Percent of companies in Cali	Employees per company	Exports per employee (US$)	Income and sales taxes paid per employee (pesos)
Foreign-owned (more than one million)	3,731	6,557	65.3	4.1	18.4	520	785	22,077
National (more than one million)	2,040	2,224	54.8	25.8	16.1	1,559	393	19,991
Foreign owned (between half and one million)	2,810	1,613	70.4	25.9	3.7	454	292	10,442
National (between half and one million)	1,729	1,206	44.4	25.0	16.7	544	370	11,345
Foreign-owned (between $100,000 and half million)	2,151	1,212	58.6	5.2	27.6	220	251	10,033
National (between $100,000 and half million)	1,537	665	50.4	19.3	9.2	354	1,090	10,830
Foreign owned (large industrial exporters)[a]	2,867	3,232	40.0	10.0	40.0	944	2,161	10,562
National (large industrial exporters)[b]	2,063	1,528	35.7	21.4	14.3	1,801	1,066	9,002

Sources and method: See text of the chapter for explanation.

[a] Ten companies.
[b] Fourteen companies, excluding sugar mills.

companies are major actors not only in the import field, but also as exporters and tax collectors for the government. Note that only income and sales tax data have been discussed; those 500 companies must also pay a very large share of all import duties.[11]

Revealed INCOMEX Criteria for Accepting or Rejecting Import License Requests

The analysis of characteristics of license requests approved or rejected (partly or totally) by INCOMEX during the second semester of 1971 can shed some light on the question of biases created by the import control system, as compared with a regime without quantitative restrictions. Table 8.5 presents a tabulation of the reasons given by INCOMEX for rejecting import requests in the sample; more than one reason is frequently given. The potential importer is handed a mimeographed sheet listing reasons for rejection; those reasons applying to his request bear a check mark.

A good share of rejections are only partial, particularly under the industry category. More serious rejections appear to be based on protectionist grounds, as reflected in reasons 1, 2, and very likely, in 8 and 9. For the commercial category these four reasons add up to 46 percent of the reasons for rejection, while for industry the corresponding figure is 40 percent. The commercial requests also seem to be particularly scrutinized for "excessive" imports (11) and tax evasion (13). Industrial requests are watched for overinvoicing (4); in this area INCOMEX claims to have saved the country several million dollars by keeping foreign-owned companies, especially those in the pharmaceutical field, from remitting excessive profits to their headquarters abroad via overinvoicing. Such claims appear to be substantially correct.[12]

The average characteristics of approved, rejected, and partially rejected import requests in the industrial and commercial categories are laid out in Table 8.6. Note first that our sample picked up a higher average of rejected requests than seems typical during the second semester of 1971. While at that time only about 10 percent of all requests in our sample were said to be turned down, 25 percent of the industrial requests and 43 percent of commercial requests were totally rejected. The companies appearing in the sample are on average larger than those in the whole industrial and commercial sector; while this fact in itself is not surprising, the sample is probably biased in the direction of over-representing larger importing firms and larger import requests.

The large standard deviations shown in Table 8.6 warn of the difficulty in generalizing with confidence about the characteristics of accepted, rejected, and partially rejected requests. Note also that the listed characteristics omit, due to lack of data, such important features of the import requests as whether or not, for example, the requested import was competitive with some local production, and also whether the requested imports originated in countries having preferential trade agreements with Colombia.

In spite of these limitations, an attempt has been made to establish what characteristics of the import requests, and of the company making them, made INCOMEX more likely to accept such petitions. As some important independent variables are left out of the analysis, we cannot expect to obtain good fits. A less ambitious goal will be to isolate characteristics which significantly influence INCOMEX in the decision to accept or reject each application, *ceteris paribus*. The analysis may be interpreted as measuring an INCOMEX supply function for import licenses, or assuming, as a not unreasonable first approximation, that the

TABLE 8.5

REASONS GIVEN BY INCOMEX FOR REJECTING APPLICATIONS FOR IMPORT LICENSES, AND TABULATION OF SAMPLE OF REJECTED LICENSES (TOTALLY OR IN PART), SECOND SEMESTER, 1971

Reason for Rejection	Commerce	Industry	Official
1. Commodity is produced within Colombia	24.5	15.9	13.3
2. Requested item can be replaced by similar Colombian goods	5.5	3.2	3.6
3. Quantity requested is excessive	0.6	0.3	1.2
4. Foreign price is excessive	0.6	4.8	2.4
5. Quantity and/or value requested is excessive relative to past record	0.9	2.1	-0-
6. Import or approval category temporarily restricted	2.5	0.8	4.8
7. Inadequate information given to justify need for requested import, modification, or addition	1.3	1.4	4.8
8. Inadequate product description (lack of catalogues, etc.)	6.1	9.0	3.6
9. Lack of exact and detailed product specification in the request, as per existing regulations	10.2	11.5	12.0
10. Adequate stocks of products are found domestically	0.6	0.1	-0-
11. Requests for identical or similar products have been approved recently to petitioner	13.4	4.6	1.2
12. There is shortage of foreign exchange	0.1	-0-	-0-
13. Requested imports out of proportion with taxes paid	5.7	0.8	-0-
14. Tax information missing	0.2	0.4	-0-
15. Data on imports provided by petitioner do not agree with those of INCOMEX	0.5	-0-	1.2
16. Excessive expenditures	0.2	0.1	1.2
17. Data on sale prices, destined for price control agency, are lacking	-0-	-0-	-0-
18. Other special reasons	9.4	11.3	44.6
19. Percentage of request granted:	17.6	33.5	6.0
20%	(0.4)	(0.3)	(0)
25%	(0.1)	(0.6)	(0)
30%	(2.4)	(0.7)	(0)
40%	(3.2)	(3.7)	(1.2)
50%	(5.1)	(16.2)	(4.8)
60%	(3.4)	(6.1)	(0)
70%	(0.2)	(0.3)	(0)
Unspecified	(2.8)	(5.6)	(0)
Total	100.0%	100.0%	100.0%

(continued)

TABLE 8.5 (continued)

	Commerce	Industry	Official
Addendum:			
a) Requests for which more than one reason was given for rejection (totally or partly)	81	75	14
b) Total of reasons given for rejecting requests (totally or partly), including partial approvals	849	710	83

Sources and method: See text.

TABLE 8.6

AVERAGE CHARACTERISTICS OF APPROVED, REJECTED, AND PARTIALLY REJECTED APPLICATIONS FOR IMPORT LICENSES, SECOND SEMESTER, 1971

	Industrial			Commercial		
	Approved	Partially Rejected	Rejected	Approved	Partially Rejected	Rejected
Number of company employees	518 (1,181)	407 (870)	331 (570)	194 (701)	126 (377)	194 (691)
Import registrations in 1970 (thousand US$)	1,257 (3,350)	1,154 (2,640)	778 (2,066)	779 (3,293)	617 (2,603)	660 (2,557)
Unused 1970 import registrations (thousand US$)	9 (28)	16 (50)	10 (37)	8 (44)	5 (16)	7 (25)
Value of requested 1971 sample license (thousand US$)	9.0 (27.5)	20.9 (28.9)	12.0 (24.7)	1.9 (9.6)	9.3 (16.0)	5.9 (12.9)
Income taxes paid in 1970 (thousand pesos)	3,520 (9,618)	2,915 (8,746)	2,387 (7,889)	1,010 (3,774)	1,068 (4,411)	1,155 (4,760)
Sales taxes paid in 1970 (thousand US$)	4,516 (31,312)	4,067 (33,380)	2,445 (26,343)	961 (4,592)	694 (3,648)	795 (3,583)
Minor exports in 1970 (thousand US$)	358 (2,040)	127 (436)	210 (1,065)	20 (94)	28 (129)	53 (695)
Average monthly wages (pesos)	2,595 (3,586)	2,605 (1,707)	2,305 (1,849)	2,436 (1,687)	2,650 (3,080)	2,451 (2,118)
Percent of licenses in nonreimbursable group	18.2 (38.6)	0	2.5 (15.5)	17.8 (38.3)	0.4 (6.6)	6.2 (28.6)
Number of requests in sample	747	212	325	466	232	517
Number of requests from foreign-owned companies	266	95	110	75	43	91
Number of requests from Bogotá or Medellín	559	167	216	373	177	384

( ) = standard deviation

demand for licenses is perfectly elastic at the going transaction costs involved in applications.

The dependent variable, to be statistically explained, is somewhat unusual. If all applications are divided simply into those accepted or rejected, that variable will only take values of zero for rejections and one for approvals. Under these dichotomous circumstances, multivariate probit analysis is known to be a superior technique to the usual least squares multiple regressions.[13] In our sample, applications partly rejected present an intermediate case, which can be handled in different ways. In what follows, the probit analysis will leave out partial rejections, will treat them as total rejections, or will treat them as total approvals. The dependent variable for partially rejected requests can also be expressed as the fraction of the value of the license granted by INCOMEX; in that case, intermediate observations will be made between zero and one. Ordinary least squares will be used to analyze this fashion of expressing the dependent variable.

Tables 8.7 and 8.8 present the best results obtained, best being determined by the number of coefficients with interesting values relative to their standard errors. Several other independent variables, not shown, were unsuccessfully tried. On the whole, the different techniques used to analyze the data yielded similar qualitative results.

Import requests under the nonreimbursable category (i.e., those which do not involve an *immediate* claim on foreign exchange resources) clearly have a much better chance of being approved than those under the reimbursable category, both under the industrial and commercial classifications. Smaller import requests also have a clearly better chance of being approved, for both the industrial and commercial classifications, than larger requests. When partial rejections are counted as approvals on the supposition that either the company will be happy to obtain a share of its perhaps inflated request, or that it can always present a new request later on, the significance of the coefficient for the absolute size of the import request declines but remains high. As seen in Table 8.6, the average value of partially rejected license applications were higher than those for complete approvals and rejections. A breakdown of requests into ten groups according to the size of requests shows the negative relation between complete approval and size of request to be quite smooth, with the percentage of total approvals declining steadily from 77 percent for the smallest to 36 percent for the largest in the case of reimbursable industrial requests. In the commercial category the decline in the acceptance rate is even steeper. On the whole, these facts indicate that INCOMEX authorities, besides their protectionist guidelines, still operated during the second semester of 1971 with an eye (somewhat myopic) to rationing foreign exchange.

Do large firms have a better chance of obtaining desired licenses than smaller firms? Size was measured by number of employees and by value of 1970 import registrations. Both measures gave substantially the same results; those using 1970 imports are shown in Table 8.7, for industrial requests, while those using employment levels are shown in Table 8.8, for commercial requests. The hypothesis being tested is that chances for approval increase steadily with size, even when other company and license characteristics are also taken into account. For the industrial category, the hypothesis receives only modest support; when partial rejections are treated as approvals, which for large companies may be quite suitable, that support is strongest. In the commercial category, the significance of the size variable is uniformly superior to that for industrials, and indicates a clear and smooth link between size and chances of approval, even after other variables are taken into account. We shall return to this issue below.

TABLE 8.7

INDUSTRIAL FIRMS: REGRESSIONS EXPLAINING APPROVAL (1) OR REJECTION (0) OF IMPORT REQUESTS IN SAMPLE

	Least Square Regressions	Probit Analysis [Partial rejections omitted]	Probit Analysis [Partial rejections as (1)]	Probit Analysis [Partial rejections as (0)]
Constant	0.383 (1.09)	-0.533 (1.36)	-0.564 (0.22)	-0.095
Nonreimbursable (1) or reimbursable (0) category	0.248 (6.60)	1.108 (5.91)	0.934 (5.15)	1.408 (7.33)
Log of value of all import registrations in 1970	0.011 (1.36)	0.043 (1.43)	0.048 (1.68)	0.029 (1.05)
Log of employees per 1970 imports	0.012 (1.02)	0.042 (0.98)	0.043 (1.09)	0.022 (0.59)
Log of value of requested imports	-0.042 (6.53)	-0.134 (5.12)	-0.047 (1.94)	-0.229 (9.58)
Log of 1970 income and sales taxes paid per 1970 imports	0.013 (2.79)	0.048 (2.71)	0.031 (1.93)	0.050 (3.20)
Log of 1970 minor exports per 1970 imports	-0.012 (2.34)	-0.047 (2.47)	-0.035 (1.96)	-0.043 (2.55)
Log of average wage	0.032 (2.01)	0.110 (1.82)	0.100 (1.97)	0.077 (1.45)
Percent of 1970 import registrations unused	-0.000 (0.33)	-0.001 (1.25)	0.000 (0.21)	-0.001 (1.26)
Bogotá or Medellín (1) or elsewhere (0)	0.062 (2.34)	0.222 (2.35)	0.246 (2.79)	0.142 (1.64)
R^2	0.102	-----	-----	-----
F-statistic	16.13	-----	-----	-----
(-2.0). log of likelihood ratio	----	115.17	72.87	228.37
Observations	1,284	1,072	1,284	1,284

( ) = ratio of coefficients to their standard errors.

TABLE 8.8

COMMERCIAL FIRMS: REGRESSIONS EXPLAINING APPROVAL (1) OR REJECTION (0) OF IMPORT REQUESTS IN SAMPLE

	Least Square Regressions	Probit Analysis [Partial rejections omitted]	Probit Analysis [Partial rejections as (1)]	Probit Analysis [Partial rejections as (0)]
Constant	0.739 (2.73)	1.134 (1.92)	0.676 (2.58)	1.023
Nonreimbursable (1) or reimbursable (0) category	0.115 (2.98)	0.421 (3.14)	0.220 (1.74)	0.535 (4.02)
Log of number of employees	0.026 (2.60)	0.093 (2.32)	0.056 (1.72)	0.098 (2.65)
Log of value of 1970 import registrations per employee	-0.002 (0.27)	0.001 (0.04)	-0.016 (0.57)	0.006 (0.19)
Log of value of requested imports	-0.116 (15.55)	-0.490 (14.22)	-0.208 (7.96)	-0.539 (16.90)
Log of 1970 income and sales taxes paid per employee	0.010 (1.43)	0.023 (0.87)	0.034 (1.50)	0.015 (0.60)
Log of 1970 minor exports per employee	0.016 (1.91)	0.042 (1.23)	0.054 (1.93)	0.037 (1.16)
Log of average wage	-0.007 (0.51)	-0.048 (0.86)	-0.014 (0.28)	-0.043 (0.79)
Percent of 1970 import registrations unused	-0.000 (0.05)	-0.000 (0.29)	-0.000 (0.18)	-0.000 (0.04)
Bogotá or Medellín (1) or elsewhere (0)	0.063 (2.20)	0.205 (1.86)	0.183 (2.01)	0.210 (2.03)
R^2	0.197	----	----	----
F-statistic	32.90	----	----	----
(-2.0). log of likelihood	----	281.74	84.98	417.87
Observations	1,215	983	1,215	1,215

( ) = ratio of coefficients to their standard errors

Company size is of course highly correlated with variables such as taxes paid and exports. Therefore, some other independent variables were defined relative to the size variable. Taxes paid, relative to either imports or employees, significantly increased chances for approval in the case of industrial license requests; somewhat surprisingly, the evidence for such a hypothesis is much weaker in the commercial group. Also surprisingly, a significant *negative* link appears for industrial requests between minor exports, relative to imports, and chances of approval. This result is inconsistent with the usual INCOMEX claims that industrial exporters are favored in the granting of import licenses. However, as shown in Table 8.12, a closer look at the data casts doubts on the robustness of this revealed negative link, at least for companies located in Bogotá or Medellín. It remains possible that some INCOMEX officials felt that large exporters (relative to their 1970 imports) were already obtaining enough fresh imports via the "Plan Vallejo," which exempts its members from prior licenses. Most participants in the "Plan Vallejo" are large firms.

Finally, a look at the correlation coefficients among the independent variables shown in Tables 8.7 and 8.8 fails to show widespread collinearity problems. Indicating the independent variables in Table 8.7 as X_1, $X_2, \ldots, X_9$, following the order in which they are shown in that table, their correlation coefficients are as follows:

	X_1	X_2	X_3	X_4	X_5	X_6	X_7	X_8
X_2	-0.01	----	----	----	----	----	----	----
X_3	0.08	-0.78	----	----	----	----	----	----
X_4	-0.20	0.16	-0.16	----	----	----	----	----
X_5	0.07	-0.24	0.36	-0.09	----	----	----	----
X_6	0.07	-0.51	0.50	-0.12	0.24	----	----	----
X_7	0.10	0.33	-0.37	0.05	-0.06	-0.13	----	----
X_8	-0.01	-0.02	0.01	0.00	0.00	0.03	-0.02	----
X_9	0.05	-0.03	-0.02	0.09	0.03	-0.14	0.02	0.02

Similar results are obtained for the independent variables of Table 8.8. Interesting relationships can be found among the size, export, wage, and tax variables discussed for major importers in the first section of this chapter and to be further explored below, but they do not appear to seriously mar the results of Tables 8.7 and 8.8.

Industrial Company Size and Chances of Approval: A Closer Look

The hypotheses dealing with the links between chances of approval and size, geographical location, and generation of minor exports will be further examined in this section for industrial companies. It will be shown that the largest industrial companies, particularly those in Bogotá and Medellín, do in fact have a better chance than smaller firms for obtaining import licenses.

The data, as shown in the last columns of Tables 8.9 and 8.10, indicate that the percentage of requests falling under the nonreimbursable category is noticeably higher for the largest companies. These tables, and those which follow, consider only license applications which had been totally rejected or approved. The link between size and share of non-

TABLE 8.9

INDUSTRIAL FIRMS: APPROVALS AND COMPLETE REJECTIONS OF IMPORT LICENSE REQUESTS, ACCORDING TO EMPLOYMENT SIZE AND REIMBURSABLE OR NONREIMBURSABLE CATEGORIES

Number of Employees of Firm Making the Request	Reimbursable		Nonreimbursable		Grand Total		Nonreimbursables as Percent of Total
	Total Requests	Percent Approved	Total Requests	Percent Approved	Total Requests	Percent Approved	
Less than 55	196	63.8	24	91.7	220	66.8	10.9
55 - 122	183	68.3	20	90.0	203	70.4	9.9
123 - 245	193	64.8	31	96.8	224	69.2	13.8
246 - 466	174	59.8	25	92.0	199	63.8	12.6
More than 466	182	72.5	44	97.7	226	77.4	19.5
Total	928	65.8	144	94.4	1,072	69.7	13.4

Sources and methods: See text of chapter.

TABLE 8.10

INDUSTRIAL FIRMS: APPROVALS AND COMPLETE REJECTIONS OF IMPORT LICENSE REQUESTS, ACCORDING TO LEVELS OF REGISTERED IMPORTS IN 1970 AND REIMBURSABLE OR NONREIMBURSABLE CATEGORIES

Imports in 1970 (thousand US$)	Reimbursable		Nonreimbursable		Grand Total		Nonreimbursable as Percent of Total
	Total Requests	Percent Approved	Total Requests	Percent Approved	Total Requests	Percent Approved	
Less than 50	217	65.4	40	87.5	257	68.9	15.6
50–200	204	65.7	22	95.5	226	68.6	9.7
200–500	189	65.6	24	100.0	213	69.5	11.3
500–2,000	206	61.2	32	100.0	238	66.4	13.4
More than 2,000	112	75.9	26	92.3	138	79.0	18.8
Total	928	65.8	144	94.4	1,072	69.7	13.4

Sources and methods: See text of chapter.

reimbursables in total request is *not* a smoothly increasing one; indeed, as one moves from the smallest to the largest firms it dips before rising most clearly for the largest firms. It was seen earlier, and Tables 8.9 and 8.10 confirm, that requests under the nonreimbursable category have a much higher chance of being accepted than those under the reimbursable classification. In other words, if unadjusted for the nonreimbursable/reimbursable variable, the largest companies and exporters seem to have a better chance of obtaining approvals, thanks to their better access to nonreimbursable licenses, associated with links to foreign credits or investments.[14]

Tables 8.9 and 8.10 also show that when only reimbursable license applications are considered, the percentage approved shows no clear trend as one moves up the size scale, until the largest size categories are reached. Firms with more than 466 employees, and/or more than $2 million in imports in 1970 show reimbursable approval rates clearly above average.[15]

The geographical pattern of approvals and rejections is explored in relation to employment and minor exports in Tables 8.11 and 8.12. Sharp differences in approval percentages between Bogotá or Medellín, and the rest of Colombia, emerge clearly for only the three largest employment categories, and the two largest categories of minor exporters. Firms from Bogotá or Medellín with at least $50,000 in minor exports in 1970 have the largest percentage of approvals in Table 8.12, while the largest employers in Bogotá and Medellín have the most successful performance of those shown in Table 8.11.

In the total number of import requests from Bogotá and Medellín under the industrial category, one finds a higher share of requests in the nonreimbursable group than the corresponding share for the rest of the country (12.2 percent vs. 8.5 percent). The same is true for the commercial category (10.4 percent vs. 5.4 percent). But even if one looks just at the reimbursable requests, the percentage of approvals is higher for Bogotá and Medellín in both the industrial and commercial categories.

Of the total requests from foreign-owned industrial companies, 68.4 percent came from those located in Bogotá and Medellín, while the corresponding percentage for national firms was 76.2. The share of nonreimbursable requests in total requests from foreign-owned industrial companies was almost identical to the corresponding share in the requests of national firms. Regardless of how requests are sliced, the percentage of approvals for requests from foreign-owned industrial companies come out very close to those from national firms, although usually slightly lower.

Table 8.13 and its underlying data show most clearly that very large industrial firms located in Bogotá or Medellín have a higher approval rate than all others. When partial rejections are omitted from the sample, the combined approval rate for firms which imported less than $2 million in 1970 *or* were located outside Bogotá and Medellín was 68.4 percent, in contrast with the 83.7 percent corresponding to the big firms in Medellín or Bogotá. The null hypothesis (i.e., that no relation exists between chances of approval and being a big firm in Bogotá or Medellín must be rejected at the 1 percent level of significance. If partial rejections are counted as approvals, the contrast is between an approval rate of 86.7 percent for big firms in Bogotá and Medellín, *versus* 73.5 percent for all others. The null hypothesis can again be rejected at the 1 percent level of significance. Finally, if partial rejections are registered as plain rejections, the relevant figures are 68.1 percent for the large firms in Bogotá and Medellín *versus* 57.2 percent for the rest. Now the null hypothesis can be rejected "only" at the 5 percent level of significance.[16]

TABLE 8.11

INDUSTRIAL FIRMS: APPROVALS AND COMPLETE REJECTIONS OF IMPORT LICENSE REQUESTS, ACCORDING TO EMPLOYMENT SIZE AND GEOGRAPHICAL LOCATION

Number of Employees of Firm Making the Request	Bogotá or Medellín		Elsewhere		Total	
	Total Requests	Percent Approved	Total Requests	Percent Approved	Total Requests	Percent Approved
Less than 50	161	66.5	41	65.9	202	66.3
50-99	112	75.0	39	66.7	151	72.8
100-199	140	67.1	53	69.8	193	67.9
200-299	112	70.5	52	57.7	164	66.5
300-499	97	73.2	48	52.1	145	66.2
More than 500	153	81.0	64	67.2	217	77.0
Total	775	72.1	297	63.3	1,072	69.7

Sources and method: See text of chapter.

TABLE 8.12

INDUSTRIAL FIRMS: APPROVALS AND COMPLETE REJECTIONS OF IMPORT LICENSE REQUESTS, ACCORDING TO REGISTERED MINOR EXPORTS IN 1970 AND GEOGRAPHICAL LOCATION

Minor Exports in 1970 (thousand US$)	Bogotá or Medellín		Elsewhere		Total	
	Total Requests	Percent Approved	Total Requests	Percent Approved	Total Requests	Percent Approved
Zero	486	72.6	139	67.6	625	71.5
1-49	152	63.2	63	71.4	215	65.6
50-399	87	80.5	54	50.0	141	68.8
400 or more	50	80.0	41	53.7	91	68.1
Total	775	72.1	297	63.3	1,072	69.7

Sources and method: See text of chapter.

TABLE 8.13

INDUSTRIAL FIRMS: PERCENT OF IMPORT LICENSE REQUESTS APPROVED ACCORDING TO LOCATION OF FIRM AND LEVEL OF 1970 IMPORTS

Location	Partial Rejections Omitted		Partial Rejections as Approvals	
	1970 Imports More than 2 Million US$	1970 Imports Less than 2 Million US$	1970 Imports More than 2 Million US$	1970 Imports Less than 2 Million US$
Bogotá or Medellín	83.7	75.5	86.7	75.8
Elsewhere	69.6	62.2	75.4	66.7

Sources and method: See text of chapter.

It should be recalled that perhaps the most serious shortcoming of the sample data is lack of information on the characteristics of requested imports, particularly on whether or not they are competitive with local production. It is conceivable, for example, that the higher share of approvals for large companies could be explained by their higher requests for imports not competitive with Colombian production, such as machinery and equipment (often brought in under the nonreimbursable category) and inputs originating in heavy industries. But while available data do not allow a test of this hypothesis, I doubt that it could fully explain the previous results.

The Import-Export-Taxes-Wages Nexus

The first part of this chapter explored some characteristics of the major Colombian importers. This section will further examine possible interrelationships among company size, imports, minor exports, and wages and taxes paid for all firms appearing in the sample.
One way of carrying out that analysis is to define, say, company "import functions" which try to explain 1970 imports per employee, depending on size, ownership, and so on. Similar attempts can be made to explain company minor exports, taxes paid per employee, and company wages. One problem with these relations is that the direction of causation is not always as clear as suggested by a model specifying dependent and independent variables. The results shown in Tables 8.14 and 8.15 should therefore be interpreted with caution; their usefulness lies primarily in presenting in a systematic fashion the import-export-taxes-wages nexus found in the sample data.[17]
Industrial companies with high imports per employee clearly tend to pay relatively high taxes per employee, high wages, and more surprisingly, also have relatively high minor exports per employee. Once this nexus is taken into account, the size variable as measured by number of employees suggests a negative link with imports and exports per employee, although such negative connection may be partly spurious. Even after the indicated nexus is taken into account, larger industrial com-

TABLE 8.14

INDUSTRIAL FIRMS: MULTIPLE REGRESSIONS "EXPLAINING" IMPORTS, EXPORTS, WAGES, AND TAXES PER EMPLOYEE

Independent Variables	Dependent Variables			
	Log of 1970 Registered Imports per Employee	Log of 1970 Registered Minor Exports per Employee	Log of 1970 Income and Sales Taxes per Employee	Log of Average Wage
Constant	-1.689	-1.609	-1.248	7.826
Log of number of employees	-0.092 (3.03)	-0.457 (9.91)	0.112 (2.40)	0.003 (0.19)
Foreign-owned (0) or national (1)	-1.339 (14.10)	-0.450 (2.81)	-0.156 (0.99)	-0.455 (9.33)
Bogotá or Medellín (1) or elsewhere (0)	0.167 (1.81)	-0.874 (6.07)	0.304 (2.14)	0.083 (1.82)
Log of average wage	0.397 (7.14)	0.183 (2.05)	0.243 (2.80)	-----
Log of income and sales taxes per employee	0.151 (8.52)	0.089 (3.10)	-----	0.025 (2.80)
Log of 1970 registered imports per employee	----	0.101 (2.30)	0.356 (8.52)	0.097 (7.14)
Log of 1970 registered minor exports per employee	0.041 (2.30)	----	0.084 (3.10)	0.018 (2.05)
R^2	0.318	0.122	0.126	0.211
F-statistic	99.28	29.64	30.75	56.96
Observations	1,284	1,284	1,284	1,284

( ) = ratio of coefficients to their standard errors.

TABLE 8.15

COMMERCIAL FIRMS: MULTIPLE REGRESSIONS "EXPLAINING" IMPORTS, WAGES, AND TAXES PER EMPLOYEE

Independent Variables	Dependent Variables		
	Log of 1970 Registered Imports per Employee	Log of 1970 Income and Sales Taxes per Employee	Log of Average Wage
Constant	-0.352	1.820	7.435
Log of number of employees	-0.114 (3.04)	-0.078 (1.90)	0.077 (3.56)
Foreign-owned (0) or national (1)	-0.568 (4.33)	-0.580 (4.03)	-0.422 (5.60)
Bogotá or Medellín (1) or elsewhere (0)	-0.246 (2.54)	-0.111 (1.04)	0.253 (4.53)
Log of average wage	0.229 (4.63)	0.010 (0.17)	---- ----
Log of income and sales taxes per employee	0.551 (26.30)	---- ----	0.003 (0.17)
Log of 1970 registered imports per employee	---- ----	0.661 (26.30)	0.076 (4.63)
Log of 1970 registered minor exports per employee	0.063 (2.19)	0.037 (1.16)	0.017 (1.00)
R^2	0.459	0.438	0.136
F-statistic	170.94	156.59	31.79
Observations	1,215	1,215	1,215

( ) = ratio of coefficients to their standard errors.

panies appear to pay higher taxes per employee, although not higher wages. For commercial companies the results, shown in Table 8.15, are clearest regarding the particularly strong per employee import-taxes link.

A traditional criticism of a system which represses imports by quotas rather than duties is that it involves public revenue losses. Tables 8.14 and 8.15 suggest that such a loss is only partial. Either because companies eager to obtain import licenses pay higher than average income and sales taxes, or because INCOMEX channels licenses toward especially efficient companies, or both, the third column of Table 8.14 shows that a 10 percent increase in imports per employee is associated with a 3.6 percent increase in sales and income tax revenues of the government. In the commercial group, the apparent feedback elasticity is nearly twice as great.

As argued by some INCOMEX officials, these results can be seen as following from a policy of channelling the still scarce imports, *ceteris paribus*, toward companies which yield the government high tax returns. It is also argued that such companies "deserve" import permits, as they have shown themselves more efficient (profitable) than the rest, as revealed by their high taxes and wages per employee. The chain of causation is unclear and likely to run both ways, in a manner difficult to untangle either statistically or a priori.

Companies with high imports per employee also pay higher than average wages. Out data have no information regarding industrial allocation nor the skill composition of a company's labor force; conceivably, high imports per employee may be correlated with the use of skilled labor commanding higher wages. But while such reasoning is plausible for industrial companies, it has much less force for commercial companies. Yet, both Tables 8.14 and 8.15 show a strong link between wages and imports. On the whole, the last columns of these two tables seem to support the hypothesis that wages are related to the profitability of each company, with access to imports being a key element in profitability.

The dummies for ownership and location emerge as significant in several regressions. Foreign-owned industrial companies have higher imports per employee than national ones, and pay higher wages. The commercial ones also clearly pay more taxes per employee. The observed results, as in earlier cases, could arise from sector and skills variables not included in the regression. Foreign-owned pharmaceutical companies, for example, are likely to have high per employee imports, and a skilled labor force, not because they are foreign-owned, but because they are in pharmaceuticals.

Industrial companies located in Bogotá or Medellín, not surprisingly, appear to pay better wages, and have both higher than average imports and tax payments per employee. For commercial companies, only the tendency to pay higher wages in Bogotá or Medellín remains.

The "minor export functions" yielded the poorest results, suggesting the importance of industrial classification and other variables in explaining export performance. Nevertheless, foreign-owned industrial companies and those outside Bogotá or Medellín are shown to have higher than average minor exports per employee. More surprisingly at first sight are coefficients for wages and per employee imports; companies with high per employee exports tend to import more and pay higher wages. Once these variables are taken into account, the size variable adopts a negative sign. But the data shown in the two bottom lines of Table 8.4, regarding the concentration of large minor exporters, cannot be gainsaid.

Combined with the information shown in Table 8.4, and those presented elsewhere,[18] Colombian *industrial* minor exports in 1970 and 1971 do not emerge as obviously intensive in unskilled labor and national raw materials. Whether this is due to a failure of the Hecksher-Ohlin hypothesis in explaining the Colombian trade pattern, or the result of distortions induced by domestic policy [such as the Plan Vallejo and Latin American Free Trade Area (LAFTA) trade] is a matter deserving further research.

Conclusions

The distribution of Colombian imports shows a substantial concentration which makes the control system easier to manage. The control system, in turn, appears to buttress such concentration, as it gives the largest companies, particularly those located in Bogotá or Medellín, a better chance of obtaining licenses. This conclusion is strengthened because it was obtained even though it could not take into account the "discouraged firm" effect. In other words, data on actual import requests were generated by a group of firms which had some hope of receiving a license; this group of companies has an average size which is larger than that for all industrial firms. Discouraged firms which do not bother to apply are in all likelihood small ones, for which transaction costs in license application loom relatively large. These smaller firms often end up buying imported items from large commercial houses.

Nevertheless, the bias toward import concentration arising *solely* from preferential treatment of the largest firms in Bogotá or Medellín, *ceteris paribus*, does not appear quantitatively very strong. Access to foreign credits and investments, allowing imports without the immediate use of foreign exchange, seems a more powerful force in biasing the operation of import controls in favor of the largest (and best connected) companies. One may speculate that much of this concentrating influence would survive a possible elimination of import controls.

This chapter has also called attention to the fact that minor industrial exports were in 1970 even more concentrated than imports. Given the tendency of large import-intensive companies paying high wages, whatever their industrial activity, to use more capital-intensive methods than other firms, some skepticism regarding the magnitude and direction of employment and income-distributional effects of minor export expansion is warranted, at least for the medium-run. This, of course, does *not* mean that the encouragement of minor exports is a mistaken policy; it is likely to generate somewhat more modern-sector employment than a comparable amount of import substitution. It does suggest, however, that for a given overall growth rate, the employment difference may be only marginally superior, so long as the 1970 industrial and export structure is maintained. Hopefully such a structure could still reflect the early stages of industrial export promotion, which may change as new exporters, less committed to earlier import-substituting ventures, enter the field.

ENDNOTES FOR CHAPTER 8

1. This essay presents results some of which are more fully developed in Carlos F. Díaz-Alejandro, *Foreign Trade Regimes and Economic Development: Colombia*, Columbia University Press for the National Bureau of Economic Research, 1976. The essay owes much to José Francisco Escandón, and the INCOMEX authorities who allowed him to gather information on a sample of import requests. Very valuable help was also provided by Lillian Barros, Stephen Kadish, Christina Lanfer and Van Whiting. Helpful comments received during seminars at MIT and Columbia University, and from Albert Berry, are gratefully acknowledged.

2. David Chu's study in Chapter 3 of supply response to changing relative prices over 1930-45 supports the idea that this sort of natural neoclassical growth process was going on in Colombian industry.

3. But evidence is available to the effect that exports respond to such price stimuli as the exchange rate, export subsidies, and so on. See Albert Berry, *Política Económica Exterior de Colombia* (Bogotá, Fundación para la Educación Superior y el Desarrollo, (FEDESARROLLO, 1972); C. F. Díaz-Alejandro, *Foreign Trade Regimes*, Chapter 2.

4. They do not allow for economies of scale, for trade based on market discrimination and decreasing costs, for the complexities of n- good factor models, for the product cycle, and so on.

5. INCOMEX officials kindly allowed the examination of about 2,500 license requests under the commercial and industrial categories. The sample includes several requests from the same company. The requests had been either accepted or rejected, totally or partially, by the "Junta de Importaciones" of INCOMEX. A smaller sample of 199 was also taken of requests under the official category. In choosing the sample of requests, no refined sampling method was followed; one basically tried to get information on those requests which were around at the time and were made available for examination. As during the second semester of 1971 relatively few applications were being rejected, a special effort was made to obtain data on rejected requests. A bias also existed in favor of obtaining requests from as many different companies as possible. No particular seasonal pattern to license requests seems to exist, except a decline in numbers in December and January, so the exclusive use of second semester information should not introduce any particular bias.

6. In establishing company ownership, heavy reliance was placed on knowledgeable Colombians, and on the United States Department of Commerce, Bureau of International Commerce, *American Firms, Subsidiaries and Affiliates-Colombia* (Washington, D.C., May 1970); The Fortune Directory of the 300 largest industrials outside the United States, *Fortune* Vol. 86 (August 1972): 152-161; Juvenal L. Angel, *Directory of American Firms Operating in Foreign Countries*, 7th ed. (1969) in Vol. 2 of the *American Encyclopedia of International Information*.

7. In several cases, a given company in the sample had import requests listed by INCOMEX under *both* the industrial and commercial cate-

gories. In all such cases, for the purposes of the tables shown in this chapter, the company was placed only under the industrial category. The same procedure was followed in the few cases for which a company was listed under both the industrial and the official categories (e.g., Acerias Paz del Rio).

8. Total income and sales taxes paid in cash during 1970 amounted to 7,220 million pesos, as reported in the *Revista del Banco de la República*. These data, as those shown in the tables, exclude tax payments made with tax certificates issued in connection with export subsidies. Total national tax revenues were 12,591 million pesos in the same year. The number of workers and employees engaged in manufacturing and registered with the Colombian Social Security Institute was 384,600 in December, 1970. See Gabriel Turbay M., "Una Política Industrial Para Estimular Las Exportaciones y Fomentar el Empleo" FEDESARROLLO, May 1972), Table 9, mimeographed. The equivalent amount for the commercial sector was 203,000. For both commerce and manufacturing, the employment figures are limited mostly to their "modern" segments, leaving out the very large "informal sector." Table 2.1 of this volume shows a total estimate of manufacturing employment around 1970 of about 850,000.

9. See Ibid., Table 9. This source reports the following number of firms in mining and manufacturing for December, 1970:

Size Category (number of employees)	Number of firms
more than 500	84
251-500	143
101-250	487

Direct comparison of INCOMEX data with those from the Industrial Census is not possible, as the latter reports on plants, not companies.

10. See FEDESARROLLO, *Coyuntura Económica*, vol. II, no. 2 (July 1972), Table X.2, p. 87.

11. Major importers under the official category have of course a different nature from those listed under industry and commerce. In our sample of official requests, the following characteristics were isolated:

1970 Registered Imports (million US$)	Number of Institutions	1970 Registered Imports (million US$)
More than one million	19	$130.83
Between half and one million	10	7.17
Between $100,000 and half a million	16	4.11
Total major official importers	45	$142.11

The largest official importers include institutions such as municipal and national public utilities (electricity, telephones, and so on), public agencies marketing basic foodstuffs (Instituto de Mercadeo Agropecuario-IDEMA) or rural inputs (Caja Agraria), the Ministries of Public Works and Defense, and so on.

Combining the largest industrial, commercial, and official importers, one can see that during 1970, 119 institutions accounted for $441 million in registered imports, or 48 percent of the total import bill.

12. See Constantine Vaitsos, "Transfer of Resources and Preservation of Monopoly Rents," Harvard Development Advisory Service, Report 168 (1968).

13. See James Tobin, "The Application of Multivariate Probit Analysis to Economic Survey Data," Cowles Foundation Discussion Paper 1, (December 1, 1953). The condition that the dependent variable must always have a value within the interval of zero to one cannot be maintained if its expected value is assumed to be a linear combination of the independent variables, as in multiple regressions. "Moreover, the multiple regression model assumes, inappropriately for this case, that the distribution of the dependent variable around its expected value is independent of the level of that expected value." (Ibid., p. 2). See also Paul L. Joskow, "A Behavioral Theory of Public Utility Regulation," (Ph.D. dissertation, Yale University, 1972), for another application of probit analysis.

14. The average value of import requests under the industrial nonreimbursable category, however, was only $3,200, compared to $12,174 for those in the reimbursable category. In the commercial group the corresponding figures were $2,285 and $5,276, respectively.

15. When partial rejections are counted as approvals, the percentage of reimbursable licenses approved according to size, as measured by 1970 imports (in thousands of dollars), are as follows:

less than 50	70.4
50-200	71.4
200-500	71.2
500-2,000	70.6
more than 2,000	81.3

16. The statistics used in the chi-square test (with one degree of freedom) are as follows:

Partial rejections omitted:	8.642
Partial rejections as acceptances:	8.811
Partial rejections as rejections:	4.617

17. Note also that Tables 8.14 and 8.15, while relying only on the census-like information of our sample, have as many observations as Tables 8.7 and 8.8. In other words, duplications were not weeded out, and data for a given company may appear several times. This is partly to avoid the laborious effort involved in this weeding-out process. It was also noted that on several occasions what appeared to be the same company had different information in different import requests; this could be due to changes in company definitions, in time coverage, or simply to errors of observation. No obvious

criteria for choosing one set of information over another could be devised. As in earlier regressions, when a given company happened to have, say, zero minor exports or imports, those zeroes were transformed into ones, so the logarithms would make sense. Finally, one may note the simple correlation coefficients among the variables appearing in the more interesting Table 8.14. Denoting by $X_1, X_2, \ldots, X_7$ the variables in the order they are presented in Table 8.14 (under the column labelled "Independent Variables"),

	X_1	X_2	X_3	X_4	X_5	X_6
X_2	-0.25	----	----	----	----	----
X_3	-0.07	0.09	----	----	----	----
X_4	0.07	-0.39	0.02	----	----	----
X_5	0.07	-0.21	0.04	0.21	----	----
X_6	0.03	-0.47	0.02	0.37	0.32	----
X_7	-0.22	-0.11	-0.14	0.12	0.12	0.15

18. Albert Berry has noted that data on Colombian industrial two-digit sectors for 1971 show a positive correlation between share of output exported and horsepower per worker. As of 1971, the major two-digit sectors in terms of gross value of exports were textiles, food products, chemicals, nonmetallic minerals, paper products, and leather products. In my "Some Characteristics of Recent Export Expansion in Latin America," in *International Division of Labour; Problems and Perspectives*, edited by Herbert Giersch, Tubingen, West Germany: J.C.B. Mohr (Paul Siebeck), 1974; pp. 215-236, evidence is presented showing a significant positive link between the share of a given sector's exports going to LAFTA, and the capital/labor ratio of that sector. Exports to LAFTA also seem to be more import intensive than those going to the rest of the world.

ANNEX A

COMPANIES IMPORTING MORE THAN ONE MILLION DOLLARS, 1970

Name	Presumed major activity
I. Industrial (foreign-owned)[a]	
1. Abonos Colombianos, S.A. (I.P.C.)	Fertilizers
2. Aluminio Alcan de Colombia, S.A.	Aluminum products
3. Armco Colombiana, S.A.	Construction materials and welding equipment
4. BASF Química Colombiana, S.A.	Chemicals
5. Bayer de Colombia S.A.	Pharmaceuticals
6. Bristol Farmacéutica S.A.	Pharmaceuticals
7. Cartón de Colombia, S.A. (Container Corporation of America)	Paper products
8. Cela Colombiana LTDA.	Printing
9. Celanese Colombiana, S.A.	Textiles (Synthetic fibers)
10. Ciba Colombiana, S.A.	Pharmaceuticals
11. Colgate Palmolive, S.A.	Soup, toothpaste, chemicals
12. Cyanamid de Colombia, S.A.	Chemicals
13. Dow Química de Colombia, S.A.	Chemicals
14. Du Pont de Colombia, S.A.	Chemicals
15. Eli Lilly Interamericana, Inc.	Pharmaceuticals
16. Enka de Colombia, S.A.	Tires
17. E. R. Squibb and Sons, S.A.	Pharmaceuticals
18. Eternit Colombiana, S.A. (Johns Mansville Corporation)	Construction materials
19. Fabrica Chrysler Colombiana de Automotores, S.A.	Automobiles
20. Fábrica de Hilazas Vanylon, S.A.	Textiles (Synethic fibers)
21. General Electric de Colombia, S.A.	Electrical equipment
22. Goodyear de Colombia, S.A.	Tires
23. Hilanderías Medellín, S.A. (Branch River Wool Combing Co.)	Textiles
24. Hilos Cadena	Textiles
25. Hoechst Colombiana, S.A.	Chemicals and Drugs
26. I.B.M. de Colombia, S.A.	Office machines
27. Icollantas S.A. (B.F. Goodrich)	Tires
28. Industrias Phillips de Colombia, S.A.	Electrical equipment
29. International Petroleum Colombia Ltda. (I.P.C.)	Petroleum refining
30. Laboratorios Life, S.A.	Pharmaceuticals
31. Laboratorios Undra, S.A.	Pharmaceuticals
32. Monómeros Colombo-Venezolanos, S.A.[b]	Petrochemicals
33. Monsanto Colombiana, Inc.	Chemicals
34. Olivetti Colombiana, S.A.	Office machines
35. Organización Farmacéutica Americana (Foremost McKesson)	Pharmaceuticals
36. Petroquímica Colombiana, S.A. (Diamond Shamrock Co.)	Petro chemicals
37. Polímeros Colombianos, S.A.	Synthetic fibers, chemicals

38.	Productos Quaker, S.A.	Foodstuffs
39.	Productora de Papeles, S.A. (Grace)	Paper products
40.	Química Schering Colombiana, S.A.	Chemicals
41.	Rhinco Productos Químicos, S.A.	Chemicals
42.	Sandez Colombiana Ltda.	Pharmaceuticals
43.	Siemens Colombiana, S.A.	Telephone material and electronics
44.	SOFASA (Renault-IFI)	Automobile engines
45.	Texas Petroleum Co.	Petroleum products
46.	The Sidney Ross Co. of Colombia	Pharmaceuticals
47.	Uniroyal Croydon, S.A.	Tires
48.	Aluminio de Colombia, Ltda. (Reynolds Metals)	Aluminum products
49.	Productos Roche, S.A.	Chemicals and drugs

[a]Companies placed by INCOMEX under *both* the Industrial and Commercial categories are here listed only under "Industrial."

[b]This is a joint Colombia-Venezuelan venture, with public sector participation. Thus, its nature is quite different from the rest of the companies in this list.

II. Commercial (foreign-owned)

1.	Distribuidora Nissan, Ltda.	---
2.	Distribudora Toyota, Ltda.	---
3.	Kodak Colombiana, Ltda.	---
4.	Productos Quimicos Esso, Inc.	---
5.	Shell Colombiana, S.A.	---
6.	Union Carbide Colombiana, S.A.	---

III. Industrial (national)

1.	Acerías Paz Del Rio, S.A.	Steel
2.	Bavaria, S.A.	Beer
3.	Britilana Benrey Ltda.	?
4.	Cano Isaza y Cia.	?
5.	Cales y Cementos De Toloviejo, S.A.	Construction materials
6.	Carvajal y Cia.	Printing
7.	Casa Editorial El Tiempo	Publishing
8.	Cementos del Caribe, S.A.	Cement
9.	Cía. Colombiana de Alcalis	Chemicals
10.	Cía. Colombiana de Tabaco	Cigarettes
11.	Cía. Colombiana de Tejidos (Coltejer)	Textiles
12.	Cía. Pintuco	Paints
13.	Consorcio Metalúrgico Nacional, S.A.	Metals
14.	Corporación de Acero (Corpacero)	Steel products
15.	David y Eduardo Puyana	Liquor and cigarettes
16.	Detergentes Limitada	Detergents
17.	Empresa Siderúrgica, S.A.	Steel products
18.	Fábrica de Hilados y Tejidos Del Hato	Textiles
19.	Fábrica Nacional de Chocolates, S.A.	Food products
20.	Gaseosas Posada Tobon, S.A.	Beverages
21.	IFI-Concesion de Salinas	Mining of salt

22.	Leonidas Lara e Hijos	Agricultural machinery and autos
23.	Lloreda, Jabones y Glicerina Ltda.	Soaps, detergents
24.	Planta Colombiana de Soda	Chemicals
25.	Productos Fitosanitarios de Colombia, S.A.	Insecticides and Fungicides
26.	Resemberg Hermanos e Hijos	Toiletries and soap
27.	Siderurgica del Pacífico, S.A.	Steel products
28.	Vitabono, S.A.	Fertilizers
29.	Empresa Colombiana de Cables, S.A.	Steel cables
30.	Tejidos Leticia Ltda.	Textiles
31.	Facomec, S.A.	Electrical equipment

IV. Commercial (national)

1.	Almacenes Angel, S.A.	---
2.	Avianca	---
3.	Central Colombiana Auto-Agrícola Ltda.	---
4.	Corpal	---
5.	Distribuidora Química Holanda-Colombia, S.A.	---
6.	Distribuidora Saja Ltda.	---
7.	Droguería Gutiérrez	---
8.	Ingenieros Civiles Asociados	---
9.	Jorge Manuel Gómez (Jomago)	---
10.	Nepomuceno Cartagena e Hijos	---
11.	Pfaff de Colombia, S.A.	---
12.	Praco Ltda.	---
13.	Almacén El Motorista	---
14.	Distribuidora Pantécnica, S.A.	---

Chapter 9

The Experience of Industrialization in Colombia: Summary and Conclusions
Albert Berry

The previous chapters described some aspects of the process of industrialization in Colombia (mainly Chapter 2) and analyzed selected issues at greater depth. This chapter draws out some of the implications for industrial policy of the findings presented earlier, after briefly reviewing the major quantitative features of industrial growth. The evidence from various chapters is of course not fully consistent, and leaves us with a variety of puzzles.[1]

During the period 1900-70, output of manufactured items rose by over fortyfold or 5.5-6+ percent per year, while the labor force only doubled or tripled, growing at about 1.5 percent per year. Output per person thus rose by somewhere around 4.5 percent per year, increasing by twenty-to-twenty-fivefold for the period as a whole.[2] The physical capital stock probably rose by about 3-5 percent per year, so that the K/L ratio rose by around 1.5-3.5 percent per year.

Together with plausible assumptions about factor substitutability, these figures indicate that the dramatic growth of labor productivity has been due more to improvements in factor productivity than to increases in physical capital per worker, this latter probably accounting for no more than one quarter of the total increase in labor productivity.[3] Total factor productivity rose by an average of perhaps 3 percent per year between 1925 and 1970, with value added measured at Colombian prices. Its rise was particularly rapid in the prewar period; our figures suggest over 4 percent per year, with a gradual decline to only a little over 2 percent per year during the sixties. The rates of output growth and of factor productivity increase would probably be lower, perhaps by half a percent or so, if international prices were used to measure growth, since some of the recently initiated industries appear to be more inefficient than were the nascent industries which Colombia protected in earlier periods.[4]

The evidence thus indicates rising total factor productivity to have been the main source of output growth. Increases in the capital/labor ratio have accounted for perhaps a quarter of the rise in labor productivity and for an even smaller share of output growth. Another 10-20 percent of the growth in labor productivity might be explained by increasing labor skills, judging from data for the shorter period 1944/45 to 1969. Much of the technological change has been associated with the shift from small, traditional firms of independent workers or few employees to large, modern firms.[5] The textile industry is one of the most notable examples. Earlier, the sharp decline in share of total labor force in cottage-shop from the late nineteenth century to about 1930 was probably more related to the rise of international trade in Colombia than to the growth of factories. Coffee exports, and hence total imports, grew rapidly over this period. Despite its declining share of the total labor force, cottage-shop still accounted for about half of manufacturing employment in 1970.

Productivity-raising innovations, whether embodied in better machines or not, form another component of technological change, as estimated quantitatively. Although the fairly common assumption that technology has not improved at all over time in cottage-shop[6] is unduly pessimistic, both statistics and observation indicate that this process of technological change has occurred predominantly in the factor subsector. Most of the embodied technological advances becoming available to the Colombian manufacturing sector are borrowed from abroad. During earlier periods virtually all machines were imported, and even today most capital equipment, especially for the factory subsector, is still imported. The transfer of technology occurs in various contexts, including foreign investment, consulting services, royalty arrangements, and so on.[7]

The effects of learning-by-doing are more difficult to gauge than either the role played by the shift from craft to large-scale production or the gains from embodied technological change. Studies in the metal-mechanical sector and in thermal power plants suggest that learning-by-doing may have contributed substantially to productivity growth.[8] Meanwhile, although the causal relationship is not clear, the process of industrial growth has been substantially associated with import substitution over most of this century, especially during 1930-45; exports did not begin to take on real importance until the late sixties. By then foreign capital probably approached one-fifth of total capital in the factory sector.

The post-World War II period saw Colombian industry move into many new areas, some of them quite capital intensive (especially in the sixties). As of 1945, the traditional consumer industries still dominated both factory output and employment. Rubber, paper, chemicals, petroleum, and all the mineral based industries accounted for only about 20 percent of both employment and output; by 1964, these industries had increased their shares of each to around 40 percent. By 1968, capital and intermediate goods constituted a little under 40 percent of output, compared to 25 percent in 1945. The trends toward increasingly sophisticated and capital-intensive industries were slowed by the export boom that began in the late sixties.

Key Issues in Colombian Industrialization

The previous paragraphs summarize a relatively successful story. Nevertheless, questions remain as to whether industrial development could have been better managed by policy makers—questions related in turn to inadequately understood aspects of the industrialization process. Several issues stand out:

1. The appropriate level and pattern of protection. Has Colombia overprotected certain industries and thereby created inefficiency in production coupled with monopoly or oligopoly power resulting in concentration of income? The inefficiency charge dates far back in time; it was directed vigorously at the nascent textile industry during the first few decades of this century before the industry became the pride of the Colombian manufacturing sector. More recently, the

very high rates of effective protection designed to foster more technologically complex and capital-intensive industries like chemicals, basic metals, metal products, electric machinery (mostly consumer durables), transport equipment, and a few others have come in for similar criticism. Other industries have received negative protection, and the variance of protection across industries has, at times, been great.

2. The appropriate forms of protection and stimulation of industry. During the last few decades quantitative restrictions have rivaled and sometimes superseded the tariff in importance. Does this, as many economists have maintained, lead to inefficient and inequitable allocation of scarce resources or, as many policy makers feel, give an added flexibility to trade policy?

3. The appropriate extent of direct public involvement in industry.

At a more specific level, key concerns/criticisms have been:

4. Capital-intensive and import-intensive biases in industrial policy, most notably in the sixties. The Instituto de Fomento Industrial's (IFI) selection of industries to be stimulated has drawn this charge. Borrowing foreign technology or letting foreigners bring it in contributes to the problem. Other elements of economic policy induced firms to use much capital and little labor; Plan Vallejo was an example of a policy inducing the heavy use of imports in production of exports, albeit designed for the entirely laudable goal of spurring exports.

5. The systematic favoring of larger firms over small ones by industrial policy. Is this a good strategy?

6. The waste of extensive underutilization of capacity.

7. The serious bias against exports of Colombian policy during most of the post-World War II period, especially with exchange rate overvaluation. Before this fact was well documented and understood, it was widely believed that Colombian manufacturers lacked the "export mentality." The manufacturing sector had generated few exports and therefore had been forced to depend on the growth of the domestic market and on import substitution. Continued import substitution into more complex and capital-intensive industries was increasingly worrying to persons who took note of its small contribution to employment and presumed that its income distribution effects were negative due to the low labor absorption of the industries in question.

8. The monopolistic or oligopolistic character of much of Colombian industry and the tight ties alleged to exist between political and business powers have drawn increasing fire as awareness of the extreme inequalities characterizing Colombian society has increased.

Most of these issues and problems are common to many developing countries. Previous chapters have attempted to review the pertinent Colombian evidence; here we summarize the conclusions toward which this evidence points.

Response Patterns of Industrial Entrepreneurs and Learning by Doing: Their Relevance to the Appropriate Level and Forms of Protection

Under the general rubric of the infant industry argument, protection is justified for industries able to achieve productive efficiency only through experience (learning-by-doing) or for industries with entrepreneurs so adverse to risk that they would not go into many potentially productive enterprises. A general instrument like a tariff applied across a wide range of products is advantageous if the industries in need of protection are not obvious, or if discriminatory controls would not be efficiently applied. Quantitative restrictions may be superior under opposite conditions and where flexibility of control is needed. A relatively high price responsiveness would seem to favor the tariff. When responsiveness is low, it is probably necessary to select specific industries for stimulation and give them very high security; the approach of letting industries select themselves according to which ones respond to a broad tariff is not feasible if that tariff would have to be implausibly high.

The single major conclusion to emerge from David Chu's analysis of the period 1920-45 is that Colombian entrepreneurs were quite price responsive. With the onset of the Depression, prices of industrial imports rose relative to prices of exports, nontraded goods, and import-competing goods; Chu's tests confirm a significant positive association between relative price and output growth in those sectors where expansion was most dramatic, especially in the textile industry. At the same time, unusually rapid growth in the thirties (rapid vis à vis the "normal" relationships to population and per capita income as estimated by Hollis Chenery and others) does not appear to be explained either by changes in the supply of credit or by any particular flowering of entrepreneurship during this period.

Chu notes that the growth of Colombian factory manufacturing between 1930 and 1945 produced a relatively efficient industrial sector, contrary to what is often believed to have been the result of the post-World War II protection. He conjectures that this was due to the concentration of growth in the "simpler" industries, and also that growth responded to a general signal from the international marketplace—the devaluation of the peso, which raised the price of all imports. In this context, domestic firms sought out profitable investments; postwar signals, in contrast, have been more industry-specific, such things as changes in the tariff designed to develop particular industries, foreign exchange allocation, and so on.

The sort of evidence provided by Chu does not constitute a case for ardent protection. It basically argues that the use of the price mechanism as an inducement device for firms in a young industry is promising; it may not be necessary to start a school for entrepreneurs, to develop a well-honed credit structure, or to invest too extensively in public infrastructure as prerequisites to industrial growth. Other things being equal (at their thirties levels), a rise in relative prices will call forward a substantial expansion of output. (The most recent experience with respect to exports is of course consistent with this.) Still, fostering industries by tariff or other protection is warranted only by the existence of entrepreneurial risk aversion at the start of an enterprise, important learning-by-doing, or some such reason for doubting the efficiency of the free market. Few would question the existence of significant risk aversion;[9] the question is how much protection it would justify.

The extent and nature of risk and uncertainty in an industrialization process would seem to vary naturally over time as increasing information about their own production activities and about the rest of the industrial sector permits entrepreneurs to make better estimates of their own costs, the nature of the competition, and so on. Ospina Vasquez felt that in early twentieth century Colombia risk aversion was a real problem and substantial protection therefore necessary to induce industrialization. Other observers felt this need to be less powerful in later periods, such as after World War II. Meanwhile, the micro-studies of Leonard Dudley and Manuel Ramirez in Chapters 4 and 5 indicate considerable technological improvement in existing plants.[10] (The over time macro-data also indicate substantial technological change, but this could be due exclusively to the superiority of new plants (or firms) over old ones, as opposed to in-plant or in-firm learning.) Dudley's analysis is particularly relevant here, since the metal-mechanical industry is one in which many products have been seriously uncompetitive initially, and protection has been relatively high, justifiable only if very substantial learning occurred in the first decade or two. He estimates that learning from experience alone explains an annual labor productivity increase of 2 to 3 percent for metal products as a whole, with considerably higher rates in some individual industries. Learning is considerably more important than the effects of either increased capital per worker or larger scale. The effect of learning on total factor productivity may be less than that on labor productivity, but it seems likely that it would also be substantial. Overall Dudley concludes that the learning process in metal products requires both time and production experience to enable firms and their workers to acquire the necessary skills. Industries vary in the level of protection needed to sustain them. Dudley's work suggests that a careful review at the industry level could provide more rational protection; he finds that, contrary to contemporary practice, protection was less desirable in assembly than in metalworking, casting, forging, and stamping. Since the study suggests that learning by firms (in the sense of development of a system for efficiently organizing production and nonproduction activities) may be as important as learning by workers, joint ventures and technical assistance would seem to have potential.

Although not an industry which competes with imports, the thermal generating plants analyzed by Ramirez provide interesting and useful insights into the process of technological change. Ramirez's learning variable was "accumulated production/maximum possible production";[11] its positive impact on total efficiency was statistically significant, but the annual improvement was relatively small. This is perhaps because of the relatively smaller number of discontinuities involved here than in something like metal products, and perhaps because of the different definition of efficiency used.[12] (Ramirez used technical efficiency—output per inputs used relative to the most efficient plant using the same input combination—rather than economic efficiency in his calculations.)

For manufacturing as a whole, our evidence on technological change comes from input- and output-series and suggests an increase in total factor productivity (treating labor as homogeneous) of 3 percent per year or more since 1925, although falling from something over 4 percent per year during the pre-World War II period to a little over 2 percent during the sixties. Some part of this residual is explicable in terms of improvements in the labor force which are independent of learning-by-doing—the gradual increase in the share of professionals, white-collar workers, and skilled workers who have received training in institutions like the Servicio Nacional de Aprendizaje (SENA). The results stemming from the introduction of newer and more efficient technologies in new plants are probably another major component. Gains due to economies of scale and public investment are also reflected. Although the increase in total factor productivity has been impressive, the many sources involved only allow one to speculate on how much of it has resulted from learning-by-doing. If, for the sixties, one concluded that only a 1 percent annual increase in total factor productivity could be attributed to learning-by-doing (half of the total estimated increase) and that the newer industries were typical of the sector as a whole, then protection in those industries starting off with costs say 50 percent above the world level could hardly be justified. However, such a sector-wide average is weighted heavily by the older industries, in which one might now expect a slower rate of technological progress.[13] Although the many statistical problems indicate a need for cautious interpretation, it is interesting that at the two-digit level Alejandro Vivas's results suggest little if any relationship between recency of installation and rate of technological change.[14] Such established industries as drinks, tobacco, textiles, printing, and rubber recorded the fastest change.

When the initial comparative disadvantage of an industry is too high, even substantial learning and modification towards the country's factor proportions may not permit the country to catch up with competitors elsewhere, whose technology also advances from year to year. The macro-statistics suggest a worrisome slowdown in the sixties for the rate of increase in total factor productivity, especially in light of the large comparative disadvantage of some recently established industries such as some petrochemicals, consumer durables, auto assembly, and so on.[15] As of the late sixties, our evidence suggests striking inefficiency in a number of two-digit sectors, especially base metals, electrical machinery, and transportation equipment; miscellaneous (in which plastics are important) and petroleum products were also inefficient (Chapter 2). The evident capital intensity of many of the industries emphasized in Andean Group programming is not reassuring with respect to the appropriate use of protection. Acquisition of a large market for inefficient industries may be attractive in the politics of such a group. The inefficient producer in a given industry can lower the burden on the buyers of his own country at the expense of those in other countries. The rapid growth of Colombia's manufactured exports, on the other hand, is reassuring, in part because the incentive to expand further in import substitutes has been diminished and the pressure on policy makers to further protect such industries curtailed. Later, under the influence of a foreign exchange surplus, import liberalization in the early years of the López government also generated competitive pressures for local producers.

Inefficiency resulting simply from below-optimal scale carries different implications than inefficiency resulting from lack of experience or poor management. We have assumed for the most part that only the latter constitutes a reason for protection. If the market is too small to achieve potential economies, production should be delayed until the market (which may include other countries if exports are contemplated) is large enough. But some of the industries developed in the late sixties and early seventies had high costs mainly because of low output levels; while this means that the protection given them may have been unwise; it is true at the same time that they may not be (or have been) burdens on the national economy for too long. A substantial cost reduction may simply await an expansion of the market; it is a matter of sliding down the cost curve rather than achieving a downward shift of the whole curve through learning-by-doing. In short, if an industry is very inefficient at present and learning-by-doing is not rapid, its stimulation by protection must be viewed as a mistake. If the problem is small market size, the mistake may be less costly since the loss of national income will not be permanent. With Colombia's healthy rate of overall growth since the late sixties, errors from investment in too capital-intensive industries or in industries requiring large markets to attain low costs are less serious than they would have been in a slower growing system. The economy will, in a shorter period of time, grow to a capital/labor ratio (i.e., to a rental/wage ratio) and/or a market size at which these industries will approach efficiency.

Protection may, of course, be justified on the grounds of external economies, but these are notoriously difficult to demonstrate or quantify.[16] If they have not been significant in Colombian industrialization, it would be difficult to avoid the conclusion that some industries have been started too soon, especially since 1960. The resulting total loss to Colombia has probably not been exorbitant. Our 1969 estimates in Table 2.18 show industries with total factor productivity below 75 percent of the average to have accounted for 10 percent of value added at Colombian prices, and their presence moderately reduced the average return to capital, with output measured at world prices, from about 9.5 percent to about 8 percent. If further research were to confirm the hypothesis that the economy could have grown substantially faster in the sixties had Colombia's international economic policy, especially her export policy, been better, then the associated loss of growth would be less attributable to protectionist policy than to ineffective exchange rate management. The problem would have been more in the discouragement of exports than in the undue encouragement of import substitutes.

Public Sector Intervention: Public Involvement in Industry and Direct Trade Controls

As noted in Chapter 2, IFI has played an increasing role as investor in Colombian manufacturing. It has fostered a number of basic industries (iron and steel, basic chemicals, and so on) and has leaned towards the capital-intensive and technologically complex ones, policies defensible only if imports become extremely expensive at some time (unlikely), if the positive external ties (or linkages) from these industries were very strong, or if their presence substantially raised national savings. Pending a good demonstration of the importance of said linkages or savings effects, IFI's previous policies must be presumed unwise. This is not to say that IFI's presence necessarily had a negative effect on Colombia's national income; its role as promoter may have been desirable, but its choice of which industries to promote has been unfortunate.[17]

On a different matter, it is natural to ask whether, given the level of protection provided to import-substituting industries, extensive use of direct trade controls (quantitative restrictions) as opposed to greater reliance on tariffs has been wise.[18] Undoubtedly some distortions have been created, and some bribery engaged in. But the management of import controls has never been blatantly bad in Colombia; by 1970 when Carlos Díaz-Alejandro studied the process in detail (see Chapter 8), he was unable to isolate strong differences in access among importers by region or even by size of firm. It must be presumed that over several decades of existence these controls worked to the disadvantage of small firms, which may or may not be counted a significant problem. But at present, no charge of "serious damage done" could be sustained against these control operations.

Policy Biases Toward Capital Intensity and Large Firms: The Issue of Employment Creation

Over the development process, the normal growth pattern involves increases in capital/labor ratios and in firm and plant size. An underdeveloped economy is characterized by artisan production of many manufactured items and by the presence of putting-out systems and small, local factories with relatively little long-distance trade. Gradually, as the economy becomes richer, more capitalized, and more integrated, large-scale firms and plants take over the bulk of production, although as recently reemphasized by a number of writers, small-scale activities remain important and usually increase in terms of the absolute level of employment.[19] Two major explanations for this pattern exist. The more common is economies of scale; as incomes rise and market size expands, production naturally gravitates towards larger units able to produce at a lower average cost. Indivisibilities of capital (e.g., of various types of machines) or of management are often considered central to this inverse relationship between output and average costs. A second proposition is that institutional factors may be paramount in the advance of large firms. First, an impetus towards production in large units exists when capitalists see the potential gains from wiping out small-scale competition, using noneconomic tactics if necessary, and thereby both increasing the size of their market and strengthening their monopoly position. Second, large firms can undertake research, and naturally search for technological improvements which will lower costs at relatively large plant or firm size. Whether comparable technological improvements could have been achieved at comparable social cost for small producing units remains untested, since these units do not have research capacity and seldom get research help from the public sector.[20] This issue is rather moot in countries where much industrial technology is borrowed, although questions of whether to encourage the borrowing of one or another type of technology remain.

A lively issue of Colombia's industrialization is whether public policy contributed to an excessive growth of large, capital-intensive firms, and thereby to a too great variance of size and capital intensity among the firms making up the industrial sector.[21] Fostering of large firms and capital-intensive ones is in considerable degree the same thing since the causal link between the two variables appears to be tight. In most developing countries, Colombia included, policy may be fairly described as favoring large firms. Size and modernity are generally believed to promote economic growth and development; large producers naturally have more political influence than small ones, and most government policies designed to aid firms involve administration of a less problematic nature when firms are large. In Colombia large firms have better credit access and foreign exchange access (whenever this input has no free market);[22] substantial legal advantages in situations where licenses or permits are required to produce, to sell, or whatever; better provision of public services like transportation; and so on. The major public policies which tend to discriminate against the larger firms are the tax system and social legislation concerning minimum wages, working conditions, and union rights; some taxes and most social legislation cannot or are not applied as stringently to small firms, nor do unions organize the workers of small firms.[23] Overall, the net policy bias seems to favor the larger firms. Thus, if all markets were perfect and all public policies neutral, the competitive position of small firms would be improved. It is, therefore, relevant to ask how this would affect static efficiency, savings, and income distribution.

Whether or not markets are perfect or public policy neutral, a gradual increase in both capital intensity and firm size would be expected, the latter because capital-intensive technologies have been developed for large-scale production. This replacement of the traditional by the modern has been discussed and modelled in the Colombian context by Richard Nelson et al.[24]

The related policy question is whether government policy should endeavor to hasten or restrain this replacement process. Although it is sometimes argued that large firms should be encouraged because they have higher savings ratios or that small firms should be favored because their effect on income distribution is preferable, there would seem to be no more than a weak presumption in either direction if factor and product markets were perfect; the likelihood that these markets are biased against smaller firms creates some presumption that public policy should lean in their direction. But empirical evidence on differences by plant or firm size in relative static efficiency, income distribution impact, savings generation, taxes paid, balance of payments impact, and so on, is essential as a base for any serious propositions. John Todd's presentation in Chapter 6 makes a strong case for relative inefficiency from a static point of view in Colombia's largest manufacturing establishments during the sixties; they had low output to fixed capital ratios and low total factor productivity compared to the sector as a whole. (The latter conclusion holds over a wide range of assumptions with respect to the relative capital stock of the various size categories, and with respect to the appropriate shadow price of different types of labor and of imported inputs.)[25] Under the most plausible set of assumptions Todd finds, more generally, that social benefit per unit of fixed capital was a decreasing function of plant size.[26] Most of the available evidence suggests that income distribution would improve with a greater share of resources in the small-scale sector, since the workers in these plants are generally less well paid than those in the large plants[27] and the capital income usually goes to lower income persons than in the case of the large firms, although this is not clear in the case of widely held corporations.

No information is available on relative savings performance of firms or plants by size, so no conclusions can be reached; savings out of income generated in corporations is substantial (Chapter 2), but the same may be true of income generated in smaller firms that are usually proprietorships or partnerships. Clearly the corporations—large on average—are big taxpayers;[28] the relative ease of levying is a major factor here.

In a system sometimes constrained by balance-of-payments difficulties, the balance-of-payments effect of a firm's operation may be important in measuring overall performance. Todd's analysis takes account of differential propensities to use imported inputs, but not differential use of imported capital (for lack of data) or differential export performance (the phenomenon was still unimportant in the early sixties). Díaz-Alejandro's evidence in Chapter 8 is intriguing: large firms do a disproportionate share of both importing and exporting. Further, in 1970 the biggest importers had more imports per worker and bigger trade deficits per worker than the next largest importers. Unfortunately, it is not clear whether these relations would hold if the same firms were classified by size of output, employment, or capital. Comparable data are not available for small firms, but it appears that both exports per worker and trade deficits per worker would be lower than for large firms. Since exporting is undertaken by only a subset of all firms, it is more relevant to the discussion of periodic balance-of-payments crises whether the right sort of large firm has a better chance at generating a positive balance-of-payments effect than the right sort of smaller firm. Evidence remains to be drawn, but the nature of the international market in many products suggests an advantage for the larger firm.

The wide range of factor proportions found in manufacturing, even within specific industries, offers strong circumstantial evidence of serious imperfections in one or both of the labor and capital markets. The efficiency advantages of small firms are based on their greater use of labor—that abundant resource—and their limited use of socially expensive capital. An interesting fact emerging from Francisco Thoumi's analysis in Chapter 7 is that the weak overall measured performance of the large firms is in spite of a more intensive use of the fixed capital available to them. A higher share of them operate their plants for two or three turns.

Summing up, both the evidence on static efficiency and our own guess on distributional implications favor smaller plants.[29] In the past, the balance-of-payments effects of larger firms were clearly more negative (e.g., per peso of value added), but their probable advantages on the export side may now help to offset their greater import intensity;[30] ease of taxing large firms goes in the positive side of the ledger. No evidence is available on relative savings generation and use; unless they have a significant savings advantage, a public policy which stacks the cards in favor of the large firms is clearly dubious.[31]

If the policies in question have not been optimal, how costly have they been? As Todd notes, the extent to which small and large firms can substitute for each other may be rather limited, in which case the higher benefit cost ratio of smaller firms may not imply that their share of output would or should be substantially increased, unless the country could alter its production bundle considerably by trade, exporting the items produced by small firms and importing those necessarily produced by large firms. But this substitution has limits. If neither direct substitution nor substitution via trade can go far, one can conclude that loss through inappropriate policy in this area has not been too large. Inefficient large firms, for the most part, are concentrated in some of the recent and/or highly capital-intensive industries; the policy error was more in protecting these industries than in making life too easy for large firms in general.[32]

A parallel conclusion may be drawn for employment creation. Although it could have been better, it was not particularly bad. The share of the labor force in total manufacturing (factory and cottage-shop) did undergo a secular decline from back in the nineteenth century through about the middle of this century; since then it has increased from a low of about 12 percent to something around 15 percent in 1970 and over 16 percent in 1978. The share in factory manufacturing has shown an essentially continuous upward trend from less than 3 percent in 1925 to 7 percent in 1970 and perhaps 9 percent in 1978. The considerable gap between output and employment growth in the factory sector prior to 1970 (7.8 percent vs. 4.5 percent or so over 1940-70) is not unusual for a developing country; some of it can be attributed to the heavy concentration, especially during the sixties, on such capital-intensive industries as petrochemicals and chemicals. With the various biases toward capital intensity, a factory labor force rising by 4 percent or more a year may surprise as much by its growth as by its stagnation.[33] During the seventies, employment growth accelerated rapidly, to the point of possibly exceeding the growth of output, although estimates are still tentative.

While employment was rising moderately in manufacturing as a whole and fairly rapidly in the factory subsector, average labor remuneration increased rapidly over most of the period from 1936 on, for which useful data are available. Average earnings of blue-collar workers in the factory sector are estimated to have advanced by about 150 percent between 1936 and 1970, while earnings of white-collar workers rose by 100-125 percent. Although earnings fell during the early seventies under the influence of accelerating inflation, by 1980 most of this lost ground was regained.

Much of the technology used in factory manufacturing is borrowed from countries with high K/L ratios, especially the United States. More workers in ancillary activities, like movement of goods, clearly reflects the lower cost of labor in Colombia. Possibilities for adapting basic production processes in this direction are less obvious. Ramirez's study of thermal electricity generation, where technological improvements come principally from abroad incorporated in the generating equipment, is instructive. He finds the learning process important in explaining the changing use of inputs. As production accumulated, both capital and fuel use diminished while labor increased; experience apparently permits a substitution of labor for capital and fuel. It was not possible to get a good reading on the importance of repairs in the process of adjusting factor proportions, but Ramirez hypothesizes that this may be a major vehicle. Learning and local inventive activity appear to be much more important in new plants, suggesting that a large part of the learning occurs during the early years. Adoption in a more labor-using direction is a particularly important phenomenon, since it helps to alleviate the negative income distribution effects of borrowing capital-intensive technologies. It is important to ascertain how general it is and whether such adaptation is becoming easier or harder in the more recent vintages. Further research in this area is of particular interest and importance.

The main policy implication of the finding that many larger firms are inefficient and create little employment is that greater attention is needed to the incentives and context within which such firms operate— not that they should be discouraged per se. Simultaneously, certain of the more obvious market imperfections working against small firms must be remedied, especially in respect of foreign exchange, where the administrative problems which could plague an attempt to equalize credit access do not appear. In other words, all it takes is a simple system of licensing, focusing on the nature of the imported items rather than on characteristics of the firm. Foreign exchange discrimination has probably been substantially less since the early seventies than it was during the early and mid-sixties, but its recurrence needs to be guarded against. Some reduction of biases operating through licensing procedures would seem possible.[34]

The policy bias in favor of larger firms may have reached its peak in the late fifties and early to mid-sixties, when a biased system of foreign exchange rationing and changes in effective protection favoring capital-intensive industries were superimposed onto the usual differential access to credit and discriminatory licensing practices.[35] At about this same time total employment in cottage-shop began to rise after a period of apparent secular decline. The relative importance of small factories, on the other hand, witnessed a substantial decline; plants of five to twenty-five workers made up about 14 percent of the manufacturing labor force in 1953 but only about 10.5 percent in 1969.[36] Could the main effect of the policy biases in favor of large firms have been to hamper small factories? Some observers discern a size range where most plants suffer discrimination in the credit, foreign exchange, and miscellaneous license departments, while being at the same time too large to avoid minimum wage and other social legislation.[37] In that event, part of the cottage-shop growth of recent decades could have resulted from the difficulties of small factories; operations which might grow into a size category of more accessible credit and foreign exchange and/or applicable labor legislation remain instead in the cottage-shop category. Thus large-firm growth may be indirectly complementary with cottage-shop. Large-firm creation of little employment[38] keeps the equilibrium wage rate of the nonprotected sector low and encourages family cottage-shop enterprises more than small factories which depend upon credit, foreign exchange, and so on. Cottage-shop is normally on its own anyway, and may not suffer much from lack of credit since it need not expand, nor from lack of foreign exchange since it seldom uses imported inputs.

In short, the set of policy biases under discussion may not so much increase the large firm's share of manufacturing employment as alter the distribution of employment and activity between small factories and cottage-shop. Testing of this hypothesis would call for time series data on small and large plants by industry, data not presently available. (The aggregate trends could be fully explained if industrial composition were moving in such a way as to favor cottage-shop over small factories.) A distinction must be made between the basic complementary and competitive relations among the large-factory, small-factory, and cottage-shop subsectors, and the effects on the latter two subsectors of policy biases in favor of the former. The first issue is a key to predicting how the small-factory and cottage-shop subsectors will develop as the normal processes of growth strengthen the large-factory subsector. The latter is clearly competitive with the small factories in such industries as wooden furniture and some food processing, and with cottage-shop in clothing and again in wooden furniture. Small and large factories seem to complement each other more frequently than cottage-shop and large factories,[39] except for the special case of some repair functions. Growth of large-scale factories due to policy bias could affect the other two subsectors differently from what we are calling "normal" large-factory growth, since biases favoring large firms (e.g., in factor markets) can affect other subsectors in different ways according to their characteristics. One might therefore hypothesize that whereas normal large-factory growth is somewhat complementary with the growth of small factories, the Colombian experience through 1970 failed to reflect this because the policy biases were particularly damaging to small factories.

Still, tentative evidence from the seventies suggests a quite different pattern, with small and medium plants (five workers to ninety-nine) showing more rapid growth than either cottage-shop or larger plants.[40] One factor at work, according to J. F. Escandon, is an increasing supply of small entrepreneurs, frequently persons who previously worked for large firms.[41] This type of complementarity between the large and the small has long been noted in Japan. Additional factors may have been the declining real wages in manufacturing, the accumulation of capital in *cesantías*, and easier access of small producers to foreign exchange and to second-hand machinery.

Only intensive analysis could reveal which cottage-shop and small-factory subsectors warrant some special consideration in public policy. Small producers of clothing, shoes, wooden furniture, and leather products, industries in which Colombia has a large comparative advantage, deserve credit access, technical assistance, and other aids. On occasion countries such as India have reserved certain industries as the exclusive domain of small-scale producers.[42] An intermediate step might be to reserve only the domestic market (or a given share of it) for small-scale producers. Even such an intermediate policy would need flexibility in a country like Colombia, since the rising opportunity cost of labor will in the foreseeable future raise costs of cottage-shop producers in a number of industries.

Low Capacity Utilization: A Weakness of Colombian Industrialization?

The underutilization of capacity frequently observed in less developed countries has been interpreted as a form of inefficiency at the sectoral level, since it suggests investment of more capital than necessary for a given level of output. Hypotheses abound as to the cause of low capacity utilization (see Thoumi's discussion in Chapter 7). In fact, capacity utilization as measured by hours of operation per week turns out not to be low in Colombia, at least when compared to G. Winston's findings in Pakistan and to calculations for the United States. And, in a subsequent sample analyzed by Thoumi, the rate is substantially higher (over 80.7 percent) when the firms' utilization rates are weighted by assets.[43] However, different indicators of the utilization of capital are not highly correlated. The share of maximum possible hours worked and the intensity of the use of capital when in operation had a correlation of only .235. Capital-intensive sectors like cement, steel, and glass are typically operated on a three-shift basis so relatively little unutilized capital exists.[44] In a wide variety of the more labor-intensive sectors, such policy variables as the night wage surcharge, the manager's preference for leisure and tranquility, and/or the high cost of nighttime management appear to be important factors limiting the number of shifts. Specific industries may have low capacity utilization for a variety of reasons; for example, in the case of shoes, a constant supply of inputs has been difficult to obtain.

Thoumi's work suggests that the problem of capacity utilization may be less serious than anticipated. Where capital is wasted in this way, resolution will be difficult and not achievable through a long-run policy of general expansion and growth of demand; frequently it will be industry specific. No easy and general prescriptions for a more effective use of the capital stock are likely to be forthcoming, although progress should still be pursued by the available means.

Lessons From the Export Boom

The last ten years or so have witnessed a reversal of the pessimism characterizing the mid-sixties, when Colombia seemed near the end of the line as far as import substitution was concerned; the country was moving into more and more capital-intensive industries, and facing with greater frequency the problems of overvaluation/devaluation with attendant inflation and inefficiency. For many years the incentive system, especially the exchange rate, made exporting of manufactured goods unattractive for the producer. Then came the breakthrough into a new world of effective exchange rate management (the floating exchange rate) and dramatic export growth. What were the preconditions for this export growth? What were its growth and income distribution implications? These and other questions are important both in the framing of future industrial policy in Colombia and also in contributing to our overall understanding of the country's trade potential in manufactured products.

The most striking aspect of the firms analyzed by Díaz-Alejandro in Chapter 8 is the concentration of manufactured exports in a few very large firms, textile producers being the outstanding ones. Other major manufactured exports are chemicals, food (especially sugar), nonmetallic mineral products, leather goods, and a few others. Exporting firms also produce import-competing goods. Data suggest that much current import substitution is done by the same firms which produce exports, though some exporting industries like textiles completed the process of import substitution some time ago. Most of the major exporting industries which bypassed a lengthy process of import substitution before becoming important exporters are foreign dominated. The textile industry, mostly national, did go through such a process. Preparation for the export phase may involve a trade-off between experience and foreign involvement.

One apparent implication of the large average size of exporting firms is the capital-intensive nature of Colombia's production of manufacturing exports;[45] the evidence therefore fails to fit expectations which might follow from the simple Hecksher-Ohlin model, whereby exports of a country with a high rental/wage ratio would be labor intensive. Conceivably, large capital-intensive firms simply jumped in first, and the average capital intensity of manufacturing exports will fall over time. But the evidence to date raises serious questions about the hoped-for income distribution benefits of the new export phase. At the same time, the distributional impact is no doubt more favorable than would be that of a comparable amount of import substitution.[46]

Conclusions

The essays in this volume have presented data and results pertinent to some of the relevant questions on Colombian industrialization. Among the more striking conclusions are the following: (1) the largest firms appear to be less efficient on average than medium and small ones; (2) labor absorption in the factory subsector has been reasonably rapid; (3) capacity utilization may not be a particularly important problem from a policy point of view; (4) Colombian entrepreneurs appear to be at least reasonably price responsive, and (5) Colombian manufacturing exports are at present produced in rather capital-intensive ways, and therefore cannot be counted on for a *large* contribution to improved income distribution or employment conditions. With respect to the nature of technological change and whether it provides a justification for protection in Colombia, the evidence of increase in total factor productivity as a result of learning-by-doing raises a definite possibility (though by no means a certainty) that substantial protection has been warranted in some industries. No reason exists for believing that protection has been given to the most appropriate industries, since the decision-making process has not reached the level of refinement necessary to sort out the promising and unpromising cases, even had it not had large nontechnical inputs.

ENDNOTES FOR CHAPTER 9

1. The methodologies employed in the different chapters are not uniform, although they are not inconsistent. Most have a neoclassical model as an explicit or implicit framework; Manuel Ramírez uses activity analysis. Although such varying specifications of economic structure can be responsible for different interpretations or judgments (e.g., of the importance of learning or of economies of scale), this is less likely when, as here, the implicit assumptions tend to differ in degree rather than in kind.

2. For these and other figures referred to here, see Table 2.1.

3. The first detailed exercise in so-called growth accounting at the economy level was Edward F. Denison, *The Sources of Economic Growth in the United States*, Supplementary Paper 13, Committee for Economic Development, (New York 1962).

4. At the same time as uncompetitive new industries were getting started, effective protection on earlier established ones was falling, so the average ratio of "output measured at Colombian prices/output measured at international prices" may not have been rising much over this period. A rough calculation in Chapter 2 suggested that between 1925 and 1970 the output of factory manufacturing grew about 0.5 percent less annually at international prices than at domestic prices (i.e., 5.9 percent per year rather than 6.4 percent.) This would imply a total factor productivity rise, measured at international prices, of about 2.5 instead of about 3.0 percent.

5. At the turn of the century only a few thousand workers were employed in plants of more than five to ten workers; they probably made up 10 percent or less of the total labor force in manufacturing. By 1969/70 workers in plants of five workers or more constituted 40-45 percent of the manufacturing labor force.

6. An assumption employed, for example, by Lester Taylor and Karsten Laursen, "Unemployment, Productivity, and Growth in Colombia," Unpublished Paper, Harvard University Development Advisory Service (Bogotá 1968).

7. For a discussion of the transfer process, see Robert W. Davenport and Miguel Bermudez P., *The Transfer of Technology to Colombian Industry through Industrial Consulting and Related Services* (Menlo Park, California: Stanford Research Institute, 1971).

8. This type of improvement bears a close relationship to what H. Leibenstein has termed x-efficiency, or how well a firm uses its inputs given those elements of its production function which are fixed by the capital equipment in use. H. Leibenstein, "Allocative Efficiency vs. X-Efficiency," *American Economic Review* 56 (1966).

9. Quantitative evidence is hard to find, since those potential entrepreneurs who do not go into a business because of risk aversion are, in general, never identified.

10. Some evidence from other Latin countries does suggest considerable adaptation. See, for example, Jorge Katz, *Importación de Tecnología, Aprendizaje Local y Industrialización Dependiente* (Mexico, D.

F.: Fondo de Cultura Económica, 1975), and Jorge Katz, *Creación de Tecnología en el Sector Manufacturer Argentino*, Monografía 1 Investigación en Temas de Ciencia y Tecnología, Banco Interamericano de Desarrollo, Comisión Económica para América Latina (Buenos Aires 1976).

11. Where maximum possible production refers to the maximum amount which could be produced in the present period.

12. Cost reduction from the vintage effect (improved technology in the more recent equipment) combined with the variables "accumulated production" and "accumulated maintenance" was a healthy 17.7 percent over five years, or a rate of about 3.3 percent a year.

13. Note though that relative price declines were not more characteristic of newer than of older industries during 1950-70. (See Chapter 2).

14. For details see Chapter 2, pp. 15-18.

15. Such a slowdown need not bring trouble, and clearly did not prevent the boom of manufactured exports in the late sixties and early seventies. Nor was it to blame for the stagnation and decline of those exports later in the seventies when the real exchange rate appreciated under the influence of the coffee and drug bonanzas. But in the long-run, a too slow rate of increase of total factor productivity is likely to be a source of difficulties.

16. The terms of trade argument would also be hard to defend in Colombia's context. The presence of economies of scale may under certain conditions constitute an argument, although it remains to be seen whether said conditions (relating to capital market imperfections and product market structure) are typically met in Colombia or not.

17. More precisely, its choice of which projects to support. IFI placed inadequate stress on project identification (i.e., on sector and subsector analysis). Part of the problem lay with the sectors selected and part of it with the projects chosen within those sectors.

18. The choice will often appear an unreal one to the policy maker who feels forced by balance-of-payments crises to apply quantitative restrictions. But ways can usually be found to soften such crises, as for example by the use of a flexible exchange rate and the maintenance of adequate levels of foreign exchange.

19. See Eugene Staley and Richard Morse, *Modern Small Industry for Developing Countries* (New York: McGraw Hill, 1965). The nature of such activities changes substantially over development.

20. Most governments apparently presume (as distinct from their presumption in the agricultural sector) that the small-firm sector lacks long-run growth potential because of real and unavoidable economies of scale. The large firms would presumably oppose activities that greatly increased the competitiveness of the small-scale sector.

21. The increase in average K/L was of course normal and desirable; the issue is the variance.

22. As of 1970, Díaz-Alejandro felt that a more powerful factor in favor of the large and well-located companies than the sort of administrative discrimination which might characterize the Instituto de Comercio Exterior (INCOMEX) processes was the access to foreign credits which obviated the immediate need for foreign exchange for firms wishing to import capital goods.

23. The appropriate comparison is not simply between larger and smaller firms (see below), since the impact of these various policy biases is not necessarily a monotonic function of size. And there may well be a size range where firms are large enough to be subjected to unions and social legislation but too small to share credit access and other benefits on an equal footing with large firms.

24. R. R. Nelson, T. P. Schultz, and R. L. Slighton, *Structural Change In a Developing Economy* (Princeton: Princeton University Press, 1971). This process is not a simple one of competition between large and small. Only detailed analysis will indicate the degree of actual displacement of cottage-shop and small-factory activities by modern ones. Much of the modern sector is noncompetitive with cottage-shop (chemicals, rubber, and so on). The presence of competition has been obvious in textiles, clothing and footwear, wood and wooden furniture, leather and the consumer nondurables in general. But various types of small-scale/large-scale complementation have also characterized these industries.

25. One of the methodological problems with Todd's study is the inability to measure total capital; if the ratio of total to fixed capital varies widely to size, the results could be affected substantially.

26. Although data permit no very precise tracing of the relationship, it is clear that the same is true with respect to firm size.

27. The import of this fact depends upon the labor market model assumed. If the labor available for work in manufacturing were homogeneous, the impact of small industry would be to raise many incomes by a moderate amount while that of large-scale industry would be to raise a few markedly. Cases could doubtless be constructed where the overall distribution impact from employment in large firms would be superior.

28. See Chapters 2 and 8.

29. This is not inconsistent with the presence of economies of scale in some or all industries (Ramirez found such economies, though not strong ones, in thermal electricity generation), or even with total factor productivity rising with size in some or all industries. If some industries are much more efficient (less efficient) than others, and most of the plants in them are small (large), small plants can emerge more efficient on average, although they are less so in most or all industries. Todd's data did not permit him to address this issue nor did Dudley's work on metal-mechanical industries permit

any strong conclusions on the size-efficiency relationship. But it seems probable that a good share of the relative inefficiency of large plants for the economy as a whole is related to the industries in which they operate. If so, the significance of the finding is less in certain respects than it would otherwise be (see text), but is by no means erased.

The results for Colombia discussed here might be usefully compared with those corresponding to developed countries, though the contexts are naturally rather different. Numerous studies have concluded that important technical economies of scale exist in many industries; some of these use engineering data. See, for instance, those reported in C. F. Pratten, *Economies of Scale in Manufacturing Industry* (Cambridge: Cambridge University Press, 1971). Others employ economic measures of efficiency, such as profit rates. The results are more mixed in the latter type of study; thus in the United Kingdom, where the cited study by Pratten reports widespread economies of scale, several studies found no relationship between profitability and scale for all publicly quoted companies. See J. M. Samuels and D. J. Smyth, "Profits, Variability of Profits, and Firm Size," *Economica* 35 (May 1968). This superficial contradiction probably results partly from the fact that most firm size/profitability studies have not disaggregated by industry, partly from the fact that economies of scale in the engineering aspects of an industry do not imply overall economies of scale, partly to the difficulties of measuring either technical or overall economies of scale, and partly to other factors. Of particular interest for Colombia is the fact that important economies of scale may exist, say, within the high capital intensity range and not within the lower capital intensity range, or be stronger in certain size ranges than elsewhere. It must also be remembered, of course, that the serious measurement and other difficulties of studying either economies of scale or the relationship between size and economic efficiency leave virtually all estimates (including those for Colombia) subject to considerable error. Much more work is needed to clarify the true patterns in question.

30. Since the mid-seventies the traditional balance-of-payments problem has been dramatically reversed, so over the second half of the decade a low import intensity was not an advantage anyway.

31. In not going beyond simple "which is better" comparisons, the above discussion with its emphasis on competition between the two subsectors clearly remains too simple. Todd notes that value added/ horsepower ratios are highest in those sectors where output is more evenly spread across size classes and lowest in those sectors dominated by large plants. Causation may run either way here, but one must at least entertain the hypothesis that the existence of competing small plants keeps the large ones from going overboard in a capital-intensive direction. The competing interpretation would be that a low output/capital ratio is characteristic of capital-intensive technologies, and that where the technology is relatively fixed, this feature will coincide with the nonexistence of small plants.

32. Large-firm inefficiency might stem from the firm's possession of monopoly power. Inefficiency can often be reduced by competition; Todd found large firms relatively better performers when they faced competition from small and medium firms in the same industry. In some of the highly capital-intensive sectors, however, large

operations are needed to achieve technical economies of scale, so the only possible competition is from abroad.

33. Low labor absorption in this sector has stirred considerable concern. Some of the more pessimistic conclusions drawn during the sixties, to the effect that factory employment was rising virtually not at all, were based on statistics which failed to catch some of the new firms and therefore underestimated employment increases. In fact there appears to have been no period of more than a year or two during which factory employment rose by less than 3 percent annually.

34. Such procedures are not usually discriminatory in principle, only in practice. An example is the closing of a small plant in the food and beverages sector by the health inspector, apparently at the request of the large plant which until then exercised monopoly power in the market. The corruption to which such licensing systems (some but not all of which do have a meaningful function to perform) are prone tends to work against the little man.

35. On the other hand, unions, relevant mainly for larger firms, may have become stronger during this period.

36. Author's estimates, based on adjusted Departamento Nacional de Estadística (DANE) data; total employment figures are those of Table A-131.

37. Large firms trying to curtail competition are more likely to block small plants than cottage-shop producers, since the latter will sometimes be less directly competitive and produce a substantially different good. Cottage-shop producers are less subject to administered restrictions because of their small size and dispersion.

38. We presume, in drawing a conclusion like this, that allowance for indirect employment effects would not alter our results. If, for example, large firms bought inputs primarily from small firms, such a presumption might not be valid. Although quite inadequate attention has been given to the extent of such transactions, they would seem unlikely to be the norm.

39. That this is the general case was suggested to me in a private communication by Helen Hughes.

40. Because of data problems it is not possible to say with any precision what was happening to employment in plants of five to twenty-five workers. For details, see A. Berry, "The Evolution of Small Scale Industry in Colombia": Toronto, 1980, mimeographed.

41. J. F. Escandón, "Análisis de los Factores que Han Determinado el Desarrollo de la Pequeña Empresa en Colombia," SSE—Colombia Working Paper 3, World Bank, Development Economics Department, (1979).

42. While this may forego some static and dynamic efficiency advantages of competition, large-scale firms often use political leverage rather than economic competition against smaller firms. If this is a serious threat, allowing them to exist may be tantamount to letting them win the competition by political or other noneconomic means. But

any step which prohibits a group of firms from competing must obviously be taken with the greatest of caution.

43. F. E. Thoumi, "La Utilización del Capital Fijo en la Industria Manufacturera Colombiana," *Revista de Planeación y Desarrollo* 10 (September-December, 1978).

44. Statistically, the main variable affecting the utilization ratio was the dummy differentiating corporations from other firms; together with the measure of capital/labor ratio, it accounted for 34 percent of the variation observed in Thoumi's composite utilization variable U (which relates actual output to output possible when the plant is operated the maximum possible number of hours and at maximum intensity).

45. For a discussion see Carlos Díaz-Alejandro and Albert Berry, "The New Colombian Exports: Possible Effects on the Distribution of Income" in Albert Berry and Ronald Soligo, ed., *Economic Policy and Income Distribution in Colombia* (Boulder, Colorado: Westview Press, 1980).

46. See F. E. Thoumi, "Estrategias de Industrialización, Empleo, y Distribución del Ingreso en Colombia," *Coyuntura Económica* IX (abril 1979).

LIST OF ACRONYMS

AID	Agency for International Development
ANDI	Asociación Nacional de Industriales
AP	Accumulated production
AW	Average wage paid
BID	Banco Interamericano de Desarrollo (Interamerican Development Bank)
BTU	British thermal unit
CAT	Certificado de Abono Tributario
CEDE	Centro de Estudios sobre el Desarrollo
CEPAL	Comisión Económica para América Latin (in English ECLA)
CFS	Casting, forging, and stamping
CIF	Cost, insurance, and freight
DANE	Departamento Administrativo Nacional de Estadística
DNP	Departamento Nacional de Planeación
ECLA	Economic Commission for Latin America
FEDESARROLLO	Fundación para la Educación Superior y el Desarrollo
FICITEC	Fundación para el Fomento de la Investigación Cientifica y Tecnológica
GDP	Gross Domestic Product
GNP	Gross National Product
HP	Horsepower
IDB	Interamerican Development Bank
IDEMA	Instituto de Mercadeo Agropecuario
IFI	Instituto de Fomento Industrial
IIT	Instituto de Investigaciones Tecnológicas
IMF	International Monetary Fund
INCOMEX	Instituto Colombiano de Comercio Exterior, the successor to SUPERCOMEX
IRTS	Increasing returns to scale
ISIC	International Standard Industrial Classification
KBTU	Kilo-British thermal units
LAFTA	Latin American Free Trade Area
LDC	Less developed country
MA	Accumulated labor on plant maintenance
MBTU	Mega-British thermal unit
MPP	Maximum possible production
NEC	Not elsewhere classified
PROEXPO	Fondo de Promoción de Exportaciones
SENA	Servicio Nacional de Aprendizaje
SSE	Small-scale enterprise
SUPERCOMEX	Superintendencia de Comercio Exterior
TO	Total employment
VA	Value added

Index

Accumulated maintenance (MA), 86, 177, 186

Accumulated production (AP) in thermal electricity, 86, 177-80

Agency for International Development (AID), 42, 50, 245, 250

Agrarian, Industrial & Mining Credit Bank. See Caja de Crédito Agrario

Agriculture, 7-8, 25, 36, 37, 50

Andean Group, 37, 48, 51

Andean Meseta, 22

Antioqueño, 60

Antioquia, 54

Appliances, 251-2

Argentina, 9, 187

Artisan class, 8, 14, 54, 58, 59

Artisan manufacturing, 198, 303-4

Assembly sector, 145, 146, 164, 252

Atlántico, 54

Automobile industry, 54, 58

Balance of payments
 crises, 37, 45, 47, 49; and large plants, 217, 305, 306

Banking, 108, 109, 118, 120, 125, 245. See also Credit; Loans
 and lending, 39, 50, 118, 125, 243

Barzel, Y., 186

Bavaria
 foreign investments by, 30

Becker, Gary S., 148

Behavior patterns
 of industry, 3

Bell, P.T., 22

Benefit/cost ratio, 193-4

Blue-collar workers, 58, 69, 71, 306

Bogotá, 278, 280, 287, 288

Bogotá exchange
 during WWII, 119

Bolívar, 54

Bonds, 118

Brazil, 9

Bribery, 303

Bureaucracy
 influence in plants, 193, 230

Caballero, Enrique, 20

Cabuya, 25

Caja de Crédito Agrario, 50, 118

Caldas, 54

Capacity utilization, 62-6, 220, 243-7, 249, 250, 251, 253, 299, 308-9. See also capital utilization
 in thermal electricity, 174, 182, 186; and wages, 242-3, 249, 253

Capital, 3, 50, 118, 119, 157-60, 172, 193-4, 217, 230. See also Foreign Capital
 inflow of, 22, 30, 42-4, 108; in metals, 151-2; and plant size, 198, 219, 305-6

Capital equipment, 192

Capital goods, 30, 39, 42, 62, 110, 148, 298
 in agriculture, 37; in thermal electricity, 176, 183-6

320 – Index

Capital/horsepower ratio, 151, 160, 194, 198, 202, 205, 210, 220

Capital income, 66-7, 217, 243

Capital-intensive industry, 39, 42, 66, 67-8, 191, 226, 298, 299, 303-8, 309, 310

Capital/labor ratios (K/L), 15, 48, 61, 73, 144, 160, 162-3, 192, 194, 219, 220, 242, 297
 and capacity utilization, 245, 249, 253

Capital market, 1, 2

Capital-output ratio, 15, 191. See also Output/capital ratio

Capital stock, 205, 217

Capital utilization, 62-3, 185, 244. See also Capacity utilization; Chapter 7

Casting, forging, and stamping (CFS), 145, 146, 148, 164

Cement, 115, 247

Census
 of 1938, 25; of 1945, 22, 62, 110, 134, 135

Central bank, 108, 109, 118, 120. See also Banking; Credit; Loans

Central Mortgage Bank, 118

Certificado de abono tributario (CAT), 47

Chemical sector, 68, 101, 115, 117

Chenery, Hollis, 99

Chenery model, 33, 104-8, 115-7, 124

Chile, 9

Chow test, 157

Chu, David, 2, 22, 30, 32, 33, 60, 300

Clothing, 54, 58, 247, 251. See also Textiles

Cobb-Douglas production function, 150, 163

Cocaine. See Drugs

Coffee, 19-20, 25, 36, 37, 47-8, 49
 exports of, 9, 19-20, 298

Colombian Ministry of Labor and Social Security, 269

Competition, 3-4, 8, 61-2, 164, 226, 242, 298. See also Plant size

Construction sector
 and capital utilization, 244

Consumer goods, 22, 30, 33, 36, 39, 42, 44, 103

Consumer industries, 298

Consumption, 8, 134, 252

Controls. See also Imports; Protectionist policy; Tariffs
 on trade, 49, 73, 99, 288, 303, 330

Corporación Financiera Popular, 50-1

Corporate bonds, 118

Corporations, 66, 245, 249, 253

Cost, insurance and freight (CIF), 134

Cost structure
 relation to technological change, 171-2

Cottage-shop sector, 19, 22, 32, 51
 employment in, 22, 25, 33-6, 58, 71, 307; and the labor force, 14, 15, 54-9, 298

Cotton, 19, 20, 30. See also Textiles

Craft industry, 2-3, 144, 191, 219. See also Artisan manufacturing; Small-scale industry; Traditional industry
 wages in, 210, 217

Index - 321

Credit, 39, 49-50, 119, 219-20, 245, 250, 253. *See also* Banking; Loans
and plant size, 50, 193, 304; supply of, 120, 124-5

Cumulative-output learning, 147, 149, 154, 160-1, 164

Cundinamarca, 54

Decree 44
impact on foreign investments, 42

Debt, 37, 100, 118

Demand, 73, 163, 174, 243, 253
domestic, 104, 112, 228; foreign, 226

Departmento Administrativo Nacional de Estadistica (DANE), 71, 198-217, 260

Depreciation, 60, 134, 186, 205, 217

Devaluation, 37, 49, 99, 108, 109, 125, 300

Development Advisory Service of Harvard Univ., 260

Díaz-Alejandro, Carlos F., 45, 210-17, 303, 305, 307

Direct taxes. *See* Taxes

Division of Industry of the *National Planning Dept.* (DNP), 260

Domestic consumption, 8, 133, 252

Domestic demand, 104, 112, 228

Domestic prices, 134

Domestic production, 104, 110, 124

Drugs, 49, 73

Dualism, 2, 157

Dudley, Leonard, 44, 301

Dummy variables, 245, 247

Dupont rayon plants, 172, 187

Economic Commission for Latin America (ECLA), 8, 9, 14, 18-19, 22, 30, 44, 101

Economic growth, 7-9, 22-33, 99, 100

Economic policy, 21-30, 47, 110, 192-3, 230, 299. *See also* Public policy

Economies of scale, 15-6, 144, 186, 193, 226

Education, 15, 120

Efficiency, 62-6, 122-4, 183, 231, 298-9, 302, 305, 307. *See also* Chapter 6
by plant size, 217-20, 264; and thermal electricity, 174-84, 186

Elasticity of substitution, 220

Electricity machinery, 163, 251-2

Electricity, 172, 174, 243. *See also* Chapter 5

Employment, 21, 32, 162-3, 165, 202, 265, 303-8. *See also* Labor; Wages
benefits, 310; in clothing, 54, 58; in consumer industries, 298; in cottage-shop sector, 22, 25, 33-6, 58, 71, 307; in manufacturing, 9-14, 59, 68-9; in metals, 162-3; by plant size, 193, 198, 220; in service sector, 0

Energy capacity, 151

Engineers, 121

Entrepreneurs, 8, 25-30, 59-60, 119, 120-2, 125, 217, 247, 300-3, 308
foreign, 122, 245, 250

322 - Index

Equipment, 19, 151, 192, 241.
See also European equipment;
Machinery
for thermal electricity, 176,
182, 183, 185, 187; for
transportation, 115, 163,
252

Equity capital, 50, 118, 119

Escandon, José Francisco, 48, 308

Europe, 8, 59

European machinery, 176, 182,
183, 185, 187, 299

Excess capacity, 242-3

Exchange control. *See*
Protectionist policies; Tariffs;
Trade

Exchange rates. *See* Foreign
exchange

Experience
effect on productivity, 144,
146, 152, 157, 182, 183

Exports, 8, 9, 21, 22, 25, 30,
32, 45-7, 61, 68, 71, 108,
243, 288, 305. *See also*
Imports; Trade
of agricultural products, 25;
of coffee, 9, 19-20, 298;
growth of, 100, 103, 104,
298, 302, 309-10; and
import substitution, 303;
by importers, 265, 269; of
manufactures, 3, 4, 36, 217;
policies, 48, 73, 263; prices,
99, 124; of textiles, 251;
subsidies, 47

Fabricante class, 14

Factor abundance, 4, 263-4

Factor markets, 3, 157-60

Factor prices, 99, 110, 112, 160,
194, 198, 220, 230
and plant size, 219; and
productivity, 163; and
thermal electricity, 186-7

Factor productivity, 163, 297,
301-2, 303

Factor proportions, 307. *See also*
Chapter 6; Factor markets

Factor use, 183-5

Factories, 8, 19, 22, 25, 32, 51,
54, 58, 59, 67-8, 69, 306.
See also Plant size

Family-owned firms, 265

Fellner, William, 147-8

Fertilizer sector, 247

Financing. *See* Credit; Foreign
loans; Loans

Firms. *See* Firm size; Foreign
firms; Plant size

Firm-embodied learning, 146-9,
152, 161, 164

Firm size, 153, 157-60, 193, 243,
278-80. *See also* Plant size

Fondo Financiero Industrial, 50

Food sector, 33, 39-42, 44, 54, 58

Foreign capital, 19, 30, 245, 250

Foreign demand, 226

Foreign equipment. *See* European
machinery

Foreign exchange, 47, 48, 49, 73,
109, 193, 210, 217, 219, 242,
288, 302, 304, 307, 309

Foreign firms, 44, 60, 99, 122, 124,
252, 264-5, 269, 271, 280, 287.
See also Entrepreneurs; European
equipment; Technology

Foreign investments, 30, 42-4, 51,
164

Foreign loans, 243, 247, 250

Foreign trade, 19, 25, 37, 48, 49, 61-2, 104, 133, 134, 164, 298. *See also* Trade

Forjas de Colombia, 39

Foss, M.R., 243

Free trade, 3, 4, 8, 21. *See also* Trade

Freight. *See* Cost, insurance and freight

Fuel, 171, 172, 183-6, 307. *See also* Petroleum; Thermal electricity

Fundación para el Fomento de la Investigación Científica y Tecnológica (FICITEC), 50

Gaitán, Jorge, 36

Gilbert, Alan, 60

Glass sector, 247

Gómez, Oscar, 62

Granadan leaders, 8

Great Britain, 8, 19, 59

Great Depression
effect of, 30-3, 49, 73, 99, 104, 108-9, 110, 115, 124, 241, 300

Gross domestic product, 30, 45, 100, 101

Gross national product, 9, 37, 99, 108, 115-7, 124, 134

Heckscher-Olin theory, 4, 48, 264, 288, 310

Hirsch, Werner, 147-8

Hollander, Samuel, 172, 187

Homothetic isoquants, 194, 198

Horsepower
as measure of capital, 151, 160, 194, 198, 202, 205, 210, 220

Human capital, 217

Hydroelectricity, 171

Immigrants, 59-60, 120-1. *See also* Foreign-owned firms; Migration

Import substitution, 3, 4, 9, 22, 33, 44-8, 60, 71, 73, 99, 103-4, 110, 112, 122-4, 125, 144, 164, 242, 263-4, 298, 299, 309

Imports, 8, 30, 32, 44-5, 61, 100, 103, 112, 133, 171, 210, 243, 264-71, 305. *See also* Chapter 8; Controls; Exports; Protectionist policy; Tariffs; Trade
controls on, 37, 252, 269, 271, 275; licensing of, 43, 47, 48, 49, 143, 217-8, 264, 271-8, 288; of raw materials, 193, 205, 210; prices of, 99, 109-10, 113, 124, 125, 134, 300; and wages, 284-8

Income, 7, 8, 25, 58, 193-4, 265. *See also* Wages
per capita, 1, 99, 104; capital, 66-7, 217, 243

Income coefficients, 106

Income distribution, 1, 69-71, 263-4, 299, 305, 310

Income taxes, 269

Increasing returns to scale (IRTS), 194

Indices
of depreciation, 186; of learning, 152-3, 154, 157, 161; of material inputs, 135; of production, 133, 134; of social efficiency, 193

Indirect taxes. *See* Taxes

Industrial census of 1945, 22, 62, 110, 133, 134

Industrial Development Institute, 118-19

Industrial growth
  overview of, 18-45; policy of, 49-73

Industrial leaders. *See* Entrepreneurs

Infant industry argument, 1, 2, 4

Inflation, 37, 69, 110, 306

Inputs, 124, 148, 210
  factor, 109-10; on material, 109-10, 135; prices, 110, 115, 193, 242

Instituto Colombiano de Administración, 50

Instituto Colombiano de Comercio Exterior (INCOMEX), 37, 264, 271-8

Instituto de Fomento Industrial (IFI), 37-9, 51, 60, 299, 303

Instituto de Investigaciones Tecnológicas, 50

Insurance companies, 119.
  See also Cost, insurance and freight

Interamerican Development Bank (IDB), 245

Interest rates, 21, 243

Intermediate goods, 30, 36, 37, 39, 42, 103, 245, 298
  price of, 110, 210

Internal funds, 50, 125

International competition, 61-2, 164, 298

International Monetary Fund (IMF), 37, 47

International standard industrial classification (ISIC), 133

Investments
  foreign, 30, 42-4, 51, 164; in industry, 8, 15-18, 20, 21, 22, 115, 187, 202, 205, 242

Jaramillo, Hernán, 37

Jipas. See Strawhats

Katz, J., 187

Kemmerer Mission of 1923, 21

Kim, C.K., 243, 244

Komiya, R., 186

Korea, 243, 244

Kwon, J.K., 243, 244

Labor, 2-4, 14, 15, 21, 22, 25, 33, 51-9, 66, 67-8, 69, 148, 151, 162, 171, 172, 193, 194-8, 205-10, 217, 230, 249-50, 287-8, 297, 305-6.
  See also Workers
  in agriculture, 7-8; in cottage-shop, 14, 15, 54-9, 298; in metals sector, 146; productivity of, 9, 15-18, 51-9, 71-3, 162-3, 165, 306-7; in textiles, 30; in thermal electricity, 183-6

Labor-embodied learning. *See* Worker-embodied learning

Labor-intensive industries, 71, 191, 309

Land, 7-8, 110

LAFTA
  and exports, 48

Large-scale industry, 2, 4, 14, 39, 198, 202-5, 217-9, 223, 303-8.
  See also Chapter 6; Plant size
  compared to small, 151-2, 157-60; policy towards, 227-30; wages in, 193

Law 63, 21

Learning, 145-57, 164, 176-7, 185, 307
  by firms, 146-9, 152, 161, 164; in metals, 146-51; model of, 150-1, 154; in thermal electricity, 186, 187; by workers, 146, 147-9, 152, 161-2

Learning-by-doing, 2, 61, 150, 161, 163, 241, 245, 298, 300-3

Learning index, 152-3, 154, 157, 161

Learning-to-learn, 147-9

Legislation
social, 304

Licensing
of firms, 243; of imports, 43, 47, 48, 49, 143, 217-8, 264, 271-8, 288

Lipman, Aaron, 60

Lleras Restrepo, Carlos, 47, 51

Loans, 118, 120, 243. *See also* Banking; Credit

Local inventive activity, 182, 187

López government, 302

McGreevey, William, 7-8, 14, 15, 19-20, 21, 22

Machinery, 163, 176, 182, 241, 251-2, 299. *See also* Equipment; European machinery
indices for, 134; in thermal electricity, 171, 183, 185, 187

Magdalena River, 8, 20, 54

Management, 66, 161, 309
and capacity utilization, 249, 253; in metals, 140

Manufacturing sector, 3, 4, 89, 100-4. *See also* Chapter 2
employment in, 9-14, 59, 68-9

Marginal social cost of labor (MSC_L), 205, 210

Marijuana. *See* Drugs

Market share
and capacity utilization, 247, 250

Market structure
and capacity utilization, 245, 250

Marris, R., 242

Maximum possible production (MPP), 176-9

Medellín, 20, 25, 278, 280, 287, 288

Medium-sized plants, 68, 223, 226-30. *See also* Plant size

Merchant class, 8

Metal products, 2, 25, 39, 44, 58, 101, 134, 143-52, 151-2, 161-3, 164, 298. *See also* Chapter 4
learning in, 146-51; price of, 115, 117, 160, 163

Mexico, 9

Middle class
consumption, 252

Migration. *See also* Immigration
rural-urban, 36

Ministry of Development, 244, 260

Ministry of Public Works, 20

Modern firms, 2-3, 144, 297-8.
See also Large-scale industry

Monetary system, 21

Monopolies, 242, 243, 250, 299

Multi-plant firms, 215, 220

Multiple-shift plants, 66, 242, 243

Nariño, 54

National firms, 264-5, 269, 280

National front, 37

National income, 193-4

National Planning Department, 244

Natural gas, 172

Nelson, Richard R., 2, 144, 219, 304

Neoclassical model, 149, 150, 154, 157

Null hypothesis, 280

Núñez, Rafael, 20

Oligopolies, 250, 299
  market, 242, 253

Ospina, Pedro Nel, 21, 49

Ospina, Vasquez, 2, 7, 301

Output, 66, 99, 108, 110, 124, 125, 134, 143, 298
  of manufactures, 61-2, 71-3, 297; in metals, 149; prices, 115, 134; in thermal electricity, 183-5

Output/capital ratio
  by plant size, 66, 194-8, 217-9, 220-3

Output-dependent learning, 152

Pakistan, 243, 246

Paper products, 39, 42, 101, 115, 117, 247

Paz del Río Iron and Steel Works, 37, 39

Petroleum, 25, 33, 51, 68, 101, 115

Pharmaceutical sector, 271, 287

Plan Vallejo, 47, 278

Plant size, 50, 182-3, 192-3, 205, 219, 217-31, 241, 275, 304, 305-6. *See also* Chapter 6
  output/capital ratio by, 66, 194-8, 217-9, 220-3

Political influence
  effect on plant size, 192, 230; on public policy, 304

Population, 104, 108

Postwar industrialization, 36-45

Prices, 108-17, 133, 226
  of coffee, 36, 37; during the Depression, 32, 33; during the postwar period, 44, 124; of exports, 99, 124; factor, 99, 110, 112, 160, 194, 198, 220, 330; of imports, 99, 109-10, 113, 124, 125, 134, 300; incentives, 99; of intermediate goods, 110, 210; of metals, 115, 117, 160, 163; of output, 134; of value, 61-2

Product class indices, 134

Production function, 143-5
  of thermal electricity, 171, 172, 183, 186

Production-task interdependence, 146, 147

Productivity, 2-3, 15-18, 144, 157-60, 297-8, 301-2, 303
  in agriculture, 8; in cottage-shop, 51; of foreign firms, 44; of labor, 9, 15-18, 71-3, 151-9, 162-3, 165, 306-7; of learning, 145-57; in metals, 143-5, 154-7, 162-3

PROEXPO, 47

Profits
  rate of, 66, 100, 191, 193, 194-8, 217-9

Protectionist policy, 1, 2, 3-4, 49-50, 298-9, 300-3, 310. *See also* Controls; Tariffs; Trade
  and imports, 37, 252, 269, 271, 275; for metals, 164; under Ospina, 21, 49; under Reyes, 20-1

Public policy, 191, 219, 220-31, 252, 299, 303-8. *See also* Economic policy

Purchaser-dependence, 146, 148

Quotas
  on assembly, 252; on imports, 287

Railroads, 19-20

Ramírez, Manuel, 301, 307

Rationing, 113

Raw materials, 103, 193, 198, 205, 210, 242, 245, 287-8

Rayon plants, 172, 187

Relative price model, 100, 110-17, 118, 124

Rentier class, 19

Repairs
in metals, 145, 146; in thermal electricity, 177, 182

Research
foreign, 176; in thermal electricity, 177, 187

Reyes, Rafael
overthrow of, 22; policies of, 9, 20-1, 50

Roads. *See* Transportation

Rojas government, 37

Rubber, 39, 42, 101, 115, 117

Rural areas, 25, 36. *See also* Agriculture
employment in, 54

Safford, Frank, 8

Salaries. *See* Income; Wages

Sales
of metal products, 145-6; taxes, 269

San Andres Islands, 252

Santander, 25

Savings
and industry, 66, 303, 305, 306

Scale factor
of productivity, 144

Scale of output
in metals sector, 146

Service sector, 9

Servicio Nacional de Aprendizaje (SENA), 50, 301

Shifts
in plants, 66, 242, 243

Shoe sector, 247, 251

Skills
learning, 145-50

Slighton, Robert L., 193, 202

Small-scale industry, 2, 14, 22-5, 50, 58, 68, 193, 219, 223, 303-8. *See also* Chapter 6; Large-scale industry; Plant size
compared to large, 151-2, 160; policy towards, 226-30; social benefits of, 198-217

Social benefits
by plant size, 198-217, 226

Social efficiency, 193-4, 217, 220

Social product
of metals, 157-60

Solow, R.R., 143

Static efficiency, 61-2

Static trade, 143

Statistical significance of learning, 154

Steel sector, 37, 39, 247. *See also* Metal products sector

Stocks, 66, 119-20

Stock market, 50

Straw hats, 25

Subsidies, 21, 47, 143, 164. *See also* Controls; Protectionist policy; Tariffs; Trade

Superintendencia de Comercio Exterior (SUPERCOMEX). *See* Instituto Colombiano de Comercio Exterior (INCOMEX)

Superintendencia de Sociedades Anónimas, 50, 66

Supplies
availability of during World War II, 118

Tariffs, 1, 8, 21, 32-3, 37, 49, 99, 109, 113, 134, 217, 300, 303. *See also* Controls; Protectionist policy; Subsidies compared to subsidies, 143, 164; under Ospina, 21, 49

Tasks, 148
managerial, 161; in metals, 146, 147, 149, 161

Taxes, 50, 66, 67, 217
and imports, 265, 271, 284-8; on large firms, 304, 306; sales, 269

Technology, 15-18, 42, 59, 143-4, 154, 157, 183-5, 217, 242, 243, 301-3. *See also* Chapter 5 foreign, 50-1, 306-7; in thermal electricity, 174-84

Terms-of-trade index, 100

Territorial Credit Institute, 118

Textile industry, 22-3, 25, 30, 32, 33, 44, 54, 58, 101, 104, 115, 117, 121, 134, 247, 251, 297-9, 309

Thermal electricity, 2. *See also* Chapter 5

Thoumi, Francisco, 48, 62, 71, 309

Thousand Days War, 8, 20, 22

Time
relationship to learning curve, 147-8; relationship to production, 144

Time-dependent learning, 152, 153, 154

Time-elapsed learning, 160, 161, 164

Times-series data, 108, 151

Tire sector, 247

Tobacco, 19, 33

Todd, John, 2, 59, 151, 160, 305, 306

Tolima, 54

Trade, 18-19, 106, 143, 284-8. *See also* Exports; Imports; Protectionist policy; Tariffs of drugs, 73; foreign, 19, 25, 37, 48, 49, 61-2, 104, 133, 134, 164, 298; free, 3, 4, 8, 21; restrictions of, 49, 73, 99, 288, 303, 330

Traditional industry, 19, 61, 297-8. *See also* Artisans; Cottage-shop sector; Craft industry; Small-scale industry

Transportation, 19, 20, 21, 22, 32

Transportation equipment sector, 115, 163, 252

Ubate Valley, 54

Underutilization of capital. *See* Capacity utilization

Unions, 304

United States, 25, 42-4, 59-60, 122 equipment from, 183, 185, 187, 306

University graduates, 120, 121

Unskilled workers, 69

Upper class, 252

Urban areas, 25, 54, 58

Utilization-of-the-plant variable, 183

Valencia, 45

Valle, 54

Value added, 134, 198, 205-17, 245

Value added/horsepower ratio, 220, 223, 226

Variance-covariance matrix, 180-2

Vintage effect, 176, 185

Violence, 36

Vivas, Alejandro, 302

Wage/rental ratio, 160

Wages, 69-71, 148, 193, 219, 309
  of artisans, 58; and capacity utilization, 242-3, 249, 253; of factory workers, 58, 69, 306; and imports, 284-8; and plant size, 193, 198, 205-10, 217-9, 304

White-collar workers, 69, 306

Winston, G., 242, 243, 244, 309

Women
  employment of, 14, 21, 22, 54

Wood products, 25, 54, 58, 251

Worker-embodied learning, 146, 147, 148, 149, 152, 161-2

Workers
  output of, 143, 147; in metals, 145

World Bank, 36, 245, 254

World War I, 25

World War II
  credit during, 118, 119; controls during, 113; effect on industry, 30-6, 73, 99; immigration since, 121; imports during, 104, 113

Yarn. *See* Textile industry